Between Two Wars

A note for the general reader

Total War and Social Change: Europe 1914–1955 is the latest honours-level history course to be produced by the Open University. War and Society has always been a subject of special interest and expertise in the Open University's History Department. The appeal for the general reader is that the five books in the series, taken together or singly, consist of authoritative, up-to-date discussions of the various aspects of war and society in the twentieth century.

The books provide insights into the modes of teaching and communication, including the use of audio-visual material, which have been pioneered at the Open University. Readers will find that they are encouraged to participate in a series of 'tutorials in print', an effective way to achieve a complete command of the material. As in any serious study of a historical topic, there are many suggestions for further reading, including references to a Course Reader, set book and to two collections of primary sources which accompany the series. It is possible to grasp the basic outlines of the topics discussed without turning to these books, but obviously serious students will wish to follow up what is, in effect a very carefully designed course of guided reading, and discussion and analysis of that reading. The first unit in Book 1 sets out the aims and scope of the course.

Open University students are provided with supplementary material, including a *Course Guide* which gives information on student assignments, summer school, the use of video cassettes, and so on.

Total War and Social Change: Europe 1914–1955

Book 1 *Europe in 1914*
Book 2 *The Impact of World War I*
Book 3 *Between Two Wars*
Book 4 *The Impact of World War II*
Book 5 *Retrospect: War and Change in Europe 1914–1955*

Other material associated with the course

Primary Sources 1: World War I, eds Arthur Marwick and Wendy Simpson, Open University, 2000

Primary Sources 2: Interwar and World War II, eds Arthur Marwick and Wendy Simpson, Open University, 2000

Secondary Sources, eds Arthur Marwick and Wendy Simpson, Open University, 2000

Total War and Historical Change: Europe 1914–1955, eds. Clive Emsley, Arthur Marwick and Wendy Simpson, Open University Press, 2000 (Course Reader)

J. M. Roberts, *Europe 1880–1945*, Longman, 2001 (third edition) (Set Book)

Total War and Social Change: Europe 1914 – 1955

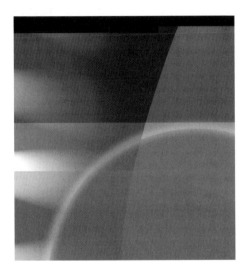

Book

3

Between Two Wars

John Golby, Bernard Waites, Geoffrey Warner, Arthur Marwick,
Annika Mombauer, Tony Aldgate and Antony Lentin

The Open
University

This publication forms part of an Open University course: AA312 *Total War And Social Change: Europe 1914–1955*. Details of this and other Open University courses can be obtained from the Course Reservations Centre, PO Box 724, The Open University, Milton Keynes MK7 6ZS, United Kingdom: tel. +44 (0)1908 653231, e-mail ces-gen@open.ac.uk

Alternatively, you may visit the Open University website at http://www.open.ac.uk where you can learn more about the wide range of courses and packs offered at all levels by the Open University.

For availability of this or other components, contact Open University Worldwide Ltd, The Berrill Building, Walton Hall, Milton Keynes MK7 6AA, United Kingdom: tel. +44 (0)1908 858785; fax +44 (0)1908 858787; e-mail ouwenq@open.ac.uk; website http://www.ouw.co.uk

The Open University, Walton Hall, Milton Keynes, MK7 6AA

First published 2001 by The Open University. Reprinted 2002

Edited, designed and typeset by The Open University

Printed and bound in the United Kingdom by The Alden Group, Oxford

ISBN 0 7492 85567

Cover illustration: Emancipate Women, Build Socialism, 1926, David King Collection, London.

1.2

20496B/aa312b3prei1.2

CONTENTS

Acknowledgements

Grateful acknowledgement is made to the following sources for permission to use material in this book:

Tables

Tables 16.1, 16.4 and 16.5: Mitchell, B. R. (1981), Table 12, Table C1 and C3, Table G9, *European Historical Statistics 1750–1975,* 2nd edn, Macmillan Press Limited; *Tables 16.2 and 16.3:* Cipolla, C. M. (ed.) (1976) *The Fontana Economic History of Europe,* Vol.6. Harpercollins Publishers; *Table 16.6:* Bairoch, P. (1982) 'International industrialization levels 1750–1980', *Journal of European Economic History,* Vol.II, Fall 1982. Banca di Roma. Reprints by Schmidt Periodicals GmbH, Dettendorf – D-8201 Bad Feilmbach 2, West Germany; *Tables 17.1 and 17.2:* Noakes, Jeremy and Pridham, Geoffrey (eds) *Nazism 1919–1945: A Documentary Reader,* Volume 2, *State, Economy and Society 1933–1939,* University of Exeter Press; *Table 18.1:* Welch. D. (1983) *Propaganda and the German Cinema 1933–1945,* by permission of Oxford University Press; *Table 18.2:* Phillips, M. S. (1971) 'The Nazi control of the German film industry', *Journal of European Studies,* vol.1, Alpha Academic.

Every effort has been made to trace all the copyright owners, but if any has been inadvertently overlooked, the publishers will be pleased to make the necessary arrangements at the first opportunity.

Unit 14 THE WESTERN DEMOCRACIES: ECONOMIC AND POLITICAL CHANGES 1918–1929

JOHN GOLBY

Open University students of this unit will need to refer to:

Set book: J. M. Roberts, *Europe 1880–1945*, Longman, 2001

Primary Sources 2: Interwar and World War II, eds Arthur Marwick and Wendy Simpson, Open University, 2000

Secondary Sources, eds Arthur Marwick and Wendy Simpson, Open University, 2000

Course Reader: *Total War and Historical Change: Europe 1914–1955*, eds Clive Emsley, Arthur Marwick and Wendy Simpson, Open University Press, 2000

Maps Booklet

Video 1

Audio 3

INTRODUCTION

The aims of Unit 14 are:

- to survey the economic and political conditions of the western democracies immediately after and in the decade following World War I, and to determine the extent to which these conditions were different from those in the pre-war years and whether the changes that occurred were a result of the war or were already discernible in the years before 1914;

- to examine the extent to which, in these years, the policies of the governments of France, Britain and Germany were constrained by the destruction caused by the war, and the ways in which the three countries coped with the problems created by the war;

- to continue the theme of historiographical controversy by looking in some detail at one particular interpretation of Europe in the years after World War I – the interpretation first put forward in 1975 by the American historian Charles S. Maier in his book *Recasting Bourgeois Europe*.

1   POST-WAR WESTERN EUROPE

There is no doubt that despite the profound relief felt by the ending of World War I the peoples of Europe faced an uncertain future. A war fought on such an unprecedented scale and for such a length of time had inevitably led to the exhaustion of both populations and capital resources. In Book 2, Units 7–10 we examined the extent to which the economies and social structures of the different European countries had been affected by the war. The Russian Revolution of 1917 and the very future of a defeated Germany also raised a whole range of political expectations and concerns. Yet, after looking at all the upheavals that had occurred during the course of the war and all the uncertainties that existed in 1918, what is remarkable is the degree of social stability achieved by the western democracies in the following decade. The questions how and why this came about lie at the centre of Charles S. Maier's study of western Europe during this period. In a political and economic climate where, so he argues, revolution or, at the least, marked internal instability might well have been expected, it is, in Maier's words, 'continuity and stability that need explanation'.

The reasons for spending time on the thesis put forward by Maier are threefold. First, and most important, Maier raises the sorts of questions which are central to the concerns of this course. Secondly, his book *Recasting Bourgeois Europe* (1975) is generally regarded as an important contribution to the study of Europe in the interwar years. The author of the set book for this course, J. M. Roberts, wrote in *History* in 1977 that *Recasting Bourgeois Europe* was 'one of the most important works of general history to appear in the last few years' (book review, *History*, 1977, vol.62, p.512). Thirdly, Maier's book is one of the few serious comparative histories of the period we are studying. In fact, the full title of the book is *Recasting Bourgeois Europe: Stabilization in France, Germany and Italy in the Decade after World War I*. Although Maier concentrates on these three continental powers, there are occasional references to and comparisons with Britain.

The Maier thesis

Brief references have already been made in the course units to Maier's thesis. In Book 2, Units 7–10, p.95 Bill Purdue makes an important comparison between the title of Charles Maier's book and that of Arno J. Mayer: *The Persistence of the Old Regime* (1981). He points out that both of them cannot be right in their analyses of pre-war Europe. Mayer, as you know by now, maintains that the old élites were still dominant in Europe in 1914, while Maier argues that by 1914 the old élites had been overtaken and Europe was essentially 'bourgeois' led. So, Purdue argues, 'if an aristocratic *ancien régime* persisted up until 1914, then a "bourgeois" Europe could not have been *recast* after the war' (Book 2, p.95).

Maier's book is not an 'easy read', so before we look at the extract from *Recasting Bourgeois Europe* in the Course Reader in some detail, it would be worth your while to read the brief general remarks on the book made by the editors of the Reader in their introduction. The relevant section runs from near the top of p.13 to just over halfway down p.14.

Exercise   I want you now to read 'From bourgeois to corporatist Europe' in the Course Reader (pp.113–24) – extracts from Maier's introduction to his book – and then answer the following questions.

1   What is the basic premise of Maier's thesis?

2   Why does Maier concentrate on France, Germany and Italy?

3   How does Maier define 'bourgeois' in this introduction?

4   What important wartime developments does Maier regard as significant in preventing a total return to the social order of pre-1914 Europe?

5   Does Maier contend that the problems facing governments at the end of 1918 were brought about by the war?

6   What does Maier mean by a change from 'bourgeois to corporatist Europe'?

7   What are the main stages in the change from a 'bourgeois' to a 'corporatist' Europe?

8   To what extent was the trend towards corporatism uniform in France, Italy and Germany? ■

Specimen answers and discussion   1   At the end of World War I, so Maier argues, it seemed as if Europe would undergo violent and disruptive upheavals. However, the extent of the disruption was limited, and by the second half of the 1920s Europe *appeared* to have returned to the comparative stability of pre-1914. But the Europe of the mid-1920s was different from that of 1914, and Maier's purpose is to explain how this change came about and how 'security was apparently wrested from profound disorder and turbulence ...' (p.113).

2   Maier chooses France, Germany and Italy because all three countries, despite quite different outcomes, participated in what he sees as the crucial developments in the post-war political cycle, finding a new area of stability which was based not on old ideological beliefs but on a cycle of periods of compromise and periods of new forms of coercion. In addition, although there were major differences between the three countries, there were also fundamental similarities, particularly in the area in which Maier is interested, that is, the ground over which power was contested. Unlike the situation in

Britain, for example, within all three countries there were deep ideological differences between the contending power élites, the political scene was fragmented and there were common 'concepts of liberalism and labels for class distinction'.

3   Maier defines 'bourgeois' primarily in terms of a 'bourgeois Europe', and he equates this with the supposed stability and values which existed in pre-war Europe and to which most conservative forces after the war wished to return. This was the crucial area of conflict in the years after the war. He argues that by the end of the nineteenth century the bourgeoisie had formed close associations with the old élites, and their major mutual concern was to defend their prerogatives from those on the left who were advocating fundamental changes in property and power relationships. Maier insists that in the 1920s the word 'bourgeois' was accepted as a word that stood for 'the basic social divisions of a market economy and industrial social order', and that for the conservative elements in the 1920s this image of a bourgeois Europe or a pre-1918 *ancien régime* was something worth striving to regain.

4   The two developments Maier regards as significant are:

(a) the growth in power of organized labour which had accelerated during the war as a result of the need to effect massive economic mobilization in converting to a war production economy;

(b) the attempts – demanded by the needs of a war economy – to control prices, the distribution of raw materials and the movement of labour. This was achieved by a variety of means but the overall effect was to erode 'the distinction between private and public sectors'.

5   No, not entirely. Maier acknowledges that the growing power of organized labour as a political force and around the bargaining table was becoming a factor before the war. More important than this, however, so Maier contends, is that during the late nineteenth century there was a significant growth in pressure groups, and that there were growing connections between these groups and political parties. This was altering the nature of representative government. Consequently, domestic policies were no longer just the preserve of the ruling interest but were achieved through bureaucratic and centralized bargaining.

6   The prime aim of conservatives in 1918 was to return to the social order of what Maier terms 'bourgeois Europe'. In fact, a social order was attained but it was not the restoration of a pre-1914 order. For one thing, as we have discussed in answer to question 5, major transformations were already taking place before the war. In addition, there was the factor mentioned in answer to question 4, namely the need for a wartime large-scale concentrated industrial production which necessitated as much industrial harmony as possible, and which had resulted in the growth in power of both business people and organized unions. Also, after the war the notable failure of liberal parliamentary leaders to solve the post-war economic and social problems by traditional methods inevitably meant a relocation of power. So what evolved was not a return to bourgeois Europe but an eventual transformation to what Maier calls a 'corporatist' Europe. What he means by this is that major political, economic and social problems became

increasingly difficult to handle in unwieldy parliamentary assemblies, and decision making was gradually relocated outside parliament to individual ministries, coalition caucuses and corporate bodies such as business corporations or trade unions. Consensus, therefore, was achieved not so much through parliaments, which depended from time to time on the approval of the electorate, but through continued bargaining between the state and the major organized interests.

The word 'corporatism' will be used quite often during the remainder of this course, and a good definition appears in Abercrombie *et al., Penguin Dictionary of Sociology*:

> A form of social organization in which the key economic, political and social decisions are made by corporate groups, or these groups and the state jointly. Individuals have influence only through their membership of corporate bodies. These include trade unions, professions, business corporations, political pressure groups and lobbies and voluntary associations.

(1984, p.55)

7   Maier divides the period 1918–29 into four key sections.

(a) 1918 to the end of 1919: a period of great turmoil during which industrial discontent and the threat of possible revolutions were stifled and contained by the élites and the middle classes uniting and combining against the claims of the militant left.

(b) 1920–21: a period in which the left was largely defeated and which resulted in crises within the ranks of socialist parties. This in turn produced schisms and the formation of communist parties. Meanwhile, governments were unable to maintain stability primarily because of both domestic and international economic problems. The problems of reparations, inflation and revaluation seemed at times insurmountable.

(c) 1922–23: years which Maier interprets as ones where nationalist or, on occasions, authoritarian remedies were attempted and which replaced the efforts of the left.

(d) Finally, the middle years of the 1920s to 1929 are, in Maier's term, ones of 'corporatist settlement', when the hopes of returning to a pre-1914 system had to be jettisoned, and when social and economic stability was achieved by government, but only as a result of considerable influence and power being transferred to various interest groups.

8   It wasn't. Maier argues that by the second half of the 1920s corporatism was most developed in Germany, it was emerging in Italy and it was in an 'embryonic' state in France. ☐

Immediate post-war problems

Before we examine Maier's thesis in any detail it is perhaps necessary to remind ourselves of the fundamental economic, political and social problems which were facing the western governments in the years immediately after the ending of the war. You have already covered this ground in section 2 of Units 7–10 and in your reading of Roberts, pp.285–7. Briefly the major issues were as follows.

1   The growth of organized labour during the war. In both France and Italy there was evidence of both greater trade-union power and working-class militancy by 1918. This growth is also reflected in Britain where trade-union membership increased from 4.1 million in 1913 to 7.93 million in 1919 and where, in the latter year, nearly 35 million working days were lost in stoppages because of strikes. In Germany, on the other hand, there was a fall in trade-union membership during the war years as more and more men were called into the army. Nevertheless, the power and influence of trade-union leaders grew during this period and, immediately after the war, in the wake of the Kaiser's departure, trade-union membership rose from 2.2 million in 1918 to 9.1 million in 1920.

2   The physical damage of the war. Much agricultural land was laid waste both in France and in eastern Europe. Industrial areas were severely changed and this resulted in the loss of production and the shortage of goods and working capital. Europe's manufacturing production in 1920 was only three-quarters that of 1913 (Roberts, p.287). We must also remember the vast loss of life occasioned by the war. The overwhelming majority of those killed came from the younger age groups and this had a profound effect not just on post-war production but also on the demographic balance of populations.

3   'The fragmentation of the old economic system' (Roberts, p.285). The hopes that with the ending of the war would come a return to pre-war economic conditions were soon shattered. The conversion of European self-contained wartime economies back to peacetime international trading economies could not be achieved overnight. In the meantime, export markets had been lost, many permanently, and overall Europe's financial and trading pre-eminence was gone.

4   In any case, with regard to international trade, the war had brought about a change of mood. Mutual distrust and an understandable concern on the part of individual governments for their own particular interests led to a 'new wave of protectionist thinking' (Roberts, p.286), and however much Europeans may have 'wished to return to the pre-war economic system, they were psychologically inhibited from doing so, even if the possibility had existed' (Roberts, p.287).

5   The international monetary system had altered markedly since the start of the war in 1914. The huge financial costs of the war on Britain, France and Germany had been borne by heavy borrowing and the sale of foreign assets, and this had resulted in the United States becoming the world's creditor. As Roberts points out, because of the vast manufacturing potential of the US, the European countries were unable to repay their debts through the export of goods or raw materials to the US. Consequently debts were paid in gold and the resulting movement of gold from Europe to the US had the effect of undermining the stability of the European currencies.

6   Other problems which affected adversely the economy of Europe, and which were caused not by war itself but by the post-war settlements, were

the reparations issue and, especially in relation to central and eastern Europe, the geopolitical changes made to the map of Europe.

One other immediate matter of concern for most European countries was the demobilization of their armed forces, and the release and resettling of millions of servicemen into the domestic labour market.

It is essential that you bear these points in mind when examining the political, social and economic events of the 1920s.

2   BRITAIN, FRANCE AND GERMANY IN THE 1920s

Exercise   I want you now to look at Britain, France and Germany in the 1920s in some detail. Start by reading Roberts: the section on France, from p.316 to the top of p.319; the United Kingdom, p.323 to half-way down p.329; and Germany, p.367 to half-way down p.372. Also consult Document I.1 in *Primary Sources 2: Interwar and World War II*, which details figures relating to industrial disputes in the three countries, and Documents I.2 and I.3 which list the votes cast for political parties in the three countries and the governments returned in this period. While reading, keep in mind the following questions:

1   Which country was faced with the greatest threat to its internal stability immediately after the ending of the war, and why?

2   How did the governments of the three countries deal with their internal problems?

3   Why do you think there were not greater threats to the stability of Britain, France and Germany in this period?

4   Look at Documents I.2 and I.3 in *Primary Sources 2: Interwar and World War II*. What electoral differences existed within the three countries, and how stable do you think political life was in Britain, France and Germany during the 1920s? ■

Specimen answers   1   Germany was the country that faced the greatest threat. With the abdication
and discussion   of the Kaiser a provisional government took over and for a few months the members of the government feared there might be violent revolution in Germany. Mutinies in the navy, disillusionment within the army, the setting up of councils of workers and soldiers in Berlin, and widespread industrial discontent all contributed to making the position of the caretaker government far from secure. In addition, the economy was run down, there were grave shortages of food and fuel, and the Allies were demanding the immediate demobilization and return to Germany of all German troops. The Allies also continued the blockade, and this could well have turned into invasion if there had been signs of the new government losing control to the forces of revolution. The birth of the new republic in Germany came at a time of real crisis. It was, in Roberts's words, 'born of defeat, mutiny and revolution, and almost its first act was the acceptance of a humiliating armistice' (p.367).

The government's task of maintaining order was a difficult one. It was challenged on all sides:

- It was challenged by those who looked towards the Bolshevik revolution for inspiration and who criticized the provisional government for being more concerned with obtaining internal stability than with effecting major socialist changes. A German Communist Party (KPD) was formed in December 1918 but it refused to take part in the elections to the National Assembly in January 1919. However, before the elections could take place there was an 'uprising' in Berlin. The extent to which this was a real threat to the new government has been argued over by historians. Roberts calls it a 'minor civil war', while Martin Kitchen has claimed that: 'Far from being a determined effort by unscrupulous bolsheviks to overthrow the regime, it was an ill-considered and chaotic demonstration' organized by those who were concerned by the apparent right-wing course that the provisional government was taking (*Europe Between the Wars*, 1988, p.162). Whatever the intention, the insurrection was crushed by the army and the newly formed *Freikorps*. The government, by approving the actions of the army, was condemned by many people on the left for betraying the cause of socialism, but its supporters argued that the prime need of government at this time was to preserve law and order. Further uprisings and strikes in other urban areas of Germany followed, and there were continuous attempts by the Communist Party to challenge the republic, from the setting up of the Bavarian Soviet Republic in April 1919 to the abortive *coup* in Thuringia in 1923.

- It was also challenged by those on the right who distrusted the socialist leaders, feared that the communists would gain power and opposed the peace terms. Within this grouping Roberts refers to the 'middle classes', white-collar workers and people who, although relieved that it was a parliamentary system which was eventually set up rather than the Soviet model republic of councils, nevertheless disliked and continually attacked the constitution of the Weimar Republic. Many of their beliefs were based on old conservative ideas of German nationalism and a desire for the restoration of the old Bismarckian era, and also the conviction that Germany had not so much lost the war but, rather, had been stabbed in the back. Consequently Versailles, to them, in Roberts's words, 'was not only brutal and unjust, it was the fruit of treason' (p.370).

In many ways the adherents of the right were just as much, if not more, a threat to the stability of Germany as those on the extreme left. In 1920 Kapp attempted to set up a rival government in Berlin which, for at least a few days, was successful. The nationalists were also involved in a number of political assassinations including those of Erzberger and Rathenau, and in 1923 there was the attempted putsch in Bavaria by the National Socialist German Workers' Party.

Compared with France and Germany, Britain's war losses in terms of men killed were not so great. Britain did not undergo the physical destruction that occurred in France, nor did it experience the traumatic political changes that took place in Germany in 1918. Yet while, in these terms, Britain emerged from the war relatively unscathed, from the point of view of industrial discontent and the maintenance of law and order the period immediately after the war was one of great anxiety for the British government.

With regard to industrial discontent, one interesting point that emerges from Document I.1 is that the number of strikes, the numbers of workers involved in strikes and days lost in strikes are high for all three countries in the two years after the ending of World War I. In 1921 the figures for France drop drastically, but they remain high for both Britain and Germany. Certainly in Britain, by the end of the war, the position of trade unions had never been stronger, and membership virtually doubled between 1913 and 1919. Real wages and expectations had risen, and there were increasing demands not just for greater controls in the workplace but also for wider social legislation involving employment, housing and health. These expectations had been fuelled partly by the events in Russia in 1917 and, in common with most other European countries, the shock waves of the Russian revolutions were felt and reflected in a militancy of feeling among certain sections of industrial workers. There is little doubt that the beliefs, held by at least some members of the British government, that there were close connections between Bolsheviks in Russia and industrial militants in Britain were vastly exaggerated. Nevertheless, there were many working men and women who were not only critical of their employers and the government, but who attacked their own trade-union leaders on the grounds that they had been too accommodating in entering into agreements with the government during the war, while at the same time neglecting local and shop-floor problems. As a result a powerful local shop-steward movement had grown up, especially in the mining, engineering and railway industries. In fact, what worried the government was not so much the growth of trade unions as the seeming inability of some unions to control their members. Churchill reflected this concern in February 1919 when he complained that 'the curse of trade unionism was that *there was not enough of it*, and it was not highly enough developed to make its branch secretaries (let alone its rank and file) fall into line with the head office' (K. Middlemas, *The Politics of Industrial Society*, 1979, pp.143–4).

In these circumstances perhaps it is not surprising that the government was extremely fearful of direct action from groups of industrial workers within the country. A government report called, significantly, 'Revolutionary feeling during the year 1919', listed a number of the workers' grievances, among which were: profiteering and high prices, bad housing, 'Class hatred, aggravated by the foolish and dangerous ostentation of the rich, the publication of large dividends and distrust of a "Government of profiteers"'. Interestingly, one of the factors recorded as offsetting the possibility of revolution was the popularity of the royal family (cited in James Cronin, *Labour and Society in Britain, 1918–1979*, 1984, p.21).

The years from 1919 to 1921 proved to be the worst for industrial disturbances in Britain during the whole of the twentieth century. But the unrest was not confined to industrial workers. At the end of 1918 there were demobilization riots and mutinies by soldiers protesting against a system which required that those most needed in industry should be released first. Eventually, most of the heat was taken out of the situation when the government changed its policy to 'first in – first out'. Potentially the most worrying of all the threatened strikes in 1919 was that by the police, which came to a head with police strikes in Liverpool and London in August of that year. The strikes were in protest against legislation recently passed forbidding policemen to belong to a trade union. This legislation had been hurriedly enacted after a strike for higher wages had taken place in August 1918 by members of the Metropolitan and City of London police forces. The government's reaction was to grant the wage rise, appoint a new police commissioner and pass legislation with the intention that this should not occur again. As it was, in August 1919 some 1,100 out of 19,000 policemen took action in London and nearly half the police force came out in Liverpool. The government's response was firm. The army was called in to put down riots in Liverpool and all the strikers were sacked.

A loyal police force was an essential prerequisite for a government expecting major industrial unrest. This expectation was especially strong with regard to the coal-mining industry and the railways, which had been taken over by the government during the war period. At some point decisions had to be made as to whether the government should return these industries to private ownership. Any decentralization was bound to meet with resistance from large sections of the workforce, especially the coal miners who were anxious to preserve the gains they had made and who were actively campaigning for the mines to be nationalized. So there was, in Roberts's words, much 'talk of industrial action for political purposes' (p.325) and the threat of a general strike was one which held some weight, especially as the pre-war 'triple alliance' of railwaymen, miners and transport workers was renewed immediately after the ending of the war.

An economic boom in the months immediately following the ending of the war provided the right conditions for workers to express their grievances. The year 1919 started with talk of a general strike and the 'battle of George Square' in Glasgow, during which the red flag was raised on the roof of the town hall. Despite the red flag the strike by engineers had limited economic, and not political, objectives, but the reaction of the government was one of great alarm. Troops with tanks and machine guns were called in and the leaders of the strike were arrested. A potentially damaging threatened strike in the coal industry in January 1919 was averted by the setting up of a Coal Mines Commission to investigate the industry, but there was a major national railway strike in the autumn of 1919. In all, as noted earlier, nearly 35 million days were lost in strikes in 1919.

In France there were fewer trade unionists (2 million) than in Britain and, as we can see from Document I.1, although there were fewer days lost in strikes in France than in Britain during 1919 and 1920, there were in fact more individual industrial disputes. Like many unions in Britain, the *Confédération Générale du Travail* (CGT) had worked closely with its government during the war, and many of the gains that unionists had made during these years had come through co-operation rather than conflict. Nevertheless, just as in Britain, some French trade unionists felt this co-operation had been too close and, as Roberts states, they found their leaders 'far too moderate' (p.318). Again, as in Britain, the threat of a general strike was freely talked about but French trade unions were not as well organized as those in Britain. Although the CGT, the membership of which had risen by over a million during and immediately following the war, was reluctantly forced into calling a strike in May 1920 in support of the French railway union who were in dispute with the government and the railway owners, the strike was a failure.

2   In Britain, France and Germany the governments acted with various mixtures of repression, compromise and conciliation, and with specific social legislation. (With reference to this legislation, see Table 7–10.2 in Book 2, pp.120–24.) In Germany, where there was the greatest threat to internal stability, the forces of law and order were applied most forcibly. Increasingly the major role of the German socialist caretaker government in 1919 seemed to be the re-establishment of stability, in order to safeguard what had already been achieved and to ensure fair elections for the setting up of a national constituent assembly. To effect this the government relied increasingly and heavily on the army and the *Freikorps* to put down the rebellions and risings of 1919 and 1920. The decision to rely on this branch of the old order which had supported the anti-democratic and anti-reformist 1914 regime was calculated and perhaps unavoidable. There is no doubt that the use of the *Freikorps* was successful in that insurrections were contained, but the often brutal manner in which the *Freikorps* acted helped to fuel working-class resentment and created bitter hatred of the government. For example, it has been estimated that at least 606 people were killed by the time the Bavarian Soviet Republic was broken up in May 1919 (I. Kershaw, *Hitler*, 1998, p.114).

In France, one indication of the strength and growth of organized labour resulting from the war was the winning of the eight-hour day in 1919. However, as Roberts states, the French workers 'had to wait until 1930 for the next instalment of social reform – national insurance against sickness and old age' (p.318). Roberts does not go on to discuss the question of law and order in France, but he does mention that the 1919 elections resulted in the most right-wing parliament since 1871. A coalition of right and centre parties (the *Bloc National*) was formed, and the government took an extremely tough and unsympathetic line towards widespread political and industrial action. From the breaking up of Paris street demonstrations in March 1919, called in protest against the release from prison in 1914 of the assassin of the socialist leader Jean Jaurès, to the abortive general strike in 1920, the police acted vigorously and often very brutally. Government action was both direct and indirect. During the rail strike the government gave money towards the formation of volunteer militias and strike breakers. It also applied to the law courts to dissolve the CGT, and union leaders were arrested on conspiracy charges. In 1921 the government took further precautions to ensure internal stability by setting up a special police force, the *garde mobile* (which became notorious for its brutality), to deal with demonstrations and other unrest.

In Britain a Ministry of Reconstruction had been set up in 1917 partly, so A. J. P. Taylor has argued, to 'allay Labour discontent' (*English History 1914– 1945*, 1965, p.93). Certainly, many of the reports which it issued, including one involving the reorganization of government departments, came to little. But implicit in most of the work of the ministry was the idea that when the war ended the government would continue to some extent in its wartime involvement in industry and industrial relations. A proposal from one of the committees responsible to the ministry, and headed by J. H. Whitley, involved the setting up of national industrial councils for individual industries. These would include both employers and trade unionists and would discuss all aspects of industrial relations, including wages and hours. The idea was welcomed especially by unskilled unions and often by the smaller unions where collective bargaining was virtually unknown. By 1920 there were fifty-six 'Whitley Councils' in existence. However, most of the industries involved in the scheme were small and it was only within the civil service that the councils played any significant role. Interest in the scheme faded and many of the fifty-six gradually disappeared. This lack of enthusiasm was mirrored in the events relating to the National Industrial Conference which was set up by the government in 1919. Intended as a forum for employers and employees to discuss industrial relations, wages and hours, as well as ways to reduce unemployment, all the major unions and the Federation of British Industries were represented. The conference made a number of proposals but eventually, in 1921, despairing of any real decisions ever being made, the trade-union members resigned from the organization.

During this period the government passed some extremely important social legislation, including a Housing Act in 1919 and two National Insurance Acts in 1920 and 1921, but with regard to improving industrial relations the government at times appeared to promise much but do little. In this respect Roberts refers to the 'conciliatory skills' of the Prime Minister, Lloyd George. Roberts argues that the setting up of the Sankey Commission and the government's acceptance of the recommendation that 'some other system' of ownership of the coal industry 'must be substituted' gave hope to the miners, and initially took the heat out of a potentially inflammatory situation with the coal miners in 1919. The fact that the government then did nothing might, in the long run, have aggravated the ill-feeling that existed in the industry, but it certainly prevented a major strike in the coal industry in 1919.

Delaying tactics were by no means the only ones used in Britain. The police force was not only used to control demonstrations but the regional special branches were co-ordinated to maintain a political surveillance of potential dissident groupings. In addition, the government set up a Committee on Industrial Unrest which was intended to deal specifically with large-scale strikes. For this purpose the country was divided into twelve departments, each with a commissioner and its own staff, so that quick action could be taken whenever any disturbance took place. During the months after the Armistice use was also made of existing wartime legislation. The Defence of the Realm Act was deployed in 1919 so that a state of emergency could be declared at the time of the rail strike. Again, in October 1920, at a time when it seemed likely that the Triple Alliance would strike in support of the miners, an Emergency Powers Act was rushed through parliament. This Act empowered the government to impose emergency regulations whenever industrial actions were threatened and might result in the disruption of essential services. The Act was again used at the time of the threatened Triple Alliance strike in 1921 when the government moved troops to the outskirts of a number of key towns, prepared for the call-up of the army reserve and approved the setting up of a special defence force of 'loyal ex-servicemen and loyal citizens'. By the time of 'Black Friday' the government's actions closely resembled, so Kenneth Morgan has argued, those 'of an anti-labour front' (*Consensus and Disunity*, 1979, p.280).

In Germany, as a result of the war and the conditions immediately after it, this was a period when workers were in a strong negotiating position. Wolfgang J. Mommsen has argued that:

> during the revolutionary period neither the government nor the employers risked antagonising the workers if at all possible. Demands for higher wages were frequently conceded without much hesitation ... government and employers alike considered relatively high wage levels and full employment politically essential, and financial policies were conducted accordingly.

> ('The social consequences of World War I', 1988, pp.39–40)

(It is important to remember that while German workers' wages mostly kept up with inflation, even in the runaway phase in 1923, it was the middle classes – those with pensions and fixed incomes – who suffered most.)

The government tried hard to distinguish between political and industrial disruption. Whereas most attempts to challenge the state were met with force, both the government and employers went to great lengths to conciliate and seek agreements with workers claiming better wages and working conditions. As has already been mentioned in Book 2, Units 11–13, p.229 in November 1918 representatives of employers and trade unions met and produced the Stinnes-Legien Agreement whereby, in return for their recognition of many trade-union bargaining rights and an acceptance of the eight-hour day, manufacturers were assured that their leadership of the various industries would not be challenged, and that there would not be a radical restructuring of industry. From the point of view of trade unionists, this agreement brought substantial material gains, while industrialists obtained a necessary compromise which, in the words of Stinnes, created a 'breathing space' (D. Geary, 'Employers, workers and the collapse of the Weimar Republic', 1990, p.97), and ensured continued control of their industries.

There were other compromises made in Germany. We have already mentioned the alliance between the socialist government and the old order in the form of the army. But this was not all. Despite the hopes of some that the Weimar Republic would be a much more unitary, centralized state, this was not the case. Like its predecessor it was essentially federal in structure, and the *Länder* remained and retained many of their executive powers.

Within this structure it was mostly the same civil servants and judiciary who now had to cope with the problems of administering Germany in the difficult years following the ending of the war. So although the government may have been in the hands of new people, many within the ranks of the old ruling groups were still in vital and important positions. It was on this series of compromises – with the army, judiciary, industrialists, trade unionists and civil servants – made in the belief that it was essential to obtain and then secure stability, that the new Weimar Republic was based, and although the new liberal constitution adhered to the principles of universal adult suffrage and proportional representation, in practice much of the real power remained in the hands of the old order.

3   The points made in answer to the previous question will have helped to explain why there was not a greater threat to stability during this period. However, there are two important factors which we have not mentioned and which need to be discussed. The first is highlighted well by Roberts, namely the lack of unity or agreement among the disaffected within the three countries. In relation to Germany, Roberts mentions the split within the SPD and the emergence of the German Communist Party (KPD) in December 1918, but within this division there were further splits and disagreements. The second factor has been highlighted by Wolfgang Mommsen, who has pointed out that in many respects the political parties of the left did not reflect much of the working-class discontent during this period. From his research in the industrial Ruhr, Mommsen concluded that the major desire of most workers was not to embrace a political ideology which demanded revolution, but rather to bring about immediate improvements in their working conditions, and they desired nationalization, especially of the coal industry. Theirs was much more a social protest movement than a wish to achieve major political and other structural changes, and their demands were not necessarily in line with the political programmes of the left-wing parties (Mommsen, 'The German Revolution 1918–1920', 1981).

In addition, although this is not touched on by Roberts, it is noticeable that the insurrections and major discontent took place in the urban areas and were not supported by workers in the rural areas. Indeed, there was considerable hostility between the urban and rural populations – a hostility which cut across class barriers. Townspeople accused the farmers of hoarding food during the last two years of the war, causing severe shortages in the towns, while the farming community resented government attempts to control the production and distribution of food even after the war, as well as during it.

On reflection, it is clear that belief in the existence of popular support for further radical changes in Germany, let alone further revolution, was exaggerated by the government and also by later commentators. After the ending of the worst and most damaging war imaginable, it is questionable whether vast sections of the population had the appetite for renewed strife and civil war. It is understandable perhaps that the government, faced with having to demobilize some 6 million servicemen rapidly in late 1918 and early 1919, was anxious about how these men would react following the defeat of Germany. In fact, most of those who had been on active service wished only to return to their homes. Richard Bessel has pointed out that the numbers of ex-servicemen who joined the anti-war Reich Association of War Disabled, War Veterans and War Dependants were double the number of those who joined the *Freikorps* (*Germany After the First World War*, 1993, p.258). It seems that comparatively few German soldiers who had fought on the western or eastern fronts were involved in the revolutionary unrest immediately after the war, and that the leaders of the revolts came from sections of the navy and workers who had spent most of their war years in Germany itself.

If, with the luxury of the hindsight of eighty years, we can conclude that the threat of a socialist revolution largely reflected the fears of the government rather than the intentions of the vast majority of the governed in Germany, the same can certainly be said for Britain and France. In Britain, despite the shop-stewards' movement and much talk and writing about the need to achieve a democratic control of industry, there was very little revolutionary fervour among the trade-union leaders, or among the Labour Party, which acquired a new constitution in 1918. Although the leaders of labour often expressed sympathy with the aims of socialism and occasionally took stands to support their fellow workers – such as when the dockers refused to load boats taking arms which might have been used against Bolsheviks in the Russo-Polish War – they more often distanced themselves from any commitment to world socialism. The Labour Party did not accept the conditions of affiliation laid down by the Third Socialist International which met in Moscow in 1920, and only a few small Marxist groups agreed to do so. They formed themselves into the Communist Party (CP) of Great Britain and immediately sought, and were refused, affiliation with the Labour Party. In 1921 the CP's membership was around 5,000 and, as Martin Kitchen has written, it 'was no more a threat to the established order than were the Jehovah's Witnesses to the established church or the Mormons to the institution of marriage' (*Europe Between the Wars*, 1988, p.187).

In France the split within the French Socialist Party (this took place around the same time as in Britain), which resulted in the formation of the French Communist Party, was almost the reverse of the outcome in Britain. In France it was the Communist Party membership in 1921 that was larger than the socialists (140,000 to 30,000), and it was the communist newspaper *L'Humanité* which sold many more copies than the socialist daily *Populaire* (200,000 to 5,000). In 1922 there was also a marked lack of unity within the ranks of the trade-union movement when the CGT, weakened after its disastrous attempt at a general strike, was itself split and the communists formed a rival, the CGTU. Again, it was the communist branch which contained the highest membership (500,000 to 370,000).

Although the communists had a greater following in France than in Britain, the militant left in France was never really strong or united enough to pose a serious threat to the established order. Although, as in Britain, the *Parti Communiste Française* was essentially a parliamentary party, just the mention of a 'Red Peril' was enough to bring together those groups who were being particularly hard hit by the escalating inflation in the country and who united under the political banner of slogans such as the protection of private property, a return to normality and law and order.

4   The first point to make is that in Germany and France there was a multiplicity of parties and that no one party ever achieved much more than 33 per cent of the popular vote. In Britain this was not the case. Far fewer parties attained representation in parliament and, apart from 1924 and 1929–31, the Conservative Party dominated every interwar government, even though during 1919–22 the government was nominally a coalition under the premiership of the Liberal leader Lloyd George, and during 1931–39 there was a National Government headed from 1931 to 1935 by the former Labour leader J. Ramsay MacDonald.

In Germany until 1933 and in France throughout the interwar years no one political party achieved a clear majority of seats in the *Reichstag* or Chamber of Deputies. The resulting political confusion can be seen in Germany where there were seventeen administrations in thirteen years. Government depended on coalitions, and at times up to six separate parties were involved in these coalitions. Obviously this state of affairs did not make it easy for governments to make decisive and unhindered policy decisions. One reason for the multiplicity of parties in the *Reichstag* was the system of proportional representation, however the large number of parties clearly reflects the fragmentation of German political life in this period. The most popular party up until 1932 was the Social Democrats (SPD), but note the figures for the Centre Party which invariably won around sixty seats in the *Reichstag* in the 1920s. The Centre Party had been formed in the 1870s, in reaction to Bismarck's attacks on the Catholic Church. Unlike many of the other German political parties, the Centre did not have a strong socio-economic base but, understandably, attracted support mostly from the Catholic electorate. Although the Centre was prominent in all seventeen administrations, unlike the SPD it was a moderate conservative party espousing the existing order and opposed to socialism and communism.

In France, too, there were a large number of political parties but the new proportional representation voting system introduced in 1919, which replaced single-member constituencies by large multimember electoral districts, favoured those parties that entered into electoral pacts or coalitions. As in Germany, there were no new popular political parties and throughout the period, again as in Germany, religion was to play an important part in politics. I have already mentioned the formation and success of the *Bloc National* at the 1919 election (a coalition of right-wing parties, nationalists and anti-socialists), but this was an uneasy alliance and there were many disagreements, particularly between the Catholics and anti-clericals within the alliance. The *Bloc* was succeeded in 1924 by another electoral alliance, this time formed between the radicals, socialists and socialist republicans and named the *Cartel des Gauches*. Again, the differences between the various groupings were not far from the surface. Indeed, at times the only belief they seemed to hold in common was a dislike and distrust of the Catholic Church and Catholic politicians. In fact, the difficulties of pursuing agreed policies were so great that within the space of nine months in 1924 there were six cabinet crises. The stalemate in French politics can perhaps best be illustrated by the figures which show that between 1920 and 1940 the average life expectancy of a French government was seven months. □

So far we have discussed the immediate problems facing governments after the ending of World War I and we have concentrated on the discontent existing within the three countries. Now I want to examine in some detail other major problems that arose as a consequence of the war.

Inflation and reparations

The dominating issue, which tended to obscure many other political and economic problems, particularly in France and Germany in the 1920s, was that of inflation. Primarily an inheritance from the war, this was a problem that governments in all three countries had to face. The war had brought shortages of many goods and a corresponding rise in prices so that, for example, by 1918 price levels in Britain were more than twice those of 1914, and in France they were three times as high. In addition, France and Germany in particular had made little attempt to finance the war through internal taxation, which would have reduced spending power and gone some way to controlling inflation. Vested interests were too strong and state powers too weak for the policy to be implemented. Consequently money was raised largely through borrowing, and by 1918 both France and Germany faced huge repayment problems which were far too large to be paid off through trade. In any case, in France during the course of the war income from exports covered only about 29 per cent of expenditure spent on imports, and so France's foreign debts in 1918 amounted to some 19 billion francs.

In Germany the financial problems were even worse. The war had been fought in the expectation that Germany would win and would then automatically solve all its financial problems by presenting bills to the losers. In November 1918 this dream was shattered. The irony is that the peace settlements then transferred the dream to the French nation, who became convinced that their financial problems could be solved by the enforcement of reparations from Germany. This way of thinking was highly damaging to both countries.

In France successive governments, fully aware that they had been voted into office on the claim that 'the Boche must pay', were extremely reluctant to grapple with their financial problems by introducing unpopular austerity measures. In order to pay off debts, governments resorted to borrowing at even higher rates of interest. More currency was put into circulation, thereby adding to the inflation, and this in turn further undermined international confidence in the franc. By 1920 price levels were five times higher than they had been in 1914.

In an attempt to accelerate the collection of reparations, 40,000 French troops were ordered, much against world opinion, to occupy the Ruhr. The move was unsuccessful in that the reparations collected in 1923 were not significantly higher than in the previous year, and the government had been forced to raise taxes by 20 per cent to cover the costs of the operation. The failure of the occupation and the success of the left wing in the elections of 1924 led to more uncertainties and a flight of capital out of the country, which contributed to a further decline of the franc from 70 to the pound in 1924 to 250 to the pound in July 1926.

It was only when Poincaré returned in 1926 as head of a coalition government which contained radicals on the left as well as politicians from the right, and armed with powers to govern by decree if necessary, that firm steps were taken to restore confidence within the country and especially among business people. Taxes were raised sharply, severe cuts were made in government expenditure and, most importantly, the drift of capital out of the country was not only stopped but reversed. In 1928 the government was able to stabilize the currency, albeit at 20 per cent of its pre-war value, but French investors at least had not been hit as badly as their German counterparts. Gordon Wright concludes:

> The French solution to the war's financial burden – an inflation that was checked short of disaster – fell midway between that of the Germans and the British and was probably healthier than either. It was, however, a solution that was more empirical than planned.

(*France in Modern Times*, 1987, p.351)

Exercise   With regard to inflation in Germany have a look at Document I.4 in *Primary Sources 2: Interwar and World War II* and then answer the following questions:

1   When did prices and the exchange rate start to increase at an enormously rapid rate?

2   Account for the vast increases in 1923.

3   From your reading of this unit so far, can you think of any additional reasons for the inflation in Germany, especially in the years immediately following the war? ■

Specimen answers   1   The first enormous change in the exchange rate took place between July *and discussion*   and August 1922, and this was reflected in the almost doubling of the cost-of-living index between August and September 1922.

2   The French occupation of the Ruhr, during which the German government called on the workers in the area not to co-operate. The response to the call for passive resistance was impressive but extremely damaging. The price for the virtual shutdown of industries in the area was that the government had to print more and more money to pay those who had ceased work.

3   Faced with severe internal unrest, there were high pay settlements. Remember Mommsen's statement: 'government and employers alike considered relatively high wage levels and full employment politically essential, and financial policies were conducted accordingly'. □

This last point must not be underestimated. It is almost impossible to appreciate the figures quoted in the inflation of 1923 (and it must be noted that because of the collapse of the currency, the figures are not as precise as those quoted for the earlier years). But even by April 1920 the cost of living was ten times what it had been in 1914.

For those people unable to work, or who were dependent on fixed incomes, inflation had been a disaster from the very start. However, the hyperinflation of 1923 not only adversely affected most sections of the German population but also threatened a worldwide financial crisis. Something had to be done to stabilize the German currency. In August 1923 yet another coalition government was formed, this time under Stresemann. While acknowledging that the German actions in the Ruhr demonstrated national unity, he also realized their disastrous consequences. He called for an end to the passive resistance and changed the direction of the government's economic policy by putting tight controls on borrowing and government expenditure. The currency was stabilized with the introduction of the Rentenmark, which replaced the Reichsmark. Most important of all, Stresemann worked towards obtaining a settlement of the reparations issue. This was accomplished in co-operation with the US. The Dawes Plan was devised in 1924 and the Young Plan, which followed five years later, ensured that Germany's payments were considerably reduced and the period for repayment extended to 1988. The Dawes Plan also paved the way for the setting up of large American loans and investments in the country which did much to stimulate the country's economic recovery.

In one sense, by the end of the war the financial position in Britain had altered more markedly than in France and Germany. As Roberts points out on p.286, 'Even before 1914, there had been signs that a slowing of industrial growth and exports might make it hard for Great Britain to go on being banker to the world.' By 1918 Britain had forfeited this position to the US. Britain, like France and Germany, was in debt to the US, and in financing the war had lost about a quarter of its overseas investments. The national debt was around fourteen times greater than it had been in 1913.

Exercise   Study Document in I.5 in *Primary Sources 2: Interwar and World War II.* In what ways do the trends in wages and prices in Britain after the war and in the early 1920s differ from those experienced in France and Germany? ■

Specimen answer   Apart from the period up to 1920, which effectively marked a continuation of
and discussion   wartime pressures, Britain did not undergo the inflation experienced by the other two countries. A brief post-war boom, continuing the inflation which had taken place during the war, meant that by early 1920 prices were about three times the 1914 figure. But this was followed by a recession, with a corresponding drop in prices and an increase in unemployment. A government committee was set up to enquire into the causes of the slump, and the recommendations that there should be drastic cuts in public spending were acted upon. Whereas Germany more or less deliberately implemented inflationary policies in the early 1920s, the British government pursued an opposite policy of deflation. □

In his book *Recasting Bourgeois Europe* Maier writes that the major aim of conservatives after 1918 was that of returning to the social order of the pre-war years. Whether or not this was the case, in Britain there was a strong desire to return to the pre-1914 situation when Britain was the financial centre of the world. Most of British economic policy was devoted largely to trying to achieve this aim. Deflation, it was hoped, would not only reduce unemployment but bring back confidence to the City. It was partly as a result of this reasoning that the British government decided to return to the gold standard in 1925 at the pre-war parity of £1 to 4.86 dollars. This was an over-valuation of the pound by some 10 per cent, but it was hoped that such an action would bring stability and confidence and raise Britain once again to the position of financial centre of the world. Also, although the over-valuation would make exports more expensive, it was hoped that these higher prices would be 'offset by lower wages, greater efficiency and the consequent reduction of unit costs' (M. Kitchen, *Europe Between the Wars*, 1988, p.195). Unfortunately the return of the gold standard did not bring the results that were hoped for and, at least in the short run, it was to have an adverse effect on British industry.

The return of industry to peacetime conditions and its consequences

In 1913 Britain, France and Germany had been responsible for roughly 60 per cent of the exported manufactured goods throughout the world. The war had interrupted this trade and these three western countries were never again to dominate the world market to such an extent. Peter Fearon, writing about European agriculture and industry after the war, argues that:

> Nowhere was Europe more severely hit by the war than in agriculture, a sector which employed more labour than all other industries together. Throughout the conflict cereal output, the main European crop, declined in spite of desperate attempts to increase it. A shortage of labour, horsepower and fertiliser explains why Europe could not feed itself in 1919 and had to import food on credit from the US. The withdrawal of Russia, traditionally the granary of the continent, from world trade in 1917 increased Europe's dependence on other continents; countries overseas responded by raising the output of their primary products, financing the expansion by borrowing from the US. However, by 1925 European agriculture was back to its 1913 levels of production and seemed set to increase output even more. At the same time, production in the rest of the world, encouraged by the golden years of high prices between 1914 and 1920, was at a much higher level than in 1913.
>
> W. A. Lewis has calculated that if the trend of output established between 1881 and 1913 in European manufacturing had been maintained the level of output that Europe eventually reached in 1929 would have been achieved in 1921. If Lewis is correct, the war set back Europe's industrial growth by eight years. It would be a grave mistake to assume, however, that all economic events of the 1920s can be traced back to the war. The economic expansion of France in this decade, for example, is a continuation of a pre-1914 trend; the overseas trade of both Britain and Germany showed a similar structure in the post-war era to that before 1914; and Britain's staple industries would have posed a problem even if there had been no war. A further example of continuity can be found in the pattern of cyclical fluctuations in the interwar period. In 1914 most major industrial countries were poised on the edge of a recession which the war delayed until 1920–21. The next major downturn began in 1929 and can be seen as a return to the normal pattern of the trade cycle. Throughout the world many countries were strengthened by the war, as their economies became more diversified and more committed to manufacturing. In Europe, however, the picture was bleak, for even by the late 1920s agriculture was not prosperous, trade was relatively depressed and in most industrial nations unemployment was high. These problems were not caused by the war but were intensified by it, and while they offer

no explanation as to why the depression began in 1929, we can accept the view that structural problems can lessen resistance to depression and make recovery more difficult.

(*The Origins and Nature of the Great Slump 1929–32*, 1979, pp.14–15)

Exercise   1   To what extent does Fearon think the economic events of the 1920s in Europe were decisively influenced by the war?

2   In what area does Fearon seemingly disagree with Roberts?

3   On what topics do Roberts and Fearon agree? ■

Specimen answers   1   Fearon sees a great deal of continuity before and after the war, especially *and discussion*   with regard to the manufacturing industries and finance. It was agriculture which was most severely hit in the years immediately following the war. Labour shortages and lack of fertilisers meant that cereal output declined. The tradition of importing grain from Russia had been halted after 1917 so that European countries had to look elsewhere for food supplies.

2   On p.316 Roberts refers to the 'lack of important growth in the economy' of France. Perhaps Roberts is referring here to the interwar years as a whole because, in fact, in the 1920s the French industrial growth rate was higher than that of any other European country. Indeed, by 1929 all production and trade figures had reached record levels. Fearon states that this economic expansion was apparent before 1914 and the French economic historian Francois Caron agrees with him. Caron states that in this period industrial growth was 'more marked in France than in the rest of Europe. It was as much a continuation of the growth of the immediate pre-war years as of the industrialist spirit of the First World War' (*An Economic History of Modern France*, 1983, p.181).

Both Caron and Fearon are correct to point to the pre-war years as the basis for this expansion but the effects of the war on French industry must be emphasized. In the first place, the recovery of Alsace and Lorraine was important in the contribution towards the production of textiles, iron and steel. Also, the acquisition of further colonies ensured export markets for French products. The necessary rebuilding of much of the industrial areas of north-west France devastated during the war also meant the replacement of nineteenth-century industrial units with more efficient modern ones. But the war had also done much to alter the attitudes of many French industrialists and this, together with the acute shortage of labour, made French industrialists more receptive than most other European industrialists to 'Taylorism' (the application of scientific methods in management and the organization of labour, named after the American F. W. Taylor) and assembly-line production methods (see Maier, 'Between Taylorism and technocracy', 1970).

Also, as we have mentioned before, the inflation that worried so many French governments played its part in this expansion. The depreciation of the franc on the foreign exchanges gave a great boost to French exports, and a relatively new industry, tourism, expanded enormously as foreigners benefited from the cheap French currency. This in its turn encouraged a great deal of investment in hotels, casinos and the development of holiday resorts. However, the major areas of investment, which had started before World War I and which carried on through the 1920s, were concentrated on plant and machinery in the productive sectors of industry. It is in the engineering, metallurgical and chemical industries that this increase can best be seen.

3   Both Roberts and Fearon agree that there was a slowing down of industrial growth in Britain and in its export markets before the war. Fearon argues that Britain's staple industries 'would have posed a problem even if there had been no war'. It was these industries which were particularly hard hit in the recession in 1920. From around 1923 there was a gradual recovery, so that by 1925 production in British industries was back to pre-war levels, but unemployment was still around the one million mark. However, all the staple industries were still producing well below capacity, largely because of the loss of export markets. In addition, as we have mentioned already, the return to the gold standard had over-valued the pound and the only way to counter this over-valuation was to attempt to make Britain more competitive by reducing production costs. Unfortunately, in such labour intensive industries as, for example, coal, it was difficult to see where these reductions could be made other than in wages, and further wage reductions in the coal industry were bound to meet with opposition from the unions. □

German industrial production had also declined during the war. By 1919 the index of industrial production was only about 38 per cent of what it had been in 1913. The drop was partly because of the loss of industrial areas as a result of the peace settlement, partly because of the rundown of machinery and industrial units during the war, but also there was a marked drop in productivity figures. The industrial discontent, as seen in Document I.1, with the vast numbers of days lost by strikes in the early days after the ending of the war, was an important factor here. Another factor was that, as we have seen, many concessions were made to German workers in 1918 and 1919, with wage increases and an eight-hour day, so in fact what had happened was that there had been both a decrease in hours and an increase in wages, which resulted in labour costs being higher and labour productivity being lower. One of the consequences of the cuts in government expenditure in 1924 was that many of the gains that German workers had obtained in the period following the war, such as the eight-hour day, were lost, wages fell and, as unemployment increased, so the membership of trade unions also fell. It was only by the end of the decade that industrial production reached the level it had been in 1913. But one particularly important development had taken place during this time. This was a move towards the development of larger units of production through amalgamation and rationalization, so that by the end of the decade, for example, IG Farben dominated the chemical industry and the United Steel Works controlled over half of Germany's coal production and nearly a half of the country's steel production.

Whereas German industrial production became increasingly concentrated in this period, German agriculture moved in the reverse direction. This was partly a result of Germany losing her eastern territories in the peace settlements, the areas where the vast majority of large estates were situated. In any case, as Fearon (1979) points out, this was a bad period for agriculture in all three countries. Increased agricultural production in other parts of the world kept agricultural prices low and land prices dropped. Although in Book 2, Units 7–10, section 2 Bill Purdue states, quite rightly, that agriculture remained France's largest industry, even here there was a transfer of the population in this period away from agriculture towards the higher industrialized sector. Between 1906 and 1931 the number of male workers in agriculture fell from 5.4 to 4.4 million, while the number of wage earners in industry rose from 3.7 to 5.4 million.

Exercise   Study Documents I.1 and I.6 in *Primary Sources 2: Interwar and World War II.*

1   Which country suffered least from industrial discontent during the period 1925–29?

2   Where and when was there the greatest amount of industrial discontent in this period? ■

Specimen answers and discussion

1   From these sets of figures it appears that the industrial disruption caused by strikes was greater in Britain and Germany than in France. Although there were often more industrial disputes in France in certain years than in the other two countries, they did not last as long, and very often fewer days were lost per strike. Again, unemployment figures were much lower in France than in Britain and Germany. For France the figure of 2.7 per cent in 1921 was high, whereas in Germany from 1923 onwards the figure was never below 3.4 per cent. Britain suffered the greatest unemployment of all three countries and the figure was never less than 9 per cent of the workforce after 1921.

2   Clearly the key dates are 1926 in Britain, when 162 million working days were lost and some 2.73 million workers involved, and 1928 in Germany when over 20 million days were lost. □

Exercise   From what you have read in this unit and in Book 2, Units 7–10 list the reasons why France had less unemployment and fewer industrial disturbances than Britain and Germany between 1925 and 1929. ■

Specimen answer and discussion

1   The loss of large numbers of men killed in the war and the very small increase in population over the previous decades compared with Britain and Germany meant that there was a scarcity of labour, or at least of French-born labour.

2   The greater growth in industrial production in France obviously helped to maintain full employment.

3   Unlike in Britain, there was little attempt until the mid-1920s to maintain the level of the currency, and the fall of the franc on the foreign exchanges helped French exporting industries. □

One could well draw the conclusion from what has been said so far that at least the French industrial workers should have benefited from these conditions. But the rise in the wages of French workers in this period does not reflect this as much as one might expect. First, French trade unions were weaker in organizational structure than those in Britain and Germany. Second, and more important, there was a large-scale immigration of foreign workers, especially Italians, Belgians, Poles and Spaniards, into France in the 1920s. These workers went into, particularly, the mines of northern France, the steel and iron mills and the construction industries. This was a largely unorganized labour force and, as is so often the case with immigrant workers, could be employed for comparatively low wages. So, although unemployment was not high, neither was there a great scarcity in the labour market.

It was partly because of this cheap labour force that, although there were changes within French society itself, French governments were never unduly pressed to make social reforms. Study again Table 7–10.2 in Book 2 and compare the social reforms and welfare policies instituted in France with those in Germany and the United Kingdom. Although legislation was passed in 1919 introducing the eight-hour day, there were few other major reforms and it is clear that in the area of social welfare France lagged well behind the other two countries.

The figures for Britain in Document I.6 show that unemployment never fell below one million after 1921, but that is only part of the story. Unemployment varied according to region and industry. It was particularly high in the old staple industries. For example, in 1927 unemployment stood at 11.3 per cent but in the five industries of coal, metal manufacture, engineering, shipbuilding, cotton and woollens, it was 15.8 per cent. It was in these industries and especially, as we have already seen, in the coal industry, which was under-mechanized and in need of reorganization and modernization, that the major industrial problems and troubles lay.

The General Strike of 1926 came about because of yet another attempt on the part of the coal owners to make their prices more competitive by reducing wages and lengthening working hours. For further information on the General Strike read Roberts, pp.328–9, where he discusses the strike and the events leading up to it.

Roberts does not discuss the reasons for the high number of days lost in Germany in 1928. In fact, the main reason was not so much a strike on the part of the workers as a lock-out by employers of some 250,000 workers in the iron and steel industries. According to V. R. Berghahn, this was a 'deliberately escalated confrontation' on the part of the employers (*Modern Germany*, 1987, p.107). The background to this, Berghahn maintains, was that the particularly conservative industrialists in the heavy industries, which had undergone cartelization (agreements whereby they divided up the market between themselves, devised production quotas and fixed prices) and rationalization and which were experiencing boom conditions, were unhappy with many of the concessions that had been made in the period immediately following the war and which were affecting their industries. They were also generally unhappy with the political liberalism of the Weimar Republic and, in particular, they resented the system of compulsory arbitration whereby wage settlements could be imposed by an arbitrator representing the state. In 1928 they deliberately challenged this procedure and refused to accept the arbitration decision for a small wage increase.

The final outcome of this lock-out was a compromise whereby the wage increase was lessened but the system of state arbitration was retained. Nevertheless, the significant fact was that these industrialists were now prepared to challenge the trade unions and the state itself. Indeed, there was growing criticism of the republic from many quarters. The ambitious Act of

Labour Exchanges and Unemployment Insurance, which covered more workers than anywhere else in Europe, soon ran into problems and was condemned by many industrialists as being too costly. Although the period 1925–29 in Germany appeared to be one of relative prosperity, bear in mind that much of the funding which brought about the industrial expansion came from the US. The American stock market crash of 1929 was therefore to have more of an effect on Germany than on Britain and France, and it was to heighten sharply any social and political discontent that existed within the country.

The Great Depression

Overall, it would be fair to say that during the second half of the 1920s economic production returned to pre-war levels, European currencies were stabilized, and as well as growing prosperity there was a new optimism in foreign relations. The 'Great Depression' was to hamper this progress seriously. Bill Purdue, in Book 2, Units 7–10, raised the question of whether this depression was at least partly caused by the economic consequences of the Great War. A key text in exploring this point is the introduction to Derek H. Aldcroft's book *From Versailles to Wall Street 1919–1929* (1987), which is reprinted in the *Secondary Sources*. If you have time, refresh your memory by rereading this extract.

Almost all the countries of Europe were affected to a greater or lesser extent by the Depression. It was regarded by some as a catastrophe almost on the scale of the Great War. William E. Leuchtenburg, in an article called 'The New Deal and the analogue of war', first published in 1964, argues that many politicians in the early 1930s used the imagery of the war when describing the Depression and, more importantly, looked back to the experiences of the war, especially in regard to the economic mobilization which took place in these years, as the most suitable means of combating the Depression. Leuchtenburg illustrates his thesis with specific reference to the New Deal and the US. He concludes that using the imagery of war was invaluable because it provided a feeling of national solidarity, but that in the last resort the New Deal would have been more successful if the economists and politicians had dealt with the basic economic and social problems rather than looking towards the 'analogue of war', that is, the economic expedients which were used in the war. Although Leuchtenburg illustrates his thesis with specific reference to the US, it is one that is worthy of consideration in relation to events in Europe, and we should bear it in mind as we discuss the impact and after-effects of the Depression.

Exercise   Read Roberts, pp.289–92, in which he outlines the reasons for the world slump.

1   Which of the three countries does Roberts believe was hardest hit, and why?

2   Which of the three countries does Roberts state was least affected, and why? ∎

Specimen answers   1   Roberts believes that Germany was hit hardest by the world slump, largely
and discussion   because of its heavy dependence on international credit, especially credit from the US.

2   Roberts believes that Britain was the least affected by the world slump. The reason for this, so Roberts states, was that British industry had 'benefited less from the boom of the 1920s and lost less ground comparatively'. □

Roberts does not mention France specifically but France was affected in a different way from the other two countries. From the unemployment statistics we can see that while unemployment increased rapidly in Britain and Germany in 1930, there was only a very small rise in France in that year. In fact it was not until 1932 that the unemployment figures in France became relatively high. However, the same sort of pattern is produced in the industrial production table. Unlike in Britain and Germany, industrial production in France did not decline in 1930 and it was only in 1932 that there was a marked drop. From all these figures it is clear that the Depression hit France later than most of the other industrialized countries of the world. The reasons for this are complex and varied, but basically France was not a producer of raw materials, was less heavily industrialized than Britain and Germany and was not so dependent on the world economy. Also, unlike Germany, France was not irrevocably dependent on loans from the US. In addition, as we have already seen, France was under-populated so that unemployment was not the problem it became in Britain and Germany.

As we have seen, Maier has argued that it was from around the mid-1920s that the hopes of returning to the pre-1914 economic system were jettisoned. This may well have been the case, but if any hopes lingered, the Great Depression finally ended them. Roberts quotes Harold Macmillan, who, writing in 1938, was able to reflect that the slump 'liberate[d] men's minds from a continued subservience to the economic orthodoxy of the prewar world' (p.291). However, it is impossible to exaggerate the effect, especially during the bleak years of 1930–32, that the Depression had on contemporaries. John Maynard Keynes, in a lecture in the US in 1931, declared that:

> We are today in the middle of the greatest economic catastrophe – the greatest catastrophe due almost entirely to economic causes – of the modern world ... the view is held in Moscow that this is the last, the culminating crisis of capitalism and that our existing order of society will not survive it ... there is a possibility that when this crisis is looked back upon by the economic historian of the future it will be seen to mark one of the major turning points ...
>
> (Cited in P. Fearon, *The Origins and Nature of the Great Slump 1929–32* 1979, p.9)

The devastating effects of the Great Slump on Germany have led many historians to contend that it was the major factor in breaking up the Weimar Republic and bringing Hitler to power. This is an issue that will be discussed in Unit 17.

3 MAIER: AN APPRAISAL

Exercise Just before we return to Maier and *Recasting Bourgeois Europe*, is there any evidence in this unit which suggests that Britain had become closer to a corporatist state in this period? ■

Specimen answer In Britain, during and immediately after the war, with the setting up of the
and discussion Ministry of Reconstruction, the National Industrial Conference and the Whitley

Councils, it appeared that ideas of collective bargaining were becoming firmly established and that there was a move towards at least a degree of corporatism. However, by the early 1920s, with the break-up of the National Industrial Conference, the comparative failure of Whitleyism and the decision of the Coalition government to extricate itself from its commitments to the coal-mining industry, it became clear that this was not the case. The attitude of the Conservative government towards trade unions certainly showed little inclination towards supporting collective bargaining. □

Exercise   Maier's book is nearly 600 pages in length. He drew on a vast range of sources, and his arguments are complex and detailed. Clearly, by just studying the introduction we are doing Maier a disservice, and by merely outlining his arguments we are open to the criticism of oversimplifying them. However, from your reading of the extract from his book and the material presented in the unit, to what extent would you agree with or question Maier's arguments? My observations are given below.

- The first stage of Maier's thesis is his contention that the period following the ending of World War I was one of great turmoil and that a revolution in western Europe was a real possibility. Certainly in Germany there were attempted political insurrections, and in all three countries there was a great deal of industrial discontent, but there is little evidence that revolutionary fervour extended beyond all but a few comparatively small groups, and there are few signs that what Maier calls the 'profound disorder and turbulence occasioned by the First World War' (Course Reader, p.113) should necessarily have been followed by revolution. If anything the notion of a threat of revolution reflected the fears of the governments in Britain, France and Germany rather than the intentions of the vast majority of the governed. So it is important to question whether the basic premise of Maier's thesis is sound or whether he is constructing an explanation for what was in any case a non-event (that is, a proletarian revolution).

- Maier's next point is that any revolution that possibly would have taken place was contained by a combination of the middle classes and élites uniting against the working-class militant left. This raises two questions.

    First, does Maier obscure the complexity of the societies in western Europe by discussing these events in specifically class terms? (Or, to put it another way, does he have a too inflexible notion of class?) Is Maier making too sharp a distinction between the working populations within France and Germany (and the same could be said for Britain) and other sections of society? We should question whether he is polarizing these societies too sharply in class terms and whether he gives due weight, for example, to the influence of Catholicism among the various classes within France and Germany and its important influence in the political, economic and social life of these two countries. To be fair to Maier, he does state later on in his book that 'The defence of bourgeois Europe must be mapped in three dimensions – in terms of class, elite and interest groups' (Maier, *Recasting Bourgeois Europe*, 1975, p.19). Also, in the introduction, he disclaims the notion that 'bourgeois defence was the stake of all political conflict in the 1920s' (p.7). Nevertheless, his thesis is based primarily on the belief that the prime motivating forces for change were economic and class conflict. The questions we must keep in the forefront of our minds are whether these claims can be sustained, and whether or not other important elements are given due weight and consideration in his analysis of European society.

Secondly, does he exaggerate the strength and unity of socialist feeling in western Europe during this period? With regard to the latter, it was not just that there were often marked and debilitating differences of opinion among leftist parties which very often prevented united action, but also the elections of 1918–19 do not show a preponderance of feeling for militancy. Indeed, the work of Mommsen and others has shown that there was a wide variety of interests, often conflicting, among different sections of the workforce, very often depending as much on job, region and religion as on socialist sympathies. Maier does attempt to answer this point by arguing that during the 1920s, as the left was gradually defeated, 'Class consciousness was undergoing a double evolution. In the world of work, identification as proletarian or bourgeois was becoming less compelling than interest-group affiliation, less a principle of common action in the economic arena.' What you have to consider is whether even in 1918 it was 'interest-group affiliations' which were the major concerns among working men and women rather than class issues.

- The final strand of Maier's thesis is that during the middle years of the 1920s, when hopes of returning to a pre-1914 Europe had finally been abandoned, some level of social and economic stability was achieved by governments, but only as a result of some of their power being transferred to various interest groups. Consequently, Germany and Italy, and to a lesser extent France, become corporatist in tendency. However, it is worth referring back to the introduction to the Course Reader where an alternative explanation is put forward for the changes which took place after 1918. Rather than going along with Maier's ideas for 'rescuing bourgeois Europe through recasting', isn't it equally justifiable to argue that there was:

> [a] simple recognition that societies had to be reorganized for peace after five years of total war? Going back to 1914 was impossible; the empiricist, searching in vain for monolithic social classes, might argue that pragmatism and the various pressures on different governments and administrations meant simply that some wartime practices were kept and others discarded.
>
> (Course Reader, p.14)

However much you may agree or disagree with Maier, he is certainly correct when he states that despite all the problems facing the European governments, some sort of stability was achieved around the middle of the decade. The major reason he gives for this state of affairs is the growing involvement of the US in Europe. But, as he states towards the end of his book, 'The equilibrium was certainly hostage to continuing American prosperity and the control of German national resentments' (p.579). Unit 17 examines the growth of German resentments and the sudden ending of American prosperity. ■

References

Abercrombie, N. *et al.* (1984) *Penguin Dictionary of Sociology*, Penguin.

Aldcroft, D. H. (1987) *From Versailles to Wall Street 1919–1929*, Penguin.

Berghahn, V. R. (1987) *Modern Germany: Society, Economy and Politics in the Twentieth Century*, Cambridge University Press.

Bessell, R. (1993) *Germany After the First World War*, Oxford University Press.

Caron, F. (1983) *An Economic History of Modern France*, Methuen.

Cronin, J. E. (1984) *Labour and Society in Britain 1918–1979*, Batsford.

Fearon, P. (1979) *The Origins and Nature of the Great Slump 1929–32*, Macmillan.

Geary, D. (1990) 'Employers, workers, and the collapse of the Weimar Republic' in Bessell, R. *et al.* (eds) *Weimar: Why Did German Democracy Fail?*, Weidenfeld and Nicolson.

Kershaw, I. (1998) *Hitler 1889–1936: Hubris*, Allen Lane.

Kitchen, M. (1988) *Europe Between the Wars: A Political History*, Longman.

Leuchtenburg, W. F. (1964) 'The New Deal and the analogue of war' in Braeman, J. *et al.* (eds) *Change and Continuity in Twentieth Century America*, Ohio State University Press.

Maier, C. S. (1970) 'Between Taylorism and technocracy', *Journal of Contemporary History*, vol.5, no.2, pp.54–9.

Maier, C. S. (1975) *Recasting Bourgeois Europe: Stabilization in France, Germany and Italy in the Decade after World War I*, Princeton University Press.

Mayer, A. J. (1981) *The Persistence of the Old Regime: Europe to the Great War*, Croom Helm/Pantheon.

Middlemas, K. (1979) *The Politics of Industrial Society*, Deutsch.

Mommsen, W. J. (1981) 'The German Revolution 1918–1920: political revolution and social protest movement' in Bessell, R. and Feuchtwanger, E. J. (eds) *Social Change and Political Development in Weimar Germany*, Croom Helm.

Mommsen, W. J. (1988) 'The social consequences of World War I' in Marwick, A. (ed.) *Total War and Social Change*, Macmillan.

Morgan, K. (1979) *Consensus and Disunity*, Oxford University Press.

Roberts, J. M. (1977) book review, *History*, vol.62, p.512.

Taylor, A. J. P. (1965) *English History 1914–1945*, Oxford University Press.

Wright, G. (1987) *France in Modern Times*, Norton.

Unit 15 A NEW CIVILIZATION: STALINISM IN THE SOVIET UNION 1929–1941

BERNARD WAITES

Open University students of this unit will need to refer to:

Set book: J. M. Roberts, *Europe 1880–1945*, Longman, 2001

Primary Sources 2: Interwar and World War II, eds Arthur Marwick and Wendy Simpson, Open University, 2000

Chapter 13 of Roberts, 'Totalitarianism and dictatorship', has a succinct account of the rise of Stalin and the development of the Soviet Union under his leadership (pp.336–49). There is also a discussion of the collectivization of Soviet agriculture in Chapter 11, 'Economy and society 1918–1939', pp.299–301. You need to read these sections of Roberts before embarking on this unit.

INTRODUCTION

On 22 June 1941 the largest invasion force ever gathered attacked the Soviet Union. Total Soviet dead in the ensuing struggle were between 20 million and 28 million, and the living suffered abysmally. No state has ever mobilized its human and material resources more 'totally' than did the Soviet Union between 1941 and 1945, and no belligerent did more to defeat Nazi Germany. Did Stalin's 'revolution from above' create the material – and *moral* – conditions for victory? He certainly thought so: in a major speech of February 1946 Stalin declared that the war had not been all bad because it had provided 'a great school of testing and verification of all the people's forces ... an examination for our Soviet system, our state, our government, our Communist party' (quoted in M. Harrison, 'Stalinist industrialisation and the test of war', 1990, p.660). Long after his death this was a Soviet orthodoxy, but the alternative view now prevails: Stalinism brought the country within an ace of defeat. On the military and 'home' fronts enormous sacrifices were made just to overcome the brutal inefficiencies of the Soviet system. Victory came despite, not because of it. This unit cannot resolve that controversy, but it should give you a better understanding of how prepared the Soviet Union was for the ordeal of total war. Furthermore, when you come to study the war's social consequences, you will be able to compare them with the extraordinary changes imposed on Soviet society after 1929 – a year that marks a critical turning point in Soviet history.

To help focus this unit on the overriding theme of the course, let me pose the paradox of total war and political petrification. By all accounts, the colossal Soviet war effort induced no significant change in the political system, the organization of the economy, and the social relations of rulers and ruled. This disparity between the death and destruction wrought by the war and its meagre consequences for Soviet society and political institutions is rather puzzling. By passing the supreme test of total war was Stalinism 'vindicated'? Did victory confirm and rigidify its structures of power? I do not know, but any student of total war and social change in twentieth-century Europe should confront these questions. But before answering them, we have to say what Stalinism was.

In the autumn of 1941 Beatrice Webb wrote a new introduction for *Soviet Communism: A New Civilisation*, which she had written with her husband, Sidney, after two visits to the Soviet Union in 1932 and 1934. They were life-long democratic socialists (Sidney was the chief author of the Labour Party's constitution and had served in the 1929–31 Labour government) and had never been attracted to Marxism. However, like many 'fellow travellers' to the Soviet Union in the 1930s, they were favourably impressed. Their account had originally been published with a question mark in the title, but the second edition dispensed with this note of uncertainty, and the 1941 introduction was a paean of praise to Britain's new-found ally. 'Stalin' – Beatrice wrote – 'is not a dictator'. The Communist Party of the Soviet Union (of which he was General Secretary) was 'democratic in its internal structure'. The USSR was 'the most inclusive and equalized democracy in the world'. Its 1936 Constitution ('a remarkable document which ought to be studied by all political students') protected every citizen against aggression and arbitrary unrest, stipulated the right to paid work and to education at every level, and guaranteed economic provision for the old, the sick and the disabled. But the crowning glory of the constitution for Beatrice Webb was its commitment to state planning of the socialized national economy:

> This fundamental transformation of the social order – the substitution of planned production for community consumption, instead of the capitalist profit-making of so-called 'Western Civilisation' – seems to me so vital a change for the better, so conducive to the progress of humanity to higher levels of health and happiness, virtue and wisdom, as to constitute a new civilisation.
>
> (1941, p.xxx)

This judgement of Stalin and Stalinism would be high on any list of great political delusions. Joseph Stalin (1879–1953) was a paranoid despot who ordered the summary execution of hundreds of thousands of Soviet citizens. On one day, 12 December 1938, he and V. M. Molotov, the Soviet premier, signed death lists for 3,167 people; most were shot without even a semblance of a trial (D. Volkogonov, *Stalin: Triumph and Tragedy*, 1991, p.339). The death toll from the forced collectivization of agriculture – for which Stalin was primarily responsible – was horrendous. Precision in these matters is impossible, but the most recent calculations indicate 8.6 million unexplained deaths in the Soviet Union between 1930 and 1936. The largest category of victims died in a man-made famine. Stalin sanctioned a reign of terror in 1937–38 that destroyed the upper echelons of the Communist Party, the intelligentsia and the military élite. According to official figures 681,692 people were executed, but these do not include unregistered deaths in confinement. In reality, probably 1–1.5 million died in the great purge (S. Rosefielde, 'Stalinism in post-communist perspective', 1996; S. G. Wheatcroft and R. W. Davies, 'Population', 1994, pp.67–77). Many more lives were destroyed by incarceration in the Gulag archipelago. The cultural policies imposed by Stalin's regime led to stultifying intellectual conformity, state-sponsored chauvinism and the absurd cult of the 'Great Leader's' personality. Stalinist art was aesthetically timid and politically corrupt: it combined surface realism and a profound mendacity as to the realities of Soviet society. Knowing all this, how can we dignify Stalinism with the term 'civilization'?

Exercise Does Roberts refer to anything that could be construed as the civilizing mission of Stalinism? ■

Specimen answer Unquestionably; he refers on p.349 to effective government being made a reality for the first time over one-sixth of the earth's surface; the transformation of a barbaric continent; the provision of universal education on an undreamed scale; the emancipation of women; and the spawning of great scientific and academic institutions. He speculates that these might have been achieved through the transformation of Russia by capitalism into a liberal, industrialized society, but writes that it was 'Stalin [who] put Russia back on the historical highroad after she had been diverted by war and revolution.' □

1 MAGNITOGORSK: THE 'SHOW CASE' CITY

Beatrice Webb's eulogy was at the back of my mind as I read Stephen Kotkin's *Magnetic Mountain: Stalinism as a Civilization* (1995), a notable contribution to

Soviet social history made possible by the partial opening of the archives to western scholars from the later 1980s. The mountain in question was a huge reserve of iron ore in a remote and inhospitable region at the southern end of the Urals. In less than decade it was turned from barren steppe into the city of Magnitogorsk, the most celebrated showcase of a new industrial age. American corporations designed and equipped the industrial complex; the German architect Ernst May helped plan the urban development.

Construction labour was provided by seasonal workers, up-rooted peasants, committed communists and prosperous farmers – so-called *kulaks* – exiled during the collectivization drive. They worked in atrocious weather and lived in tents and primitive barracks. Except for the penal labourers, this labour force was too fluid to be effectively coerced by the authorities. The huge internal migrations of the early 1930s created what has been called a 'quicksand society' of transient, barely literate, ill-disciplined workers with few industrial skills. Internal passports were reintroduced in December 1932 to restrict the movement of famished peasants to the towns and bring order to the construction sites, but they did little to stabilize the Magnitogorsk labour force. The regulations were evaded through a black market in forged and stolen documents, and industrial managers desperate for labour ignored them when hiring workers. There were too few officials to handle the paperwork (S. Kotkin, *Magnetic Mountain*, 1995, pp.99–101). It is a telling illustration of the difficulties of implementing 'totalitarian' controls in conditions of social upheaval.

Paradoxically, communist idealism did put down roots in Magnitogorsk's shifting social sands: men and women felt they were constructing not just an industrial complex but a new social order based on the dignity of labour and production for use. John Scott, an American who worked at Magnitogorsk, later wrote that when the first steel was poured nearly all workers sensed they were making history. As it became a stable 'show piece' city there developed a 'lived culture' whose core values were the communal organization of housing and other basic services, the centrality of labour in personal identity, the criminalization of private trade, and the primacy of revolutionary politics in all matters. 'It was', writes Kotkin, 'this set of distinct characteristics, expressing a dream for a better way of life attendant upon the transcendence of capitalism, that accounted for the admiration Magnitogorsk elicited at home and abroad. [This was] the world's first newly constructed socialist city' (p.150).

Coercion was overt and pervasive, but workers were not passive objects of the state's heavy-handed designs. At production meetings they groused quite freely, criticizing the works' director, complaining about the wages, bad living conditions, the lack of things to buy in the store – about everything, in fact, except the general line of the Communist Party and its half-dozen sacrosanct leaders. They reacted to the oppressive terms of work by absenting themselves, going slow, and stealing tools and materials with which to work 'privately' in the illicit 'market' sector. But there were real gains for men and women workers: paid vacations and paid pregnancy leave, free health care, vocational training, retirement pensions. Landless rural labourers moving into industrial employment entered a more secure world where job rights were taken seriously. In the first half of 1937 the local court tried 120 'labour cases', mostly involving alleged improper dismissal. In 91 cases the complaint was upheld and the dismissals were reversed (Kotkin, 1995, p.66). Sacking a woman because she was pregnant became a criminal offence. An élite of so-called *Stakhanovites* or 'shock workers' who greatly exceeded production norms were well rewarded financially and given access to luxuries, such as motor cycles and Black Sea holidays. Furthermore, communist rhetoric seeped into ordinary speech, and workers participated in the regime's ideology and purpose by adopting its idiom and ethical norms, even in private. They learned to 'speak Bolshevik'. We're inclined to choke on ascribing ethical norms to Stalinism, but consider this extract from an unpublished letter by the wife of a *Stakhanovite* worker to the wife of another worker who hadn't been pulling his weight:

> I ask you, Marfa, to talk to your husband heart to heart, read him my letter. You, Marfa, explain to Iakov Stepanovich that he just can't go on working the way he has. Persuade him that he must work honourably, conscientiously, like a shock worker. Teach him to understand the words of comrade Stalin, that work is a matter of honour, glory, valour, and heroism ... I will ask my [husband] to take yours in tow, help improve himself and become a shock worker, earn more. I want you, Marfa, and [your husband] to be honoured and respected, so that you live as well as we do.

> (Quoted in Kotkin, 1995, p.219)

It is quite possible that the letter writer was 'coached' by a party activist, but it seems she had genuinely absorbed the regime's values. The letter's combination of idealism and pragmatism was wholly characteristic of Stalinism's public ethics by the later 1930s. Magnitogorsk was conceived at the end of the 1920s during a phase of 'cultural revolution' when party radicals were urging a leap into utopia. The 'bourgeois' family was to be superseded as the basic cell of society; religion was to be extirpated by militant atheism; professional hierarchies – at work, in the armed forces, in the universities – were to be overthrown by an equally militant egalitarianism; personal relations were to be unshackled from an outdated morality. From 1932 the regime began to disown this utopian agenda, without retreating from the central objectives of state socialism. It recognized the family as indispensable if the nation's children were to be socialized and rampant hooliganism controlled: a decree of June 1936 made divorce complicated and expensive. Civil marriage was solemnized. Abortion, which had been available on demand in the cities throughout the 1920s and early 1930s, became tightly restricted. Financial and other rewards were offered to multiple-child families. Authority in professional hierarchies was re-established, and huge differentials in income and material privileges opened between management, élite workers and the toiling masses. But, at the same time, massive social mobility occurred through the drafting of hundreds of thousands of worker-communists into the higher technical institutes where they acquired the skills to manage the new industrial society. Magnitogorsk registered this shift from utopianism to the Soviet-style managerial revolution. By the later 1930s more than 40,000 people in the city were enrolled in full- or part-time education progammes, ranging from elementary schooling to technical instruction in the so-called workers' academies; another 12,000 were enrolled in literacy courses, part-time trade courses or night school. Virtually everyone in the city who could study was studying (Kotkin, 1995, p.361).

2   PLANNING AN INDUSTRIALIZED ECONOMY

Magnitogorsk has to be seen in the context of an unprecedented project of societal engineering: from 1929 the Soviet government attempted to transform an entire continental economy, through conscious state planning, as part of the strategy of constructing socialism in a single country which was surrounded by a hostile capitalist world. The objectives were to achieve self-sufficiency in capital goods (industrial plant, machinery, etc.), to surpass the most advanced capitalist countries in per capita industrial output, and to outstrip them technically (R. W. Davies, 'Industry', 1994, pp.136–8). Despite chaotic mismanagement and waste during the first Five Year Plan, the industrialization drive must be judged a success in economic terms. According to western estimates, industrial output trebled between 1928 and 1940. Employment in industry grew by about 9.5 per cent a year. Small-scale manufacturing, which employed about two-fifths of industrial workers in the 1920s, declined absolutely while employment in certain priority industries (such as iron and steel and machine-building) was concentrated in giant factories. By 1940 the output of iron and steel was four times the 1928 level, and ten giant works produced more than half the tonnage. Coal output increased five-fold and electric power generation six-fold. The 'gap' between the Soviet Union and the leading industrial powers was dramatically – no other word will do – narrowed: in 1928 total Soviet industrial output was equal to only 6.9 per cent of total US industrial output, but by 1938 total Soviet output was 45.1 per cent of US output (D. Lane, *Politics and Society in the USSR*, 1970, p.67). The Soviet Union began the industrialization drive heavily dependent on advanced-technology imports (and was the United States' best customer for capital goods throughout the 1930s). By the eve of the war the Soviet Union was basically self-sufficient in industrial technology, with an efficient machine-tool industry well adapted to its needs. Tractors, combine-harvesters and motor lorries were being produced in large new factories adapted from American designs, and the technological level of the basic production lines and their products was high. The vastly expanded defence industry made the Soviet Union virtually self-sufficient in armaments and a world leader in certain military technologies, such as rocketry.

As all accounts now stress, planned industrialization was not an unqualified success, and different policies could probably have achieved a comparable rate of industrial growth while maintaining a more even balance in the economy. Even after the fantastic objectives of the first Five Year Plan were scaled down, industries were set unrealistic targets that bred inefficiencies (such as the hoarding of materials and labour). The output of consumer goods lagged far behind capital goods. Fewer textile fabrics were produced per head of population in the early 1930s than in 1913. Less than half the residential construction scheduled under the first two plans was actually built. Real wages outside agriculture fell by nearly 50 per cent between 1928 and 1940, though household incomes were sustained by full employment, wives going out to work, and the halving of the number of dependants per wage earner. (In 1928 the average wage had to support 2.46 people; by 1940 this had dropped to 1.28.) But the greatest failure was in agriculture: food production fell disastrously in 1931, and for the rest of the decade there was less food available per head than during the years of the New Economic Policy (NEP) (for this see Roberts, p.343). Even in 1940 per capita consumption had not returned to its 1928 level.

3 THE TRAGEDY OF COLLECTIVIZATION

The transformation of agriculture from small-scale peasant farms based on animal power and human muscle to large-scale mechanized collectives was Stalinism's most ambitious and least successful societal project. From the point of view of Marxist revolutionaries – supported exclusively by urban industrial workers – collectivization was undertaken for cogent economic and political reasons. All Bolshevik leaders believed that moving to a higher mode of production depended on expanding the productive forces: a socialist civilization would rest on material abundance. Soviet peasant farming in the 1920s was technically backward and its yields were lower than in any other major European country. The revolutionary land settlement of 1917–18 had compounded historic problems of low productivity. The great estates responsible for most pre-1914 agricultural exports were dissolved, and the prosperous farmers created by the Stolypin land reforms (see Roberts, pp.155–6) fared relatively badly from the nationalization of land. Peasant society became more egalitarian through a redistribution which tended to assimilate rich and poor to the middle stratum of *serednyaks*. Furthermore, virtually all holdings were returned to communal ownership and managed by the traditional organ of village government, the *Mir*, which guaranteed each household a holding in perpetuity, but periodically reallocated land. This discouraged investment and hampered efforts to improve farming. Coupled with the low productivity of agriculture was the chronic problem of supplying the towns and securing an export surplus to pay for imported capital goods. Though total harvests during the best NEP years were only slightly less than before 1914, the proportion marketed by the peasants was considerably lower. Post-revolutionary peasant society was more oriented to subsistence farming, more inclined to feed its surpluses to animals and directly improve its own way of life.

Politically, the Bolsheviks had always considered the peasantry 'an awkward class'. Lenin had described the typical 'middle' peasant as 'partly a property owner, partly a worker ... the problem of our attitude towards this vacillating class is one of enormous difficulty'. Though peasants and their families were the vast majority of the population, they provided a small fraction of party members (only 14.5 per cent in October 1928). There was only one rural party member for every 420 rural inhabitants (compared with one for every twenty-five urban inhabitants) (R. W. Davies, *The Socialist Offensive*, 1980, pp.51–2). The rural soviets were unpopular and relatively few peasants voted in elections for them. To many Bolsheviks – especially on the left – NEP appeared to be strengthening the property-owning elements within the peasantry and laying the social basis for counter-revolution. In 1925 the restrictions on the hiring of labour by richer peasants and their long-term leasing of land from poorer neighbours were removed. The 1926 census revealed that over three-quarters of a million peasant households were hiring permanent wage labour, while about 66,000 craft enterprises had two to three employees on average. Including dependants and working family members, the 'capitalist' group enumerated by the census was nearly 4 million or 3.5 per cent of the rural population. In fact, numerous female-headed households that relied on hired help were – absurdly – designated 'capitalist', while many peasants who had prospered through commerce were excluded. However, from very questionable data, radical Bolsheviks deduced a class differentiation in the countryside with the re-emergence of rural capitalists or *kulaks* (a pejorative term originally applied to village loan-sharks and petty traders rather than farmers). Most so-called *kulaks* were simply the more able and harder working farmers who hired out equipment, loaned money and traded on the side; only about half employed labour on a permanent basis. They were poor by western European standards, and there was no clear distinction between them and the great mass of *serednyaks*, many of whom employed labour occasionally. The most readily identifiable group in rural society lay at the bottom – the million or so day-labourers (*batraks*) – though very few had no plot of land at all. Their living and working conditions were awful: there was 'no domain of Soviet life in which the gulf between doctrine and reality was more blatantly obvious, and more compromising for the socialist idea ...' (M. Lewin, *Russian Peasants and Soviet Power,* 1968, p.52).

Was collectivization of some kind *necessary* for accelerated socialist development in an overwhelmingly agrarian society? Perhaps a viable alternative to Stalinist modernization lay in the ideas and 'programme' of Nikolai Bukharin, Stalin's ally on the Politburo from mid-1925 until his expulsion in November 1929. Bukharin argued that the *smychka* or 'link' with the peasantry forged when private trade in grain was conceded under NEP was essential for social stability and state security. Growth could come, he believed, by allowing market forces to raise peasant income and increase the demand for consumer goods (S. Cohen, *Bukharin and the Bolshevik Revolution,* 1980). Whatever might have been, Stalin responded to a critical shortage of grain in the cities in late 1927–28 (due to a refusal to sell at the price offered by the state) by reverting to the outright expropriations of War Communism. Peasants were compelled to hand over their stocks at gunpoint; the recalcitrant were arrested for 'hoarding', and deported. With the resort to force, the NEP truce between the state and the peasantry was over.

Collectivization had not been part of the original Five Year Plan, but in 1929 a programme for accelerating the development of collective farms was improvised, as much by local and regional party organizations taking the initiative as by the centre imposing a policy from above. In fact, by the autumn, the central authorities were confronted 'from below' with plans which exceeded their own expectations (R. W. Davies, *The Socialist Offensive,* 1980, p.133). Stalin's role was pivotal: his *Pravda* article of 7 November, 'The year of the great breakthrough', was the decisive signal for all-out collectivization, and by expelling Bukharin from the Politburo he silenced the party moderates. On 27 December he announced 'the liquidation of the *kulaks* as a class' to a conference of agronomists. It would seem that he 'stumbled into a bloody civil war with the peasants', and the central authorities had to ride the tiger of provincial party radicalism (C. Ward, *Stalin's Russia,* 1999, p.99). His *Pravda* article strongly emphasized the voluntary nature of collectivization, but it was characterized nonetheless by chaotic coercion and escalating violence. Urban collectivization brigades descended on the villagers to harry them into the collectives, and *kulaks* were brutally stripped of their property. Their barbarous treatment was intended to frighten the masses into conformity. Tens of thousands were executed. Between 1930 and 1933 about 2.1 million men, women and children were exiled to other regions, usually in remote parts of the country, where they became 'special settlers' under the control of the Soviet security police, known as the OGPU (later NKVD, and later KGB). According to the official records, 241,355 died in exile in 1932–33 alone. Between 2 and 2.5 million were exiled within their own region, and 1–1.25 million 'dekulakized' themselves by fleeing to the towns (S. G. Wheatcroft and R. W. Davies, 'Population', 1994, p.68). Activists from the Young Communist League attacked rural religion with carnivalesque fervour: churches, mosques and synagogues were desecrated; clergymen were deported *en masse*; icons, church bells, plate and other valuables were destroyed. Villagers were compelled to give up their household icons on entering collectives (Sheila Fitzpatrick, *Stalin's Peasants*, 1994, pp.59–62).

The speed and brutality with which collectivization was implemented had catastrophic consequences for Soviet agriculture. Production declined very substantially in 1928–32, chiefly because of the collapse in animal husbandry. Peasants initially slaughtered their livestock rather than see them collectivized, though the turning of pastures over to grain was an additional incentive to cull the herds (and made re-stocking much harder). The number of cattle, pigs, sheep, goats and horses fell by between half and two-thirds – a greater loss than had occurred during the years of world war and civil war (S. G. Wheatcroft and R. W. Davies, 'Agriculture', 1994, p.113). Horses were the main source of tractor power and manure, and without them all forms of agricultural production were severely affected. The labour force was weakened by the sudden exodus of young men who formed the large majority of the 6.5 million moving from village to town in 1930–31. While agricultural capacity declined, the demands placed on agriculture grew remorselessly. The largest cities expanded at a phenomenal rate between 1929 and 1932: Moscow's population rose from 2 million to 3.7 million; industrial centres such as Sverdlovsk, Perm and Stalingrad more than doubled in size. The state's exactions were relentless, and were without doubt the major cause of the famine that devastated vast regions in 1932–33. Because the collectives were compelled to hand over a large proportion of their crops, the amount retained in the villages for food and sale on the market was drastically reduced. Additionally, the collectives were grossly inefficient, basically because the peasants cajoled into them were utterly demoralized. A Smolensk party secretary reported in February 1931 on the 'absence of labor discipline in them [and] "anti-moral phenomena" like drunkenness and thievery ...'[1] (Merle Fainsod, *Smolensk Under Soviet Rule*, 1958, p.258). Mass pillage of communal property was such that draconian penalties (including death) were introduced in August 1932 for pilfering. By the beginning of 1933 more than 50,000 people had been sentenced for appropriating *kolkhoz* property.

---

[1] The Smolensk provincial archives were captured by the Germans in 1941 and turned over to US forces in 1945. For decades, they were the major primary sources on Soviet rule available to western scholars.

In the summer of 1932 Molotov, who had just returned from Ukraine, warned the Politburo, 'we definitely face the spectre of famine, especially in the rich bread areas'. The Politburo nevertheless decided that 'Whatever the cost, the confirmed plan for grain requisition must be fulfilled' (R. Conquest, 'Victims of Stalinism', 1997, p.1319). Not only did the regime insist on its deliveries, but it refused to open the state grain reserves in early 1933 to prevent starvation, it continued to export grain for hard currency, never sought international food aid (such as Russia had accepted in 1921) and deployed the militia and Red Army to stop peasants leaving the stricken areas. Why did it countenance millions of needless deaths? One possible answer is that the state followed a policy of genocide – both in Ukraine, which had put up a stubborn nationalist resistance to Soviet rule, and against non-Russian minorities in the North Caucasus (R. Conquest, *The Harvest of Sorrow*, 1986). Nobody would expect abundant documentary evidence for genocidal purpose – even from such a meticulously bureaucratic regime – but at present it is insufficient to convince most experts. In our present state of knowledge, a more plausible explanation is that the regime thought no sacrifice was too great in pursuing industrialization and maintaining its urban support. During the civil war Soviet power had barely survived mass flight from the starving cities; the need to keep the workers supplied with bread was a lesson the authorities could not forget.

Between the 1926 and 1939 censuses adult employment in agriculture fell by about a fifth, from 61.6 million in 1926 to 48.2 million, and the urban population rose from 26.3 to 56.1 million. Two-thirds of the urban increase came from migration. By any estimation, this was tumultuous social change. But it is worth insisting that the Nazis attacked an agrarian empire in which 57 per cent of the labour force still worked in the primary sector and about 115 million people still lived in villages. Labour-intensive, low-productivity agriculture constrained Soviet mobilization for war just as surely as industrialization produced the means for victory: a smaller proportion of the population was drafted into the armed forces than in Germany for the simple reason that to have taken more men from the farms would have spelt starvation. As it was, three-fifths of the Red Army was of rural origin. Collectivization was almost universally perceived by country folk as a second serfdom; it imposed state economic exploitation, and denied farm workers civil and economic rights granted to industrial workers. The unpopularity of the collective farms was such that Ukrainian and southern Russian peasants initially welcomed the invaders, or at least were prepared to tolerate them, because of the hope they would dismantle the collectives (Sheila Fitzpatrick, *Stalin's Peasants*, 1994, p.314). Rather surprisingly, there is little evidence that the traumas of the 1930s left *muzhik* (peasant) soldiers morally ill-prepared for the ordeal of total war. The argument that apathy and resentment lay behind the mass surrenders of 1941 is not confirmed by German sources. A captain in the 18th Panzer Division wrote about the first days of the campaign that 'there was no feeling, as there had been in France, of entry into a defeated nation. Instead there was resistance, always resistance, however hopeless' (quoted in R. W. Thurston, *Life and Terror in Stalin's Russia 1934–1941*, 1996, p.262). We need to think about the sources of Soviet patriotism.

4   RECUPERATING THE RUSSIAN PAST

For Stalin and other Soviet leaders industrialization meant much more than economic development; it entailed, they believed, intensified class war against putative domestic enemies, and deepening international antagonism as imperialist states sought to crush the emerging socialist society. In 1927 a war scare – prompted by the breakdown of diplomatic relations with Britain – triggered the regime's offensive against the peasantry, and formulating the Five Year Plan was accompanied by an ideological offensive against the 'bourgeois' specialists who had co-operated in the reconstruction of the economy under NEP. In May 1928 the first of a series of highly publicized trials of industrial 'saboteurs' opened when fifty-three engineers (including three Germans) from Shakhty in the Donbass mining region were accused of wrecking equipment. The regime drummed up the trial's 'social-political significance as an element in the class struggle against the implacable hostility of the bourgeoisie at home and abroad ... [The proceedings] riveted attention on the bourgeois affiliations and sympathies of the accused rather than their specific acts' (E. H. Carr and R. W. Davies, *Foundations of a Planned Economy*, 1969, pp.622, 624).

This background is essential to a full understanding of Stalin's speech to a conference of industrial managers on 4 February 1931 (substantial extracts are reproduced in Document I.7, *Primary Sources 2: Interwar and World War II*). Stalin delivered few memorable speeches, but this one was emotionally charged. He gave his audience an ideological rationale for the enormous tasks they were engaged in, and he redefined the ties between Soviet citizens and the state.

Exercise   Summarize the main points Stalin was making here and say what section of the speech you find most emotionally resonant. With what was Stalin identifying himself, and his policies, in this passage? In terms of the allocation of industrial resources, what would be one practical consequence of the arguments Stalin was advancing? What are the special problems of handling this kind of evidence? ■

Specimen answer   Stalin begins by referring to the pledge to meet 'control figures' (that is, targets laid down in the Five Year Plan) ahead of schedule. In the subsequent paragraphs he calls on communists to become masters of industrial technique and management, and cites the Shakhty case as evidence of the 'wrecking' activities of non-party specialists. Stalin warns that the 'class enemy is seriously resisting the socialist offensive' – a constant theme of his speeches and articles at this time. A communist monopoly of industrial expertise was required for the one-man management needed to enforce discipline in industry. Stalin alludes to those who had asked for a slackening in the tempo of industrialization, and rejects this in what I find the most emotional part of his speech where he refers to the many occasions on which Russia had been beaten because of its backwardness (by the Mongol *khans*, the Turkish *beys*, the Swedish feudal lords, and so on). What is remarkable is Stalin's identification with the Russian past: he was readmitting national patriotism to the value system of Soviet society. He warns that 'our socialist fatherland' will similarly be beaten if it does not 'put an end to its backwardness in the shortest possible time'. He then goes on to say that the Soviet Union's obligations to the world's proletariat require the elimination of its backwardness: 'in ten years we must make good the distance which separates us from the advanced capitalist countries'. In conclusion, he reiterates his demand that Bolsheviks master industrial technique. If, as Stalin maintained, international antagonism towards the Soviet Union was mounting, the country would need to allocate more industrial resources to defence, and re-establish itself as a great military power.

Stalin's public addresses are difficult to assess as evidence because he frequently used 'coded' language to allude to conflicts within the party hierarchy. (Who were the people pressing for a slackening of the tempo? What arguments in the Politburo were being hinted at here?) Moreover, one can't be sure how the speaker took his own propaganda: did Stalin and his audience believe the chiliastic rhetoric ('We must march forward in such a way that the working class of the whole world ... may say: This is my vanguard ...')? Or was it the sort of incantation of faith, equally evident in other political cultures, which leaders make and audiences expect on certain public occasions, although they know that policy will be conducted in the light of more practical considerations?

Discussion   It is entirely consistent with Stalin's speech that in subsequent years he took a personal interest in the teaching of Russian history to Soviet schoolchildren. In September 1931 history was reintroduced as an independent classroom subject in Soviet schools, but the curriculum was marred by a dogmatic historical materialism. Stalin wanted the teaching to catch people's imagination and promote a unified sense of national identity. He berated a conference of historians in March 1934 over the quality of history textbooks: '[They] aren't good for anything ... What the heck is "the feudal epoch", "the epoch of industrial capitalism", "the epoch of formations", – it's all epochs and no facts, no events, no people, no concrete information ... History must be history' (from a diary kept by one of the historians, cited in D. L. Brandenberger and A. M. Dubrovsky, ' "The people need a tsar" ', 1998, p.875). According to some accounts, Stalin was coming to identify with Ivan Grozny ('The Terrible') – the Muscovite ruler who had thrown off the Tatar yoke, destroyed the boyars, and unified the early Russian state. He encouraged (or ordered) the Soviet cinema towards heroic historical biography. The quintessential Stalinist films celebrate great men from the national past: *Peter the First*, *Alexander Nevsky*, *Suvorov* and, of course, *Ivan the Terrible*. Their subliminal message was that the Soviet people, too, needed a tsar. History teaching and historical films promoted a very Russian view of the past. The tsarist empire's 'progressive' historic role in unifying a vast region and diverse peoples under a dominant nation became part of Soviet historical discourse. □

5   THE REMAKING OF A GREAT MILITARY POWER

If Stalin's warnings of foreign threats to the Soviet Union were somewhat baseless in 1931, Hitler's coming to power and Japanese aggression in the Far East meant they were well grounded by 1933–34. The major industrial achievement of Stalinism was the creation of a technologically advanced armaments industry, virtually from scratch, to meet these external threats. In 1929–30 Soviet factories produced 170 tanks and 204 combat aircraft; in 1940 they turned out 2,794 tanks and 8,232 combat aircraft of a quality at least equal to the *Wehrmacht*'s (R. W. Davies *et al.*, *The Economic Transformation of the Soviet Union*, 1994, Table 28). By 1940 armaments accounted for 22 per cent of industrial production, and nearly a third of capital investment was allocated to the defence industry. Until 1935–36, rising defence expenditure was deliberately hidden from the outside world (partly because the Soviet Union had joined the League of Nations and participated in its disarmament conference) but at this juncture Stalin ordered a complete reorganization and expansion of the Red Army. That the Soviet Union was becoming a great military power could no longer be disguised; indeed, there were compelling reasons for advertising the fact.

Since 1921 the Soviet Union had relied on a mixed military system in which a small professional standing army was combined with a large territorial force of conscripted, but part-time, soldier-citizens. Broad social categories (such as *kulaks*) and many national minorities were exempt from conscription, and in remote areas most young men escaped military service altogether. Soviet staff officers acquired expertise by playing clandestine war games with their Weimar counterparts,[2] but their forces – especially the technical branches – were poorly equipped. The military system was relatively low cost and essentially defensive.

In 1935 it was decided to convert the Red Army into an all-regular force. Over the next few years the draft age was lowered from 21 to 19, and exemptions on grounds of class, nationality or religion were removed. (Those previously identified as *kulaks* or children of *kulaks* became subject to military service in 1936, as did minority nationalities such as the Uzbek and Turkmen.) As a result of widening the conscription base, the Red Army's standing strength rose from 940,000 men in 1936 to nearly 5 million on the eve of Barbarossa. To command these additional troops, about 255,000 new officers were needed – so more opportunities were created for smart young communists to rise from the ranks. Soviet youths were obliged to undergo more than 200 hours of military instruction in the two years *prior* to their induction into the army, though their training was left largely to the party and for this reason was poorly organized. Conscripts had a five-year obligation, but until 1939 active service lasted only two years, after which they were sent on long-term leave. Despite the recruitment of minorities, Russians, Ukrainians and Belorussians were over-represented in relation to their numbers in society: they comprised 84.7 per cent of troops in 1941 (Roger Reese, *Stalin's Reluctant Soldiers*, 1996, p.15). The Red Army was a means by which a Russian national identity was superimposed on the Soviet Union's diverse population. At a basic level, military service was 'civilizing': men were taught personal hygiene, heavy drinking was discouraged, and illiterates learnt to read and write. They also imbibed the socialist values of the 'new civilization'. Though titles and insignia of rank were reintroduced in the forces in 1935, class distinctions were formally prohibited and, on paper at least,

---

[2] Under the Weimar Republic the *Reichswehr* collaborated with the Red Army as a way of evading the restrictions on the size of German forces imposed by the Treaty of Versailles. A German tank school was set up near Kazan in 1929 and a flying school was built at Lipetsk.

Soviet soldiers retained all their civil rights. Officers and men addressed each other with the respectful '*vy*'. Political indoctrination and the teaching of Soviet patriotism were vital parts of military training. The army's total subordination to the party's power structure was ensured by the reinstitution of dual command at regiment level and higher in August 1937. This meant that all military orders had to be counter-signed by a military commissar who was a party functionary appointed by the political administration of the Red Army.

By the later 1930s the Red Army's equipment reflected the qualified success of the first and second Five Year Plans. The standard rifle division doubled its firepower during the 1930s through the addition of heavy artillery, and more guns were tractor-towed. Regiments were supplied with armoured vehicles and radios. After Hitler's seizure of rump Czechoslovakia (16 March 1939) Soviet motorized armoured units expanded and specialized at a staggering rate; there were, for example, 61 tank divisions in 1941 compared with none in early 1939. But, just as in the *Wehrmacht*, the infantry continued to rely on foot marches for tactical movement and on horses to pull guns and supplies.

The effectiveness of the Red Army as a military instrument on the eve of Barbarossa has been widely debated. Soviet forces defeated Japanese units in major battles on the Manchurian–Mongolian border in July and August 1939, but were savagely mauled by the numerically much inferior Finns during the 'Winter War' of 1939–40. The Manchurian conflict demonstrated the technical superiority of Soviet tanks and the competence of the army commander in the Far East, General Zhukov. The Finnish War revealed gross deficiencies in training, tactical skills and the chain of command. Zhukov was one of the few generals to escape the purges that decimated the officer corps in 1937–40, and his presence was an important – maybe crucial – factor in explaining superior military performance against the Japanese. It was long thought that the purges destroyed about half the officer corps but we now know that the proportion dismissed, imprisoned and executed was much smaller. About 11,000 army officers were discharged for political unreliability in 1937 (compared with 4,474 arrested by the NKVD) but of these more than a third were reinstated in 1938–39. Taking account of reinstatements, the 1937 purge removed slightly fewer than one in ten officers. The 1938 purge included more arrests and executions, but touched fewer than one in twenty officers (R. R. Reese, 'The Red Army and the great purges', 1993). However, the purges fell disproportionately on the highest ranks: nine out of ten generals were removed. Those arrested (and mostly executed) included three out of five marshals; 13 out of 15 army commanders; 57 out of 85 corps commanders; 110 out of 195 division commanders; 220 out of 406 brigade commanders; all eleven vice commissars of war; 75 out of 80 members of the Supreme Military Council; all the military district commanders. When Colonel-General Halder told Hitler, on 5 December 1940, 'Die [Rote] Armee ist führerlos' ('The Red Army is leaderless') he was spot on. If the best military brains had not been blown out, they either mouldered in the Gulag or were too demoralized to function effectively. As Roger Reese has argued in his path-breaking social history of the Red Army (*Stalin's Reluctant Soldiers*, 1996), the purges are not the complete explanation for the military catastrophes of 1941. The military expansion had been too rapid and poorly planned to maintain efficiency. Hundreds of new divisions were created without the cadres to organize and train them. The military academies could not cope with the vast influx of trainee officers, and too many were promoted beyond their competence, education and command experience. But the purges grievously exacerbated a bad situation. They shattered the military *esprit de corps* by persuading many officers and men that the highest ranks had been riddled with traitors.

6   THE TOTALITARIAN PARADIGM AND ITS REVISIONIST CRITICS

Exercise   Until now, little has been said about the notion of totalitarianism, yet it was obviously a key term for Roberts when he wrote his textbook, and most people would regard it as essential to our understanding of the twentieth century. From your reading, write down a short definition of 'totalitarianism' (consult a dictionary if necessary). Do you know the origins of the term? Roberts clearly regards the Soviet Union under Stalin as the 'model' totalitarian state: what features of the regime would you identify as *typical* of totalitarian institutions, political practices and ideology? ■

Specimen answer   The dictionary I consulted defines the adjective 'totalitarian' as 'belonging to a form of government that includes control of everything under one authority, and allows no opposition', and then simply adds 'totalitarianism' as the noun (*Chambers Twentieth Century Dictionary*). Your dictionary may have told you that the word derives from '*totalitarismo*', the official doctrine of Mussolini's Italy. The English equivalent was widely used by 1940: an American political analyst, James Burnham, wrote that 'Totalitarianism is so striking a feature of the present social transition that it seems, to many persons, to define the character of the transition. They tell us that the "issue" is "totalitarianism v. democracy" ...' (*The Managerial Revolution*, 1941, p.131).

Your list of 'typical' features might include:

1   a single party monopolized political power; representative assemblies were stripped of their functions and authority;

2   a dictator exercised despotic power and became the object of a national 'cult';

3   the state sought to control and direct the entire economy through its bureaucracy;

4   terror was used to coerce large sections of the population and destroy supposed enemies within the party and state apparatus;

5   the regime's ideology legitimized the control of all aspects of social life, including art, literature and religion. I referred above to the *chiliasm* in Stalin's rhetoric. This a religious term for a perfect final state of mankind which the ideology projected and which justified the regime's actions and programme;

6   a large proportion of national product was devoted to armaments expenditure, and the armed forces were totally subordinated to the political party and the dictator.

Discussion   The six points I have identified are fairly close to those itemized by two political scientists, Carl J. Friedrich and Zbigniew K. Brzezinski, in a once-influential study, *Totalitarian Dictatorship and Autocracy* (1956). When Roberts wrote his textbook, the 'totalitarian paradigm' was the dominant analytic framework in western scholarship – a scholarship which relied heavily on 'deciphering' official published documents, the censored Soviet press and emigré testimony. The theoretical framework of the political scientists was bolstered by empirical studies, such as Robert Conquest's seminal *The Great Terror* (1968), but key issues in Soviet history could only be matters of heroic conjecture. □

Glasnost and archival research have put paid to the 'totalitarian paradigm', at least amongst western specialists. It is no longer *the* conceptual framework for the study of Stalinism. One 'revisionist' scholar writes: 'Theories of totalitarianism are ... simply irrelevant to most of what went on ... in the Soviet Union in the 1930s. The desire of the Soviet government to control its people must not be confused with what actually happened' (R. W. Thurston, *Life and Terror in Stalin's Russia 1934–1941*, 1996, p.xvii). 'Revisionists' do not deny the brutalities of the Stalinist dictatorship. They are not suggesting that the six listed points are erroneous, and any serious analysis of Stalinism would address all of these points. What they are contesting is the paradigm's basic premise that the dictatorship obliterated the distinction between state and society. The monolithic image of a terroristic regime imposing all its policies on a passive people is, they argue, false. A clamour for the radicalization of the regime's policies welled up 'from below' at the end of the 1920s when Stalin and his henchmen were almost embarrassed by 'cultural revolutionaries' proclaiming the withering away of the state, law and formal schooling. Stalin initiated collectivization but did not control the party militants and Komsomol zealots who drove the process forward in the countryside. We now have empirical studies of popular opinion which show that the Orwellian notion of a people in the thrall of the regime's lies is not accurate: the powerful – 'them' – were constantly represented as deceiving 'us', the people. The media may have been saturated with stories of happiness and prosperity, but private letters, graffiti, and conversations recorded by the police told a different tale. An 'honest' factory worker expressed himself thus:

> What is there to say about the successes of Soviet power? It's lies. The newspapers cover up the real state of things. I am a worker, wear torn clothes, my four children go to school half-starving, in rags. I, an honest worker, am a visible example of what Soviet power has given the workers in the last twenty years.

> (Quoted in S. Davies, *Popular Opinion in Stalin's Russia*, 1997, p.135)

Have the 'revisionists' scored an own goal by unearthing such testimony? I think not. What they have gone some way to demonstrating is that, despite the denial of a free press and freedom of association, people criticized the regime quite freely in everyday life. But they also supported it quite freely. The reverse side of popular dissent was the active consent by *Stakhanovites*, those entering higher education for the first time, the upwardly mobile, and – as is evident from private letters – large numbers of national servicemen. Families, not just individuals, gave their loyalty. An illiterate 65-year-old mother wrote (through her son) to Kalinin in 1939: 'All my children had and are having education thanks to the state and, I would say, thanks to the party, and especially comrade Stalin, for he, along with Lenin, opened the way for us simple people ...' (quoted in Davies, 1997, p.156).

7   'TOTALITARIAN' AND 'REVISIONIST' INTERPRETATIONS OF STALINIST TERROR

Nothing has contributed more to the 'totalitarian' image of Stalinism than the political terror of 1937–38 (known as the *Ezhovshchina*, after its principal executor, N. I. Ezhov, the Commissar of Internal Affairs). This dreadful period in Soviet life is poignantly evoked in the memoirs of Nadezhda Mandelstam, and the experiences of arrest, interrogation and incarceration were brilliantly reconstructed from survivors' accounts by Solzhenitsyn. None of the post-*glasnost* revelations have led us to question the truth of this personal testimony. Yet, paradoxically, the most forceful 'revisionist' challenge to the totalitarian paradigm has arisen from reinterpreting the origins and development of the great purge. In this final section I will outline the controversy. First comes a skeletal narrative, then a discussion of the scale of the terror, finally an analysis of rival interpretations of its dynamics and of how the 'totalitarian–revisionist' debate affects our broader understanding of Stalinism.

Narrative of the great terror

There was, of course, nothing new about political terror in the Soviet Union in the 1930s – the *Cheka*, Lenin's political police, had exercised sweeping powers of arrest and summary execution – but, until the early 1930s there was a sancrosanct prohibition against shooting Communist Party members. What changed matters was the assassination of the Leningrad party boss, S. M. Kirov, on 1 December 1934, by a party member apparently acting alone. Stalin promptly issued a secret party directive (only later approved by the Politburo) prescribing summary execution of those accused of 'terrorist' offences, who were to be denied defence lawyers. A hundred or so 'non-party' people already in custody in Leningrad were immediately executed. More portentously, Stalin capitalized on Kirov's murder to strike at known party 'oppositionists': there were sweeping arrests among the Leningrad party supporters of his old right-wing opponent, G. E. Zinoviev. In mid-January, Zinoviev and Kamenev (who had been expelled in September 1932 for political misdemeanours), together with a number of middle-ranking Bolsheviks, were charged with 'politically encouraging' Kirov's murder – for which they agreed to accept 'moral responsibility'. They were not tortured, did not confess, and energetically contested the court proceedings. Their prison sentences ranged from five to ten years. Surprisingly, the number of registered executions for counter-revolutionary crimes at this time seems to indicate a relaxation, not an escalation of terror. There were 20,201 'political' executions in 1930, but only 1,229 in 1935 and fewer still in 1936.

In August 1936 Stalin instigated the first of the 'show trials': Zinoviev, Kamenev and others were now charged with Kirov's murder, and with conspiring on Trotsky's instructions to murder Stalin and other leaders.[3] Stalin's speeches and articles had been harping on 'enemies of the people' for some months, and the international situation had become more threatening with the re-militarization of the Rhineland in March and the outbreak of the Spanish Civil War in July. Stalin warned that the class struggle abroad was intensifying and linking up with the class struggle at home. Even before the accused were brought to court, the newspapers and radio screwed up the public tension by demanding the death penalty. The accused made grovelling confessions, incriminated major figures not in the dock (including Bukharin) and unanimously asked to be shot: their co-operation had been secured by psychological torture, threats against their families and promises of clemency. They were shot. Subsequently, their families were either exiled or killed off. In January, a group of less senior Bolsheviks who had once been associates of Trotsky were put on show trial. The most important, G. L. Piatakov, was Deputy Commissar for Heavy Industry and the most able of Stalin's industrial managers. His destruction began a witch-hunt in the industrial administration and the hounding to suicide of his immediate boss, S. Ordzhonikidze, one of Stalin's oldest and closest associates.

Public opinion had been 'softened up' for the show trials by vituperative press campaigns, but the arrest, trial and execution of the Red Army generals in June 1937 was without warning, and for that reason all the more shocking. The announcement that the military élite had been conspiring with Germany and Japan to bring about a *coup d'état* and dismember the Soviet Union induced a psychotic paranoia in the NKVD and regional party committees. They began to compete among themselves to fulfil arrest 'quotas'. One regional party secretary reported in October 1937: 'We are now unmasking and destroying enemies: Bukharinites, Rykovites, Trotskyites, Kolchakites, saboteurs, we are crushing all the swine in our region' (quoted in D. Volkogonov, *Stalin*, 1991, p.307). The terror among bureaucrats and managers became so widespread it threatened to bring rational administration to a halt. The recall and execution of numerous diplomats harmed the regime's international prestige. A climacteric was reached with the final show trial of Bukharin, A. I. Rykov, G. G. Iagoda and others in March 1938. Unlike Kamenev and Zinoviev (who had been expelled from the party some time before their trial and execution), the accused had only recently been at the heart of the Soviet power structure. Iagoda was Commissar of Internal Affairs until mid-1937; Rykov was Commissar of Communications and, like Bukharin, a candidate member of the party's Central Committee. Their destruction brought the most publicized and most acute phase of terror to an end. In the spring and summer Stalin's favoured lieutenant, A. A. Zhdanov, warned the Politburo that repression was endangering national security and economic efficiency. The regime admitted miscarriages of justice and rehabilitated some political prisoners. Ezhov was dismissed in the autumn (and later shot) after Stalin had ordered a commission to check into the work of the NKVD. Though the tempo of repression slowed considerably, the Gulag

---

[3] Trotsky was banished from the Soviet Union in February 1929. He was given asylum in Norway in 1935 and settled in Mexico in early 1937.

population peaked in 1940. The camp numbers tumbled in 1941–45, chiefly because of the appalling deterioration in camp conditions. Over a fifth of prisoners died of malnutrition and disease in 1942, and nearly a quarter in 1943. On a home front wracked by privation, these were the most deprived.

The scale of the purges

Just how many were arrested by the political police in 1937–38 was long a bone of contention. Conquest conjectured about 8 million – an enormous figure which accorded with the notion of all-pervasive terror; Volkogonov, Stalin's post-*glasnost* biographer, cautiously estimated 4.5–5.5 million (R. Conquest, *The Great Terror*, 1968, p.702; D. Volkogonov, *Stalin*, 1991, p.307). Revisionists were sceptical about these kinds of figures: assuming arrests were highly concentrated among men well into their careers, they implied a staggering proportion of mature manhood behind bars. This scepticism seems warranted. The figure for NKVD arrests in 1937–38 culled from police records by an official Russian commission is 1,372,392. Some NKVD atrocities went unrecorded (they include the massacre of Polish officers in 1940), and the completeness of the published documentation has been called into question. The NKVD data for custodial sentences are seriously discrepant with data for the Gulag population. But, even if we assume only one in two arrests were recorded, the terror sucked in a narrower social segment than was once believed. This has a crucial bearing on how we interpret the role of repression in mobilizing and controlling the society as a whole. Workers and peasants appear to have experienced the terror 'at a distance', as something that happened to remote 'high-ups'. It was not – revisionists argue – a major factor in securing their compliance with the regime's policies (S. Davies, *Popular Opinion in Stalin's Russia*, 1997, p.119; R. W. Thurston, *Life and Terror in Stalin's Russia 1934–1941*, 1996, p.xx, *passim*).

Revisionists have drawn attention to another quantitative issue: the mass purging of party members for apolitical offences, such as drunkenness, embezzlement or sheer passivity, and the general re-registration of membership ordered in 1935. In the 'totalitarian' interpretation these were too casually lumped under the rubric 'terror', but they require separate consideration if we are to grasp the extraordinary changes in the Communist Party at this time. Apolitical purging, weeding out the 'dead wood' and the drive to recruit new members among the upwardly mobile cadres rejuvenated the party. Less than a fifth of the membership at the beginning of 1921 remained party members in 1939: loss of the party card and 'natural wastage' accounted for more of the attrition than political repression. Over 70 per cent of the 1.589 million members in 1939 had been recruited since 1929, and about half were under thirty-five. As Stalin destroyed old enemies, he simultaneously created a youthful technocracy, and the continuity of this emergent political class was to be a major factor in the durability of the Stalinist socio-economic system beyond the dictator's death.

Explaining the terror

The sharpest controversy between 'revisionists' and those upholding the 'totalitarian paradigm' has been over the cause and direction of the terror. Put simply, in the 'totalitarian' interpretation Stalin planned and directed the bloody business from beginning to end. It has long been known that the calamities of collectivization and the first Five Year Plan provoked furious opposition within the party, which was far from Stalin's pliant instrument in the early 1930s. A former district secretary, M. N. Riutin, who had already been expelled for 'rightist (i.e. pro-peasant) opposition', circulated a platform in August 1932 castigating the General Secretary's 'personal dictatorship', his 'theoretically illiterate' ideas on the development of agriculture, and 'the rule of terror in the party and the country...'. Riutin was arrested in September, and it was then that Zinoviev and Kamenev were expelled for receiving Riutin's platform but not denouncing him. Stalin demanded the death penalty for Riutin but the Politburo would not countenance this; Kirov, in particular, spoke out strongly against it. Kirov was immensely popular in the party and had a reputation as a social conciliator. At the 1934 Party Congress he may have received more votes than Stalin in the elections to the Central Committee (though this cannot be confirmed) and there is evidence that he was approached by a cabal of Old Bolshevik Party secretaries seeking to depose the General Secretary. According to the 'totalitarian' interpretation, Stalin suspected Kirov had become the focus of moderate opposition and ordered his assassination. His long-term intention was to extirpate all party elements remotely sympathetic to the Riutin platform and remould it into a new type of political instrument. What stood in the way of a radical renovation of the party were disputatious Old Bolsheviks (and their followers in the rank and file) and the prohibition on shooting party members. Robert Tucker, whose biography of Stalin generally supports the 'totalitarian' interpretation, argues that the dictator 'needed a Soviet equivalent of the Reichstag fire: a heinous crime and politically shocking event in which numbers of prominent Old Bolsheviks could be implicated'; the outrage would legitimize the introduction of emergency measures and 'The bar to terror against the party ... would be broken' (*Stalin in Power*, 1991, p.275).

Exercise Do you know why the comparison with the Reichstag fire might work against the thesis that events unfolded as a result of Stalin's premeditation? ∎

Specimen answer It is now beyond doubt that the Reichstag fire was started by one man acting entirely alone. The Nazi leadership immediately convinced itself that there was a communist plot, and turned the terror on their political enemies.

Discussion Some Russian and western scholars still hold Stalin responsible for Kirov's murder, but the balance of the evidence indicates he had nothing to do with it. If that was so, then the terror's origins lay in improvisation, rather than premeditation. □

This is the starting point for 'revisionism': Stalin had no long-term plan to destroy Old Bolsheviks. He improvised on Kirov's death to make an example of former opponents (who were treated comparatively leniently in early 1935) but there was no inevitable progression towards the mass executions of 1937–38. In 1935 and early 1936, public life was dominated by the framing and discussion of the new constitution, with its provisions for direct elections by universal franchise and secret voting and its guaranteed freedoms of speech, press and assembly. Prominent Soviet lawyers – such as A.Vyshinsky, chief prosecutor at the show trials – were insisting in the legal journals on the need for due process, careful judgments on the basis of evidence, firm legal codes, a strong role for defence lawyers. The total discordance between the constitution, legalism and Soviet realities is a commonplace, but 'revisionists' argue that some élite figures (notably Zhdanov) were serious about liberalization and that the public took their new rights seriously. The regime's liberal rhetoric does not square with the notion of a premeditated strike against the party, and contrasts strongly with the paranoia whipped up in late 1936, with its war and spy scares, xenophobia and demands for constant vigilance against the traitors within. In the 'totalitarian' interpretation, Stalin is presumed to have cynically invented a Trotskyist conspiracy, but some 'revisionists' credit him and Ezhov with a genuine fear for the regime's security. Evidence is now available that Trotsky and his son had indeed formed a 'bloc' with dissidents inside the Soviet Union. The show trials, argues Thurston, were not concocted out of thin air (though it still seems pretty rarefied to most!).

Perhaps the most important point to emerge from 'revisionist' scholarship is that the party rank and file and the lower ranks of professional groups (such as junior officers) were active participants in the terror, denouncing their superiors for suspected treason and urging the security authorities to take more extreme measures. The party bureaucracy, state administration and military élite were destroyed from above *and below* in a wave of voluntarism, chaos and even a kind of perverse revolutionary puritanism. Stalin's public calls, in February and March 1937, for moderation in party expulsions and an end to the arrests of those who had forsworn oppositional activity were, 'revisionists' argue, unfeigned attempts to restrain dangerous forces he had himself unleashed. This does have an important bearing on our understanding of Stalinism more generally. It is a personalized name for a complex historical phenomenon, and perhaps it ties 'the system' too closely to one man. No one questions that Stalin was a 'hands-on' dictator: an immensely hard-working and talented administrator with a formidable grasp of detail and a retentive memory, he personally supervised the destruction of his most eminent opponents while running vast areas of Soviet government. But he was not a one-man band. He had many thousands of willing collaborators, not just NKVD professionals but ordinary party members who took the initiative in rooting out 'enemies of the people'.

CONCLUSIONS

Beatrice Webb and a parade of fellow travellers were pathetically deluded about the nature of the new Soviet civilization, but they were nevertheless right to see it as a type of modernizing state-cum-society qualitatively different from any seen before. Since its politics were manifestly uncivilized by our standards, we jib at calling it a civilization at all. I think, however, that the term is apt and can provoke us into thinking about how the Soviet Union prepared for war, materially and morally. It is apt because the Soviet Union was a vast, self-contained empire of domination that was coercively but also ideologically unified by a secular clerisy – the CPSU – inspired by an exceptional sense of historic purpose. The subjects of this empire were compelled, as well as inspired, into creating a great industrial and military power at break-kneck speed. For most of them, Stalinism represented something hopeful. By and large, they were sufficiently inculcated with a sense of national purpose to recover from the military catastrophes of 1941 and resist a ferocious invader with equal ferocity.

References

Burnham, J. (1941) *The Managerial Revolution*, Penguin.

Brandenberger, D. L. and Dubrovsky, A. M. (1998) ' "The people need a tsar": the emergence of national Bolshevism as Stalinist ideology 1931–1941', *Europe-Asia Studies*, vol.50, no.5, pp.873–92.

Carr, E. H. and Davies, R. W. (1969) *Foundations of a Planned Economy 1926–1929*, vol.1, Penguin.

Cohen, S. (1980) *Bukharin and the Bolshevik Revolution*, Oxford University Press.

Conquest, R. (1971) *The Great Terror*, Penguin (*The Great Terror: A Reassessment* published 1990, Hutchinson).

Conquest, R. (1986) *The Harvest of Sorrow*, Hutchinson.

Conquest, R. (1997) 'Victims of Stalinism: a comment', *Europe-Asia Studies*, vol.49, no.7, pp.1317–19.

Davies, R. W. (1980) *The Socialist Offensive: The Collectivisation of Soviet Agriculture 1929–1930*, Macmillan.

Davies, R. W. (1994) 'Industry' in Davies, R. W. *et al.* (eds).

Davies, R. W. (1998) *Soviet Economic Development from Lenin to Khrushchev*, Cambridge University Press.

Davies, R. W., Harrison, M. and Wheatcroft, S. G. (eds) (1994) *The Economic Transformation of the Soviet Union 1913–1945*, Cambridge University Press.

Davies, S. (1997) *Popular Opinion in Stalin's Russia: Terror, Propaganda and Dissent 1934–1941*, Cambridge University Press.

Fainsod, M. (1958) *Smolensk Under Soviet Rule*, Macmillan.

Fitzpatrick, S. (1994) *Stalin's Peasant: Resistance and Survival in the Russian Village After Collectivization*, Oxford University Press.

Friedrich, C. J. and Brzezinski, Z. K. (1956) *Totalitarian Dictatorship and Autocracy*, Harvard University Press.

Getty, J. A. (1985) *Origins of the Great Purges: The Soviet Communist Party Reconsidered 1933–1938*, Cambridge University Press.

Getty, J. A. and Manning, R. T. (eds) (1993) *Stalinist Terror: New Perspectives*, Cambridge University Press.

Harrison, M. (1990) 'Stalinist industrialisation and the test of war', *History Workshop Journal*, vol.29, pp.65–84.

Kershaw, I. and Lewin, M. (eds) (1997) *Stalinism and Nazism: Dictatorships in Comparison*, Cambridge University Press.

Kotkin, S. (1995) *Magnetic Mountain: Stalinism as a Civilisation*, University of California Press.

Lane, D. (1970) *Politics and Society in the USSR*, Weidenfeld and Nicolson.

Lewin, M. (1968) *Russian Peasants and Soviet Power*, Macmillan.

Radzinsky, E. (1996) *Stalin*, Hodder and Stoughton.

Reese, R. R. (1993) 'The Red Army and the great purges' in Getty, J. A. and Manning, R. T. (eds).

Reese, R. R. (1996) *Stalin's Reluctant Soldiers: A Social History of the Red Army 1925–1941*, University of Kansas Press.

Rosefielde, S. (1996) 'Stalinism in post-communist perspective: new evidence on killings, forced labour and economic growth in the 1930s', *Europe-Asia Studies*, vol.48, no.6, pp.959–87.

Thurston, R. W. (1996) *Life and Terror in Stalin's Russia 1934–1941*, Yale University Press.

Tucker, R. C. (1991) *Stalin in Power: the Revolution from Above 1928–1941*, Norton.

Volkogonov, D. (1991) *Stalin: Triumph and Tragedy*, Weidenfeld and Nicolson.

Ward, C. (1999) *Stalin's Russia*, Arnold (second edition).

Webb, B. and S. (1941) *Soviet Communism: A New Civilisation*, Longman (first published 1935; second edition 1937, reissued with a new introduction 1941).

Wheatcroft, S. G. and Davies, R. W. (1994) 'Agriculture' in Davies, R. W. *et al.* (eds).

Wheatcroft, S. G. and Davies, R. W. (1994) 'Population' in Davies, R. W. *et al.* (eds).

Unit 16 ITALY 1918–1940

GEOFFREY WARNER, EDITED BY ARTHUR MARWICK

Open University students of this unit will need to refer to:

Set book: J. M. Roberts, *Europe 1880–1945*, Longman, 2001

Primary Sources 2: Interwar and World War II, eds Arthur Marwick and Wendy Simpson, Open University, 2000

Secondary Sources, eds Arthur Marwick and Wendy Simpson, Open University, 2000

Maps Booklet

Arthur Marwick, who has edited this unit, has occasionally inserted comments in the text. These are shown in square brackets and are italicized.

INTRODUCTION

This unit deals with the history of Italy between 1918 and 1940. For all but the first four years of this period, of course, Italy was ruled by Benito Mussolini, the *Duce* or 'Leader', with the support of his *Partito Nazionale Fascista* or 'National Fascist Party' (PNF). For this reason, fascism naturally bulks large in the unit, and, in accordance with the theme of the course, much attention will be given to the relationship between fascism and war. By the end of the unit you should be able to answer the following questions:

1   What were the consequences of World War I for Italian politics and society?

2   What was the nature of fascism and to what extent was it a product of World War I?

3   How and why did fascism come to power in Italy in 1922? What other possible outcomes were there – for example, the continued development of democracy?

4   What was the nature of the Fascist regime? How much support did it enjoy and how does it fit into the so-called 'totalitarian model'?

5   How far was war basic not only to Fascist theory but also to Fascist practice?

1   ITALIAN POLITICS AND SOCIETY AT THE END OF WORLD WAR I

Exercise   Read Roberts from the beginning of the section on Italy at the foot of p.358 as far as the sentence 'The nature of fascism, and the context in which it appeared, made this impossible' at the foot of p.360. (Don't bother with the cross-reference to Fiume on p.359, since we shall look at this later in the unit.)

When you have finished the passage from Roberts, try to answer the following related questions:

1   Why, in Roberts's opinion, did World War I precipitate a crisis in Italian politics and society?

2   Was this crisis primarily economic or political? ∎

Specimen answer   Pre-war Italy's constitutional and parliamentary foundations were weak, and World War I undermined them still further for two main reasons. The first was that Italy's economy, being less strong than those of its allies, suffered proportionately more from the economic consequences of the war, such as inflation and unemployment. The second reason was political. First of all the war, in Roberts's words, 'accentuated the divorce between patriotism and the left which had lain in the teachings of pre-war Socialism'. This led to increasing polarization between the left and the nationalist right. Furthermore, successive Italian governments seemed unable to cope with either the economic or the political situation. This was because the political system in which they were accustomed to operate depended upon the absence of mass parties and, unfortunately for them, the aftermath of World War I saw not only an increase in the strength of the Socialists, but also the emergence of a second mass party, the Roman Catholic *Partito Popolare* or 'People's Party'.

Roberts does not directly address the question of whether Italy's post-war crisis was primarily economic or political, but the implication of his analysis is, surely, that political factors were more important. Even if we accept his contention that the Italian economy was more severely affected than those of other countries, his emphasis is much more upon politics than economics: the polarization between left and right; the threat of revolution; and the impotence of Italian governments. Of course, you could argue that it was economic developments which produced the political problems that Italian governments were unable to tackle, but I would rather not explore this particular example of the chicken and egg.

Discussion Since we are principally concerned with the impact of World War I, I think it is important to emphasize that Roberts makes it clear that the war did not create Italy's problems; it merely exacerbated them. Despite the rhetoric of the *Risorgimento* or 'Revival' (the process which led to Italian unification in the nineteenth century), Italy was not united by a mass movement from below, but by conquest from above. One state, Piedmont, had extended its control over the rest of the peninsula by a mixture of war, diplomacy and subversion. This left a profound legacy of alienation between rulers and ruled, made worse by regional differences (most 'Italians' did not speak Italian, but a local dialect), ignorance (as late as 1911 four-fifths of Italians were illiterate), poverty (Italy's infant mortality rate was among the highest in western Europe) and religious antagonism (the Roman Catholic Church, which claimed the allegiance of most Italians, was at daggers drawn with the anti-clerical state which had annexed its temporal lands). The outcome was that, until the eve of World War I, Italy's political system could hardly be called democratic. It was characterized by what was known as *trasformismo* or 'transformism', a shifting pattern of loose parliamentary coalitions based upon a restricted suffrage and local patronage.

Although Italy remained a predominantly agricultural economy well into the twentieth century, there had been a rapid expansion of industry in the 1890s and 1900s and, in common with other countries, this had encouraged the growth of socialism. The *Partito Socialista Italiano* or 'Italian Socialist Party' (PSI) was formed in 1892, and the parallel trade-union movement, the *Confederazione Generale di Lavoro* or 'General Confederation of Labour' (CGL), in 1906. As Roberts indicates, the PSI had not supported the war – its official policy was summed up in the slogan *ne aderire ne sabotare* or 'neither support nor sabotage' – but its anti-militarism had already been forged during the experience of an earlier conflict, the war of 1911–12 against Turkey, as a result of which Italy annexed Libya. It was, indeed, in 1912 that the so-called *massimalisti* or 'maximalists', with their intransigent and revolutionary views, defeated the reformists and gained control of the PSI. Contrast the situation in Italy with that in Britain, France and Germany, where the socialist parties were controlled by reformists and supported their countries' war efforts. Although the wartime consensus had begun to break down in these countries by 1917, it had never existed in Italy. As Roberts also points out on p.360, the PSI was one of the two mass political parties whose growth helped to destabilize the post-war Italian political system. What he does not mention here, however, is that the growth of the PSI was greatly assisted by another pre-war development, namely, the expansion of the franchise, which took place in 1913. This almost trebled the proportion of adult males eligible to vote, from 32 per cent to 90 per cent. Women did not obtain the right to vote in Italy until after World War II. □

Having looked at what Roberts has to say about the causes of the post World War I crisis in Italian politics and society, and commented on the extent to which it was rooted in developments prior to 1915, let us now examine the post-war scene in more detail.

The economy

The only effective way of ascertaining the extent to which Italy suffered economically as a result of World War I is to make comparisons with other belligerents. Unfortunately, the necessary statistics are not always available, and those that are often leave much to be desired in the way of accuracy. The comparisons which follow, therefore, should only be taken as a very rough guide.

   In terms of military casualties, Italy does not appear to have come off too badly. Although a higher proportion of the male working population was killed than in the United Kingdom (6.2 per cent as opposed to 5.1 per cent) this was much lower than in France (10.5 per cent) or Germany (15.1 per cent). On the other hand, Italy suffered much more in the great influenza pandemic of 1918 than any other west European belligerent. Thus 274,000 died of the disease in Italy, compared with 188,000 in Germany, 112,000 in the United Kingdom and 91,000 in France.

   The position with regard to inflation is set out in Table 16.1, which reproduces the cost-of-living index for the same four countries between 1914 and 1922.

Table 16.1   Cost-of-living indexes 1914–22

	France	*Germany*	*Italy*	*UK*
1914	100	100	100	100
1915	118	125	109	123
1916	135	164	136	146
1917	159	245	195	175
1918	203	293	268	203
1919	259	401	273	215
1920	359	987	359	249
1921	312	1,299	427	226
1922	300	14,576	423	184

(Source: B. R. Mitchell, *European Historical Statistics 1750–1975*, 1981, Table 12)

Exercise   How would you compare Italy's wartime and post-wartime rate of inflation with those of the other countries in Table 16.1? ■

Specimen answer   Inflation in Italy was certainly worse than that in the United Kingdom, but nowhere near as bad as in Germany, especially in the post-war period. While the pace varied in the two countries, the French and Italian rates ended up at exactly the same point in 1920, although inflation in France then fell back much more sharply. While Italian prices continued to rise until 1921, these figures would not suggest that inflation in Italy was particularly severe in comparison with that in other countries.

Discussion   This conclusion clearly casts some doubt upon the thesis put forward by Roberts on p.359 that 'Italy had in comparison with them [its allies] undergone a *much greater* financial and economic strain' (emphasis added). Ironically, he goes on to demolish a possible counter-argument by stating that 'Wages during the war did not lag far behind prices', for if they had, the position of the Italian wage-earner could still have been a lot worse than that of his or her opposite numbers elsewhere. It all depends, of course, on what you mean by lagging far behind. For the record, while prices in Italy rose more than one-and-a-half times between 1914 and 1918, wages only rose by three-quarters. This seems quite a large gap to me. □

Turning to unemployment, we once again face a dearth of comparable statistics. On the face of it, it would seem that the peak figure for unemployment in Italy during the period 1919–22 was only about 3 per cent of the labour force, compared with 6 per cent in Germany and 22 per cent in Britain. However, it is only fair to point out that the Italian figures are almost certainly a gross underestimate.

We are on slightly firmer ground when it comes to output. Once again, Italy does not fare at all badly in comparison with other countries. Take, for example, the index of industrial production shown in Table 16.2 (note that 1913=100).

If we turn to agricultural production we find a similar picture. Thus, if we take the average annual output of a country's five main grain crops over the years 1910–14 as 100, the index for 1920–24 is as shown in Table 16.3.

It is only when we look at foreign trade that there is a substantial deterioration in Italy's position compared with pre-war. Italy is poor in natural resources and had to import both raw materials and foodstuffs. In 1913 its exports paid for 68 per cent of its imports; in 1919 the proportion was only 36 per cent.

Table 16.2   Index of industrial production 1919–22

	France	Italy	UK
1919	57	104	90
1920	62	104	98
1921	55	95	80
1922	78	107	93

(Source: Carlo M. Cipolla (ed.), *The Fontana Economic History of Europe*, 1976, vol.6, part 2, pp.687, 689–90, 692–3)

Table 16.3   Index of grain crops output 1920–24

France	86
Germany	66
Italy	96
UK	99

(Source: Cipolla, 1976, vol.6, p.670)

Despite this last statistic, the argument that Italy suffered proportionately more economically than other west European belligerents as a result of World War I does not hold water. It seems more likely, therefore, that the roots of fascism are to be found in politics rather than in economics.

The polity

The main developments on the Italian political scene in the aftermath of World War I were:

1   the growth and increased combativeness of the socialist trade-union movement and of the PSI;

2   the birth and rapid development of the Catholic People's Party and of the Catholic trade-union movement;

3   the ferment of nationalist forces, which were hostile to both socialism and the liberal parliamentary system;

4   the founding of the *Partito Comunista Italiano* or Italian Communist Party (PCI).

The first two phenomena have already been mentioned. In the elections of November 1919, for which the last barriers to universal male suffrage were removed and proportional representation introduced, the PSI obtained 32.4 per cent of the vote and trebled its strength in comparison with the last pre-war election (1913), becoming the largest single party in the Chamber of Deputies, with 156 seats out of 508. At the same time, the CGL, which had 250,000 members in 1918, saw its strength increase to 1,150,000 in 1919 and to 2,200,000 in 1920.

We have alluded (see above, p.58) to the militancy of the Italian socialists. An indication of the way in which this manifested itself was labour unrest. Once again, this becomes clearer if we compare the situation in Italy with that in other west European countries. In Table 16.4 I have computed (very roughly!) the number of hours lost through strike action per 1,000 workers in France, Germany, Italy and the United Kingdom in the immediate post-war period.

Table 16.4   Hours lost through strikes (per 1,000 workers)

	France	Germany	Italy	UK
1918	45	45	49	303
1919	713	1,034	1,221	1,806
1920	1,064	523	1,672	1,372
1921	324	808	447	4,436
1922	181	866	378	1,025

(Source: adapted from B. R. Mitchell, *European Historical Statistics 1750–1975*, 1981, Tables C1, C3)

It will be seen from this table that labour unrest was widespread in west Europe during this period and that it peaked in the two years 1919 and 1920. These were known in Italy as the *biennio rosso* or 'red two years'. (The main reason the unrest decreased in 1921, incidentally, albeit not in Britain, was because that year saw a sharp downturn in the economic cycle.) It also emerges from the table that Italian labour was more militant than French and German labour, although less militant than labour in Britain. [*It may be, rather, that labour in Britain was more self-confident and better organized, rather than more 'militant'.*]

There were two particular features of Italian labour unrest to which I should like to draw attention, as they were of great concern to contemporaries. The first was that the industrial unrest culminated, in September 1920, in large-scale factory occupations in such northern cities as Turin, Genoa and Milan, where Italian industry was concentrated. The Prime Minister at the time, Giovanni Giolitti, who was the great political manipulator of pre-war Italy, did not take the occupations too seriously, reasoning that the workers were less dangerous inside the factories than on the streets and that they would sooner or later have to come to terms. He was right, but his alleged passivity in the face of what looked like the revolutionary expropriation of private property, and his pressure upon the bosses to grant concessions to their workforce in order to bring the occupations to an end, antagonized the employers and the middle classes generally.

The second special feature of post-war Italian labour unrest was that it extended into agriculture. Indeed, during the *biennio rosso* four out of ten Italian strikers were in the agricultural sector. Since Italy was still a predominantly agricultural economy, it is perhaps not surprising that there should have been trouble in the countryside, although agrarian unrest was not a feature of post-war discontent elsewhere in west Europe. It was accompanied, moreover, by widespread seizures of land by the poorer peasantry and landless labourers, who had been encouraged by wartime promises of the 'land fit for heroes' variety. It is estimated that the number of peasant proprietors in Italy doubled to 3.5 million between the censuses of 1911 and 1921. Although much of the land seized in this way was barren or uncultivated, landowners, like industrialists, felt that the government was not doing enough to protect their property and was even encouraging the agitation by such measures as its September 1919 instruction to its local representatives to legitimate seizures of uncultivated land.

Neither the factory occupations nor the land seizures were revolutionary in intent – there are, after all, few people less revolutionary than peasant proprietors – but the rhetoric of the PSI and its allies made them appear so. The consequences were serious for the stability of the political system. As the British historian Martin Clark has pointed out:

> The PSI's revolutionary posturing meant that it was not 'available' to friendly politicians like Giolitti; it could not be tacitly 'absorbed' into the system by public works schemes or union concessions, as in pre-war days ... The PSI's public Bolshevism, its support for strikes and factory occupations, frightened the respectable middle classes away from a Liberal regime that seemed incapable of dealing with overt subversion.

(*Modern Italy 1871–1982*, 1984, p.212)

The second main development in Italian politics after World War I was the emergence of a powerful Roman Catholic party and trade-union movement. Italy had been united in the face of the opposition of the papacy. The papal lands in central Italy, including the city of Rome, had been forcibly incorporated into the new kingdom, and Piedmont's liberal, anti-clerical legislation was extended throughout the peninsula. It was not surprising, therefore, that relations between the Italian state and the Vatican were very bad. Indeed, in the early years after unification, the Church even tried to prevent Catholics from voting in parliamentary elections by threatening them with excommunication if they did so. By January 1919, however, Pope Benedict XV had come to the radical conclusion that 'a democratic party with an advanced political and social programme ... [was] the surest instrument for furthering the church's interests in Italy' (C. Seton-Watson, *Italy from Liberalism to Fascism,* 1967, p.514). Although the *Partito Popolare Italiano* or 'Italian People's Party' (PPI) was not formally set up by the Vatican and was careful, even in its title, to avoid too close an identification with the Church, it could never have been established without the latter's permission and its leader, Luigi Sturzo, was in fact a priest. A Catholic trade-union organization, the *Confederazione Italiana de Lavoratori* or 'Italian Workers' Confederation' (CIL), had already been formed in September 1918.

In the election of November 1919 the PPI won 20.5 per cent of the vote and 100 seats, making it the second largest party after the Socialists. As for the CIL, its membership rose from 500,000 in 1919 to 1,250,000 in 1921. As indicated above, the new Catholic mass movements were socially progressive, drawing much of their inspiration from the encyclical *Rerum Novarum,* or 'Concerning New Phenomena', promulgated in 1891 by Pope Leo XIII, which had criticized the excesses of unrestrained capitalism. Thus, Catholic organizations played their part in the post-war social unrest which affected Italy. This was particularly true in the countryside, where priests and PPI activists frequently organized the land seizures by a predominantly Catholic peasantry. One Catholic peasant leader, Guido Maglioli of Cremona, was even known as 'the white Bolshevik'.

Nevertheless, the PPI was not a 'revolutionary' party in the way that the PSI purported to be, and it even took part in government. Like the PSI, however, it did represent a group which had been outside the mainstream of Italian political development since unification. In some degree, therefore, it too was an 'anti-system' party which found co-operation with Italy's traditional ruling élite none too easy. Unfortunately, it did not find co-operation with the anti-clerical and atheistic PSI any easier – and vice versa – so that we have the alarming situation in which the country's two largest political parties were, to a greater or lesser extent, alienated both from the political system in which they operated and from each other.

Both the growth of the PSI and the emergence of the PPI were a direct result of World War I. One should not posit too much of a connection between death and deprivation, whether in the trenches or on the home front, and political radicalization, but it is surely significant that increased unionization of labour, greater industrial militancy, and heightened demands for political, economic and social reform were well-nigh universal phenomena in all belligerent countries. The old order had failed. Indeed, the war itself had underlined the failure. It was time for a better tomorrow, and ordinary men and women seemed more inclined to organize and agitate for it.

The ferment of right-wing nationalism, which was the third major development in post-war Italian politics, also grew directly out of the war, but in a different way. Although 1918 had witnessed the disintegration of Italy's traditional enemy, the Austro-Hungarian Empire, and although the subsequent peace settlement awarded Italy some additional territory at its expense (see the map of Italy in the *Maps Booklet*), the nationalists who had propelled the country into war in 1915 were still not satisfied. In order to find out why, you should read the relevant passage from Roberts, beginning on p.270 with the sentence 'It would be superficial to begin the story of Italian revisionism in 1918 ...', and ending just over half-way down p.271 with 'Giolitti hastened to come to terms and agreed that the Italians too should leave (2 August 1920)'.

Exercise   Why, in Roberts's opinion, did Italy fail to obtain all that it had been promised under the Treaty of London, and what were the consequences for post-war Italian politics? ■

Specimen answer   The chief obstacle to Italian ambitions was President Woodrow Wilson, who refused to be bound by the Treaty of London and similar inter-allied agreements to which the United states had not been a party. It was he who objected most strongly to Italy's claims upon the new state of Yugoslavia, the existence of which he supported, and to Italian aims in Albania. The French, however, were also opposed to Italian gains at the expense of Yugoslavia, a state which they saw as 'a future ally and client'. The Italo-French quarrel had repercussions upon the redistribution of non-European territory, as did the failure to partition Turkey. Nationalist rhetoric and resentment over these issues, according to Roberts, 'combined to weaken the prestige of the government and the parliamentary system'.

Discussion   Although Roberts describes the intervention of the nationalist poet Gabriele d'Annunzio in Fiume as 'almost comical', it illustrated not only the strength of nationalist feeling, but also the connivance of some sections of the armed forces – the local Italian commander allowed d'Annunzio to take over – and the relative impotence of the Italian government, which was unable to retrieve control of the situation for more than a year. This connivance in right-wing defiance of the government on the part of sections of the state apparatus, and the apparent inability of the government to deal with either the defiance or the connivance, was to be a feature of the rise of fascism.

At a more symbolic level, d'Annunzio's occupation of Fiume provided a foretaste of Fascist theatricality. As the British historian Christopher Seton-Watson has written:

> The uniforms and the black shirts [originally worn by the *arditi* or 'shock troops' in World War I], the 'Roman salute', the 'oceanic' rallies, the party hymn, *Giovinezza* ['Youth']; the organisation of the militia into cohorts and legions, commanded by consuls; the weird [and meaningless] cries of *Eia Eia Alalà*, the demagogic technique of 'dialogue' between orators and massed audiences; all the symbolism, mystique and 'style' with which the world was later to grow so familiar, were plagiarized from d'Annunzio ...

> (*Italy from Liberalism to Fascism*, 1967, p.596)

Right-wing nationalists like d'Annunzio were, of course, bitterly opposed to the PSI, which they accused of trying to undermine the country's war effort. Yet like the PSI, they had nothing but contempt for the effete parliamentary democracy which had failed to win the peace and brought about instead what d'Annunzio called a *vittoria mutilata* or 'mutilated victory'. All the major developments on the Italian political scene after World War I, therefore, were a challenge to the existing system. □

2   THE RISE OF FASCISM

A brief sketch of the rise of fascism is provided on pp.360–63 of Roberts. You should read this now, from the sentence beginning 'The first organization of Fascism ...', near the foot of p.360 as far as the end of the first paragraph at the top of p.363.

Roberts glosses over the fact that, while fascism was part of the post-war nationalist ferment in Italy, its size and influence was minimal until the end of 1920. Its leader, Mussolini, had begun his political career as a revolutionary socialist and was, in fact, the director of the PSI's newspaper, *Avanti!* (Forward), at the outbreak of World War I. Before the end of the year, however, he had broken with his erstwhile comrades over the issue of Italian participation in the war, believing that this was essential in order to create the necessary conditions for a socialist revolution. He founded his own newspaper, *Il Popolo d'Italia* or 'The Italian People', and his was undoubtedly the most powerful voice on the left arguing for Italian intervention. It was only at the end of the war that Mussolini began to move towards the right, and the programme of the *Fasci di combattimento* or 'fighting groups' still contained many left-wing ingredients, such as the seizure of Church property, the replacement of a standing army by a short-term people's militia, and a swingeing tax upon capital. As the Italian historian Marco Revelli writes:

> In this phase Fascism ... was still a volatile and fluid amalgam of frustrated minorities drawn from the most varied political and cultural backgrounds ... Their common denominator was a radical rejection of the political realities of the day and, characterised above all by the *combattentismo,* the war-veteran's cult of the fighting spirit. It was first and foremost an *urban* phenomenon, a phenomenon of the big cities in fact, almost exclusively confined to the North and found especially in Milan, the only large-scale concentration of industry and commerce in Italy. Of the 112 'founders' of the Fascist movement at the meeting of 23 March 1919 ... as many as 60 were Milanese and another 14 came from the immediate surroundings ... Among these 112 there were nine lawyers, five army or navy officers, five professors, five doctors, three accountants, two parliamentary deputies and one senator. All the rest appear to have had no particular professional or academic qualification.
>
> (In D. Mühlberger, *The Social Basis of European Fascist Movements,* 1987, p.11)

Although the movement claimed 137 fasci (fighting groups) and 40,385 members in October 1919, it only succeeded in picking up about 2 per cent of the vote in Milan in the general election of 16 November, a performance which puts it roughly on a par with the late David ('Screaming Lord') Sutch's Monster Raving Loony Party in this country. If fascism does indeed appear to have been a direct outgrowth of World War I, it was a very tender plant, and by the end of 1919 its strength had fallen to 31 fasci and 870 members.

What undoubtedly kept it alive was Mussolini and his newspaper, *Il Popolo d'Italia*. This appears to have been financed by the Perrone brothers, who controlled the giant Ansaldo armaments combine and other Milanese industrial interests. You may wonder why these people bothered to hand out cash to a party which could command so little support, but it should be remembered that Mussolini was a skilled and influential journalist, and that *Il Popolo d'Italia's* fierce anti-socialism and nationalism were grist to the mill of industrialists, and especially of arms manufacturers. In any case, Mussolini and his newspaper were not the only beneficiaries of their largesse.

Three developments in the last quarter of 1920 rescued fascism from the doldrums and transformed it from the status of an irrelevant sect to that of a mass movement contending for power. These were: first, the factory occupations of September and the parallel agrarian unrest; secondly, the local elections of September/ October, as a result of which the PSI gained control of 2,022 communal and 26 provincial governments compared with 400 and 4 respectively in the previous elections in 1914; and thirdly, the Treaty of Rapallo between Italy and Yugoslavia in November, by which the former renounced its claims to Dalmatia, Fiume was declared a free city, and d'Annunzio and his supporters were subsequently driven out by the Italian armed forces. For the right, the first two developments constituted a major challenge to the existing structure of property relations and political power, while the third was regarded as an act of treachery on the part of the government.

Doubtless defeated by the demands of compression, Roberts's account implies that fascism had been growing steadily since its foundation in March 1919 but, as we have seen, this was not the case. Moreover, Roberts fails to bring out the crucial significance of the developments mentioned in the previous paragraph. Particularly significant for the expansion of fascism was the reaction of landowners in the Po Valley and Tuscany to the agrarian agitation and land seizures. Despairing of effective support from the government, they turned to private enterprise, in the shape of squads of Fascist thugs, for help in fighting the peasant unions and their political allies. From the end of 1920 a kind of civil war raged in the countryside between the Fascists and the left. A near-contemporary account of a typical example of what took place is provided by the Italian anti-Fascist historian Gaetano Salvemini, and you will find it reproduced as Document I.8 in *Primary Sources 2: Interwar and World War II*. You should read it now.

Exercise   What impression do you get from Salvemini's account of the attitude of the forces of law and order to the activities of the Fascists? ∎

Specimen answer   To judge from Salvemini's account, their attitude was one of passivity or complicity. The *carabinieri,* the military police force in the countryside, made no attempt to stop the Fascists from attacking socialist property in Foiano on 12 or 17 April 1921. They did nothing to prevent the Fascist reprisals against the alleged perpetrators of the ambush on 17 April either. Indeed, they appear to have collaborated with the Fascists in hunting down the latter. Finally, while the courts handed out heavy sentences to those convicted of participation in the ambush, no Fascists received any punishment whatsoever.

Discussion   If anything, Salvemini's account of events at Foiano underplays the complicity of the state authorities in Fascist violence. Christopher Seton-Watson sums up their involvement as follows:

> Fascism could never have prospered so rapidly without at least the tolerance of the state authorities. Many prefects, police and military commanders went far beyond tolerance. In Venezia Guilia the *squadre* ['squads'] enjoyed virtually official status. Elsewhere, particularly in Tuscany, they were supplied with lorries and arms, and serving officers joined the fasci with the approval of their superiors. Sometimes soldiers and *carabinieri* accompanied the *squadre* on punitive expeditions, fully armed and in uniform. Long-suffering policemen and state officials, after years of forced subservience to provincial socialist bosses, took little trouble to conceal their delight at the turning of the tables.
>
> (*Italy from Liberalism to Fascism*, 1967, p.576) □

Seton-Watson goes on to emphasize that this complicity was local in origin, and that the central government repeatedly enjoined its local representatives to curb the activities of the squads and punish crimes of violence. This may have been true in general, but as we shall see, even Prime Minister Giolitti was prepared to turn a blind eye to Fascist thuggery during the election campaign of May 1921.

Fascism grew in leaps and bounds during this period, although its point of departure was nowhere near as high as Roberts suggests on p.360. The official Fascist figures for the end of 1920, which are unlikely to be an underestimate, were for 88 fasci with 20,615 members. By the end of March 1921 these had risen to 317 and 80,476, and by the end of June to 1,192 and 204,506. Originally heavily concentrated in the north of the country (75 per cent of the membership in March 1921), it did gradually extend its influence into other parts of Italy, but as late as October 1921 only a quarter of Fascists were to be found in the south compared to over one-third of the population as a whole. The reason for this was that the old political élite still retained much of its control over this backward part of the country. Like the PSI and the PPI – over four-fifths of whose parliamentary seats in 1919 had been won in north and central Italy – fascism was essentially a northern phenomenon.

It must be stressed that the Fascist surge was a counter-revolution and not, as it was so often portrayed by apologists at the time and since, a defensive action against the threat of 'Bolshevism'. As you will recall from Table 16.4, labour unrest in Italy had peaked in 1920 and fallen back sharply in 1921. In addition, the *Partito Comunista Italiano*, or 'Italian Communist Party' (PCI), split off from the PSI in January 1921 in response to the dictates of Lenin and the Third International. Mussolini himself wrote in *Il Popolo d'Italia* on 2 July 1921, 'To maintain that the Bolshevist danger still exists in Italy is to mistake fear for reality.' What was happening was that the 'victims' of the *biennio rosso* were getting their own back, with interest. However, we should always keep in mind the great fear of communism and socialism there was everywhere in the west: to many, the split between Socialists and Communists simply meant that they had *two* threatening parties to deal with.

When Giolitti had originally formed his government in June 1920, he had persuaded the PPI to join it. The latter had loyally supported him, but was becoming progressively more disillusioned with his failure to implement some of the more cherished parts of its programme. Giolitti was aware of its growing disillusionment and, mindful also of the split in the PSI, decided to go to the country in May 1921 in order to obtain a new parliamentary majority. As Roberts says, he even offered the Fascists a place on the government ticket. Although he no doubt hoped that he could thereby trim the claws of the movement, he was perfectly prepared to make use of its organized thuggery in his election campaign, explaining to a British official, 'These Fascists are our Black and Tans.' Among the thirty-five Fascists elected was Mussolini himself. The other results, which Roberts cites, show that Giolitti had failed in his bid to create a new majority at the expense of the socialist/communist left and the PPI. When Mussolini repaid his patron by withdrawing his support, Giolitti did not so much 'step off the stage ... to leave others to discover they could not do without him' (Roberts, p.361) as find himself pushed over the edge. Italy seemed more ungovernable than ever.

The extent of Mussolini's own opportunism at this time is illustrated by the fact that he toyed with the idea of an alliance with the PSI and the PPI, and he actually concluded an agreement in August 1921 which promised a cessation of hostilities between the Fascists and the socialist trade unions. In doing this, however, the *Duce* had over-reached himself. The local Fascist bosses, or *ras* as they were called after Abyssinian chieftains, men like Dino Grandi of Bologna, Roberto Farinacci of Cremona, and Italo Balbo of Ferrara, were not prepared to have deals of this kind struck above their heads. Mussolini was forced to backtrack. In October 1921 the *Partito Nazionale Fascista* (PNF) was founded. Its programme, adopted a month later, was unabashedly right-wing and nationalist. As the American historian Charles Delzell has written:

> It is clear ... that the tenuous 'socialism' of 1919 had given way to 'integral' nationalism. The abolition of 'demagogic' fiscal measures such as taxes on inheritance and bondholders was called for, as were strikes in the public services. The program ... demanded complete freedom for the Catholic Church in the exercise of its spiritual office. It repudiated the League of Nations and called for a large standing army instead of the short-term militia that had been favoured in 1919.

> (*Mediterranean Fascism 1919–1945*, 1971, p.27)

We are fortunate in having a picture of the social composition of the PNF in November 1921, drawn from a sample of about half the total membership. It is instructive to compare it with the composition of the Italian population as a whole, taken from the 1921 census, which was held at about the same time. Marco Revelli writes:

> The social structure of the party was a fairly faithful reflection of the general distribution of classes and occupational groups (achieving in a sense the ambition of representing organically and faithfully the whole nation), except for some significant cases of over- and under-representation in certain categories. Industrialists, for example, accounted for 2.8 per cent of [party] members (while ... the entire *haute bourgeoisie* numbered at the time only 1.7 per cent [of the population]). The figures tally almost perfectly for the middle classes (56.5 per cent in the party compared with 53.3 per cent in society), but there was a conspicuous imbalance in favour of the petty bourgeoisie formed by white-collar workers in the public and private sectors (15.7 per cent in the party as against 3.2 per cent in society). On the other hand workers were under-represented ...
>
> (In D. Mühlberger, *The Social Basis of European Fascist Movements*, 1987, p.19)

Exercise How far do you think the above figures support the traditional view of fascism as the protest movement *par excellence* of the lower middle classes against inflation and working-class militancy? ■

Specimen answer Although the much higher proportion of members of what Revelli calls 'the petty bourgeoisie' (which is another name for the lower middle class) in the PNF as opposed to the country as a whole gives some support to the traditional view, the figures clearly imply much more than that. As Revelli himself points out, the PNF could justifiably claim to be representative of the nation as a whole and not just of a particular class.

Discussion In fact, the PNF was more representative than Revelli's figures suggest. This is because even the corrected figure for workers which he gives is misleading, since it applies only to those in industry: 15.4 per cent in the party; 19.6 per cent in the country as a whole. If the agricultural workers, who were over-represented in the party, are included within the working class, then on that basis the under-representation of the working class in the party virtually disappears: 24.3 per cent in the party compared with 21.8 per cent in the country as a whole. Depending upon your point of view, this last figure either signifies a degree of resentment on the part of some agricultural labourers at the closed shop implemented by the socialist unions, or the success of the intimidatory tactics employed by the Fascist squads.

More significant than class, perhaps, was age. One scholar has estimated that no less than a quarter of the PNF's membership at this stage was under 21. Certainly 13 per cent were students. And while Mussolini himself was approaching 40 in 1921, the three powerful *ras* mentioned above – Grandi, Farinacci and Balbo – were still in their twenties. Youth is no doubt an asset when you are going around beating up your political opponents.

In January 1922 Pope Benedict XV died. He was succeeded by Pope Pius XI (1922–39), who was much less sympathetic to the PPI than his predecessor had been, especially as Mussolini was showing signs of withdrawing from his earlier anti-clericalism and was hinting that the Church could expect favourable treatment from a Fascist government. In a confidential circular to Italian bishops at the beginning of October, the Vatican formally dissociated itself from the PPI, a step which was bound to benefit the Fascists in their drive to power. As for the socialists, they became even more fragmented after the unions called a general strike on 31 July in protest against Fascist excesses. Support was not strong outside the major cities, and even there, the Fascists gained credit with the public by using their own personnel to break the strike in key services such as transport. On 3 August the unions ordered their members back to work. The Fascists launched a counter-offensive by physically driving out Socialist councils in such cities as Milan, Genoa and Leghorn and taking control in their place. Once again the authorities did nothing to prevent this crude exercise in brute force. When the reformist socialist Filippo Turati had the temerity to suggest that the opponents of fascism should actually form a coalition to fight it, hard-line purists in the PSI expelled him and his followers from the party in October. He formed a new, moderate socialist party, the *Partito Socialista Unitario* or 'United Socialist Party' (PSU). Italian socialism was now split three ways – PSI, PCI and PSU – at precisely the time it most needed to be united. The feeling was growing that, sooner or later, Mussolini and the PNF would have to be taken into the government, if only to turn these rather vicious poachers into gamekeepers. Unfortunately Mussolini did not want to serve under anyone else; he wanted to be Prime Minister himself. Roberts has described the *dénouement* on pp.361–2. The motive for the King's refusal to support Facta and his ministers is unclear. Some say that it was because he felt he could not rely upon the army. 'Your Majesty,' he is reported to have been advised, 'the army will do its duty. However, it would be well not to put it to the test.' Others believe it was because he feared that his pro-Fascist cousin might usurp the throne, or that he was persuaded by the equally pro-Fascist Queen Mother. □

Exercise   Going back to Roberts's account of these events, why do you think I have not ended this section of the unit with 'the march on Rome' and Mussolini becoming Prime Minister? (Hint: concentrate on what Roberts says on p.362 at the end of the first paragraph and the start of the second.) ■

Specimen answer   Mussolini's accession to power did not at first seem to signify a fundamental change in the governmental system. His was a coalition government; it contained only four Fascists and the special powers it took were only for a limited period. As Roberts says, 'It was clear that Italy was to have vigorous, strong government; it was not yet clear that the constitutional state had been set aside. The imposition of dictatorship was gradual.'

Discussion   What we need to know is how and why Mussolini became a fully-fledged dictator, or how and why his government became a regime. Unfortunately, I do not think that Roberts's account (on pp.362–3) is terribly clear, although he does provide most of the information necessary to address the question. In particular, it seems to me, he fails to bring out the full importance of the 1924 elections, the Matteotti murder and the so-called 'Aventine secession'.

It was not just the electoral law that enabled Mussolini's supporters to win the 1924 elections but also the widespread fraud and intimidation which accompanied its implementation. It was this that was denounced by the PSU's Secretary-General, Giacomo Matteotti, in the Chamber on 30 May 1924, and it was his denunciation which led to his disappearance on 10 June. Although Matteotti's body was not discovered for some weeks, it was widely and correctly assumed that he had been murdered by the Fascists on account of his accusations.

While the 'Aventine secession' (named after an incident in the history of Ancient Rome) was an unfortunate tactic on the part of the opposition parties, it might have achieved more if they could have agreed on something else as well. As it was, the PCI soon returned to the Chamber, while Pius XI vetoed a promising initiative for an alliance between the PPI and the PSU. Even then Mussolini's position remained weak, especially as evidence of Fascist complicity in Matteotti's abduction and murder mounted. Once again, however, the King failed to act; the general and admiral serving as war and navy ministers refused to join some of their civilian colleagues in resigning, thus in effect pledging the support of the armed forces for Mussolini; and Italian business, enjoying the effects of a mini-boom and good labour relations, came out in favour of the government. Most decisively of all, perhaps, the Fascist leadership itself urged Mussolini to take the offensive. He did so in a famous speech to the Chamber on 3 January 1925 in which he took 'full political, moral, and historical responsibility for all that has happened' and warned that 'when two irreducible elements [fascism and anti-fascism] are locked in a struggle, the solution is force'. This speech is usually seen as marking the inauguration of the Fascist dictatorship. Even so, this did not happen overnight. Thus it was not until December 1925 that the Decree on the Powers of the Head of the Government made Mussolini responsible only to the King and not to the Chamber; elected local governments were abolished in two stages in February and September 1926. If the rights of opposition trade unions were effectively removed by the Palazzo Vidoni pact of October 1925, under which employers agreed to negotiate only with the Fascist trade-union confederation, it was not until 1926 that all opposition political parties were banned. This latter step took place after the latest in a succession of attempts on Mussolini's life and was accompanied by other measures, including the establishment of a Special Tribunal for the Defence of the State to try political offences.

There was nothing 'inevitable' about the course of events in Italy between 1918 and 1925. Before 1922 fascism could have been stopped in its tracks at almost any time if its opponents had (a) got their act together and (b) displayed sufficient resolution. Even at the time of 'the march on Rome', the evidence suggests that the forces of law and order could and would have disarmed the Fascists if both King and government had not caved in before the threat of violence. The trouble, as Roberts suggests on pp.361–2, was that too many politicians thought they could 'use' the Fascists when the Fascists were in fact 'using' them. It was also true that too many anti-Fascists were as, if not more, suspicious of each other as they were of their common enemy. The balance became harder to redress once Mussolini was in power, especially after a hitherto largely neutral Roman Catholic Church and big business had swung into line behind him. Even then, however, the *Duce's* position was not impregnable, as the Matteotti crisis had shown. □

Going back to the principal theme of this part of the course – the impact of World War I – our analysis has, I think, clearly shown that while Italy was not destabilized economically by the conflict, it was destabilized politically. The emergence and/or growth of the PSI, the PPI and the Fascist movement itself, all of which were attributable in large measure to the war, posed a powerful threat to the pre-war liberal regime which was, in the end, insurmountable. However, this is not the same thing as saying that World War I led to the accession of fascism to power. The weakness of the Italian political system was due not so much to the war as to the way in which Italy had been united and the way that it had been ruled since unification. There had been neither the time nor the inclination to lay the foundations of a stable democratic tradition. Fascism proved more able to profit from this state of affairs than its rivals.

3   FASCISM AND TOTALITARIANISM

The purpose of this section of the unit is to examine the nature of the Fascist regime in Italy and, in particular, to explore the extent to which it was 'totalitarian'.

Exercise   You should now read Roberts, from the paragraph beginning 'To understand Italian fascism one must in the end focus on Mussolini', near the top of p.363, down to the end of the section on Italy on p.367. When you have done this, write down how far you think Roberts addresses the question of whether the Fascist regime was totalitarian and what his conclusions are. ■

Specimen answer   Roberts begins with a discussion of ideology, refers to Fascist control of the economy, and discusses the question of terror. On the other hand he does not examine the role of the party or the monopoly of mass communications.

As to the degree of conformity of the Fascist regime to totalitarianism, Roberts clearly does not believe that it was very close. 'As a totalitarian system', he writes on p.364, 'Fascism was far less impressive than Bolshevism.' He seems to reach this conclusion for three main reasons:

1   The weakness of Fascist ideology. 'Fascism', he writes on p.363, 'never presented any real ideological coherence.' He adds a little later on that there was a 'lack of positive content in Fascism'.

2   The relative independence of certain sectors of society. In this context Roberts refers specifically to the monarchy, the Church, and the economy.

3   The inefficacy of Fascist terror. Although Roberts concedes that 'terror had been a weapon of Fascism from the start', he nevertheless argues that 'when all is said and done, it is difficult to see terror as Fascism's mainspring in Italy' (pp.366–7). This was because the regime was never able to terrorize its opponents into total submission, and he cites the widespread evasion of the anti-Jewish racial laws of 1938 in support of his contention.

Discussion   In one sense, of course, the rest of this section of the unit is a discussion of the issues raised by this exercise, but for the moment I should merely like to draw your attention to two points. The first is a relatively simple one, although easily overlooked. Roberts says that 'as a totalitarian system Fascism was far less impressive than Bolshevism'. But this can be put another way, as indeed it is by the American scholar A. James Gregor, when he writes, 'By the commencement of World War II the Fascist government exercised more control over the lives and activities of its citizens than any other government save the Soviet Union' (in P. V. Cannistraro, *Historical Dictionary of Fascist Italy*, 1982, pp.540–1*)*. In other words, just because fascism was less totalitarian than Stalinist communism, this does not mean that it was not very totalitarian at all. Fascist Italy should be compared not only with the Soviet Union, but also with other contemporary regimes, and particularly with Nazi Germany. [*Most scholars today would say that there was not the same systematic terror in Italy as there was conducted by the Gestapo in Germany and the NKVD in the Soviet Union.*]

The second point relates to the definition of totalitarianism. Roberts is very scathing about the 1932 encyclopaedia article which, he says, was 'the main theoretical document of the [Fascist] movement' (p.363*)*. This article was actually called 'The doctrine of Fascism' and was supposedly written by Mussolini himself, although it seems that the philosopher Giovanni Gentile had a hand in it. Repetitive and disorganized though it is, the article does emphasize one crucial element in Fascist thinking: the centrality of the state. Extracts from the article are reprinted as Document I.9 in *Primary Sources 2: Interwar and World War II,* and you should read them now.

If 'outside the State there can be neither individuals nor groups (political parties, associations, syndicates, classes)', if 'the Fascist State ... is a force ... which takes over all the forms of the moral and intellectual life of man', and if 'it is the State alone that grows in size, and power', the definition of totalitarianism which emerges is one characterized not so much by any descriptive 'list' of its features, as by its purpose: the progressive annihilation of the boundaries between state and society.

Roberts clearly believes that fascism failed more or less completely to achieve this objective. Thus he argues, on p.363, that 'Fascist rule was important in Italian foreign policy, yet effected no substantial changes at home.' Even in foreign policy, he goes on to say on p.364, Fascist theory and practice were combined with only disastrous results. The theory and practice of Fascist foreign policy are the subject of the final section of this unit. For the remainder of this section, let us take a closer look at developments on the home front. □

Much of the confusion as to whether or not Fascist Italy was a totalitarian political system arises out of a consideration of the role of the Fascist Party. To begin with, it did seem as though Mussolini was building up the PNF as a rival to the state apparatus. Thus, on 1 February 1923 he turned the blackshirted Fascist squads of bully boys into the *Milizia Volontaria per la Sicurezza Nazionale* or 'Voluntary Militia for National Security' (MVSN), which superficially looked like a parallel security force. However, the real purpose of the move was to bring the squads – and, even more, the *ras* who ran them – under central control. This was clearly demonstrated when the MVSN was brought under army authority in August 1924.

Similarly, although the highest authority of the PNF, the Fascist Grand Council, was given what looked like impressive powers in December 1928, including the right to be consulted over the succession to the throne and the royal prerogatives, international treaties involving boundary changes and the succession to Mussolini, it rarely met after 1929 and, when it did so, merely acted as a recipient of the *Duce*'s wishes and decisions. Only in July 1943, when Italy had been defeated and invaded by the Allies, did the Grand Council seize the initiative and carry the motion of no confidence which led to Mussolini's dismissal by the King.

The true nature of the relationship between party and state power was shown in the circular which Mussolini sent to all prefects – the central government's local representatives – on 7 January 1927:

> The prefect ... is the highest authority of the State in the provinces. He is the direct representative of the central executive power. All citizens, and in the first instance all those who have the great privileges and the highest honour of being Fascist militants, owe respect and obedience to the highest political representatives of the Fascist regime, and must work with him under his control in order to make his task easier. Where necessary, the prefect must stimulate and harmonise the activity of the party in its various forms. But it must remain clear to all that authority cannot be exercised on a shared basis, nor can slippages of authority or responsibility be tolerated. Authority is single and uniform. If this is not so, there is a collapse into complete disorganisation and the disintegration of the State, thereby destroying one of the fundamental bases of Fascist doctrine ... Now that the revolution has been completed, the Party and its hierarchy, from top to bottom, are merely a conscious instrument of the will of the State, both at the centre and at the periphery.
>
> (Quoted in A. Aquarone, *L'Organizzazione dello Stato Totalitario*, 1965, p.485)

It is an interesting commentary upon the above text that between 1922 and 1929 only 20 out of 86 new prefects appointed came from outside the prefectoral corps, and that even at the end of the regime in 1943 only 37 out of a total of 117 prefects in office were political appointees. There was, therefore, no large-scale 'colonization' of this key sector of the state apparatus.

Of course, the very fact that Mussolini felt obliged to send a circular such as that of 7 January indicates there was a problem of rivalry between the PNF and the state. The *ras,* in particular, had been, and could still be, a threat to the *Duce*'s authority, and the latter took good care to see that they did not become too influential. Farinacci, for example, who had become Secretary-General of the PNF in February 1925, was dismissed in March of the following year and remained in the political wilderness until 1933, while Balbo, who became an international celebrity as an aviator in the late 1920s and early 1930s, found himself exiled to the governorship of Libya at the end of 1933.

Farinacci's successor as Secretary-General of the PNF, Augusto Turati, presided over a transformation of the nature of the party. In the words of the British historian, Philip Morgan:

> In a drastic reshaping of party membership, at its height before the official closing of party rolls in 1927 but continuing into 1928–29, many thousands of ex-squadrists and extremist Fascists were expelled from the party, their numbers swollen by the spontaneous defections of other disillusioned old members. There was a corresponding recruitment drive attracting to the party an influx of opportunists and white-collar public employees in

particular, a more passive membership that mirrored the consensus at the basis of Mussolini's dictatorship.

(Quoted in P. V. Cannistraro, *Historical Dictionary of Fascist Italy*, 1982, p.405)

Until 1932 there were never more than a million members of the PNF, or about 2.5 per cent of the population, but subsequently more and more of the opportunists described by Morgan were allowed to join, so that by June 1943 membership had reached a total of 4,770,000. No wonder that some wits alleged that the initials PNF really stood for *Per Necessità Familiari* or 'for family reasons'!

Although one can therefore agree that Fascist Italy possessed a single, hierarchically organized mass party, led by one man, which was either superior to, or (in the case of the PNF) intertwined with the government bureaucracy, its influence was not on a par with the German NSDAP or the Russian CPSU. At the same time it must be recognized that Hitler's 'night of the long knives' in June 1934 and Stalin's purges in the late 1930s are sometimes described in terms of 'victories' by the dictators concerned 'over' their parties. Indeed, one is entitled to ask: how important is a single mass party to the concept of totalitarianism?

As for the system of terroristic police control, there is no doubt that this existed at one level in Fascist Italy. It has been calculated that, in a typical week, the political police alone would conduct 20,000 visits, searches, arrests, seizures of literature, and so on. On the other hand, throughout its history the Special Tribunal for the Defence of the State imposed only twenty-six death sentences, and seventeen of these were during the war years 1940–43. The preferred penalty for political offences was imprisonment – some 3,000 individuals were sentenced to a total of 28,115 years – or the so-called *confino* or 'banishment', which gave northern anti-Fascist intellectuals their first revealing glimpse of life in Italy's backward south. While not wishing to condone fascism's persecution of its political opponents, it has to be conceded that this was small beer compared to what went on in Nazi Germany and the Soviet Union.

In the nineteenth century the press was the only genuine mass medium; today there is cinema, radio, television and video. Together with the press, cinema and radio were available to the totalitarian regimes of the interwar period. How did Fascist Italy make use of them?

Even before the abolition of the opposition political parties in 1926 there had been close censorship of the press. Afterwards there were no opposition papers at all, and detailed guidelines were issued to editors. Nevertheless, not all newspapers were owned or run by the PNF or the government, and it seems that Italians preferred to read the ones they had always read. In 1933, for example, the Milanese daily, *Corriere della Sera* or 'Evening Courier', had a circulation of over 600,000 compared with the official *Popolo d'Italia*'s 100,000.

It was the Italian radio pioneer Guglielmo Marconi who suggested to Mussolini in 1923 that there were advantages in setting up a national radio network in Italy. An organization was duly set up in August 1924 and taken over by the state in November 1927. The number of radio licences grew as shown in Table 16.5.

Impressive though this expansion may appear at first sight, its importance should not be exaggerated. In 1938 there was still only one radio licence for every forty-three Italians, compared with one for every seven Germans and one for every five Britons. The problem was that radios were still too expensive for

Table 16.5   Radio licences in Italy, 1928–40

1928	63,000
1930	176,000
1931	239,000
1932	305,000
1933	373,000
1934	431,000
1935	529,000
1936	697,000
1937	826,000
1938	978,000
1939	1,142,000
1940	1,321,000

(Source: Mitchell, *European Historical Statistics 1750–1975*, 1981, Table G9)

most Italians and so the government tried to attract a collective audience by distributing free sets to schools, municipal buildings and local Fascist Party headquarters. It would also be wrong to assume that the Fascist radio carried a high proportion of political propaganda. Most programmes consisted of popular entertainment, such as music, sports commentaries and comedy. Even for news it was always possible to tune in to the independent Vatican Radio or, in the north of the country, to the Swiss Italian language station. On the positive side, radio did feature in the state-sponsored working-men's (*Dopolavoro*, literally 'after work') clubs.

Although Mussolini once claimed that 'the cinema is the strongest weapon', the state did not take over the entire film industry as it did radio. It exercised its influence indirectly through the following steps. In 1926 it was laid down that 10 per cent of films shown in Italian cinemas had to be Italian. This was raised to 25 per cent in 1928. Finally, in 1938 the government took a decisive step in eliminating the American domination of the market by taking direct control of the importation of all foreign films. This led to a reduction in the number of licences granted to American films from 163 in that year to only 58 in 1939, which was below the Italian output of 79 for the same year. As in the case of radio programmes, however, it would be a mistake to believe that most independently produced Italian films were overtly Fascist in content. All the time, of course, there was a strict censorship.

Purely propaganda films came mainly from the LUCE Institute, which was made a state agency in 1925 and which was responsible for newsreels and documentaries. (LUCE stands for *L'Unione Cinematografia Educativa* or 'Educational Cinematographic Union' and is also the Italian word for 'light'.) From 1926 all cinemas were required to show a LUCE film as part of each programme.

What the above analysis of the Italian mass media under fascism shows, I believe, is that while government influence was considerable, it would be a gross exaggeration to claim that the regime possessed anything approaching a monopoly of them. Its greatest achievement probably lay not so much in propagating its own values as in preventing the expression of those of the opposition.

Totalitarianism is often said to involve the central control and direction of the entire economy through the state bureaucracy. You should note straight away that 'control and direction' is not the same thing as ownership, although if the state did 'own' the entire economy – as was more or less the case in the Soviet Union under Stalin – that would clearly imply 'central control and direction'. The latter can also exist in a predominantly privately owned economy, as for example in Britain, France and Germany during World War I.

Before turning to a more detailed examination of the way in which the economy functioned in Fascist Italy, however, it is important to dispose of one red herring: corporatism or corporativism (the two terms are interchangeable – 'corporatism' is the version used by Maier and in John Golby's discussion of him in Unit 14). If you go back to pp.365–6 of Roberts you will see that he devotes a couple of paragraphs to this phenomenon in the context of his discussion of fascism's lack of control over the economy. Unfortunately, he never explains what it means. For some enlightenment, let us turn to the American historian Alexander de Grand, who defines corporatism/corporativism as:

> ... a system of institutional arrangements by which capital and labour are integrated into obligatory, hierarchical, and functional units (corporations) recognized by the state, which become organs of self-government for issues relating to the specific category as well as the basis for participation with other corporatively organized interests in policy decisions affecting the whole society ... The corporations may be the controlling power in the state, or they may, as in Italy, be controlled by a political authority that exists independently of and outside the corporative system.
>
> (*Italian Fascism*, 1982, pp.79–80)

As both Roberts and de Grand indicate, Fascist Italy displayed the characteristics of a developed corporatism. Since this corporatism was inspired and organized by the state, Italy was a corporate state. If these state-controlled corporations ran the economy, this could clearly imply the 'central control and direction' of totalitarianism, as generally understood.

Fascist theorists tried to describe the corporate state as 'a third way' between capitalism and communism, according to which employers and employees ran their industries under the benign supervision of the state. The foundation stone of the corporative system had been laid by the trade-union law of 3 April 1926, which permitted only one officially recognized association of workers and employers for each branch of production, prohibited all strikes and lock-outs, and created a system of compulsory arbitration of labour disputes. 'In essence', the American historian Shepherd B. Clough has written, 'it created machinery to serve the government in handling all problems between employers and employees' (*The Economic History of Modern Italy*, 1964, p.233).

The supposed equality between capital and labour in the system was undermined by the decision in November 1928 to break up the Fascist trade-union confederation, which had getting on for 3 million members, into six smaller units. This was done partly in order to appease the business community, but also because Mussolini feared that the head of the single confederation, Edmondo Rossini, might otherwise become too powerful. This possibility was all the more likely since the electoral reform of May 1928 had given the Fascist unions the right to nominate candidates for the new nationally constituted Chamber of Deputies.

In March 1930 a kind of corporative parliament was set up in the shape of the National Council of Corporations, which was made up of the seven large employer and worker organizations for the main branches of agriculture, industry, services and the professions [*yet the first actual corporations only came into being in 1934*]. Finally, in January 1939, the Chamber of Deputies itself was replaced by a new Chamber of Fasci and Corporations. These are no doubt the '[F]urther changes ... which, on paper at least, appeared to extend the corporative structure beyond the purely economic sphere to become a new form of political and social control' to which Roberts refers on p.366.

Roberts's scepticism about the role of corporatism in Italy's economic life is justified. The National Council of Corporations, for example, was a purely consultative body. But, as he indicates, the object of the corporate structure was primarily political and social, rather than economic. Unfortunately Roberts goes on to undermine the force of his own argument by suggesting that the *Istituto per la Ricostruzione Industriale* or 'Industrial Reconstruction Institute' (IRI) was part of the corporate structure. It was not and, as we shall see, it did play an extremely important part in the 'central control and direction' of the economy.

There was little need for such control and direction in the early stages of Fascist rule, since the accession to power of Mussolini fortuitously coincided with an upturn in the economic cycle. His first Finance Minister, Alberto De' Stefani, who occupied his post from October 1922 to July 1925, adopted a more or less completely non-interventionist approach, abolishing the remaining wartime controls and tax surcharges. The economy grew, although whether this was due more to the international boom than to De' Stefani's policies is a moot point. In any event, the budget was balanced in 1925 for the first time since before World War I, and in the following year pre-war levels of production and consumption were regained. There had also been a remarkable improvement in the balance of payments. Whereas Italy's exports had financed only 47.6 per cent of its imports in 1921, the proportion had risen to 75.7 per cent by 1924.

The continuing deficit on the balance of payments did, however, lead to a steady depreciation of the lira. At around 90 to the pound when Mussolini came to power, it fell to 145 in 1925. In August 1926 Mussolini announced that the lira's value would be restored to 90 to the pound. This was a much higher value than Italy's economic position warranted and was only achieved as a result of harsh deflationary measures.

The government also took steps to reduce the balance of payments deficit. One of the most spectacular was the so-called 'battle for grain', launched by Mussolini in June 1925 and designed to end Italy's dependence on imports of wheat. Tariffs on imported wheat were raised and domestic producers were thereby enabled to charge more for their crops. As a result Italian wheat production rose from an annual average of 5.2 million tonnes in 1922–25 to 7.6 million tonnes in 1936–39, which was a position of self-sufficiency. Italy's overall

OXFAM

VAT 348 4542 38

Last year our Christmas cards
raised enough to fund 4 years
of a water & sanitation project
in Ethiopia

Find cards that fight poverty
in-store and online

ELENA   SALES   F0823/POS1
MONDAY 9 DECEMBER 2019   11:56 146820
1   NON FICTION   £1.49
      GIFT AID 20127626450823
1   NON FICTION   £1.49

                        2 Items
      TOTAL   **£2.98**
      £20   £20.00
      CHANGE   £17.02

          Oxfam Shop: F0823
          33 King Street,
          Sheffield S3 8LF
           0114 2494919
        oxfam.org.uk/shop

TAKE HOME SOME NECTAR POINTS

Donate your unwanted items to Oxfam and you can collect Nectar points when they're sold.
Find out more at:

www.oxfam.org.uk/nectar

LIFT LIVES FOR GOOD | OXFAM

WARM FUZZY GLOW – TO GO

Every item you buy or donate helps lift lives worldwide. Just £6 raised could train a health volunteer, helping communities in Bangladesh prepare for disaster.

www.oxfam.org.uk

balance of payments deficit was reduced from 19.5 billion lira in 1920–24 to 8.6 billion in 1925–29 and 165 million in 1930–34, although there were, of course, many other factors at work in this process. Moreover, it rose again in the second half of the 1930s, totalling 3.9 billion lira in 1935–39.

Two developments led to a much greater degree of state intervention in the economy in the 1930s than in the 1920s. These were the onset of the Great Depression in 1929 and Italy's increasingly belligerent foreign policy, commencing with its invasion of Abyssinia in 1935 and its involvement in the Spanish Civil War in 1936. Both gave rise to growing pressure for autarky, or self-sufficiency, a process by which Italy could become less dependent upon the outside world and particularly upon potential enemies.

IRI, to which reference has already been made, was set up in January 1933 in order to help the banks out of the difficulties caused by the depreciation during the depression of the shares they had acquired in industry and commerce. By purchasing these shares it gradually acquired a stake in many industries. Indeed, it has been estimated that on the eve of World War II IRI controlled 90 per cent of Italy's merchant shipping, 80 per cent of its shipbuilding, 77 per cent of its pig iron production, 75 per cent of its metal tubes, 67 per cent of its iron ore, 50 per cent of its arms and ammunition, 44 per cent of its steel, 39 per cent of its power machinery, 23 per cent of its engineering and 22 per cent of its aircraft construction. As the Italian economic historian Rosario Romeo has observed:

> If one adds to the industries controlled by IRI those which the state already managed in various forms, beginning with the railways, it will become clear that from 1936 onwards the Italian state owned a proportionately larger share of industry than any other European state apart from the Soviet Union.
>
> (*Breve Storia della Grande Industria in Italia 1861–1961*, 1982, p.173)

And Martin Clark has added that, with its new generation of managers trained in the running of state and semi-state enterprises, IRI, which still exists today, was 'the key economic legacy of the Fascist period' (*Modern Italy 1871–1982*, 1984, p.266).

If the existence and role of IRI suggests that the state was indeed responsible for the 'central control and direction' of the economy during the 1930s, that picture must be modified by taking into account the fact that large private firms also played a significant part. Government policy did, in fact, encourage the process of industrial concentration in this period with the result that, also on the eve of World War II, the chemical giant Montecatini controlled the output of rayon and three-fifths of that of chemical fertilizers; Snia Viscosa controlled between 60 and 65 per cent of artificial fibre production; Fiat controlled 83 per cent of automobile production; Pirelli enjoyed a monopoly in the field of rubber and, in addition, controlled 60 to 70 per cent of cable production; and Edison was responsible for 45.5 per cent of the output of electric power.

Shepherd B. Clough sums up Fascist economic policy in the following words:

> It may be said with justice that Fascism helped to preserve private capitalism, although it should be added quickly that capitalists were frequently pushed around – were made to pay heavy taxes, take workers that they did not need, and to pursue policies of which they did not approve.
>
> (*The Economic History of Modern Italy*, 1964, p.238)

Together with the information contained in the previous few paragraphs, this judgement implies, I believe, that while Roberts's dismissal of the totalitarian nature of the Fascist economy is too severe, it would be equally wrong to argue that Italy did fulfil the criterion of 'central control and direction of the entire economy through the state bureaucracy'.

The above analysis, of course, says little or nothing about the success or otherwise of the Fascist economy. Compare these two statements:

> Economic growth was slow: National income at 1938 prices went from 115.1 billion lire in 1925 to 138.2 billion in 1938 and on a per capita basis increased between the same years from 2,923 to only 3,201 lire. So far as labour was concerned the index of real wages appears to have fallen from 111.8 (1913 = 100) to 100.5 in 1938.
>
> (S. B. Clough, 1964, p.238)

> Italy by 1939 was more industrialized than she had been in 1922, and rather more prosperous. Gross domestic product [another term for national income] had increased by 1.2 per cent per year on average, more than double the growth of population; manufacturing production had gone up by 3.9 per cent p.a.
>
> (M. Clark, 1984, p.267)

Both statements are correct, and it is not simply the choice of dates which is responsible for the different – one might even say opposite – impression conveyed by them. What you need to bear in mind is the point of departure and the comparison with other countries. The Swiss economist Paul Bairoch has made some estimates of levels of industrialization in various countries over a period of more than 200 years. Table 16.6 selects some of these estimates in order to measure Italy's performance against those of the same countries we used at the beginning of this unit. They show the per capita level of industrialization measured against the United Kingdom level in 1900 (= 100).

Table 16.6   Levels of industrialization

	1913	1928	1938
France	59	82	73
Germany	85	101	128
Italy	26	39	44
UK	115	122	157

(Source: P. Bairoch, 'International industrialization levels from 1750 to 1980', 1982, p.302)

What this table shows is that while Italy had gained on the other three powers since 1913, it was still behind them all in 1938, and well behind Germany and the United Kingdom.

It should also be pointed out that fascism had done nothing to narrow the gap between the more prosperous north of Italy and the backward south. Indeed, that gap had widened. On the eve of World War II, the Turin-Milan-Genoa 'industrial triangle', with only a quarter of the Italian population, had half the industrial employees, more than half the installed horsepower, and almost two-thirds of the share capital.

On p.73 I wrote of an alternative view of totalitarianism, one that sought to encapsulate the concept in the notion of the progressive annihilation of the boundaries between state and society. That this is, perhaps, a more fruitful approach to the subject is shown by the fact that it enables us to discuss an important aspect of the Fascist regime, the question of mass socialization.

The American historian E. R. Tannenbaum has written:

> One of the most novel, yet typical, features of Italian Fascism was its effort to regiment large segments of society, particularly youth and labour, into mass organizations. By the mid-1930s Nazi Germany and the Soviet Union were equally totalitarian in this respect, but the Italian effort was the first and was all the more remarkable for having had practically nothing to build on from the nation's liberal past.
>
> (*The Fascist Experience,* 1972, p.119)

What we are concerned with here, essentially, are the regime's educational, youth and leisure policies.

Although the Fascist government's first education minister – the philosopher Giovanni Gentile – carried out a reform of Italy's educational system as early as May 1923, it was not until the end of the decade that the 'fascistization' of the schools began seriously. It was in February 1929 that all schoolteachers were compelled to take an oath of loyalty to the regime. University staff had to follow suit in October 1931, and after 1933 all new appointees to any post in the public educational system had to belong to the PNF. During the same period the state began to publish its own school textbooks and to exclude all others from state schools. Fascist propaganda permeated the entire curriculum. Tannenbaum cites the example of the timetable of a class of 8-year-olds in 1937:

> The largest number of hours was devoted to practice in the Italian language [the use of dialect had been banned in 1934]; about half of the drill material was on Fascist topics – the regime's public works, the Ethiopian war, the Mediterranean Sea as *mare nostro* ['our sea']. The geography class also emphasised *mare nostro,* while the history class discussed famous naval battles and the First World War ... In arithmetic the following problem was to be solved: 'In 1902 the salary of Mussolini the teacher was 56 lire a month. How much a day? A year?
>
> (1972, p.164)

As students progressed through the educational system, the amount of specifically Fascist indoctrination they encountered declined, partly no doubt because of the exigencies of public examinations. If they went on to university, they found a completely different atmosphere, with no state textbooks and few compulsory courses. The regime's influence in universities was exercised through its student organization, the *Gioventù Universitaria Fascista* or 'Fascist University Youth' (GUF), but this also sponsored non-political, and popular, activities such as sport and film shows.

The GUF was only one of a number of organizations which sought to regiment the nation's youth. The most prominent was the *Opera Nationale Balilla* or 'National Balilla Institution' (ONB), which was founded in 1926 and named after an eighteenth-century boy who became an early hero of the Italian nationalist movement. The ONB was divided into a number of sections according to age and sex: the *Figli della lupa* or 'children of the she-wolf' for boys and girls of 6 and 7; the *Balilla* proper for boys between 8 and 13; the *Piccole Italiane* or 'Little Italian girls' for girls between 8 and 13; the *Avanguardisti* or 'Vanguard' for boys between 14 and 17; and the *Giovane Italiane* or 'Young Italian girls' for girls between 14 and 17.

Exercise   You will find reproduced as Document I.10 in *Primary Sources 2: Interwar and World War II* extracts from the decree law of January 1927 setting out the functions of the *Avanguardisti* and the *Balilla*. You should read these now and then answer the following questions:

1   From these extracts, what would you say was the principal objective of the *Avanguardisti* and the *Balilla*?

2   Do you note any particular connection with Italy's past?

3   Would you say that there was anything in these extracts which casts doubt upon the totalitarian nature of the *Avanguardisti* and the *Balilla*?∎

Specimen answers   1   The principal objective of the two bodies, as it appears from these extracts, is the preparation of boys for the army. Note in particular the military organization of both the *Avanguardisti* and the *Balilla* and the emphasis upon 'discipline and obedience'. Physical training, of course, also fits in with this objective.

2   The historical allusions in these extracts are to Ancient Rome. Almost all the sub-divisions of both bodies are named after Roman precedents: centuries, maniples, cohorts and legions.

3   Two items in the extracts which cast doubt upon the totalitarian nature of the two bodies are the fact that membership is voluntary and not compulsory (Article III) and that Roman Catholic religious beliefs be inculcated in members (Article XXXVIII).

Discussion   Membership of the ONB was made compulsory in the early 1930s, although this was difficult to enforce once children had left school, which was as early as 11 for many Italian boys and girls. In October 1937 it was amalgamated with the non-student movements for young people between the ages of 18 and 21 to form the *Gioventù Italiana del Littorio* or 'Italian Youth of the Lictors' (GIL), another Roman allusion. The new organization was under direct party control, whereas the ONB had been run from the Ministry of Education. In June 1939 the GIL had a membership of around 6,700,000, which was about half the relevant age group. Membership was proportionately much higher in the north of Italy than in the south.

The third principal agent of mass socialization in Fascist Italy was the *Opera Nazionale Dopolavoro* or 'National Afterwork Institution' (OND), which was set up by a decree of 1 May 1925 with the purpose of providing 'healthy and profitable leisure-time activity for the workers by means of institutions that develop their physical, intellectual, and moral qualities'. By 1939 the OND had 3.5 million members: a majority of white-collar employees, nearly 40 per cent of industrial workers, and a quarter of the eligible peasants. The secret of the OND's success, as Martin Clark points out, was that it 'was fun, not propaganda; it was recreation, not self-improvement'. The *Dopolavoro* clubs, he writes:

had bars, billiard halls, libraries, radios and sports grounds, they put on concerts and plays; they provided virtually free summer holidays for children; they organized charabanc trips, ballroom-dancing, mountain walks, and days at the seaside. They also handed out welfare relief in poor areas; both circuses and bread. No wonder they were popular. It was the first time in Italian history that mass leisure activities had existed, let alone been encouraged and subsidized by politicians.

(*Modern Italy 1871–1982*, 1984, p.245) □

There may seem little that was political in all this, but many of the OND's cultural activities, with their emphasis on Italian traditions as opposed to twentieth-century cosmopolitanism and 'Americanization', were distinctly nationalistic in tone. And at the time of the Ethiopian war in 1935–36 the OND was used, and used successfully, to help mobilize public opinion in support of the regime's objectives. It was the OND, for example, which organized the famous 'plebiscite of gold' in which, among other things, women gave their wedding rings to be melted down to help pay for the war effort.

If one thinks of a young Italian in the 1930s, being educated by Fascist teachers on the basis of Fascist textbooks, joining the ONB for out-of-school activities, beginning work as a member of a Fascist trade union and with his or her spare time organized by the OND, totalitarianism does not seem such a fanciful concept. Nevertheless, it is important to bear in mind that, as we have seen, membership of the ONB and the OND, while high, was nowhere near universal, and that since there were no free elections, let alone anything approaching modern opinion polls, it is not easy to assess the effects of all this indoctrination in the shape of the degree of support which the regime enjoyed.

It should already be clear from what has been said in this unit that fascism was opposed by a great many Italians from Mussolini's accession to power in October 1922 down to the consolidation of the regime after the Matteotti crisis in 1924. Nevertheless, the impression is that from the mid-1920s most Italians accepted the Fascist regime and gave it credit – however grudging at times – for its achievements. Most historians seem to agree that its popularity peaked at the time of the Ethiopian war in 1935–36, but that it declined thereafter, especially with Italy's growing alignment with Nazi Germany and the danger of a general war. It was certainly the case that when Mussolini did take Italy into World War II in June 1940 the prefects reported that this decision was not popular. The position is perhaps best summed up by Martin Clark:

> Did all this Fascist effort at 'social control' actually work ...? The judicious historian gives a prosaic answer: yes and no. Yes, in the sense that until 1936 most people swallowed most of the propaganda most of the time, at a fairly superficial level. Italy was stable, the *Duce* was popular, open dissenters were rare. It made sense to go along with the regime, and patriotism is a natural feeling even in Italy. But there was little enthusiasm for Fascism – as opposed to patriotism and Mussolinism – and the regime's claims to 'totalitarianism' were laughable. Religion, family sentiment, individual ambition and cunning, the parish pump, the art of *arrangiarsi* ['fixing'] – all these traditional institutions and values survived and flourished ... In short, there was acceptance but not devotion, consensus but not commitment, let alone 'hegemony'. Still, even the Fascist consensus was a

great deal more than most Italian regimes had achieved. On balance the ideological efforts paid off. It took years for most people to see through Fascism.

(*Modern Italy 1871–1982*, 1984, p.247)

There also existed, as Roberts points out on pp.364–6, important political forces that were largely independent of fascism. He refers specifically to the monarchy and the Roman Catholic Church. Roberts refers to the concessions accorded to the latter under the terms of the Lateran treaties of 1929, and rightly maintains that these were more important than those which the Church gave in return (p.365). But they were not the only concessions to the Church by any means. We have already seen how Roman Catholicism was to be inculcated in members of the ONB (see above, p.82). It was the same in the schools. Fascism broke with the traditions of the liberal state in instituting compulsory religious instruction in state schools, and it was taught at the secondary level not by lay teachers but by priests.

Roberts should also have mentioned the armed forces as one of the independent organizations in Fascist Italy. Although the regime made ample use of them in its propaganda, they were careful to brook no interference from Fascist busybodies in running their affairs. Even the *Duce* largely confined himself to acting as an arbitrator in conflicts between the different branches of the armed services.

Of course these organizations went along with Mussolini and fascism for most of the time, but this was because their interests temporarily coincided. They had no particular love for Mussolini, or he for them, as we shall see in the final section of this unit. They retained a capacity for independent action and, indeed, opposition, and it is significant in this connection that it was a coalition between the King and the armed forces which was mainly responsible for the downfall of Mussolini in July 1943. It is also significant that the new political élite which eventually replaced the Fascists after World War II had mostly served their apprenticeship in the ranks of Catholic Action, a network of lay organizations controlled by the Church and set up, not in 1931 as Roberts claims (p.365), but well before World War I.

[*Geoffrey Warner did not pick up Martin Clarke's comment (p.83) that 'the regime's claims to "totalitarianism" were laughable', though this strong statement does seem to run counter to Warner's apparent argument that the term can, exceptions and problems being noted, be applied to Italy.*

Two recent books, Emilio Gentile, La Via Italiana Totalitarismo: Il Partito e lo Stato nel Regime Fascista *(The Italian Road to Totalitarianism: The Party and the State in the Fascist Regime) (1995), and R. J. B. Bosworth,* The Italian Dictatorship: Problems and Perspectives in the Interpretation of Mussolini and Fascism *(1998) both stress that Mussolini boasted that he had created a totalitarian state. If we are trying to distinguish Mussolini's Italy from, say, France and Britain, it is worth noting that French and British leaders, of course, made no such boasts. In terms of state control and mass mobilization, Italy was indeed 'totalitarian' in ways that neither Britain nor France were or aspired to be.*]

4   FASCISM AND WAR

This final section of the unit is related specifically to the article by the American historian MacGregor Knox, 'Conquest, foreign and domestic, in Fascist Italy and Nazi Germany', extracts from which are printed in your collection of *Secondary Sources*. Profoundly dissatisfied with the results so far of the historical and political debate on the nature of fascism, which purports, among other things, to draw out the common features of Italian fascism and German Nazism, Knox makes his own comparison of the two regimes in terms of what he sees as the inseparable connection between their domestic and foreign policies.

Exercise   You should now read the article.

I want you to concentrate on the second section of the article, which is entitled 'From mission to program' (*Secondary Sources*, pp.145–55).

Try to answer the following questions in a couple of short paragraphs:

1   What, in Knox's opinion, were the sources of Mussolini's world view, and how did World War I affect it?

2   What, according to Knox, was Mussolini's vision of Fascist Italy, and how did he intend to realize it? ■

Specimen answers   1   Mussolini's underlying assumption was that life was a perpetual struggle. This was linked with two myths: the idea of revolution, which he took partly from Marx and partly from Sorel; and the idea of the nation, which he took from Mazzini and other Italian nationalist thinkers. World War I removed the contradiction between these two myths and indeed permitted their fusion. If Italy's participation in the war was motivated by nationalist considerations, it would also lead to revolution.

2   Mussolini wanted, in his own words, 'to fascistize the nation, so that tomorrow Italian and Fascist, more or less like Italian and Catholic, will be the same thing'. This new Italy would reject old stereotypes – 'mandolin players' and 'exquisite manners' – in favour of a tough, ruthless image. Expansion and war would be the means of achieving this objective. □

Discussion   The importance of war in Fascist ideology is, of course, brought out in Document I.9 in *Primary Sources 2: Interwar and World War II*, the extracts from Mussolini's article 'The doctrine of Fascism' (1932). As he stated in that article:

> Above all, Fascism ... believes neither in the possibility nor in the utility of perpetual peace ... War alone brings up to their highest tension all human energies and puts the stamp of nobility upon the peoples who have the courage to meet it. All other trials are substitutes, which never really put a man in front of himself in the alternative of life and death.
>
> (*Primary Sources 2*, p.32)

Knox shows how the 'battle for grain', which I discussed in section 3 of this unit in a different context, was also launched in order to create the demographic prerequisites for Italian power and expansion. Indeed, the regime adopted a whole panoply of measures in the 1930s in order to boost Italy's birth rate: family allowances, marriage loans (part of which was written off each time the happy couple produced a child), job discrimination in favour of family men (women, of course, were encouraged to stay at home and breed), and a surtax on bachelors. Despite all these incentives, the birth rate continued to decline: from 26.7 per 1,000 of the population in 1930 to 23.5 per 1,000 ten years later. On the eve of World War I the rate had exceeded 30.

If you cast your mind back to the previous section of this unit, you will no doubt recall other facets of the regime's policies which were designed for preparation for war, notably the emphasis upon military-style training in the ONB and the drive for economic autarky.

You will find a brief account of the approach to World War II in Chapter 15 of Roberts and a more detailed analysis in Antony Lentin's Unit 19. I do not wish to go over this ground again, but I should like to address the question of what I see as, if not the inevitability, at any rate the strong likelihood of Italy's eventual alignment with Germany as opposed to Britain and France. □

Knox states (*Secondary Sources*, p.155) that Mussolini 'remained uncommitted to a specific alliance structure until 1936'. This is true, but Britain and France would have found it extremely difficult to win the *Duce*'s permanent allegiance. This was not only because of the 'humiliation' which they, together with the Americans, heaped upon Italy at the end of World War I, but also, and more importantly, because of Mussolini's geopolitical vision, which Knox outlines in *Secondary Sources*. It was not the Germans who were the principal obstacle to Fascist Italy's Mediterranean ambitions, but the British and the French.

Mussolini himself spelled it out in a speech to the Fascist Grand Council on 4 February 1939:

> States that cannot communicate freely with the oceans and are enclosed in inland seas are semi-independent ... Italy ... does not have free connection with the oceans. Italy is therefore in truth a prisoner of the Mediterranean, and the more populous and prosperous Italy becomes, the more its imprisonment will gall. The bars of this prison are Corsica [French], Tunis [French], Malta [British], Cyprus [British]. The sentinels of this prison are Gibraltar [British] and Suez [British]. Corsica is a pistol pointed at the heart of Italy; Tunisia at Sicily; while Malta and Cyprus constitute a threat to all our positions in the eastern and western Mediterranean. Greece, Turkey, Egypt have been ready to form a chain with Great Britain and to complete the politico-military encirclement of Italy ... From this situation, whose geographical rigour leaps to one's eyes and which tormented, even before our regime, those men who saw beyond considerations of momentary political expediency, one can draw the following conclusions:
> 1 The task of Italian policy, which cannot have and does not have continental objectives of a European territorial nature except Albania, is first of all break the bars of the prison.
> 2 Once the bars are broken, Italian policy can have only one watchword – to march to the ocean. Which ocean? The Indian Ocean, joining Libya with Ethiopia through the Sudan, or the Atlantic, through French North Africa.
>
> In either case, we will find ourselves confronted with Anglo-French opposition ...
>
> (Quoted in M. Knox, *Mussolini Unleashed 1939–1941*, 1982, p.40)

If Fascist Italy's principal expansionary thrust was to be directed towards the south, Nazi Germany's was to be directed towards the east and north. As Hitler told Mussolini's son-in-law and Foreign Minister, Galeazzo Ciano, on 24 October 1936, 'by steering our two dynamisms in these two exactly opposing directions, there can never be a clash of interests between Germany and Italy' (R. Mosca, *L'Europa verso la Catastrofe,* 1964, vol.1, p.101). Hitler's sense of direction may have been somewhat astray, and notwithstanding their joint protestations, both dictators were keenly interested in the fate of the Balkans and hence potential rivals in the peninsula, but the Axis was probably based more on this convenient division of spheres of influence than upon ideological solidarity.

Exercise   I should now like you to look again at the final section of Knox's article, 'Unholy war' (*Secondary Sources*, pp.155–63), and then describe briefly the attitude of the independent forces in Fascist Italy – the monarchy, the armed forces and the Roman Catholic Church – to Mussolini's expansionism from 1935 to 1939. ∎

Specimen answer   In order to launch his war against Ethiopia, Mussolini had to overcome army (though not navy and air force) opposition, and hesitancy on the part of the King. Only the Church was enthusiastically in favour of his policy. The Church, too, favoured the 'anti-Communist' intervention in the Spanish Civil War, although, once again, both the monarchy and the armed forces were doubtful. By September 1939 the Church, which was upset by the regime's new racial laws and the alliance with Germany, joined forces with the King, the military and others to restrain Mussolini from plunging into World War II at Hitler's side.

Discussion   This section of Knox's article brings out the growing antagonism between the independent forces and the regime. He even alludes to the possibility of a royal coup against Mussolini in March 1940, something which materialized in a slightly different form in July 1943 in the wake of Italy's comprehensive defeat in World War II. Knox's analysis shows not only the limits of Mussolini's totalitarianism, but the *Duce*'s awareness of those limits and his own determination to do something about them, as for example in his plans to get rid of the monarchy.

Finally, I should like to focus upon Knox's principal conclusion: that 'Foreign policy was internal policy and vice versa; internal consolidation was a precondition of foreign conquest, and foreign conquest was the decisive prerequisite for a revolution at home that would sweep away inherited institutions and values' (*Secondary Sources*, p.164). This is clearly of considerable importance in the context of a course that is specifically concerned with the relationship between total war and social change.

Some elements of Knox's proposition do not seem to take us very far. After all, there is a close connection between foreign and domestic policy in most modern states, and not only Fascist regimes would attempt to consolidate their position at home before embarking upon adventures abroad, although some governments have, of course, used war as a means of rallying support. Knox, however, goes much further than this. What he appears to be saying about Fascist Italy – and, I repeat, I am not talking about Nazi Germany – is that Mussolini's totalitarian revolution had gone off at half cock, and that it required war and foreign conquest to complete it.

This is not the same thing as saying that war and foreign conquest were essential ingredients of fascism. I think they were, but this could have been for other reasons; ideological conviction, a desire to strengthen the regime by constant mass mobilization in support of external objectives, or the perceived need to distract the population from problems at home. Knox, on the other hand, is arguing that the motive for war and foreign conquest was precisely to overcome the remaining obstacles to his totalitarian rule.

In order to make his case, Knox would have to show that the opposition from King, armed forces and Church prompted the wars, and that Mussolini saw no other way of neutralizing these independent forces except by means of war. I don't think he does. The *Duce* was undoubtedly hostile to what Knox sometimes calls 'the Establishment', and was exasperated by its criticisms of his policies, at home as well as abroad. But where is the evidence that Mussolini embarked upon expansion because of this hostility and these criticisms, as opposed, for example, to the geopolitical ideology, which Knox so convincingly demonstrates the Italian dictator held from the very outset? □

5   CONCLUSION

Returning to the questions we asked at the very beginning of this unit, we can conclude that although the economic effects of World War I were no worse in Italy than in other west European countries, the conflict did have important political consequences in the form of the growth or emergence of powerful mass parties and movements which challenged the old liberal regime. Fascism itself grew out of the war as one of the currents in the ferment of nationalism produced by the conflict and Italy's alleged mistreatment in the peace settlement, but it did not become a mass movement, let alone a major threat to the parliamentary system until the end of 1920, when it was able to take advantage of the reaction against the industrial and agrarian unrest of the *biennio rosso*. The mass Fascist movement was broadly representative of Italian society as a whole, but its accession to power was by no means inevitable. This occurred because of the failure of the liberal regime to crack down on Fascist violence, the illusion on the part of some politicians that they could 'use' fascism for their own ends, the divisions in the ranks of the opposition, and the benevolent neutrality of organizations such as the monarchy, the armed forces, and the Roman Catholic Church.

After surmounting the Matteotti crisis of 1924, the Fascist regime managed to build a degree of consensus which was probably greater than that created by any of the liberal governments which had preceded it. It may legitimately be described as 'totalitarian', although it was Mussolini and the state apparatus rather than the Fascist Party as such that exercised the control, and its mobilization of the populace and of the economy was by no means complete. Most significant of all, important independent focuses of power remained in existence, notably the monarchy, the armed forces and the Church, which in the crisis brought about by the regime's participation in World War II were able to move decisively against it. The fact that war brought about fascism's collapse was in a sense paradoxical, since war and foreign conquest were essential to both Fascist theory and practice.

References

Aquarone, A. (1965) *L'Organizzazione dello Stato Totalitario*, Einaudi.

Bairoch, P. (1982) 'International industrialization levels from 1750 to 1980', *Journal of European Economic History*, vol.11, no.2, fall, pp.269–333.

Bosworth, R. J. B. (1998) *The Italian Dictatorship: Problems and Perspectives in the Interpretation of Mussolini and Fascism,* Arnold.

Cannistraro, P. V. (ed.) (1982) *Historical Dictionary of Fascist Italy*, Westport Greenwood Press.

Cipolla, C. M. (ed.) (1976) *The Fontana Economic History of Europe*, vol.6, part 2, *Contemporary Economics*, 2, Collins/Fontana.

Clark, M. (1984) *Modern Italy 1871–1982*, Longman.

Clough, S. B. (1964) *The Economic History of Modern Italy*, Columbia University Press.

de Grand, A. (1982) *Italian Fascism: Its Origins and Development*, University of Nebraska Press.

Delzell, C. F. (1971) *Mediterranean Fascism 1919–1945*, Macmillan.

Gentile, E. (1995) *La Via Italiana Totalitarismo: Il Partito e lo Stato nel Regime Fascista* (The Italian Road to Totalitarianism: The Party and the State in the Fascist Regime), La Nuova Italia Scientifica, Rome.

Knox, M. (1982) *Mussolini Unleashed 1939–1941: Politics and Strategy in Fascist Italy's Last War*, Cambridge University Press.

Mitchell, B. R. (1981) *European Historical Statistics 1750–1975*, second revised edition, Macmillan.

Mosca, R. (ed.) (1964) *L'Europa verso la Catastrofe*, vol.1, Il Saggiatore.

Mühlberger, D. (ed.) (1987) *The Social Basis of European Fascist Movements*, Croom Helm.

Romeo, R. (1982) *Breve Storia della Grande Industria in Italia 1861–1961*, Cappelli.

Seton-Watson, C. (1967) *Italy from Liberalism to Fascism*, Methuen.

Tannenbaum, E. R. (1972) *The Fascist Experience: Italian Society and Culture 1922–1945*, Basic Books.

Further reading

Bessel, R. (ed.) (1996) *Fascist Italy and Nazi Germany: Comparisons and Contrasts*, Cambridge University Press.

Clark, M. (1996) *Modern Italy 1871–1995*, Longman.

de Grazia, V. (1981) *The Culture of Consent: The Mass Organization of Leisure in Fascist Italy*, Cambridge University Press.

de Grazia, V. (1992) *How Fascism Ruled Women: Italy 1922–1945*, University of California Press.

Koon, T. (*c.*1985) *Believe, Obey, Fight: Political Socialization of Youth in Fascist Italy 1922–1943*, University of North Carolina Press.

Whittam, J. (1995) *Fascist Italy*, Manchester University Press.

Williamson, D. (1998) *Mussolini: From Socialist to Fascist*, Hodder.

Willson, P. R. (1993) *The Clockwork Factory, Women and Work in Fascist Italy*, Clarendon Press.

Unit 17 STATE, ECONOMY AND SOCIETY IN NAZI GERMANY 1933–1939

ANNIKA MOMBAUER AND BERNARD WAITES

Open University students of this unit will need to refer to:

Set book: J. M. Roberts, *Europe 1880–1945*, Longman, 2001

Primary Sources 2: Interwar and World War II, eds Arthur Marwick and Wendy Simpson, Open University 2000

Secondary Sources, eds Arthur Marwick and Wendy Simpson, Open University 2000

INTRODUCTION

This unit deals with an immensely wide-ranging topic and, given the confines of space, cannot be in any way all-encompassing. It will therefore focus on some aspects of the Third Reich only. For example, little attention is devoted to German foreign policy in these crucial years, which is discussed by Antony Lentin in Unit 19. We will also not deal in detail with the important topic of resistance to the Nazi system. These areas, only touched upon briefly here, are discussed in more detail in Roberts, and there are suggestions for further reading at the end of the unit should you want to pursue any aspect of National Socialist German history in more detail.

At the end of this unit you will have:

1   encountered different historical approaches to the Third Reich;

2   learned how the Nazi Party came to power and how the Nazi State was consolidated;

3   studied society in the Third Reich, with particular emphasis on the importance of racial ideology;

4   learned of the Nazi economy, both in terms of stabilizing the new government by way of its apparent successes, and in terms of preparing Germany for the Second World War;

5   be familiar with some of the different approaches historians have adopted in an attempt to make sense of Nazi Germany, and you will have encountered some important debates. You will also be aware of the most important of Nazi ideologies, the racial ideology, and will know some of the ways in which the regime tried to implement changes in order to put that ideology into practice, particularly regarding Jews, but also regarding women. This unit will provide you with essential background knowledge for moving on to study the Second World War later in this course.

1   HISTORICAL APPROACHES TO THE THIRD REICH

In the course of studying the Third Reich, different historiographical debates have divided historians in their approaches to Nazi Germany. They have argued, for example, over a definition of the phenomenon, asking whether it was a form of fascism (as Marxists would argue), whether it is best described as totalitarianism (and as such bears many similarities with Soviet Russia), or whether it was a uniquely German phenomenon which could only have arisen given particular and unique German circumstances and historical development.

Historians have also advanced differing interpretations of Hitler's role and significance within the Nazi system. Was he the 'Master of the Third Reich' (Norman Rich), or was he a 'weak dictator' (Hans Mommsen)? Did he exercise total, unrestricted power, or was he simply at the top of a polycracy of power, in which he was able to exploit opportunities as and when they arose, rather than following his own preconceived plans? Historians who stress the significance of

Hitler's personal power have been labelled 'intentionalists'. They include Klaus Hildebrand, Andreas Hillgruber and Eberhard Jäckel. Those who stress the role of 'supra-personal' factors, of interest groups, and state and party apparatus, are called 'functionalists' or 'structuralists'. These include Martin Broszat, Hans Mommsen and Wolfgang Schieder (Enrico Syring, 'Intentionalisten und Strukturalisten', 1990, pp. 169ff.) The central problem of such differing interpretations of Hitler's role is, in Ian Kershaw's words, 'the moral issue – the feeling that the evil of the central figure of the Third Reich is not being adequately portrayed, that Hitler was underestimated by contemporaries and is now being trivialized by some historians' (I. Kershaw, *The Nazi Dictatorship*, 1993, pp.59ff.).

More recently, historians have debated how 'modern' Hitler's Germany was, by examining the nature of National Socialist economic and social policy, or how modernizing some of its policies proved for German society. National Socialism used to be seen as a reaction against modernity, but recent literature portrays it 'both as a product of and as warmly embracing the modern world'. (Mark Roseman, 'National socialism and modernization', 1996, p.197) Historians have also debated whether any such modernization was accidental or deliberate.

This is a particularly difficult area of investigation, because to some commentators the barbaric and inhumane nature of the Third Reich can almost by definition not be associated with any positive, modernizing attributes. And yet, to name one example, Germany in 1933 was a modern, industrialized state, claiming a leading role in technology and production world-wide and, if anything, these trends in modern industrial economy were further advanced by the military-economic preparations for war in the 1930s. The problem for historians is how to reconcile this apparent 'modernity' with, for example, the regressive and irrational 'blood and soil' mystique of Nazi ideology and, more crucially, with the fact that a modern and civilized state like Germany could have regressed into the barbarity of million-fold murder (B. J. Wendt, *Deutschland 1933–1945*, 1995, pp.690–2). In Roseman's words, 'untangling the relationship between the barbaric and the modern lies at the very heart of understanding National Socialism' (Roseman, p.198).

This leads us to another problem encountered by historians of Nazi Germany: how to 'historicize' National Socialist Germany, i.e. how to place it in a historical context and even compare it to other states and yet not to 'relativize' its horrors by relating them to other atrocities. The *Historikerstreit* (historians' debate) of the 1980s made the problems obvious: is it even legitimate to attempt a comparison between Nazi atrocities and those of Stalinist Russia, for example, as some historians have done, or would this result in a 'relativization', and thus in an apologetic account of Nazi history?

More recently still, the controversial publication *Hitler's Willing Executioners* by the American historian Daniel Goldhagen and a controversial travelling exhibition detailing the crimes against humanity committed by the *Wehrmacht* in south-eastern Europe and in particular in the Soviet Union have demonstrated that the history of Nazi Germany is still far from unemotive, if indeed it ever can be. What was the role of 'ordinary Germans' in the atrocities committed against Jews, and against enemy soldiers, prisoners of war and partisans on the eastern front? Recent research has demonstrated that the persecution of Jews in

Germany could not have been carried out as effectively without informers among ordinary Germans, as for example Robert Gellately's study of the Gestapo files in Würzburg shows, and that soldiers of the *Wehrmacht* were as implicated in war crimes as the SS, a fact that used to be denied by former *Wehrmacht* members (R. Gellately, *The Gestapo and German Society*, 1990; Omer Bartov, *Hitler's Army, Soldiers, Nazis, and War in The Third Reich*, 1991; Hamburger Institut für Sozialforschung (ed.), *Vernichtungskrieg. Verbrechen der Wehrmacht 1941–1944*, 1996.) While Goldhagen's thesis that ordinary Germans were 'willing executioners' of Hitler's anti-Jewish designs has been the subject of much criticism and debate, the fact remains that many Germans were either unwilling or unable to intervene when they were confronted with the barbarity of the Hitler regime. In the following sections, we will examine some of these debates more closely. First, we will investigate how Hitler was able to come to power in 1933.

2   THE NATIONAL SOCIALISTS' ACCESSION TO POWER

The nature of the Nazi Party

As one of the many anti-democratic parties of the Weimar Republic, the National Socialist movement originated on the semi-legal fringe of extreme nationalist politics in Munich in 1919 and was reconstituted as the National Socialist German Workers' Party (NSDAP) at a mass meeting in February 1920. By this time, Hitler was already the foremost propaganda speaker of the new organization. In the spring of 1920, the NSDAP, assisted by officers from the national *Freikorps* and Defence Leagues, organized the 'Storm Detachments' (*Sturmabteilungen* – SA), and this military arm of the party made physical force or the threat of force 'an established instrument in the Nazi struggle for power' (M. Broszat, *The Hitler State*, 1981, p.19). The SA closely resembled Mussolini's 'Action Squads': both organizations served to protect party meetings and demonstrations, they carried out punitive forays against opponents, and with their uniforms, banners and parades they helped infuse politics with a martial, 'front-line' spirit.

The twenty-five-point programme of the new party was eclectic and essentially negative: it was anti-Marxist and anti-capitalist, anti-parliamentarian and anti-Semitic, but above all it was against the Versailles settlement. It called for the recreation of the national community, such as was deemed to have existed after the outbreak of war in 1914, but was utterly vague as to how this *Volksgemeinschaft* (community of Germanic people) was to be achieved. Some specific points – such as the demands that all income not earned by work and all war profits were to be confiscated – were 'Leftish' and conformed with the self-stylization as a socialist workers' party. (Members addressed each other as 'comrade' and party flags and posters were red.) Other demands reflected the hostility of the *Mittelstand* (middle classes) to big business: department stores were to be turned over to small tradesmen and land speculation outlawed to protect small farmers. Appended to the programme was a specific reference to 'breaking the shackles of finance capital', which indicates that, whatever its later evolution, the party did not originate from capitalism's most reactionary and chauvinist elements, as Marxist commentators have argued. Other points – such as the demands for living-space and for measures against the Jews – were derived from nationalist and *völkisch* (ethnic nationalist) sects, notably the Pan-German Thule Society, to which many of the original members (although not Hitler) had belonged. These sects had promoted the racist ideology of 'Aryanism' and had first used the swastika as a symbol of political racism.

Hitler was later to describe this programme as 'unalterable', although many points – particularly the socially radical proposals – were tacitly abandoned, even before 1933, principally to secure the co-operation of Germany's traditional élites in industry, and the support of the army and the bureaucracy in the accession to power and the rearmament programme. However, it would be unwise to dismiss it *en bloc* as mere expediency. Hitler was obsessed by the absolute truth of his basic ideas. To over-estimate his opportunism and not take ideology in National Socialist policy seriously is to repeat the mistake made by Hitler's contemporaries at home and abroad. The anti-Semitism of the programme, and its racist and expansionist ideas and formulations, were never officially rescinded or changed (K. D. Bracher, *The Nazi Dictatorship*, 1969, pp.314–15).

Moreover, the diverse programme had a particular functional importance in relation to the party membership and its wider constituency. Both were remarkably heterogeneous: the old lower middle class of small producers and traders was somewhat over-represented among the membership, but the party became a genuinely 'mass' movement joined by men from all social strata. (Women were much under-represented until the later stages of the Second World War; in 1935 they made up only 5.5 per cent of members. However, the share of female voters for the party was much greater.) Perhaps more importantly, members joined for varying, even contradictory, reasons. Many party activists saw it as egalitarian and revolutionary, and hoped that it would break the authority of the traditional élites and introduce a new and more meritocratic social order. Others were attracted to it for socially conservative reasons: they saw it as a movement reasserting traditional German values, above all national pride. Later, many came to vote for it as an act of protest against the discredited Weimar Republic. The eclecticism of the party programme, and the vagueness of its goal of national integration, 'encouraged individuals and groups to identify their own particular hopes and aspirations with the party and its leader. In other words, Nazism came to mean many things to many people' (J. Noakes, 'The Nazi Party and the Third Reich', 1980, p.2).

The first phase of National Socialism's history ended in fiasco in November 1923 when Hitler, Field Marshal Ludendorff and other extreme nationalists attempted a *coup* in Bavaria as a preliminary to a 'March on Berlin', modelled on Mussolini's 'March on Rome'. The failure of the putsch of 8/9 November, which led to a widely publicized trial, persuaded Hitler that he had to adopt 'a policy of legality' and take the electoral road to power. By this time, the NSDAP's membership had already increased from only 1,100 in June 1920 to 55,000 by the autumn of 1923 (R. Eatwell, *Fascism*, 1996, p.91). A sizeable proportion of members consisted of young men who had served in the war and were disillusioned by what the new state had to offer them.

Hitler used his short prison sentence (he had been treated very leniently by the judges in a system that tended to be harsh in sentencing left-wing activists, but rather more sympathetic regarding right-wing anti-democratic behaviour) to plan this new strategy, and also famously to commit to paper his vision for the future in *Mein Kampf.* After only seven months in prison, Hitler was released in December 1924, but by now the ground was less well prepared for National Socialist action. In the winter of 1923–24, the government used its emergency powers to undertake a number of measures (including monetary reform in late 1923) which promoted economic and social stabilization and helped protect the Republic from insurrectionary overthrow either by the Left or the Right. The political success of these measures can be gauged from the ebbing popular support for anti-Republican forces which, for the next five years, reduced the Nazis to an electorally insignificant splinter group (for the Weimar electoral figures, see *Primary Sources 2: Interwar and World War II*, Document I.2).

Although popular support eluded Hitler until 1929, a number of developments occurred within his movement which were to have a powerful bearing on the Nazi state. First, the socially radical faction in National Socialism, led by Gregor Strasser, was subordinated by Hitler. In this process he was able to reassert his position as undisputed leader of the party and establish a relationship with its disparate and often disputatious elements that was transferred into the Nazi power structure after 1933. The *Gauleiter* or regional leaders, for example, were his personal agents: he appointed them and they reported directly to him. The Führer did not attempt to bind his party together by forbidding factions (as Lenin had attempted to do in the CPSU in 1921) or through regular control of the party machine. Rather, he made personal subordination to his unique leadership the party's cohesive element and acted as the arbiter of intra-party conflicts, almost 'as if he was "floating" above the party' (M. Broszat, *Hitler and the Collapse of Weimar Germany*, 1987, p.64). Both the 'leadership principle' and the arbiter's role above factions characterized the later dictatorship.

Secondly, a mythology grew up around Hitler which helped secure rank-and-file loyalty to his movement. Even before Hitler's career began, the cult of the heroic leader who would redeem Germany from squabbling petty interests was a notable feature of political discourse and imagery. Hitler and his myth-makers (notably Joseph Goebbels) both exploited and developed this existing cult in a way which skilfully set him above, and apart from, the NSDAP. Hitler was perceived as dedicated, endowed with a religious sense of mission and purpose, ascetic, incorruptible. These perceptions of him bound together his heterogeneous party following; after he became a national leader they were shared by most Germans (even those hitherto hostile to National Socialism) and acted as a crucial integratory force in the Nazi system of rule (I. Kershaw, *The 'Hitler Myth'*, 1987).

Thirdly, there began a process by which the conflicting interest groups of Weimar Germany came to be represented within the National Socialist movement itself. Leagues of Nazi lawyers, doctors and teachers, among others, were established, and in 1928 the NSBO (*Nationalsozialistische Betriebszellenorganisation*), or National Socialist shop-floor organization, was set up. During the economic crisis of 1929 to 1933 this process of sectional representation was accelerated; National Socialist organizations were established for farmers, civil servants and white-collar workers. Although interest-group representation obviously facilitated the growth of a mass movement, it had the dysfunctional effect of 'introducing the fragmentation of German society into the party itself' (J. Noakes, 'The Nazi Party and the Third Reich', 1980, p.13).

The Nazi breakthrough from electoral insignificance to mass following began with the 1929 referendum on the Young Plan for the rescheduling of reparations. In alliance with the German National People's Party (*Deutschnationale Volkspartei*, DNVP) and the ex-servicemen's *Stahlhelm* organization, the National Socialists forced a plebiscite designed to reject the Young Plan. Their opposition was couched in such extreme terms that it won the support of only 12 per cent of the voters, but the campaign brought Hitler the great advantage of political respectability as an acknowledged spokesman of the 'National Opposition', and gave the party a platform from which to outdo all others in their denunciation of Versailles. Furthermore, Alfred Hugenberg, the leader of the DNVP, was Germany's leading press magnate and henceforth Hitler and the National Socialists were sympathetically treated in his newspapers. That the Young Plan campaign brought the NSDAP greater electoral popularity was almost immediately evident from the provincial elections in Thuringia in December 1929, when the party trebled its previous share of the vote.

Exercise   Study the electoral statistics in Document I.2 in *Primary Sources 2: Interwar and World War II* (and discussed in Unit 14), and the discussion in Roberts on pages 373–5. Then answer the following questions:

1   What were the main changes in popular support for Germany's political parties between 1929 and 1933?

2   Which parties suffered least from a loss of voters to the NSDAP?

3   How could you relate the changes you describe to economic developments?

4   Can you speculate which major groups in society were likely sources of resistance to the NSDAP? ■

Specimen answer   1   There is clear evidence for the radicalization of popular opinion, with the
and discussion   extreme Right and Left both gaining ground. The Communists were as hostile to Weimar as the NSDAP, and while the growth of Nazi support (up to mid-1932) is the most striking feature of the table, the large increase in communist votes is also notable. There were many first-time voters in this period, who may well have voted disproportionately for the Nazis who proclaimed themselves a party of youth. However, there is a close correlation between Nazi gains and DNVP losses, and we can infer that the NSDAP grew chiefly at the expense of its conservative ally and of the bourgeois liberal parties. The figures indicate that the Nazis also attracted some disaffected socialists since the combined socialist and communist vote declined by about 4 per cent between 1928 and July 1932. Another important point is that there was a higher turnout at these elections; 1928: 75.6 per cent; 1930: 82 per cent; 1932 (July): 84 per cent, 1932 (Nov.): 80.6

per cent. Previous *non*-voters were voting in the depression. When the number of votes overall declined between July and November 1932, votes for the Nazi party declined by 2 million.

2   Although political allegiance was flowing away from the bourgeois conservative and nationalist parties to the Nazis, with other parties it was fairly stable. The Catholic Centre Party's vote scarcely altered. Similarly, electoral support for the left remained quite solid; although there was some erosion of the combined left vote, the Nazis made relatively few gains among the industrial working-class constituencies of the SPD and the KPD. At the same time, as Jill Stephenson explains, 'as myriad tiny, single-issue splinter parties fragmented an already fissiparous landscape, support for the parties of the political centre haemorrhaged' (J. Stephenson, 'The rise of the Nazis: *Sonderweg* or spanner in the works?', 1997, p.302).

3   It is tempting to see a straightforward connection between the growth of Nazi electoral support and the catastrophic slump which hit the German economy. However, the Nazis did not make their gains among those groups most affected by mass unemployment (chiefly the industrial working class) and the connections between Hitler's rise to power and the economic crisis were more indirect than is often assumed. Before the collapse of the industrial economy, major gains were made among the stricken farming communities of Protestant northern Germany. Because of falling prices, greater foreign competition and higher tax bills, many farmers faced bankruptcy and foreclosure; the Nazi party was able to mobilize their discontent and that of many of the independent artisans, shopkeepers and merchants of small-town Germany. The NSDAP thrived on the disappointments of all classes, but the most solidly pro-Nazi sector of the electorate was to be found among Germany's large self-employed labour force, whether in agriculture or handicrafts.

4   You could have concluded that under free elections two major groups or communities – the Catholics and industrial workers – had largely lain outside the Nazi constituency, and we might therefore have supposed that they would have been sources of resistance to the Nazi state. In section 4 we will discuss the extent to which they actually were. □

The NSDAP and business interests before 1933

The amount of support that the National Socialists received from 'big business' before 1933 has been a matter of dispute among historians. As we have seen, this question is important when analysing the relationship between capitalism and Nazism. Contemporary commentators, particularly from the left, blamed monopoly capitalism for Hitler's rise to power. The response of the Left – particularly the German Communist Party – to Hitler's accession to the chancellorship was partly determined by the ideological dogma of the monopoly-capitalist manipulation of fascism which dated back to the early 1920s. In line with this dogmatic interpretation, the left expected the new regime to fall apart under the weight of its internal contradictions, and adopted a fatal policy of waiting upon events (Broszat, 1981, p.60). Even non-communist intellectuals subscribed to the general features of the dogma; in the summer of 1932, the influential left-liberal historian, Eckart Kehr, privately described Hitler and his following as 'whores' to Fritz Thyssen, the Ruhr steel magnate, and other industrialists (H. A. Turner, *German Big Business and the Rise of Hitler*, 1985, p.351).

No historian now seriously contends that Hitler was the puppet of monopoly capitalism, and those arguing that the support of business interests was an important factor in his rise to power do so in a much more nuanced fashion. They stress the many divisions within the business community, particularly that between heavy industry (coal, iron and steel), which was highly dependent on the domestic market during Weimar, and the electrical and chemicals industries whose export record and profitability were much better. Export-oriented industrialists, led by men such as Carl Duisberg of IG-Farben, were much more supportive of the democratic system, favoured free trade and economic liberalism and were prepared to co-operate with the unions. With the onset of the world economic crisis, the informal accord between 'progressive' industrialists and Weimar broke down and an increasing number of industrialists were prepared to tolerate the NSDAP in a bourgeois coalition which was intended to shore up capitalism and dismantle Weimar's welfare and labour legislation (D. Geary, 'The industrial élite and the Nazis in the Weimar Republic', 1983, pp.85–99, summarizes the arguments of those who attribute weight to the attitudes of business in Hitler's accession to power).

H. A. Turner has argued forcibly against even the most nuanced interpretations of recent years; for him the role of business in Hitler's rise to power is simply a comprehensive myth, which has persisted because historians have preferred to 'theorize' about the relationship between capitalism and fascism, rather than engage in research. Turner shows that most employers were thoroughly hostile to the NSDAP before its electoral breakthrough in 1930 (which was achieved without their aid).

According to Turner, economic power did not easily translate to political power under Weimar, and big business played only a secondary part in the disintegration of the Republic between the elections of 1930 and the winter of 1932–33. The major participants in setting up a regime based on presidential authority were military officers, President Hindenburg's immediate advisers and representatives of the traditional aristocratic élite. The executives of Germany's great industrial corporations simply had no role in effecting the transition from parliamentary to presidential rule (Turner, p.341). It is true that after their near extinction in the 1930 elections, the 'businessmen's parties' were denied their customary subventions and business interests began 'a flirtation' (Turner's phrase) with the NSDAP. On their part, the Nazis tried to neutralize businessmen's understandable fears of the party programme's social radicalism, and Hitler muted his anti-Semitism when addressing business audiences for this prejudice was uncommon among leading industrialists.

The 'flirtation' of big business with the NSDAP did not last beyond the early summer of 1932. Businessmen on the whole supported the authoritarian cabinet of Franz von Papen, which the Nazis attacked vociferously, and in the later months of 1932 it seemed that the socially radical elements in National Socialism were once more coming to the fore. In November, the Nazis lost a great deal of middle-class and élite support when they allied with the Communists in supporting the Berlin transport strike. Although the repercussions were serious for the NSDAP, creating, for example, an open enemy in the DNVP, Goebbels explained the reasons for this: 'Many bourgeois circles are frightened off by our participation in the strike. But that's not decisive. These circles can later easily be won back. But if we'd have once lost the workers, they'd have been lost for ever' (quoted in I. Kershaw, *Hitler 1889–1936: Hubris,* 1998, p.391).

Turner's research demonstrates that most of the support for the Nazis from the business community came from lesser industrialists, whose businesses were outside the cartels and price-setting arrangements of 'organized capitalism', and poorly supported by the great national business associations. It was among such lesser businessmen that the Nazis made inroads before the accession to power, but they had no part in the backstairs intrigues that 'jobbed Hitler into office' (in Alan Bullock's words, *Hitler. A Study in Tyranny,* 1962). It is an indication of the modest financial resources they afforded Hitler that by the end of 1932 his party was bankrupt from incessant electioneering. Hitler's appointment came just when relations between his movement and the most powerful sectors of the business community had reached their lowest ebb. Some leading German industrialists actually attempted to dissuade Hindenburg from according Hitler a prominent place in the new cabinet formed at the end of January 1933.

Hitler's accession to power

The collapse of democracy and the slide into authoritarianism began during the chancellorship of Heinrich Brüning (March 1930 to May 1932). His cabinet did not enjoy a *Reichstag* majority and Brüning relied on President von Hindenburg's constitutional authority to rule by emergency decree. This routine use of quasi-dictatorial powers made authoritarian solutions to the simultaneous crises in the political system and the economy increasingly attractive. The elections Brüning called for September 1930 simply compounded his problems; the number of Nazi deputies increased from 12 to 107 giving Hitler, the notorious opponent of parliamentary democracy, the prospect of office. Brüning rejected all efforts to form a broadly-based administration and the *Reichstag's* functions were reduced to tolerating his cabinet, which grievously undermined public confidence in parliamentary processes. When confronted in November 1931 with clear evidence of Nazi plans for a terrorist regime after a *coup*, the government and the judiciary demonstrated their own inability to defend democracy by failing either to prosecute Hitler for treason, or to deport him as an undesirable 'stateless' person. (The Austrian Hitler did not acquire German citizenship until February 1932, following his nomination to the civil service position of government councillor (*Regierungsrat*) for Brunswick.)

Government by decree also enabled the ultra-conservative clique around Hindenburg and the army leadership to play major roles in political intrigues. Nazi demands for rearmament and 'military preparedness' harmonized with the professional interests and ideology of the officer corps, some of whom wanted to use the SA as a border militia to supplement the limited numbers of the professional German army, the *Reichswehr*. The fact that, by 1932, the army leadership was willing to countenance Hitler's claim to office was an important, even decisive, factor in his accession to power.

After his re-election as President in April 1932, Hindenburg dismissed Brüning at the end of May. Acting on the advice of the *Reichswehr* Minister, General von Schleicher, he appointed to the chancellorship Franz von Papen, who had no popular base whatsoever and whose cabinet of aristocratic 'gentlemen' was avidly anti-republican. Papen hoped to use Hindenburg's prestige to overthrow the constitution and install an authoritarian, corporate state. He looked for Hitler's support in this and, as a concession to the Nazi leader, lifted the ban on the SA which had been imposed in many German states. After a meeting with Hindenburg that day, Hitler told Joseph Goebbels, the NSDAP's propaganda chief: 'The SA ban will be dropped. Uniforms are to be allowed again. The *Reichstag* will be dissolved. That's the most important of all. v. Papen is foreseen as Chancellor. But that is not so interesting. Voting, voting! Out to the people. We're all very happy' (quoted in Kershaw, 1998, p.367). The lifting of the ban led to unprecedented political violence that summer. There were dozens of politically motivated murders, and hundreds more were injured in street fighting. In the most infamous incident seventeen people died in the mayhem caused by a Nazi march through the working-class district of Hamburg-Altona on 17 July, and sixty-four were injured. In Kershaw's words, 'the latent civil war that had existed throughout the Weimar Republic was threatening to become an actual civil war' (ibid., p.368).

Lifting the ban on the SA did not achieve its ulterior political objective of securing Hitler's co-operation; indeed, with cool effrontery and their customary venom, the Nazis began to defend the prerogatives of parliament and to attack Papen's presidential 'cabinet of barons'. Papen was completely dependent on ruling by emergency decree, as he lacked a majority in the *Reichstag*. In response to Nazi attacks, in a reckless attempt to break out of his political isolation by a display of authoritarian self-confidence, Papen (with the support of the President and the army) staged a *coup d'état* against the SPD-led Prussian government of Otto Braun. On the pretext that the Prussian ministry was incapable of maintaining public order, he appointed himself Reich Commissioner and thus gained control of Prussia's substantial police forces. The Prussian administration was purged and reorganized in a foretaste of the Nazi *Gleichschaltung* ('co-ordination') of the state apparatus in 1933.

The elections of 20 July 1932 in Prussia had given Hitler, as leader of the largest party, a strengthened claim to the chancellorship, although even with the nationalists he could not command a majority, and their common 'front' had been temporarily fractured by running different candidates for the presidency. However frightening the prospect of a Hitler government, scarcely any of the political parties would tolerate Papen who was anathema to the democrats and too insubstantial a figure to fill the power vacuum created by the deadlock of social and political forces. He suffered a massive vote of no confidence when the *Reichstag* reassembled at the end of August but avoided resignation by calling fresh elections. In the interim, he had attempted to incorporate the National Socialists within the government and control their seemingly inexorable advance by suggesting that Hindenburg offer Hitler the vice-chancellorship in August. However, Hitler would accept nothing less than the chancellorship, telling Hindenburg that he demanded 'the leadership of the state to its full extent for himself and his party' (ibid., p.373). As a result, Hitler suffered a major political defeat; his 'all-or-nothing' gamble had not paid off. His rejection by Hindenburg was also a severe personal defeat.

In the autumn of 1932, the Weimar State was in severe crisis, as Germans faced the fourth year of the Depression. The November elections only made matters worse – the parties that supported the government (DNVP and DVP) received only around 10 per cent of the vote. Both the NSDAP and the Centre Party lost votes, and the Nazi Party's momentum seemed halted. Papen had been unable to find a support base for his government, and his entire government resigned on 17 November. The deadlock continued until, among fears of civil war breaking out, Hindenburg regretfully dismissed Papen on 2 December before the new *Reichstag* assembled and appointed Schleicher Chancellor.

As *Reichswehr* Minister, Schleicher had been an indispensable conduit of influence between the military and the government, and was responsible for securing the army's support for the coup against Prussia. He entertained the idea of installing a military-dominated, populist regime (such as existed in Pilsudski's Poland) by allying Strasser and the non-communist labour movements. As long as Hitler demanded the chancellorship in a presidential cabinet, Schleicher's plan could be realized only after a split in the NSDAP, and that seemed quite likely: many of the rank and file were fed up with Hitler's intransigence, depressed by election losses and were leaving the party. The scheme was scotched by the fatal indecision of Gregor Strasser, the leader of the Nazi left, whose nerve failed him when it came to promoting a mass defection from Hitler. In an extraordinary display of ferocious will, the Führer re-imposed his authority on his fragmenting party, and in the process dismantled Strasser's organizational framework, the basis of his power within the party. Under Rudolf Hess, a new Political Central Commission was established, and Strasser's two *Reich* Inspectorates were abolished (ibid., p.401).

The *Reichstag* refrained from passing an immediate vote of no confidence in Schleicher, and the Christmas recess gave him a respite in which to seek either an extra-constitutional solution to the political crisis or an accommodation with a coalition within the *Reichstag*. Even before his appointment, Schleicher had been negotiating with Hitler over the terms on which the Nazis would enter government. Hitler's patience in hanging out for the highest executive office was finally rewarded on 30 January: Schleicher had suggested to Hindenburg that the Constitution be broken, but this the President would not countenance. A constitutional alternative was made possible by the revival of the 'front' between the Nazis and the DNVP and by Alfred Hugenberg's publicly declared willingness to serve under Hitler. Like Papen, who acted as the President's agent in the final political crisis, Hugenberg deluded himself that Hitler could be constrained within a coalition. After Schleicher's entire ministry had resigned, Hindenburg appointed Hitler Chancellor in a cabinet numerically dominated by nationalists and with Papen enjoying, on paper, wide powers as vice-Chancellor. Papen was also *Reich* Commissioner of Prussia. Hitler had only two National Socialist colleagues in the cabinet, Hermann Göring and Wilhelm Frick. However, since Göring was appointed to the Prussian Ministry of the Interior, and Frick was *Reich* Minister of the Interior, formidable police powers fell into National Socialist hands throughout the greater part of Germany. Following these momentous decisions, Ludendorff expressed his concern about Germany's future to Hindenburg at the end of January: 'I solemnly prophesy that this accursed man will cast our *Reich* into the abyss and bring our nation inconceivable misery. Future generations will damn you in your grave for what you have done' (ibid., p.377). Hitler's reign over Germany began on 30 January 1933.

Although he had never disguised his intention of destroying the parliamentary republic, Hitler's accession to power was formally constitutional. He had calculated that his revolutionary purpose would be more effectively achieved by observing legal formalities; even when he became Chancellor he preferred to postpone a ban on the KPD until he had secured a *Reichstag* majority to enact a draconian 'Enabling Law' (*Ermächtigungsgesetz*). To many on the left it appeared that the real beneficiaries of 30 January were the reactionary Nationalists who, it seemed, had made a 'prisoner' of Hitler. They assumed that they would be able to control and contain Hitler – a tragic error of judgement.

Exercise   While such political manoeuvres were occurring behind the scenes, the German people were trying to carve a living out of increasingly difficult circumstances. Read the extract from Ian Kershaw in your *Secondary Sources* collection and comment briefly on the effects of the Depression on the German people. What was its most damaging result for Germans? Comment on how different social groups were affected, in particular the young and women. What is the connection between the Depression, and the fact that so many Germans opted to vote for the NSDAP? What was the effect of the Depression on anti-Semitic feelings and general intolerance in Germany? ∎

Specimen answer   The Depression led to a drastic fall in industrial production, but also hit the
and discussion   agricultural sector particularly hard. The most important effect of the Depression was undoubtedly the mass unemployment, which reached the unprecedented number of over 6 million in January 1933, although the total figure including hidden unemployment was even more staggering, reaching over 8.7 million in October 1932. This meant that almost half the workforce was out of regular, full-time employment. Unemployed youths flocked in great numbers to fill the ranks of both the KPD and the NSDAP, although many others failed to become radicalized by their plight, and were simply resigned to their fate. According to Kershaw, the young were particularly badly affected by the Depression years, with four consecutive school-leaving cohorts of pupils facing dismal employment prospects. Evidence for the lack of perspective and general despair is the growing suicide rate, as well as youth criminality rates.

In urban as in rural Germany the mood was depressed and despondent, intermingled with political radicalization, leading to a rejection of the Weimar parliamentary system. No party was excluded from criticism. In towns and country, there was a deep-seated anger towards those deemed responsible for the crisis, but also, crucially, a desire for social harmony and unity.

Women, of course, were also badly affected by the Depression. It heightened the existing level of discrimination against women in the job market, and there was a growing intolerance of 'double-earning' families, and in particular of the small number of women in professional jobs. Single women were often hostile to employed married women who had a 'male breadwinner'. The view that the married woman's place was in the home was widely held and strongly propagated by the churches. Most parties shared an anti-feminist message. It is worth noting that this did not stop women from voting for parties with an anti-feminist agenda, but that women voted much like men at that time.

For German Jews, these were difficult times, as they became easy targets for discrimination and were faced with an upsurge of anti-Semitism. In general, the years of Depression had left Germany, in Kershaw's words, 'a more intolerant society', not just with regard to its Jews. The fact that the death penalty was reintroduced in the early 1930s is seen as evidence by Kershaw that the humane principles of the Weimar Republic were being eroded. Radical views on 'racial hygiene' and eugenics are another indicator of a changing climate in German society (although eugenics was by no means an exclusively German phenomenon), as the costs of keeping mental patients, for example, led to demands for voluntary sterilization of those with hereditary defects. Clearly, the ground was well prepared for National Socialist racial policy to expand on popular discontent and prejudice, and to implement increasingly radical solutions to perceived social problems.

As Kershaw points out, the statistics for unemployment 'provide only an abstract glimmer of the human suffering' in those desperate years. Even today, Germans who remember the early 1930s emphasize the incredible numbers of unemployed, the dole-queues that stretched around whole buildings, and the dire poverty and hunger suffered by millions of Germans. Hitler offered an alternative and he promised better times. At first, he was even able to deliver, at least to the majority of Germans who conformed to the new government's racial ideology. Ordinary Germans, no more than Weimar's politicians, could not have foreseen what price would have to be paid for such economic recovery. □

The Nazi seizure and consolidation of power

Hitler consolidated his one-party regime in two stages. During February, March and April of 1933 he used the police and the SA to crush the left-wing parties and the trade unions, and then he compelled the middle-class and Nationalist parties to renounce their political independence. The Nazi consolidation of power followed the established tactic of legality; one of Hitler's first acts was to persuade his cabinet to hold fresh elections which would provide a majority to enact the legal instruments of the National Socialist 'co-ordination' (*Gleichschaltung*). After the *Reichstag* was dissolved, a presidential decree (actually drafted by a previous government) 'For the Protection of the German People' was used to suppress the left-wing press and political meetings on the grounds of 'disseminating false information' which 'endangered vital interests of the state'. The Prussian *Landtag* was dissolved against the wishes of its majority, and Göring continued the purging of pro-republican civil servants, councillors and police chiefs which Papen had begun.

The Prussian police were given *carte blanche* to use arms against the government's opponents and ordered to co-operate with the 'National' paramilitary organizations (the SA, SS and the *Stahlhelm*) whose members were, in late February, enrolled as auxiliary police volunteers. The Communist and Social Democratic parties in Prussia were quickly driven into a half-clandestine existence by police raids, newspaper bans and unchecked Nazi terrorization. There was some juridical mitigation of Göring's draconian measures by the *Reich* and Prussian Supreme Courts, but little to hinder the creation of extraordinarily favourable electoral advantages for the governing coalition by a combination of force and a near monopoly of the means of mass communication. The constitution of the Reich Broadcasting Corporation, in which the government had a dominant position, allowed Hitler and Goebbels to make masterly use of radio for domestic propaganda. Furthermore, Hitler was able to exploit the prestige of his office at a meeting of leading industrialists on 20 February 1933 when a substantial election fund for the Nazis was secured (M. Broszat, *The Hitler State*, 1981, pp.60–9).

On 27 February 1933, the Nazis' intimidation of their opponents was aided and accelerated by the burning of the *Reichstag*, allegedly by a Communist. The incident seemingly confirmed the existence of a Communist insurrectionary conspiracy, which the Nazis had often invoked and in which they may even have believed. All KPD deputies and leading officials in Prussia were immediately arrested and the party's papers banned indefinitely. On 28 February, a presidential decree introduced a far-reaching state of emergency which ended the hitherto constitutional rights of personal freedom, freedom of the press and of association, and protection of property and homes, and authorized the Reich government to exercise the powers once reserved for the governments of the *Länder* (the individual German states). This improvised decree typified the *ad hoc* process of establishing the despotism of the police state: it did not put forward any clear legal definition of changes in the law and in the powers of authority, and instead made do with the general abolition of existing basic and constitutional rights (ibid., p.71). The decree forced Communist Party officials who had escaped capture either to emigrate or go underground and led to a wave of arrests among the intellectual and literary left.

Given the circumstances it is unsurprising that the election of 5 March secured for the governing coalition a majority of the votes (51.8 per cent), with the NSDAP itself receiving 43.9 per cent. Yet, the number who resisted intimidation and were not swayed by government propaganda seems remarkable; despite its persecution, the KPD polled 4.8 million votes and the SPD's vote scarcely changed. However, the election underwrote the decisive preponderance of the NSDAP within the coalition: because of the arrest of communist deputies, the Nazis commanded a *Reichstag* majority irrespective of their coalition partners who were now treated with disdain. Up to the election, Hitler had been careful to speak of a 'National' government. The results inaugurated the process of National Socialist revolution, 'which although it was directed and legalized from above, was first made possible through pressure and terror from below' (ibid., p.77).

The unguided revolutionary impulse coming 'from below' took the form of the occupation of town halls, newspaper and trade-union offices, banks, courts and other public buildings by SA and SS detachments who compelled the dismissal or detention of 'unreliable' or Jewish officials. A wave of enforced vacations and resignations swept through local government and speeded the 'co-ordination' of the *Länder*. On their own initiative, the auxiliary police hunted down communists and other known opponents of National Socialism and the SA organized boycotts of department stores and Jewish businesses. Attempts by the Nazis' Nationalist allies to persuade Hitler to restrain the militants' excesses were rebuffed: he told Papen that he would permit nobody 'to deflect him from his mission' of 'destroying and exterminating Marxism', and this was to be the standard justification for the subversion of constitutional and legal order (ibid., p.79). The first concentration camps for political prisoners, run by the SA and SS outside normal police and juridical control, sprang up in Dachau, Oranienburg and elsewhere.

To orchestrate the revolution, Hitler created a Reich Ministry of Information and Propaganda headed by Joseph Goebbels. He promptly stage-managed the first great state ceremony of the new regime with the convening of the *Reichstag* on 21 March at the garrison church in Potsdam where the Hohenzollern kings of Prussia were buried. In contrast to the uncontrolled violence on the streets, this occasion established the regime's legitimate descent from the Prussian authoritarian state, emphasizing the links between the new Germany and Prussia. The new, young Chancellor and the 85-year-old Hindenburg exchanged a handshake on the church steps which was subsequently reproduced a million-fold on postcards and posters. Inside, the Kaiser's seat was kept empty, but behind it sat the Crown Prince in full-dress uniform, while Hindenburg, in his Prussian Field Marshal's uniform, was the symbolic link between the old Reich and the new (J. C. Fest, *Hitler*, 1974, pp.601–2; Kershaw, 1998, p.465). It was an occasion when Hitler and National Socialism represented themselves as the bearers of traditional German virtues with, apparently, great emotional effect. A host of new members – 'the March converts' – flocked into the NSDAP at this

Hitler as a youthful Chancellor in March 1933 (in Potsdam) shakes the hand of the 85-year-old President, Field Marshal Hindenburg. Photo by Theo Eisenhart, courtesy of Bildarchiv Preussischer Kulturbesitz, Berlin.

time, many no doubt climbing aboard the bandwagon, but others were persuaded that the movement stood for the reassertion of national pride and Christian values, as well as recovery from economic misery. It was a perfect, stage-managed illusion. Only three days later, that illusion was shattered with the grim reality of the Nazi take-over of power (B. J. Wendt, *Deutschland 1933–1945*, 1995, p.98).

The only task of the new *Reichstag* was to enact the 'Act for the Removal of Distress from the People and Reich', the so-called 'Enabling Law' (*Ermächtigungsgesetz*) of 24 March 1933, which empowered the government to take the legal measures, including constitutional changes, necessary 'to relieve the distress' of the German people and the German Reich. This measure, which amounted to a change of the Weimar constitution, required a two-thirds majority (and also depended on at least two-thirds of the deputies to be present), and could not be passed without the support particularly of the Centre Party. A majority of Catholics was persuaded to support the law by promises to protect confessional schools, to preserve good relations with the Vatican, and by Hitler's publicly expressed regard for the Catholic and evangelical churches 'as among the most important factors of our nationality' (Broszat, 1981, p.83). The Centre Party deputies also allowed themselves to be swayed by the law's limiting provisions: Clause 5 stated it was to lose its validity 'if the present federal cabinet is replaced by another'. This meant – or should have meant – that the law could only be applied by the government formed in January in which the Nationalists predominated, and would lapse if the government's composition was changed. The only protest against the law came from the Social Democrats, whose leader Otto Wels made a courageous speech against Hitler's motion. The result of the voting was 444 votes in favour of the law, against only 94 votes from the Social Democrats (Wendt, p.104). The *Reichstag* had surrendered all its powers.

The law was of fundamental importance in securing the collaboration of non-party civil servants, judges and prosecutors in the National Socialist revolution, whose allegiance to the existing state hierarchy and social order had to be co-opted. The law satisfied their professional commitment to the *Rechtsstaat* – the legal state – and secured for the Nazi revolution expertise in spheres where the NSDAP was weak. The legality of the seizure of power rested on these alliances and compromises with non-Nazi office and influence holders and formed a marked contrast to the Bolshevik revolution (K. D. Bracher, *The Nazi Dictatorship*, 1969, p.342).

Since the Communist deputies were either in hiding or under arrest (and their party effectively proscribed), the only opposition to the law came from the SPD. The days of its legal existence were numbered: its combat organization, *Reichsbanner*, was banned in several states and, after the SPD had suffered dissension between those who wished to go into emigration to fight the regime and those who wished to continue within Germany, a directive of 22 June outlawed the SPD. The socialist trade unions were dissolved on 1 May and their members and assets were transferred to the new German labour front even before the SPD was dissolved. Other political parties and organizations were soon wound up or banned. The Liberal parties – which had been insignificant for some time – dissolved themselves. The organizational independence of the Nationalists was ended by defections to the NSDAP, police harassment and Nazi concessions allowing former DNVP deputies to be included in the NSDAP parliamentary group, and the *Stahlhelm* to merge with the SA. Hugenberg, who had grossly over-estimated his ability to 'contain' Hitler and had lost the support of Hindenburg, resigned his posts of Minister of Economics and Agriculture on 26 June. The Centre Party, whose membership and electoral support had been so solid up to March, was gravely weakened by the fact that the Catholic hierarchy began to negotiate directly with the government in order to preserve the position of the Church; as part of the new *Reich* Concordat the Vatican agreed to forbid any political activity on the part of the German clergy. Now that it was disowned at the top, large numbers deserted political Catholicism for the first time. The Nazis' call for the dissolution of the Centre Party was acceded to on 5 July. On 14 July, a salvo of decrees battered the remnants of political pluralism: the NSDAP was declared the sole legal party and anyone undertaking political activity outside its ranks was liable to three years' penal servitude; the assets of the SPD, KPD and political and Jewish expatriates were confiscated. Rule by charismatic leadership became the fundamental principle of the state and dictated the formalities of everyday official life; civil servants were instructed to employ the Hitler salute. Henceforth, after taking major decisions (such as leaving the League of Nations on 14 October 1933) the regime used plebiscites to proclaim the popular legitimacy of its actions.

3   THE PARTY AND THE STATE AFTER THE SEIZURE OF POWER

Liquidating the revolution

Simultaneously with the establishment of one-party rule Hitler was calling for the winding up of the revolution. He told a meeting of *Reich* Governors on 6 July: 'Revolution is not a permanent condition ... The ideas in our programme do not commit us to behaving like fools and destroying everything, but to realising our conceptions wisely and carefully ...' (quoted in Broszat, 1981, p.204). What 'programme' did he have in mind and why was the continuation of the revolution a threat to it? It is reasonable to assume that he was thinking of the intimately connected goals of rearmament and economic recovery, and probably also of the aggressive foreign policy for which these were the instruments. The spontaneous turbulence of the revolution 'from below', and its frequent violence, threatened these goals by arousing foreign hostility, and thus the possibility of concerted international action (such as an economic boycott) against Germany. Furthermore, the militants' demand for 'the Second (social) Revolution' to complement the seizure of political power, and their brutal indifference to law and order, profoundly disturbed the businessmen and civil servants whose co-operation was indispensable for the realization of Hitler's 'programme'. Germany's professional military establishment, too, was increasingly distrustful of the pretensions of the SA under Ernst Röhm to set itself up as the rival of the *Reichswehr*, and even to submerge the professional army in a mass revolutionary 'People's Army'. Although the officer corps generally welcomed the SA as a supplement to Germany's exiguous forces, subordination to the likes of Röhm was a thoroughly abhorrent prospect. In this dispute, Hitler – who wanted a mass army but under total professional control – sided with the generals. The power of Röhm and the SA had to be curbed if Hitler was to secure total power for himself.

In July and August 1933, a series of measures was taken to discipline the SA and dismantle its 'private' concentration camps and torture chambers. The auxiliary police were disbanded and, in Prussia, a prosecuting office set up to investigate and punish SA and SS illegalities. The Secret State Police (*Geheime Staatspolizei* or Gestapo*)*, formed by Göring out of the old Prussian political police, were given a major role in suppressing SA terror, initially under the auspices of the Ministry of Justice and Central State Prosecutor's office, although the political police were to grow into an autonomous empire in a way which typified the multiplication of uncoordinated nuclei of power.

Hitler was determined to crush the SA leadership. This was apparently linked with the allaying of foreign apprehensions about his regime for, in February and again in April, he confided to Anthony Eden, then Lord Privy Seal in the British government, that he intended to reduce the SA by two-thirds and place the rest under international supervision (I. Kershaw, *Hitler. 1889–1936: Hubris*, 1998, p.506). Rumours of an intended SA coup were circulated, as well as defamations of the moral characters of Röhm (a homosexual) and his associates, in order to prepare party and public opinion for a purge. In close collaboration with the *Reichswehr,* which supplied weapons and transport, SS detachments purged the SA, killing Röhm and dozens of other high-ranking SA leaders on 30 June/1 July 1934. Hitler also took the opportunity to settle political scores with old opponents: Schleicher, Gregor Strasser, and reactionaries who had deserted him during the 1923 putsch were also murdered, together with an unknown number of victims of 'private' feuds. Some estimates put the total number of victims at between 150 and 200 (ibid., p.517).

The purge both demonstrated and ensured that Hitler exercised untrammelled power. His erstwhile conservative allies were now quite insignificant: Papen was placed under house arrest, and later relieved of the vice-chancellorship and given a diplomatic post in Vienna. A terse retrospective law of 3 July legalized the murders as 'justifiable acts of self-defence by the state'; on 13 July Hitler was declared 'Supreme Judge of the German people'. The death of Hindenburg on 2 August allowed Hitler to assume formally the roles of Chancellor and Head of State; shortly after this the army swore a personal oath of loyalty to the Führer. The purge also quickened the process by which Hitler's public image and popularity were dissociated from that of the Nazi Party. The Führer's personal standing in the eyes of the great majority of Germans was, all the evidence suggests, greatly enhanced by his sanctioning of the state murders. These met the traditional bourgeois demands for 'peace and quiet' and 'law and order' which the unruliness, arbitrary violence, and public outrages of the SA had threatened (I. Kershaw, *The 'Hitler Myth'*, 1987, p.93).

Despite Hitler's untrammelled power, neither the purging of party veterans nor acts of blatant, murderous illegality characterized Nazi rule between 1934 and 1939. Unlike Stalin, Hitler did not massacre old comrades with whom he disagreed and he retained their fidelity virtually to the end. After the Röhm purge, the regime preferred to pursue its internal opponents (of whom very few were from the political or social élites) by legal procedures and through the judicial system. The SA's terrorist violence against domestic foes ceased to be a regular part of the regime's *modus operandi*, although the notorious pogrom of November 1938 (described below) was an important exception. True, the courts were now applying draconian legislation which defined treason and subversion in extraordinarily wide terms. Special courts with streamlined procedures were created to try infringements against the '*Reichstag* Fire Decree' and a 'Decree on malicious gossip' which made even spoken criticism of the regime an offence punishable by penal servitude. Between 1934 and 1937, as a result of the use of judicial proceedings, the number of political prisoners detained in the regular prison system was greater than those held in the concentration camps (M. Broszat, *The Hitler State*, 1981, p.302). The camps were reduced in number, their staff even made liable to proceedings for maltreating political prisoners, but they were nevertheless firmly institutionalized and the Gestapo was able to decide for itself what constituted 'political' acts. Consequently there arose a persistent dualism in the prosecution of political 'offenders', with the coexistence of the traditional legal system, derived from the authoritarian *Rechtsstaat,* and an improvised system uncontrolled by the regular organs of state government and justice, whose dubious legality came from 'emergency' decrees. There were numerous parallels to this dualism in the Nazi state, which many have discerned as its basic characteristic.

The party and the state after 1934

The Nazis themselves, and later historians and political scientists, sometimes asked: What is the sovereign power in National Socialist Germany? On what theory does its sovereignty rest? These questions are important because they lead us to ask whether the regime ever established the institutional conditions for a peaceful persistence. Much of the reckless instability of Nazi Germany, it has been argued, resulted from the absence of any impersonal and rule-governed authority structure, which in the modern state is normally identified with a public office or a complex of offices and institutions. Sovereign power was invested in the Führer, who embodied the will of the people, and the legitimizing principle of this sovereignty was charisma – the idea that the leader was endowed with super-human qualities which emanated from him and pervaded the state, party and people (F. Neumann, *Behemoth*, 1942, p.75). Charismatic rule is an irrational and inherently unstable mode of domination. It usually originates during political crises, and is difficult to prolong and renew without recurrent crises which justify the leader's exalted position and allow him to display his exceptional qualities. One of its consequences for Hitler's Germany was that collective decision-making rapidly fell into disuse; there were seventy-two cabinet meetings in 1933, but only four in 1936. Government came to resemble a feudal court, where a minister's real power depended on his access to the Führer.

We have here a schematic and partial explanation for the 'adventurism' of Hitler's foreign policy, particularly after changes in the Foreign Office and High Command in early 1938 removed the restraining influences of conservative diplomats and generals. However, we can supplement this explanatory sketch by considering how relations between the state and the party exacerbated the instability of charismatic rule.

Germany had a strong state tradition which the Nazi dictatorship could, and to a certain degree did, exploit to secure its rule. The Italian fascist regime had developed the theory of the totalitarian state which the Nazi leadership initially appropriated as the official doctrine of the new Germany. On several occasions in 1933 Hitler spoke of establishing the 'totality' of the state and, in November, Goebbels declared: 'The goal of the revolution must be a totalitarian state pervading all spheres of public life' (quoted in Neumann, p.47). However, totalitarian theory had not figured in Hitler's political conceptions before 1933; in *Mein Kampf* he rejected unconditional obedience to the state, which he described as only a means for the preservation of the racial community. He affirmed a people's 'biological' right to resist in the interests of its own self-preservation. As a racist Social Darwinist he valued the 'dynamic' virtues he discerned in the *Volk* and the movement above the 'static' formalism of the state and its bureaucracy. It can be argued that Hitler espoused totalitarian theory during the seizure and consolidation of power only because it met the practical needs of the moment: the doctrine was useful in restraining the SA, and in legitimizing the co-ordination of the *Länder*, and the unification and concentration of legislative power in the Reich. After the liquidation of the revolution in June 1934 Hitler discarded totalitarian theory; at the NSDAP Congress of September 1934 he asserted the sovereignty of the movement as the authentic representative of the racial community: 'It is not the state which commands us but rather we who command the state. It was not the state which created us but rather we who created our own state' (J. Noakes and G. Pridham (eds), *Nazism 1919–1945*, 1984, p.236). Evidence for consistency in Hitler's thinking is provided by his party address in 1935, when he reiterated the idea of the state merely being an instrument for the organization of the *Volk*, whose vital will was given immediate expression in the Nazi movement (ibid., p.237). Hitler's address belied the unity of state and party which the decree of December 1933 had theoretically established and, in practice, there was constant tension between the sovereignty claims of the NSDAP and the state apparatus.

In principle, the party was, after 1934, assigned the functions of politically training and educating the people, and preparing them psychologically for war, while administration was left to the state. This division of roles foundered on a number of factors. As we have noted, the Nazi leadership was able to take over the existing machinery of the state intact and secure the co-operation of the bureaucracy. Purges of the higher administration under the Law for the Restoration of the Professional Civil Service (April 1933) mainly affected Jews and fell far short of 'Nazification'. Consequently a traditional state bureaucracy, with its legally trained personnel, coexisted with a party whose organization and collective outlook was quite different. This coexistence was made chronically antagonistic because there was no means of internally integrating the party itself, and after the seizure of power its component parts either infiltrated the state apparatus or set up quasi-official agencies which rivalled those of the state. The *Gauleiter*, for example, acquired senior state offices but at the same time shook off the last vestiges of control by the central party organization when, as a result of the dismantling of Strasser's administrative structure, they were answerable only to Hitler. In some instances, this penetration of the state by party bodies resulted from an individual's personal union of party and state officers: Goebbels, who became Minister for Propaganda, and Walther Darré, who headed the party's agrarian organization and became Minister for Agriculture, are two examples (J. Noakes, 'The Nazi Party and the Third Reich', 1980, p.15). However, in many instances party and state institutions existed alongside each other, with overlapping competencies that gave rise to institutional confusion and a chaos of personal rivalries (Noakes and Pridham (eds), pp.203–4). We have already noted how the SS, a party organization, usurped some of the functions and powers of the police. During the war it encroached on those of the army. Mention should also be made of the rival state and party bodies influencing the conduct of foreign affairs.

Hitler may have promoted what has been called 'institutional Darwinism' (D. Schoenbaum, *Hitler's Social Revolution*, 1967, p.206) because he believed that only through organizational struggle could the fittest to rule survive. However, this polycratic system also served two distinct political purposes: first, it reinforced his position as the sole co-ordinating authority in the government of the Reich. Secondly, the fact that the totalitarian movement, with its hard core of committed racists, was not incorporated into the 'establishment' meant that it could act as a goad for the civil service, and its dynamic fanaticism could be held in reserve for the more radical policies adopted in 1938 (such as the anti-Jewish pogrom on 9 November). From the point of view of our course, institutional Darwinism, and what has been called the 'shapelessness' of the Nazi state, were of fundamental importance because they were preconditions for an unrestrained will to war from 1938 and the horrific mass murders which occurred during the war. As Broszat concludes in his remarkable study of the Third Reichs' internal structure, 'the more the organizational jungle of the National Socialist regime spread out the less chance there was of restoring any rationally organized and consistent policy-making and governmental process' (Broszat, 1981, pp.358–9).

Economic recovery and the Nazi economy

The economic recovery of Germany fell into two phases – 1933 to 1936, and 1936 to 1939 – distinguished by the role of rearmament in promoting revival and growth. In both phases, state expenditure and investment were basic instruments of economic policy, but during the first, spending on the military represented a relatively modest proportion of government outlays. During the second, spending on rearmament, and on projects intended to ensure Germany's strategic self-sufficiency, became the dynamo of economic expansion. (R. J. Overy, *The Nazi Economic Recovery, 1932–1938*, provides a clear summary of economic recovery.) This second phase, inaugurated by the 1936 Four Year Plan to put the economy on a war footing, is discussed in more detail below; first, we will examine the overall features of Germany's economic revival.

The Nazi Party was generally ill-prepared for power in terms of specific policies, but during 1932 it established the broad outlines of an economic programme to restore production and employment, and to finance rearmament. In terms of Germany's place in the international economy, the programme's main objective was autarky (or economic self-sufficiency) within a 'large economic area' *(Grossraumwirtschaft)*, dominated by Germany and protected by tariff barriers. This idea had a long pedigree in German economic nationalism and closely resembled the plans for *Mitteleuropa* which had been a key German war aim in 1914 (Noakes and Pridham (eds), p.260; see also Units 5 and 6). The project had been given renewed vitality by the collapse of the international economy and the emergence of protected trading blocs in the British Empire, Japan and the United States of America.

With respect to the domestic economy, the Nazis planned greater state intervention and a policy of reflation by deficit-spending through a major series of public works. The Papen and Schleicher governments had put forward similar 'work-creation' proposals and the coalition formed in January 1933 contented itself with continuing a programme launched by Schleicher. This resulted in 600 million marks being allocated to public contracts for agricultural improvement, and house and street building. While Hugenberg remained Minister of Economics, no purely National Socialist measures to deal with unemployment were implemented. His chief concern was to relieve the plight of German farmers, particularly the large estate owners, on whose behalf a ban on the foreclosure of farms for debt and increased agrarian tariffs were introduced.

One of Hitler's main purposes during the spring and summer of 1933 was to keep the economy out of the hands of the SA and to reassure financiers and industrialists that the National Socialist revolution would leave the capitalist system basically untouched. When, in early June, a programme was enacted to supplement the work-creation scheme, this was done after talks with leading industrialists, although these discussions did not allay their many reservations about the Nazi proposals for the economy. A billion marks was provided to finance public building works – including the construction of the *Autobahnen* – and to subsidize certain private sector buildings, while tax concessions were given to domestic machinery producers. Various measures reflected Nazi ideology and the government's obligations to the Nazi rank and file: women were encouraged to leave the labour market through marriage loans (this is discussed in more detail below, section 4) and, in the provision of work for the unemployed, SA and SS members enjoyed priority. From the summer of 1933, the regime turned to tackling unemployment with the frenetic energy and in the style that had brought National Socialism to power. As in other spheres, propaganda – the art of political rhetoric in mass society – was as important as the substantive content of policy. The campaign against unemployment served to divert the party rank and file from the incompleteness of the National Socialist revolution; it mobilized many non-Nazis behind the new regime and offered a kind of compensation for the destruction of civil liberties and trade unions (Broszat, 1981, p.137).

A long-term objective of Nazi economic policies was the establishment of a *Wehrwirtschaft* or military economy. On 8 February 1933, Hitler told his cabinet that 'every publicly sponsored measure to create employment had to be considered from the point of view of whether it was necessary with respect to rendering the German people again capable of bearing arms for military service. This had to be the dominant thought, always and everywhere' (Noakes and Pridham (eds), p.263). Although this certainly expressed Hitler's intentions, the circumstances of the early years of Nazi rule meant that it was impossible to pursue rearmament with such fixity of purpose. An initial political priority was the re-absorption of the unemployed for which the defence industries, being capital-intensive, were ill suited (besides, the army, which was enlarged after 1933 but remained a voluntary force until 1935, simply could not have coped with a huge input of weapons).

Policies pursued from 1933 greatly increased the powers of the state over the economy and initiated the process by which 'politics' established its primacy over economics. The regulation of the economy which the Nazis introduced, without following any preconceived plan, effectively superseded the capitalist system in several essentials by 1938. True, private property rights were guaranteed by the Nazi state which returned some state and municipal property to the private sector. However, although the means of production remained legally in private hands, the freedoms of contract normally enjoyed by employers and employed in capitalist societies were severely curtailed, and the market was displaced as a key regulative institution by state agencies or private agencies endowed with new powers by the state.

Compulsory labour service for young men (*Reichsarbeitsdienst*) was introduced in 1935 (in theory, all young Germans were obligated to work in a labour service, but the Women's Labour Service remained voluntary until the outbreak of war) and the state's power to direct labour was greatly extended in June 1938. Employers lost their right to sack workers – for after 1934 dismissals had to be sanctioned by the Labour Exchanges – and wage ceilings were imposed to stop employees selling their labour to the highest bidder and to control inflation. To compensate labour for wage restraint and protect living standards, the prices of consumer goods and services were decided administratively after 1936, rather than by market forces; food prices, rents, professional and school fees, transport rates, cinema charges – all now had to be authorized by a Federal Commissioner whose rulings were enforced by severe penalties. It has been argued that the state's panoply of economic controls brought the economy 'closer in character to [that] of Stalin's Russia than to those of the capitalist West' (R. J. Overy, *The Nazi Economic Recovery*, 1982, p.66), although we cannot push this comparison too far, because the Nazis introduced nothing approaching the central economic planning discussed in Unit 15, and they pursued their objectives of recovery and rearmament by *ad hoc* methods and agencies. They preferred to work with, rather than against, private enterprise but, when private corporations would not co-operate with their plans, the state set up rival institutions which were fiefs of the NSDAP.

The tight political control of the German economy distinguishes the Nazi economic revival from the rapid expansion during the Wilhelmine period and the post-1945 'economic miracle'. It also distinguishes it from the economic recovery in Britain during the 1930s, where market forces and the growth of private consumption were far more important. In a long-term historical perspective, the performance of the German economy under the Nazis was not particularly remarkable. Although growth accelerated sharply between 1933 and 1938, there is much evidence that thereafter the weight of rearmament in the economy made further rapid expansion unsustainable. Veiled inflation, and material and labour shortages, were seriously endangering economic performance on the eve of the Second World War, and internal economic difficulties may have contributed to a war psychosis in 1939. (This is a matter referred to in the next section, and in the article by Richard Overy in the Course

Reader that you will read in connection with the establishment of a 'war economy'.)

Yet, Nazi economic policies did enjoy a fair measure of success, a fact which many historians have been rather loath to acknowledge. Ever since Allied intelligence agencies revealed extensive under-utilization of productive resources until the later stages of the Second World War, the inefficiency of the Nazi economy and its unsystematic improvization have been bywords of progressive folk-wisdom. It is rather refreshing, therefore, to read one economic historian's assessment:

> Though certainly not frictionless, the German economic machine worked and worked quite well, on a narrowly economic level, compared to the other economic systems of the time ... Contempt for the political and social doctrines of the Nazis should not interfere with a dispassionate analysis of their economic system. The Nazis subscribed neither to central planning along Soviet lines nor to the market economy of the Western world, but selectively and without dogmatic qualms used those economic tools that seemed to serve their purposes.
>
> (K. Hardach, *The Political Economy of Germany in the Twentieth Century*, 1980, p.66)

All the objective indices of economic performance bear this out. Total industrial production rose extremely rapidly from its nadir in late 1932 and by 1938 had more than doubled. This was twice the rate of growth in contemporary Britain, although since Germany had suffered far more during the Depression it had much more to recover (D. Landes, *The Unbound Prometheus*, 1969, p.391). The rate of inflation in Germany between 1933 and 1938 was about half that in Britain and America, which testifies to the effectiveness of Nazi price controls. Above all, Nazi Germany did far more than any other industrial society to restore employment. In fact, by 1938, Germany (with year-round average unemployment of 1.3 per cent) was experiencing acute labour shortages; America (with 18.9 per cent of its labour force unemployed) and Britain (with 8.1 per cent) must have wished they had Germany's problem (figures in Hardach, p.61. See also Table 17.1).

Table 17.1 Level of unemployment in Germany, 1933–39

	January	*June*	*Total industrial production-index*
1933	6.014	4.857	100
1934	3.773	2.481	130.8
1935	2.947	1.877	149.5
1936	2.520	1.315	168.9
1937	1.853	0.648	187.2
1938	1.052	0.292	205.1
1939	0.302	0.049	?

(Source: J. Noakes and G. Pridham (eds), *Nazism, 1919–1945*, 1984, pp.296, 359)

4   STATE AND SOCIETY IN NAZI GERMANY

Attempts to co-ordinate German society

Drawing a boundary between the state and society is not easy in any circumstances. It is particularly difficult for the Third Reich – where the state was so amorphous – for the Nazis sought to obliterate all distinctions between public and private life by creating an array of institutions which would organize the major social groups (workers, youth, women) behind the leadership of the NSDAP. After 1933, nearly all voluntary organizations of a professional or social type were dissolved, and their members and functions absorbed by satellites of the Nazi party enjoying official status. For example, the Nazi Women's Group – *NS Frauenschaft* – displaced women's voluntary organizations, and the regime attempted to mobilize the great mass of women through official unions of German women and girls: *Deutsches Frauenwerk* and *Bund deutscher Mädel.* The task of representing women in society, which in Weimar had been undertaken by self-governing women's organizations, now fell on parts of a very complex party-cum-state apparatus (for details see Jill Stephenson, *The Nazi Organisation of Women*, 1981). Nazi ideology of a *'Volksgemeinschaft'* did not allow for any independent organizations, be they for women, for religious groups, workers, youth etc., although Catholic groups were protected up to a point by the Concordat and were able to outlast virtually all other non-Nazi groups.

National Socialism also implemented a large number of welfare policies which, at first glance, suggest that the state cared about the well-being of its citizens. Indeed, this is another area of popular folk-memory of those who remember the 1930s. However, such achievements in social policy cannot be evaluated without stressing their limitations or their underlying intentions. National Socialist welfare policy only ever extended to those who were considered racially, biologically and politically 'deserving', and was used towards implementing 'social hygiene', eugenics and 'racial hygiene' (B. J. Wendt, *Deutschland 1933–1945*, 1995, pp.232–3).

The Nazi utopia was a racial political community unified behind a single leader, summed up in the slogan: *Ein Volk, Ein Reich, Ein Führer*. This ideal represented a reaction against the relative autonomy of society from the state which had resulted from the economic and political liberalization of nineteenth-century Europe. Although Hitler rejected the totalitarian doctrines of Fascist Italy which elevated the state above the race, he and Mussolini shared the objective of re-fusing state and civil society in new political totalities with monopolistic claims to allegiance. Hitler wrote in *Mein Kampf:* 'the [National Socialist] *Weltanschauung* is intolerant ... and peremptorily demands its own exclusive, and complete recognition as well as the complete adaptation of public life to its ideas' (quoted in K. D. Bracher, *The Nazi Dictatorship,* 1969, p.315). In conformity with this precept, the regime attempted to impose a 'co-ordination' (*Gleichschaltung*) of intellectual and cultural life through institutions like the Reich Cultural Chamber, set up to censor critics and inculcate the leadership principle and martial values, and the 'Strength through Joy' organization which was meant to control the private lives of workers through communal leisure and holidays.

This drive to shape society from above might be termed the creative aspect of Hitler's totalizing ambition; its negative aspect was the determination to purge society of internal foes (notably Jews and Communists) and 'racially unhealthy' elements (such as homosexuals and the mentally ill). From the previous unit on Fascist Italy, you will already be familiar with the thesis put forward by MacGregor Knox that the common essence of Mussolini's and Hitler's regimes was the intertwining of domestic and foreign conquest. Both dictators regarded war against domestic enemies as inextricably linked with foreign aggression. What Knox calls their 'visionary programs' blended demography and geopolitics, but in Hitler's case, the rationale for his bellicose 'world view' lay in a racist external and internal Social Darwinism, which took foreign aggression and domestic revolution to create fitness for war to be inescapable in the struggle for survival. In his unpublished 'Second Book', Hitler was quite explicit about the interdependence of foreign and domestic policy:

> Domestic policy must secure the inner strength of a people so that it can assert itself in the sphere of foreign policy. Foreign policy must secure the life of a people for its domestic political development. Hence domestic policy and foreign policy are not only most closely linked, but must also mutually complement one another.
>
> (Quoted in *Secondary Sources*, MacGregor Knox, p.154)

The following sections will examine the deeper historical motives behind the Nazis' attempt to obliterate the distinction between state and society, and ask how far this intention was realized. By looking at four instances of state/society relationships – anti-Semitism, the adaptation of the Catholic community to Nazi rule, the regime's relationship with the working class and the policies it implemented regarding women – we will see how the regime attempted to remodel society according to the dictates of ideology, but also how certain social groups were able to resist (in an apolitical way) total domination by the state. At the same time, the emphasis will be on the ideology of the 'racial state', identifying both the aims and the limitations of implementing National Socialist racial ideology.

The racial state: viewing Nazi society from the bottom up

We have identified some of the basic premises of the Nazis' programme for society. Understandably they have acted as powerful influences on the historical interpretation of Nazi Germany: in 1945 the world was confronted with horrifying evidence of the internal war against the Jews, and other acts of grotesque barbarity, and it was highly plausible to think that these could only have been accomplished by a totally dominant state whose combined ideology and terror had subverted and destroyed autonomous society. An influential version of this thesis was Hannah Arendt's famous study *The Origins of Totalitarianism* (first published in 1951), in which she argued that the totalitarian movement sprang from the break up of the class structure of civil society, the decay of its social ties and the 'atomization' of individuals torn out of their customary roles and allegiances by the First World War and the economic catastrophes of the interwar period. In power, Arendt argued, the movement made this atomization a fundamental principle of its rule by tolerating no ties except those which bound the masses to the leader and his élite.

The crucial flaw of this interpretation was that its view of the German 'masses' (a term with a heavy conceptual load which harked back to the theory of mass society) was no different from that enjoyed by Hitler from his podium. The Nazis' own claim to have eradicated class division and class consciousness, as well as other sectional ties, and to have created a mass community of sentiment between leader and led, was taken as an achieved fact. The traditional preoccupation of German historiography with the state and high politics, and the fact that the sources for the study of the regime are almost entirely official, have meant that, even for scholars sceptical of the totalitarian concept, the same view from the podium has been the dominant perspective on the Third Reich. Only relatively recently have historians begun to look at Nazi Germany 'from the bottom up' by reconstructing everyday experiences and popular mentalities. Research into these social aspects of the Third Reich has revealed the incompleteness of the regime's hold on the hearts and minds of the people and the existence of strong currents of popular dissent, amounting (in the opinion of some historians) to a massive challenge to the regime. Even if the challenge has been exaggerated, it is clear that German society was not simply a passive instrument of the Nazi state.

Admittedly research into popular mentalities has confirmed the extraordinary position of Hitler in the affections of his people; that the regime was able to function effectively was in no small part due to the fact that Hitler was loved rather than feared by the Germans. However, Hitler's role in domestic politics was symbolic rather than executive, and the myth built around him was all the more effective because he was perceived as being above the party and the bearer of traditional values that emanated from society. Wherever the Nazis confronted these values, especially religious sentiments, then their ideology was relatively weak. It was where they worked with the grain of existing values that they were successful in carrying public opinion with them and pushing on with their political goals (R. Bessel, 'Living with the Nazis', 1984).

Case I: Anti-Semitism

The years 1933–39 in Germany were, in Saul Friedländer's words, 'years of persecution' for Jews, Gypsies, and other 'non-Aryans', but also for the mentally and physically handicapped, the 'asocial', for homosexuals and anyone not deemed able or fit to form part of the German *Volk*. Anyone who was considered a risk to the purity of the German, 'Aryan' race, was victimized and persecuted in National Socialist Germany. This persecution developed in different stages and was dependent on domestic and foreign policy considerations. Room for manoeuvre for the regime was much more limited in 1933 than after the beginning of the war in 1939, when there was no longer any need to make concessions to the outside world (B. J. Wendt, *Deutschland 1933–1945*, 1995, p.166). However, in what is surely the most depressing aspect of Nazi Germany, the new government proceeded as soon as it was in power to act against those whom it considered 'internal enemies', particularly, but not exclusively, against Germany's Jews. With the accession of Hitler to power, racism practically became Germany's official 'state religion'. Anti-Semitic measures and legislation were implemented almost immediately, as were anti-left wing measures (in fact, the Nazis' association of Jews and Bolshevism led to a muddying of the waters for a while). The new regime was able to pick up on already existing anti-Jewish feelings in the country. During the bitter years of the Depression, Jews had served as scapegoats, and even before this time, anti-Semites in Germany had found willing listeners for their pseudo-scientific theories. Although there was only a tiny minority of Germans of Jewish affiliation (about half a million, or 0.77 per cent of the population), and although most of them were highly assimilated and secularized, their disproportionate role in certain sections of employment, for example in business and the professions, made them easy targets for anti-Jewish agitation and gave anti-Semites a pretext for denunciations and attacks. As Ian Kershaw points out, most people did not vote for the Nazi party because of its anti-Semitic message, but the underlying hostility towards Jews meant that voters were not deterred by the Nazis' anti-Semitic rhetoric, either (I. Kershaw, *Hitler. 1889–1936: Hubris*, 1998, p.410). It should also be noted, however, that the Nazis had toned down their anti-Semitic message during election campaigns from 1929/30 onwards as a concession to their coalition partner (Wendt, p.160). This would have made it easier for voters to ignore the unpalatable anti-Semitic rhetoric, if indeed they ever took it seriously.

Nazi anti-Semitism did not spring from religious intolerance, but was a biological, *racial* prejudice. Therefore, conversion to Christianity could not alter the perceived racial difference of the Jews. This anti-Semitism combined Social Darwinism and racism and claimed to be based on exact scientific knowledge of a combination of biology, human genetics, eugenics and anthropology. By presenting itself as a pseudo science, it managed to gain a peculiar legitimacy (Wendt, p.162). Propagating anti-Semitism had, for the Nazis, the functions of raising a more general race consciousness and universalizing that sense of incessant strife which was central to their world view, in which racial struggle was the determining force of all history. The values attached to anti-Semitism – martial hardness, rejection of common humanity, indifference to human suffering, *a rejection* of Enlightenment ideas – were the values needed for the primitive tribal warfare and domination which Hitler envisaged as the more or less permanent future of eastern Europe (E. Nolte, *Three Faces of Fascism*, 1965, p.516). Sexual paranoia was an important factor in the psycho-pathology of anti-Semitism: the most vicious of the Nazis' racist papers, *Der Stürmer* (which had a semi-official status after 1933), frequently portrayed Jews as monstrous sexual perverts, and many of the worst propaganda films echoed this. Significantly, the element of anti-Jewish legislation which seems to have given the party rank and file greatest satisfaction was the outlawing of miscegenation. Anti-Semitism also accorded with the Nazis' political ideas, especially their hostility to parliamentary democracy and to the fissure between state and society in liberal politics. The inclusion of Jews within the nation-state exemplified a more general process of emancipation which the Nazis strove to reverse. Their anti-Semitic legislation set at nought the category of secular citizenship and was a crucial expression of the new political totality created by the Nazis. At the same time, it was claimed that Jews had a close affinity with Bolshevism, the other declared enemy of National Socialism.

An example of how anti-Jewish measures were first implemented soon after Hitler's accession to power, and what happened to those who put up resistance, is the story of Hermann Umfried, a pastor of the Lutheran church in south-west Germany. In the small towns of Niederstetten and Crelingen, about thirty SA men had broken into Jewish homes on 25 March 1933 and had beaten the men they found, after taking them to the town hall. Two of the victims, 67-year-old Hermann Stern, and 53-year-old Arnold Rosenfeld, died as a result of those savage beatings. At the following morning's Sunday service, the local pastor of the Lutheran church, Hermann Umfried, spoke out against this act of violence in a carefully phrased sermon: 'Only authorities are allowed to punish, and all authorities lie under divine authority. Punishment can be meted out only against those who are evil and only when a just sentence has been handed down. What happened yesterday in this town was unjust. I call on all of you to help see to it that the German people's shield of honor may remain unsullied!' Saul Friedländer outlines what happended next:

> When the attacks against Pastor Umfried started, no local, regional, or national church institution dared to come to his support or to express even the mildest opposition to violence against the Jews. In January 1934 the local district party leader (*Kreisleiter*) ordered Umfried to resign. Increasingly anguished by the possibility that not only he but also his wife and their four daughters would be shipped off to a concentration camp, the pastor committed suicide.
>
> Seven years and eight months later, at 2:04 p.m. on November 28, 1941, the first transport of Jews left the Niederstetten railroad station. A second batch boarded the train in April 1942, and the third and last in August of that year. Of the forty-two Jews deported from Niederstetten, only three survived.
>
> (S. Friedländer, *Nazi Germany and the Jews*, 1997, pp.41–2)

Exercise Reflect on what the above account reveals about how Germans reacted to anti-Semitism. How representative do you think the pastor's behaviour was? ∎

Specimen answer This account demonstrates that not everyone in Germany was willing to accept the new regime's anti-Semitic measures without voicing their protest, but also testifies to the difficulties and hardship one could encounter as a result of speaking up against prejudice and maltreatment of others. The pastor received little, if any support for his brave action, and it would seem as if such heroic acts of defiance were out of the ordinary. It is important to consider, however, what great personal risk was involved for anyone wanting to help victims of Nazi persecution. You might want to ask yourself if you would have taken such a risk. As the new government consolidated its power, it became increasingly difficult to resist such acts of inhumanity openly. □

How did the Jews react to the rise of Nazism? With hindsight, we cannot imagine why any of them chose to stay in Germany when conditions began to deteriorate for them after the National Socialists came to power. And yet, it is important to remember that these people were Germans foremost, and Jewish second. In most cases, they no longer had any affinity with their Jewish roots or faith which now came to determine their 'racial' attributes. They were as German as their Catholic or Protestant neighbours. Germany was their home – where else should they go? They had experienced discrimination before, or at least known of it in other counties and many considered this to be a passing phase, unpleasant but not ultimately life-threatening. The Central Association of

German Citizens of Jewish Faith took the threat more seriously than the average German Jew, who might have been more complacent in thinking that the danger would blow over. Many simply could not believe what was happening to them. As conditions became increasingly difficult for the German Jews, the Central Association and other such organizations concentrated on making it possible for Jews to emigrate. Most, however, had nowhere to go, like the philologist Victor Klemperer, whose diaries of the Nazi Years have recently been published. They provide a chilling account of the fear and hopelessness encountered by German Jews during the Nazi 'seizure of power'. On 30 March, 1933, he recorded:

> Mood as before a pogrom in the depths of the Middle Ages or in deepest Tsarist Russia. During the day the National Socialists' boycott call had been announced. [Klemperer is referring to the boycott of Jewish shops on 1 April discussed below.] We are hostages. The dominant feeling ... is that this reign of terror can hardly last long, but that its fall will bury us. Fantastic Middle Ages. 'We' – threatened Jewry. In fact I feel shame more than fear, shame for Germany. I have truly always felt a German. I have always imagined: the 20th century and Mitteleuropa was different from the 14th century and Romania. Mistake. –
>
> [A few days later, on 7 April 1933, his diary records:] The pressure I am under is greater than in the war, and for the first time in my life I feel political hatred for a group (as I did not during the war), a deadly hatred. In the war I was subject to military law, but subject to law nevertheless; now I am at the mercy of an arbitrary power.
>
> (V. Klemperer, *I Shall Bear Witness. The Diaries of Victor Klemperer, 1933–1941*, 1998, pp.9–11)

The National Socialist programme demanded the disfranchisement of Jews and their exclusion from economic life, but at first there were few detailed proposals as to how this could be achieved. During the seizure of power after the March elections, anti-Semitism chiefly manifested itself as SA violence and local boycotts of Jewish businesses which, although condoned from above, were part of the 'revolution from below'. Partly to reassert its authority over the rank and file and restrain random violence, the Nazi leadership called for a national boycott of Jewish shops, doctors and lawyers on 1 April. Despite the regime's claims, the boycott was not a complete success. In a number of places, the public responded by demonstratively buying from blacklisted businesses, thus registering their disapproval of the boycott. Some Nazis were sufficiently dismayed by the failure to mobilize anti-Semitism among the general population as to suggest that future actions against Jews should be kept secret (R. Bessel, *Political Violence and the Rise of Nazism*, 1984, pp.107–8). Moreover, Hitler's concern at the hostile foreign reaction was such that the boycott was broken off prematurely and the regime turned to legislation to provide more orderly and systematic means for excluding Jews from public life, and one that was less likely to alarm the general public. On 7 April, a hurriedly prepared 'Law for the Restoration of the Professional Civil Service' was promulgated; Article 3 required the retirement of civil servants of 'non-Aryan' descent, while those considered 'politically unreliable' were also affected (the law was passed with the approval of the National Socialists' conservative coalition partner!). Other decrees of the same date aimed to exclude Jews from the legal profession and a number of other public and free professions; as a result of local initiatives by Nazi bureaucrats, Jewish doctors were excluded from the state health insurance system. The effect of these measures was considerably mitigated by President Hindenburg's insistence that those who had been in office or their professions in 1914, or had fought in the war, or whose sons or fathers had been killed during the war, should be exempted from these laws. Because of these exemptions, over 70 per cent of Jewish lawyers remained in their profession (J. Noakes and G. Pridham (eds), *Nazism, 1919–1945*, 1984, p.528). The 'Law against Overcrowding of German Schools and Universities' of 25 April 1933 limited the number of new Jewish pupils and students to be admitted to educational institutions, a first step towards their eventual complete exclusion.

In January 1934, as part of the moves to restrain the radicalism of the SA, the Minister of the Interior instructed local authorities not to extend 'Aryanization' to the economy, and the year proved to be one of relative calm for German Jews. There are a number of reasons why the boycotting of Jewish businesses and anti-Semitic violence did not revive until May 1935, and why the regime waited until the annual party rally in September to promulgate the racist Nuremberg Laws, criminalizing marriage and sex between Jews and Gentiles and depriving Jews of their citizenship. (Shortly afterwards most of the Jewish civil servants exempted under the April 1933 Law were dismissed.) The renewal of SA violence is probably best explained as the stormtroopers' disgruntlement with Hitler's conciliation of the conservative élites and his failure to implement the social radicalism of the Nazi programme; anti-Semitism expressed SA race hatred but was also a tolerated way of venting other resentments. Several factors may explain the regime's delay in introducing the laws. In the early days, the new leaders had to make concessions to their conservative coalition partner, the president, the army, the bureaucracy and the economy, and consider foreign trade, especially with the US and Britain, which might have been adversely affected by strong anti-Jewish actions (Wendt, p.166). Furthermore, there were practical difficulties of defining 'Jewishness' and identifying a tiny, well-assimilated minority; conservative and religious objections; even sheer bureaucratic inertia. The exemptions for Jews who had served during the First World War could only be abolished following Hindenburg's death in 1934.

As a result of such practical considerations and irreconcilable priorities, anti-Jewish policies and measures were often of a contradictory nature in those early months of the regime. On the one hand, for example, there was the desire within the National Socialist leadership to discriminate against the Jews, on the other hand the urgent need for economic recovery. Goebbels made this plain at a meeting of propaganda officers at Nuremberg on the occasion of the declaration of the anti-Jewish legislation of 1935:

> We have absolutely no interest in compelling the Jews to spend their money outside Germany. They could spend it here. One should not let them into every public swimming resort, but we should say: We have up there [in the North] on the Baltic Sea, let's say, one hundred resorts, and into one of them will go the Jews; there they should have their waiters and their business directors and their resort directors and there they can read their Jewish newspapers, of all of which we want to know nothing. It should not be the nicest resort, but maybe the worst of those we have, that we will give them (amusement in the audience) – and in the others, we'll be among ourselves.

That I consider right. We cannot push the Jews away, they are here. We do not have any island to which we could transport them. We have to take this into account.

(Quoted in S. Friedländer, *Nazi Germany and the Jews*, 1997, p.143)

Among the many schemes the Nazis thought up to deal with 'the Jewish problem', the German Foreign Office did actually propose in 1940 to ship all Jews to the French colonial island of Madagascar off the East African coast for resettlement. However, British control of the sea lanes rendered this plan impossible (Stanley Payne, *A History of Fascism, 1914–1945*, 1995, p.381).

The Nuremberg Laws of September 1935 affected almost every aspect of German-Jewish life. The preamble to the third law testifies to what extent the state was motivated by 'racial' concerns. It stated that the *Reichstag* had unanimously decided upon this legislation, 'fully aware that the purity of the German blood is the condition for the survival of the German *Volk*, and animated by the unwavering will to secure the German nation forever ...' (quoted in Friedländer, p.142).

As part of the Nuremberg Laws, the 'Law for the Defence of German Blood and Honour' forbade marriages and relationships between Jews and non-Jews, and such marriages were considered invalid. Jews were also not allowed to employ German women under 45 years old in their households. The 'Citizenship Law' distinguished between 'citizens of the Reich' with full political and civic rights, and 'subjects', without such rights. Citizens had to be of German or related blood (whatever that might actually be!). This law effectively gave German Jews the status of foreigners in their home country. This exclusion was further underlined by the fact that Jews were forbidden to hoist the German flag, although they were allowed to fly their own colours (again, whatever those might be, considering that we are talking about German Jews).

For everyone in Germany, it now became increasingly important to prove one's 'Germanness' by demonstrating an 'untainted' list of 'Aryan' ancestors, a matter that today seems almost tragically comical in its petty concern with detail. The reality of life in Germany for anyone unable to prove a 'clean' ancestral bill of health was no laughing matter, however. Inability to prove an 'untainted' list of ancestors could lead to refusals of marriage certificates, to job losses or denial of promotion, and of course, if 'pure' Aryan ancestry could not be proved, to increasing discrimination. The following citation is an example of questions and answers printed in the 'Information Bulletin of the Reich Association of Non-Aryan Christians' of March 1936, giving an indication of how seriously the quest for definition was taken:

Question: A man has two Jewish grandparents, one Aryan grandmother and a half-Aryan grandfather, the latter was born Jewish and became Christian only later. Is this 62 per cent Jewish person a *Mischling* [of mixed race] or a Jew?

Answer: The man is a Jew according to the Nuremberg Laws because of the one grandparent who was of the Jewish religion; this grandparent is assumed to have been a full Jew and this assumption cannot be contested. So this 62 percent Jew has three full Jewish grandparents. On the other hand, if the half-Aryan grandfather had been Christian by birth, he would not then have been a full Jew and would not have counted at all for this calculation; his grandson would have been a *Mischling* of the First Degree.

(Quoted in Friedländer, p.158)

The years 1936–37 were comparatively peaceful for German Jews and many were persuaded that they could retain a tolerable niche within German society. Nazi propaganda only had a limited success in raising popular race consciousness; although anti-Semitism was a widespread prejudice, relations between individual Jews and their Gentile neighbours were often cordial. Attacks on Jewish property by Nazi stormtroopers were frequently condemned as sheer hooliganism, and police reports noted with regret that Jewish middlemen still enjoyed the confidence of their clients. The Munich Gestapo complained in August 1937 that 80–90 per cent of the cattle trade in one Bavarian locality remained in Jewish hands. 'The deeper reason for it', according to the report, 'lies in the attitude of the peasantry who show a complete lack of awareness of race ... particularly in those districts where political Catholicism is still in control, the peasants are so infected by the teachings of an aggressive political Catholicism that they are deaf to any discussion of the racial problem' (Noakes and Pridham (eds), p.546). Protestant, as well as Catholic clerics opposed the Nazis' racist extremism, as did conservatives in the government (such as Hjalmar Schacht), the bureaucracy and the army; and they acted as a brake on anti-Semitic policies.

During these 'quiet years' the SS, that most ideologically rigid but also most methodical of Nazi power machines, became increasingly important in formulating official policy towards Jews. It pressed for the radical solution of mass emigration and, logically, persecuted assimilationist organizations and encouraged Zionist ones. There were difficulties which hindered the implementation of emigration on a grand scale: firstly, the regime had introduced measures which stripped Jewish emigrants of virtually all their property when they left Germany, so there was a strong disincentive to leave. Secondly, a wave of anti-Semitism in Poland, Romania and other parts of eastern Europe had left a flood of stateless people trying to enter developed countries who now had strict controls over immigration. Furthermore, Britain, the mandate authority over the Jewish Home in Palestine, restricted settlement in order to appease Arab opinion.

A radicalization of anti-Semitic measures was initiated in the autumn of 1937, at the same time as important conservatives were removed from the bureaucracy, the diplomatic corps and the army, and the regime quickened the tempo of its rearmament programme and aggressive foreign policy. The scale of the changes was such as to be likened to a 'second seizure of power', and the quickening pace of anti-Semitism was no coincidence: it signalled the determination to grapple with internal as well as external enemies, to remake society as part of the drive towards war. At the September party rally, Hitler launched his first major attack on the Jews since 1935 and in the following months the 'Aryanization' of Jewish businesses accelerated as their owners came under increasing pressure to sell out at unrealistic prices. The *Anschluss* of Austria ('union of Austria and Germany') brought a further 190,000 Jews under National Socialist rule and led to the unrestrained seizure of Jewish companies by Nazi officials. In order to regulate this rapacity, and ensure that his Four Year

Plan organization benefitted most from 'Aryanization', Göring ordered a general registration of Jewish property which was clearly a preliminary to its confiscation. Simultaneously the regime introduced further restrictions on Jewish professionals and excluded them from many commercial occupations. In July 1938 a decree compelled all Jews to carry special identity cards, and in August they were forced to adopt the additional first names 'Israel' or 'Sarah'.

On the night of 9/10 November Goebbels seized the opportunity of the assassination of Ernst vom Rath, a German diplomat in Paris by a young Polish Jew, Herschel Grynszpan, to instigate a massive pogrom, the *Reichspogromnacht*[1] (or *Kristallnacht,* named after the smashed glass littering the pavements after Nazi thugs ransacked Jewish shops and houses). Grynszpan had probably reacted to the forcible expulsion of thousands of Jews of Polish origins from Germany to Poland – including his own family in Hanover – with an act of protest. He could not have realized the terrible repercussions of his actions. Like the *Reichstag* Fire in 1933, when the new leaders were quick to react against Communists, this presented the regime with an excellent pretext for extending and intensifying its anti-Jewish programme, and for justifying its actions outwardly. As Friedländer points out, the pogrom of November 9 and 10 marked a major turning point in the pre-war persecution of Jews in Germany. Hitler and Goebbels waited until Rath's death was confirmed in the afternoon of 9 November, and at a dinner that evening in Munich, Goebbels, alluding to anti-Jewish violence that had already erupted in some parts of Germany, and that he regarded as an expression of the 'justified anger of the German people', stated that 'the Führer had decided that such demonstrations should not be prepared or organized by the party, but in so far as they erupted spontaneously, they were not to be hampered'. The party leadership was careful to ensure that no written orders existed, but that the regional party and SA leaders knew what was expected of them, while pretending to the outside world that the events of that night amounted to spontaneous actions that had not been organized by the party (B. J. Wendt, *Deutschland 1933–1945*, 1995, p.176; S. Friedländer, *Nazi Germany and the Jews*, 1997, pp.270ff.)

During the violence that erupted that night, between ninety and one hundred Jews were murdered all over Germany, most of them beaten or stabbed to death, thousands were psychologically tormented and physically abused, and hundreds more either committed suicide or died as a result of mistreatment in concentration camps in the following months. More than 260 synagogues were burnt down, many more were vandalized and at least 8,000 businesses were destroyed (Wendt, p.177; Friedländer, p.276). Sleeping people were dragged from their beds, their homes stripped of their belongings, and graves were defiled in what has been called a 'quasi-medieval orgy of destruction' (I. Kershaw, *Popular Opinion and Political Dissent in the Third Reich,* 1983,

[1] Scholars in Germany now prefer to use the less euphemistic term *Reichspogromnacht* (pogrom night) or *Novemberpogrom* to *Reichskristallnacht* (crystal night). The slang-term *Kristallnacht* was coined in Berlin on 10 November 1938, as Berlin residents awoke to streets filled with shattered glass, and was adopted into official usage both in Germany and abroad. However, as Bernd-Jürgen Wendt points out, that night was not just about broken glass, but about an inestimable amount of suffering that was inflicted on the Jews, and the terminology we use to describe such an event should adequately reflect this (B. J. Wendt, *Deutschland 1933–1945*, 1995, p.177).

p.261). Between 20,000–30,000 Jewish men were arrested and placed in concentration camps. The pogrom gave a huge impetus to Jewish emigration: 40,000 Jews left Germany in 1938, and 78,000 in the first five months of 1939. Following the pogrom night, Göring commented: 'I would not like to be a Jew in Germany' (quoted in Friedländer, p.283). The *Novemberpogrom* was just a small taste of what was yet to come.

Exercise   The American Consul in Leipzig wrote an account of events in the city on the night of 9/10 November, based on personal observation and interviews. This is reproduced as Document I.11 in *Primary Sources 2: Interwar and World War II.* What does it tell us about the reaction of the general population to the atrocities? ■

Specimen answer   The Consul describes local crowds as benumbed over what had happened and aghast over the unprecedented fury of Nazi acts. Spectators viewing the wreckage and the gutted synagogues were bewildered. Witnesses to the sadistic humiliation of Jews recalled the spectacle with nausea. The account makes clear that only its perpetrators condoned the wanton violence, although it also indicates how ineffective their opponents were. Those who wanted to help the Jews were themselves in danger of attack, and, faced with the fury of the SA men in the streets, ultimately lacked the courage of their convictions.

Discussion   The reaction described by the Consul appears to have been quite representative of German popular opinion. Although some reports spoke of casual bystanders looting shops and baiting Jews, most indicated a general abhorrence at the senseless destruction, and in Catholic areas the condemnation of barbarity was particularly vociferous. Only a minority, including uniformed Hitler-youths, took an active part in the pogrom, while the majority remained silent and was either intimidated, frightened or disgusted by the events. Many simply looked away. Few actively sought to help, an act that would have required more courage than most were capable of. Perhaps most sadly of all, if criticism were voiced, it tended to be about the physical damage to properties and goods, or the fear of what such a regime might be capable of next, or how Germany might be regarded abroad, following such events (Wendt, p.178). We should perhaps consult other documents in addition to the Consul's account, such as the reports smuggled abroad by socialist informants for the 'Reports on Germany' of the Social Democrats in exile. The following excerpt is from the reports of November 1938, and indicates perhaps a higher level of popular discontent than the Consul's report suggested:

> The brutal measures against the Jews have caused great indignation among the population. People spoke their minds quite openly, and many Aryans were arrested as a result. When it became known that a Jewish woman had been taken from childbed, even a police official said this was too much: 'Where is Germany heading, if these methods are being used?' As a result, he was arrested too. ... After the Jews, who are going to be the next victims? That is what people are asking. Will it be the Catholics? Or will an emergency general capital levy be imposed? One clear example of this was when the SA smashed up a shop after dark and were pelted with stones from an orchard opposite, under cover of darkness ... Many people are

looking after the Jewish women and children and have put them up in their homes. Housewives are shopping for the Jewish women, because it is now forbidden to sell food to them. It has also been established that the violence of the measures taken varied considerably from place to place ... But among the people the action was certainly a cause of great intimidation ... People no longer dared to speak so openly. Everyone realised that the Nazis have got the power to do whatever they want ... The protests by the people of Berlin against the robberies and arson and the evil deeds done to Jewish men, women and children of all ages were plain. They ranged from looks of contempt and gestures of disgust to overt words of revulsion and harsh abuse.

(SOPADE report, cited in D. Peukert, *Inside Nazi Germany*, 1987, pp.58f.) □

Clearly, if the leadership had hoped for a general approval, this expectation was disappointed. The alienation of opinion appears to have persuaded the Nazi leadership that such a tactic should never again be tried, and that anti-Jewish measures should take a more 'rational' course (Kershaw, 1983, pp.257–71). However, Nazi propaganda had not entirely failed in its aim of instilling racism: despite evidence for much human sympathy and good neighbourliness, the dominant concern of popular opinion appears to have been with property, rather than human rights. There was widespread approval of the further legal discrimination and the added humiliation which followed the pogrom, when the Jewish community was forced to pay for the devastation created by the party and the SA. The Reich confiscated all the insurance payments that would have been due to Jews, a total of 225 million *Reichsmark*. In addition, as a 'tough penance' for the assassination of Ernst vom Rath, Göring imposed a fine of 1 billion *Reichsmark* on the Jewish community. In total, the pogrom brought 1,127 billion *Reichsmark* into the state coffers (Wendt, p.177).

Most crucially the Germans were now generally persuaded by Nazi propaganda that there was a 'Jewish Question'. The *Völkischer Beobachter* provided the 'rationale' for such thinking, when it printed Goebbels's summary of the events on 12 November: 'The Jew Grynszpan was the representative of Jewry. The German vom Rath was the representative of the German people. Thus in Paris Jewry has fired on the German people' (quoted in Friedländer, p.280). The violence of 9/10 November was thus portrayed as acts of self-defence.

Following the November pogrom, the Nazi leadership may have concluded that, if the methods to solve the 'Jewish Question' did not visibly offend the sensibilities of the German people, they would be indifferent to its solution. Even before the beginning of the war, more than half of Germany's Jews had been driven into exile. The outbreak of war less than a year later after *Reichspogromnacht* would make an escalation of the National Socialists' anti-Jewish policies possible and would result in the murder of more than six million European Jews. This dreadful holocaust is discussed further in Unit 20.

Case II: Catholics and the Nazi state

The role of the churches in National Socialist Germany is a controversial topic which historians have debated in great detail. How the churches reacted to the totalitarian regime differed and ranged from collaboration and adaptation to a position of critical distance and even opposition. Although we concentrate here on the Catholic church, that is not to say that there was not also Protestant dissent (and approval).

You will recall that political Catholicism had withstood the rise of Nazism until the signing of the Enabling Law, and the previous section has indicated how Catholic communities could be points of moral resistance to Nazi anti-Semitism. What explains this? Chiefly the fact that during and after the conflict of the 1870s (known as the *Kulturkampf*), the Catholic Church had developed a defensive armour against the state. The Church gave the faithful a firm and coherent 'world view' and it had secured a popular loyalty through its newspapers, trade unions and a dense network of youth and welfare organizations. The Catholic ideological community, which was much more homogeneous than the Protestant community, was autonomous and self-sufficient in ways which the Nazis envied and tried to emulate; its autonomy was an affront to their 'totalizing' ambition. Until the spring of 1933, the Catholic Church's attitude to National Socialism was so negative that it even threatened to excommunicate party members.

A cynic might argue that the political views of the Catholic hierarchy, especially in Bavaria, were such that the Church should have been able to accommodate itself fairly comfortably to the new regime, provided that the near paganism of a minority of Nazi zealots was held in check and the rights of Catholic schools and congregations acknowledged. A regime that proclaimed itself the bastion of western cultural values against atheistic Bolshevism was bound to strike a sympathetic chord among churchmen; the attack on the USSR in June 1941 was applauded by Catholic bishops as a 'holy crusade' (Kershaw, 1983, p.340). Many leading clerics were patriotic and authoritarian conservatives who detested Socialism, had a pronounced antipathy for parliamentary democracy and hankered after a monarchical state. The head of the Church in Bavaria, Cardinal Faulhaber, was such a type, though he had roundly condemned anti-Semitism from the pulpit, and strongly protested during the violence suffered by Catholic youth and other organizations at the hands of the SA during the seizure of power, he wished to avoid conflict with the Nazi state with which he had much in common politically. Priestly and lay subordinates were generally behind their superiors in seeking a *modus vivendi;* for example, Catholic teachers' associations at national and local levels voluntarily joined the Nazi teachers' organization during 1933. The National Socialist government became more validated and perhaps more attractive following the Concordat with the Pope on 20 July 1933.

The basic cause of the long-running 'Church struggle' in Nazi Germany was not political incompatibility, but the constant friction of the Nazi *Volksgemeinschaft* against the Catholic 'way of life' with its rich pattern of custom and ritual. In the Nazi ideal, the local party leader would have taken on most of the pastoral functions of the priest, and the ceremonies, which gave common meaning to social life, would have been inspired by National Socialist ideals. Both priests and congregations were determined that this would not happen, and they reasserted the distinctiveness of Catholic culture in response to the 'totalizing' pretensions of the regime. For example, the first mass of a newly ordained priest in Bavaria (often celebrated in the priest's home parish) became a particularly marked demonstration of Catholic feeling and solidarity.

These were occasions for the expression of a form of dissent which was anxiously monitored but proved difficult to repress, although in 1939 the Gestapo banned all festivities outside the church building itself (Kershaw, 1983, pp.196–7).

To assert that the 'Church struggle' arose basically over social practices is not to deny doctrinal divisions between Catholicism and the state. One source of church-state conflict was the anti-Catholic fantasies of Alfred Rosenberg, the Nazis' leading ideologist. He wanted to create a religious myth of the blood community of the *Volk,* a myth so exalted that it would tolerate no values in its vicinity higher than its own. Hatred for the Church – which contested this supremacy (and was allegedly Jewish-inspired) – ran through his writings. It is doubtful whether even Hitler took them seriously (they rivalled his own in tedium), but they had an impact when local party zealots seized state offices regulating the churches and schools and expected teachers to treat them with respect. This occurred in Oldenburg, a northern-German town with a very pious Catholic minority, as the prelude to a protracted struggle over the attempt to ban crucifixes in schools (or other denominational symbols such as portraits of Luther) and to forbid their religious consecration (J. Noakes, 'The Oldenburg Crucifix Struggle', 1978, pp.210–34). The ban, proclaimed in November 1936, was a piece of 'private enterprise' by a local Nazi on the make that appalled the regional authorities who correctly anticipated the public outcry it would provoke. That the ban was decreed at all was due to the chaos of Nazi administration. Protests took various forms: a virtual mass demonstration of ex-servicemen (where a priest declared their determination to 'fight and bleed and if necessary die for Christ and ... the crucifix'); a flood of protest letters; deputations to the Oldenburg government; the setting up of an illuminated cross that could be seen for miles; even the ostentatious wearing by women of jewellery crucifixes. A local mayor warned that 'trust in the state has been as seriously shaken by this decree as one can possibly imagine'. As well as dividing the people from the regime, it split the party apparatus in the districts most affected; many resigned their membership and in one village the SA disbanded itself. In the face of this opposition, the offending decree was revoked. The public humiliation of the Nazi authorities was all the greater because at the packed meeting announcing the revocation, the *Gauleiter* was furiously barracked and the SA and police openly defied.

This dramatic victory over the Nazi state was, however, a short-lived triumph for religious symbolism, made possible by the solidity and piety of local Catholic communities and the simplicity of the issue. In 1938 the authorities were able to abolish denominational schools in Oldenburg (as they had already done in other regions after referenda held under conditions of intimidation), although they felt obliged to proceed circumspectly. When they did encounter parental opposition in the villages, the Gestapo arrested the protesters and sent them to concentration camps.

The 'Church struggle' subsided into an uneasy and partial truce during 1938–39, but then revived into bitter opposition between Christian denominations and the state over the 'euthanasia action' of 1939–41. For the sake of completeness we will touch on it here, although it is slightly outside the chronological span of this unit. Shortly after the beginning of the war, Hitler secretly ordered the murder of the mentally and physically handicapped, many of whom were patients in Catholic and Protestant asylums. The selective Nazi 'welfare' policy did not cater for those considered undesirable, or those who did not contribute to the 'racial state'. The order was inspired by racist-eugenic ideas quite widely current in the medical profession, and resulted in the deaths of more than 70,000 helpless victims. The action violated Christian doctrines on the sanctity of human life and was undertaken clandestinely for fear of popular outrage. Murder on this scale is difficult to keep secret and, inevitably, knowledge of the action seeped out, provoking categorical condemnation by Catholic and Protestant leaders and great public unease. Admittedly many lay protesters did not dispute the principle of 'euthanasia' so much as the utter lawlessness of instituting it by administrative initiative. Catholics were the most resolutely opposed to it; priests organized demonstrations against the action and its most famous condemnation came from the Catholic Bishop of Münster. The Nazi leadership was urged to hang him, but Goebbels advised that this would lose Münster – indeed the whole of Westphalia – to the war effort. Hitler ordered the action to cease. Ian Kershaw has described this as a victory without parallel during the Third Reich for the force of popular opinion in a matter which lay not far from the heart of the Nazi racial-eugenic creed of Social Darwinism. He attributes this to the willingness of Church leaders not merely to respond to public opinion, but to channel and direct it. Sadly it was the only occasion when they gave this leadership in an issue which concerned not merely their denomination, but the most basic human right to life itself. Regarding other atrocities committed against human beings, they did not speak out so vociferously.

Case III: The state and the working class

We turn now to another controversial topic in the historical analysis of Nazi society: the relationship between the regime and industrial workers, particularly those who had supported the SPD and KPD before 1933. The controversy has a dual significance for this course: it forces an examination of the nature and extent of conflict between the working class and the employers and state in Nazi Germany, and it begs the question whether this conflict was a determining factor in the decision to go to war in 1939. In various publications, Tim Mason has been the chief protagonist of the view that class conflict was the 'fundamental reality' of the Nazi system, that it re-emerged in the form of a 'Workers' Opposition' to the regime with the restoration of full employment, and that working-class intransigence generated an 'inner' socio-economic crisis which affected not just the decision for war, but also its strategy. If – as many would maintain – the wars which the Third Reich actually fought bore very little relation to the wars which Hitler appears to have wanted to fight, then (argued Mason) 'this was so because of the domestic pressures and constraints which were economic in origin and also expressed themselves in acute social and political tensions' (T. W. Mason, 'Intention and explanation', 1981, p.39 and *Social Policy in the Third Reich*, 1993). According to Mason, the economic problems of the regime amounted to a 'domestic crisis' in 1938–39, which increased the temptation to solve them by a war of conquest.

The relationship between military strategy and internal, social politics is something we return to in the final section. Here we will explore the nature of workers' opposition to the regime and question some of the significance which

Mason attached to it by drawing on research into industrial relations in the Ruhr coal mines.

The German Communist Party was banned in March 1933, the Trade Unions dissolved in May, and the SPD banned in June. It only took the Nazis six months to crush 'the largest and best-organized workers' movement in the world' (D. Peukert, *Inside Nazi Germany*, 1987, p.103). How was this possible? In 1933, workers were neither politically nor industrially united and their disunity goes far to explain the speed and completeness with which the Nazis destroyed the working-class movement. The parties of the left and the trade unions had been powerless to protect workers against the worst effects of the depression, and with dividing numbers of trade union members the left had no political muscle left by 1932. Moreover, Hitler's rise to power was regarded as nothing more than yet another change of government, a fact which helps explain the lack of resistance by the working class (ibid. p.103). Vis-à-vis the workers, the party followed a 'carrot and stick' policy – while their political and union organizations were outlawed and persecuted from January 1933 onwards, the workers themselves were wooed and even 'bribed' by the regime. At the same time, the terror emanating from raids by SA, SS, Gestapo and police on working-class houses created an atmosphere of insecurity and undermined working-class solidarity (ibid. p.104). The once so powerful German workers' movement did not put up a fight, and many workers were taken in by Goebbels's propaganda, such as the declaration on 1 May of putting an end to class struggle and creating a unity within the German *Volk* (Wendt, pp.231–2). Moreover, the Nazis' intentions were poorly gauged by the trade unions. Even in April, some leaders of the free trade unions hoped that their organizations would retain their independence in exchange for dissolving the tie with the SPD. Corporatist ideas were influential among labour leaders and they publicly offered 'to cooperate in the corporative structure of the ... economy as planned by the Government' (J. Noakes and G. Pridham (eds), *Nazism, 1919–1945*, 1984, p.329). In fact, corporatist policies were never seriously entertained by the Nazis; they ordered the 'co-ordination' of the trade unions, under the provisional local leadership of their own factory cell organization (the NSBO). This was too radical a body to be permanently entrusted with workers' interests and in May new Reich Trustees of Labour (that is, state officials) were created with ultimate authority for the regulation of wages. At the same time the German Labour Front (DAF) was set up under the leadership of Robert Ley as a sop to the workers for the destruction of their unions and to keep the NSBO in hand. With about 25 million members by 1942, the DAF was to become the largest of Nazi social organizations, incorporating employers as well as workers. For Hitler, it symbolized the new class harmony. It was a compulsory organization for all wage earners. An agreement with the Ministries of Labour and Economics narrowly defined its role as educating all Germans at work to support the state and indoctrinating them in the National Socialist mentality. Membership was more or less compulsory for workers and a contribution of 1.5 per cent of a worker's salary was automatically deducted (Wendt, p.236).

The basic legal instrument governing labour in the Reich was the 'Law for the Ordering of National Labour' of 20 January 1934. It brought a neo-feudal division of industry into 'leaders' (employers) and their 'retinues' (workers), set up advisory 'Councils of Trust' (*Vertrauensräte*) to increase the mutual confidence within a company's community, and created 'Courts of Social Honour' to try 'leaders' for maliciously exploiting labour and 'retinue' for endangering social peace. In practice, only small employers had anything to fear from the courts. The key adjudicating role on industry was taken by thirteen 'Trustees of Labour', appointed by Hitler, whose general support for 'leaders' was guaranteed. The fig-leaf of workers' representation was stripped from the system when election results revealed too much opposition and the 'Councils of Trust' ceased to be elected bodies after 1936 although, even before, few had been taken in by the pseudo elections. The DAF's educative and integrative roles were mostly pursued by two welfare organizations established under its aegis: 'Beauty of Labour', which tried to persuade employers to improve working conditions, and 'Strength through Joy', the workers' holiday and physical fitness organization. Workers did take advantage of what was often their first opportunity for travel and tourism, but they appear to have seen this for what it was: the superficial glitter on a repressive industrial system (I. Kershaw, *Popular Opinion and Political Dissent*, 1983, p.313). More than 10 million Germans had been on organized holidays by 1938, and 35 million day-trips had been organized. For the first time, statutory holidays were introduced (6–12 days), and this ushered in the age of mass tourism. However, what was intended as class levelling did in practice not quite achieve its aim. Workers could still only afford the cheaper destinations, and were often regarded as a nuisance by wealthier holiday makers (Wendt, pp.240f.). Behind the veneer of better conditions the state limited, and all but removed, the privileges of free choice of workers, who could no longer freely decide where to live and work. The introduction of the compulsory labour service for 17–25 year-olds, the *Reichsarbeitsdienst,* in June 1935 aimed to ensure that as many 'Aryan' young people as possible worked for Nazi Germany. Earlier, we already encountered some of the other measures designed to limit the freedom of choice of employers and employees alike. In Detlev Peukert's words, 'the labour policy of the Third Reich was an attempt simultaneously to mobilise and straightjacket the workers' (*Inside Nazi Germany*, 1987, p.112.).

Between 1933 and 1936 the restoration of employment and the threat of the Gestapo kept labour quiescent; many were grateful to the Nazis for providing jobs and shared the sense of national revival. But, after 1936, the discipline of the labour market was much less effective and, argued Mason, 'economic class conflict re-emerged in Germany on a broad front' (T. W. Mason, 'The workers' opposition in Nazi Germany', 1981, p.120). Workers' criticism and protest began to make itself heard. It manifested itself through spontaneous strikes, defiance of work-place rules, absenteeism, going-slow, and such forms of collective pressure on employers as threatening to leave *en masse* unless wage demands were met. The last tactic was particularly successful in the building industry where smaller and medium-sized firms had to reckon with the solidarity of their whole labour force. Such was the truculence of workers in the Ruhr that DAF officials had to make wage demands on their behalf in order to maintain credibility. The rearmament boom brought acute labour shortages and the poaching of labour by one employer from another publicized the new balance of forces in the labour market and encouraged workers to assert themselves. By the end of 1938 there were one million vacancies in German industry; labour turnover was so rapid that on average workers were changing their jobs every twelve months. The state had to intervene by directing labour and workers responded by lowering productivity and with poor discipline which Mason sees as 'the direct and conscious expression of resentment against the new measures of regimentation'. The outbreak of war brought no improvement; indeed, Mason discerned in workers' behaviour during its first months 'a broad denial of co-operation by the working class' (pp.129–30).

Assessing the 'political' content of such sporadic and, in the absence of overall leadership, uncoordinated industrial action is obviously difficult. Virtually the only sources at historians' disposal are official (usually police reports) which tend to attribute unrest to unidentified communist subversives and deny large-scale political disaffection. Mason argued that 'workers' opposition' displayed the solidarity of a largely unbroken class consciousness and drew upon notions of social justice nurtured in trade unionism and social democracy before 1933. Workers were manifesting a sense of collective independence fundamentally incompatible with the Nazi *Volksgemeinschaft*. Others have failed to discern in workers' industrial behaviour any general spirit of opposition to the political system as such; they explain it in terms of the increasing frictions in the German economy caused by labour shortages, official wage restraint, longer hours and a dearth of consumer goods on which to spend growing weekly incomes. Detlev Peukert's conclusions are particularly noteworthy: although he characterizes workers' attitudes as 'non-compliance', he argues that 'lack of enthusiasm for the character and policies of the regime, and lack of zeal in the workplace, went along with a wary retreat into privacy' (Peukert, pp.110–17). Similarly, Bernd-Jürgen Wendt concludes that the signs of discontent and resistance which increased towards the end of the 1930s and during the war, such as working slowly, taking sick-leave or producing inferior goods were an expression of an increasing bitterness over pressures to perform, as well as a result of greater self-confidence due to the realization that one was badly needed, rather than large-scale industrial action or collective political resistance (Wendt, p.246).

The Ruhr coalfield is an interesting case in which to test Mason's thesis: labour-management strife had been frequent before 1933 and workers were often politically radical, although divided by religion and ethnicity. Because mining operations were inherently difficult to supervise, the management, through wage differentials and welfare policies, had tried to create a core group of skilled and loyal miners, but after 1930 their wage levels declined relative to other industries, and mining lost the social status it had once enjoyed among the working-class. Germany was extraordinarily dependent on coal for energy supplies and synthetic products (much more so than any other great power), so the labour force was in a position to hold the rearmament programme and the war economy to ransom. These background conditions should have proved fertile soil for the growth of 'workers' opposition', but in fact they did not. Although there were problems with malingering, the regime succeeded in imposing maximum production at minimum cost on the mining labour force. From 1937, record outputs were achieved because of the willingness of miners to work longer, even without adequate compensation. This growth in production continued during the war, in contrast to Britain where coal output slumped (both in aggregate and per manshift) and strikes and absenteeism rose. Of course, terror and the use of slave labour partly explain the German coal industry's far better wartime production record, but it seems inescapable that what Albert Speer called 'the soldierly bearing of our German workforce' was of fundamental importance (J. Gillingham, 'Ruhr coal miners and Hitler's war', 1982).

Exercise   Consider the arguments drawn from Mason and Gillingham and say whether you regard 'Workers' Opposition' as a justifiable term to describe German industrial workers' behaviour and whether we can characterize it as a form of *political* action. ∎

Specimen answer   The fact that there was more evidence for so-called 'workers' opposition' in British than in German coalfields in the early 1940s should have given pause for thought about what exactly the term means. The comparison underlines the fact that industrial militancy and labour-management conflict do not necessarily entail opposition to the political form of the state. The term 'workers' opposition' appears, therefore, to be an interesting but unproven thesis. On the whole, any protest actions by German workers were motivated by personal concerns, rather than constituting a political protest. □

Case IV: Women in National Socialist Germany

'In my state, the mother is the most important citizen', Hitler declared in a speech in September 1934, while Goebbels eulogized that 'a woman's primary, rightful, and appropriate place is the family, and the most wonderful task that she can perform is to present her country and people with children.' (Both citations in M. Burleigh and W. Wippermann (eds) *The Racial State*, 1991, p.242). Despite such clear statements from the leaders of the party, the National Socialists never developed a unified, clearly defined policy or ideology towards women and the family. Moreover, as in other areas, their policies were hampered by a gap between ideological expectations and the constraints imposed by reality (Wendt, p.248). Only 'racially desirable' and politically reliable women were cast as 'mothers' and given incentives to reproduce.

On the whole, leading Nazis had reactionary attitudes to women and were hostile even to the limited emancipation that had taken place. Their policy towards women was illiberal and paternalistic. In the first instance, they wanted to encourage women to adopt their 'traditional' mother role and to produce more children. They introduced incentives to boost birth rates, such as rebates for large families on rent and utilities. Interest-free loans were provided for young married couples, while single people had to pay extra tax (see Burleigh and Wippermann (eds), pp.249f. for this and the following).

The regime attempted to heighten the social status of motherhood, for example with the introduction of the 'Honour Cross of the German Mother' (*Mutterkreuz*), an honour which was given to women who had given birth to four or more children; with Honour Cards entitling mothers of three or more children to preferential treatment in shops; and with the national celebration of 'Mother's Day'). Many women appreciated the respect suddenly afforded to their maternal role. Perhaps they were unaware that the state's real interest was not an elevation of the private status of traditional motherhood, but to support and encourage mothers of the German race (in contrast, for example, with Italy's pro-natalist policy) (G. Czarnowski, 'The value of marriage for the *Volksgemeinschaft*', 1996, p.95).

With a variety of social policy measures, the Nazi state encouraged women to reproduce, supported and fostered marriages, for example with the provision of loans (in the shape of vouchers for household goods, exchangeable in non-Jewish shops, rather than cash!). Over a million such marriage loans were given to German couples between 1933 and 1938, conditional on the wife giving up work. Nazi family policy reflected their anxiety about falling birthrates. One measure to encourage reproduction was the provision that the marriage loans could be 'paid off' by producing offspring. For each child, the loan would be reduced by 25 per cent. At the same time, abortion of 'healthy Aryans' was severely penalized and the death penalty was imposed for this crime during the war (Burleigh and Wippermann, (eds), pp.249–50).

Nazi family policy was only partially successful. Although more marriages were contracted following the introduction of these measures, they produced fewer children on average. (The figures are 2.3 children per family in 1920, and 1.8 children in 1940.) The reason for this decline have been seen in the fact that the marriage loans were inadequate in covering the actual costs of a three-child family, and in the lack of a housing policy to provide the space needed for larger families (ibid.).

All Nazi social policy was essentially motivated by racial ideology. Despite the desire to ensure an increase in birth rate, for example, racially 'undesirable' children were to be eradicated. Part of this racial policy was the supervision and regulation of births, marriages and sexuality in an attempt to 'improve' the race. Loans, for example, were dependent on racial criteria. Nazi family and women policies must be seen against the background of their aim of improving the German race, and of 'cleansing' the racial body (*Volkskörper*) of 'inferior' individuals and members of 'alien races' (Czarnowski, p.95). The introduction of a 'certificate of fitness to marry' (*Eheeignungszeugnis*) which proved 'Aryan' descent and genetic health, as well as a number of restrictive laws introduced in September and October 1935, limited the freedom to choose marriage partners. The regime made it increasingly impossible for 'undesirable' marriages to be concluded, and the certificate was one way of ensuring that the wrong kind of people did not have a chance to procreate. In 1934, for example, a couple applied for a marriage loan, and had to endure a racial examination. As a result, it was recommended to have the wife sterilized for 'feeblemindedness', because she had had to resit two classes at school (Burleigh and Wippermann, pp.249–50).

After the Nazis came to power, many, particularly married, women were dismissed in the public sector to make room for men (a system that had already been mooted by the Brüning government) (R. Eatwell, *Fascism. A History*, 1996, p.126). Moreover, those who took advantage of the government's marriage loans were also forced to stop work. Women were not, however, completely removed from the workforce, and the Nazis considered certain jobs, such as nursing or welfare services, particularly suitable for them. Moreover, general female input into the labour market was essential by the mid-1930s to ensure economic expansion and low inflation. In 1939, the number of women in paid employment was actually almost double that of 1933, although well-paid or prestigious jobs were generally reserved for men (ibid., p.127). By the time they got married, however, women were generally expected to give up work and look after the family.

Many married working-class women welcomed the regime's policy allowing them either to stay at home to look after their families or have a less physical job away from the factories they were used to, while men welcomed the removal of competition on the job market that was brought about by Nazi social policy. As soon as the Nazis had come to power, they removed women from certain sectors of the labour market. Restrictions applied to female doctors, pharmacists, lawyers and civil servants. At the same time, the number of female university students was reduced to only 10 per cent of the new intake. In other employment sectors, however, female workers were indispensable, and their numbers even increased under the new regime. The numbers of female doctors, for example, increased from 2,455 (5 per cent) in 1930, 2,814 (6 per cent) in 1934 to 3,650 (7.6 per cent) in 1939 (J. Stephenson, *Women in Nazi Society*, 1975, p.166; B. J. Wendt, *Deutschland 1933–1945*, 1995, pp.252ff). It should also be noted that the number of industrial workers, for example, actually increased from 1933 to 1934, as did the total number of working women.

As Bernd-Jürgen Wendt points out, one cannot talk only of the Nazis' aim of a 'reintroduction of the honour of the German woman and mother' without appreciating the other side of a system that is basically an anti-humane, primarily materialistic and racially oriented image of the role of women in society. One must also not overlook the issue of forced sterilization and the fact that women in occupied eastern territories were encouraged, if not compelled, to use birth control or have abortions (ibid., pp.262–3). Social welfare was only ever aimed at those who were considered 'deserving'.

In conclusion, it must be reaffirmed that Nazi policy towards women was motivated by concerns that had very little to do with to a woman's private status as housewife and mother. In Gabriele Czarnowski's words, 'this policy should rather be regarded more as a functional strengthening of and control over women's efficiency as housewives and mothers while at the same time undermining their traditional legal status and marriage and family' ('The value of marriage', 1996, p.112).

5   THE ROAD TO WAR

Armaments and economic preparations for war

In *Mein Kampf* Hitler had made clear that he was not interested in pursuing the *Weltpolitik* of pre-war Germany, nor did he make the recovery of the frontiers of 1914 one of his objectives. National Socialists, he wrote,

> have purposely drawn a line through the line of conduct followed by pre-war Germany in foreign policy. We put an end to the perpetual Germanic march towards the South and West of Europe and turn our eyes towards the lands of the East. We finally put a stop to the colonial and trade policy of pre-war times and pass over to the territorial policy of the future. But when we speak of new territory in Europe today we must principally think of Russia and the border states subject to her.
>
> (Document I.22, *Primary Sources 2: Interwar and World War II*)

Hitler made far fewer public references to eastward expansion during the 1930s and his ostensible policy was the revision of Versailles. However, there is evidence that on his accession to power his ultimate goals were unaltered. At a meeting with the German generals on 4 February 1933, Hitler asserted that Germany's economic prospects would improve only when it recovered its military and political power. He envisaged as the long-term solution to the problems of lost export markets and living space 'the conquest of land in the east and its ruthless Germanization' (W. Carr, *Arms, Autarky and Aggression*, 1972, p.22). Although he often spoke for effect, and not all his listeners took his bellicose ramblings seriously, we have little reason to doubt his sincerity. True, the low level of Germany's military forces and fear of a French attack during the early stages of the Nazi regime dictated caution in foreign affairs, in whose conduct conservative professional diplomats initially had a major role. Moreover, Hitler's frequent public declarations of his desire for peace were in one sense quite genuine; his regime had only negligible means of waging war. In 1933, Germany possessed only 80 aircraft and 450 flying personnel, and had none of the reserve strength on which states who had maintained conscription could call. The work of building modern armed forces would take years and Hitler, it would seem, did not contemplate war with the major powers before 1942. In February 1934, when the show-down with Röhm loomed (see above section 3) and Hitler had to choose between the professional army and the SA, he reviewed foreign and military policy with local army commanders and party leaders and for the first time drew up a timetable for attaining his objectives. He anticipated a recurrence of acute economic difficulties in about eight years' time and stated that Germany would then be obliged to acquire living space to accommodate its surplus population and to avoid 'frightful destitution'. Opposition from the western powers was certain; therefore, 'short decisive blows to the west and then to the east would be necessary'. Germany, he said, required a powerful mass army, based on the *Reichswehr*, ready for defensive action in five years and for offensive action in eight years (ibid., pp.36–7).

All historians accept that foreign policy was the sphere in which Hitler's personal power had freest rein; not surprisingly many have taken these and other pronouncements as evidence in support of 'intentionalist' explanations of the course of German policy after 1933. There is some dispute as to just how grandiose those intentions were. Certain scholars (most prominently Andreas Hillgruber) have argued that Hitler's ambition was a world dominion, to be achieved stage-by-stage: after the conquest of Europe and the establishment of an autarkic German-dominated economy (*Grossraumwirtschaft*), Hitler envisaged an apocalyptic intercontinental war between 'the Teutonic Empire of the German Nation and the American World Empire'. The ideological dynamic behind this global megalomania was an unshakeable belief in the racial superiority of the *Herrenvolk* ('master race'). (The argument is summarized in M. Hauner, 'Did Hitler want a world dominion?', 1978.) Other 'intentionalist' historians have argued that Hitler's ambitions were continental, and that his expansionist plans did not go beyond territorial conquest in Russia and hegemony throughout Europe.

Some scholars have disputed the 'intentionalist' orthodoxy. In Britain, one of the most famous critics is A. J. P. Taylor, whose controversial study of the origins of the Second World War you will encounter in Unit 19. More pertinent here are the views of Martin Broszat who asserts that *Lebensraum* (living space) should be understood as an essentially symbolic and metaphorical concept which represented unrestrained power politics in the international sphere rather than concrete territorial objectives. 'Living space', it could be said, had an ideological function comparable to that of the 'White Man's Burden' for late-Victorian imperialists. For Germans, *Lebensraum* connoted the mythology of the Teutonic knights, the ideal of a self-sufficient agrarian community and a master-race of yeoman farmers; it was these secondary significations which made it a crucial symbol in sustaining the dynamic momentum which Hitler had unleashed. In support of this interpretation, Broszat cites the absence before 1939 of any clear thinking on the position of Poland (despite the fact that its geographical position ought to have made it a central component of any concrete notions of an attack on Russia) as demonstrating the nebulous, unspecific and essentially 'utopian' nature of Hitler's foreign policy goals (Broszat's views are summarized in I. Kershaw, *The Nazi Dictatorship*, 1985, p.110). Whether you find Broszat's analysis of *Lebensraum* convincing or not, it is clear that with respect to Poland, Hitler initially behaved with a high degree of pragmatic flexibility, even concluding a non-aggression pact in January 1934 which was quite contrary to the nationalist and revisionist tendency of German *Ostpolitik* (eastern policy) since 1919. Germans had resented the division of their state by the Polish Corridor, Polish suzerainty over Danzig (which local Nazis attempted to overthrow), and successive German governments had refused to recognize the eastern frontier. Hitler brushed aside these powerful anti-Polish prejudices in the interests of detaching Poland from France and of pursuing an increasingly anti-Soviet policy.

While Hitler was displaying considerable diplomatic flexibility, he was also initiating the rearmament of Germany which was the prerequisite to its assuming a power-political role commensurate with its basic industrial and demographic strength. This led to the withdrawal in October 1933 from the Geneva disarmament conference and League of Nations – so bringing Germany's determination to rearm into the open – and could have resulted in international action, but Hitler correctly calculated that Anglo-French differences would neutralize this danger. In March 1935, he assumed equally correctly that Britain and France would not unite to oppose effectively Germany's reintroduction of conscription in breach of the military clauses of the Treaty of Versailles. The military occupation of the demilitarized Rhineland in March 1936 was a similar 'calculated risk'.

The domestic, financial obstacles to rearmament were more serious than the international. Nonetheless, National Socialist economic policy became an armaments and defence policy. For the general public, the early years of Nazi Germany appeared like an 'economic miracle'. However, behind the glittering façade of economic growth the economy was in increasing crisis (a fact that has led to speculation over whether war was used as a means of escaping this crisis in 1939, or whether the crisis was of only secondary importance) (Wendt, pp.210–11).

Hitler was assisted in surmounting the financial obstacles by the ingenuity of Hjalmar Schacht (known as Hitler's 'financial wizard'), the President of the *Reichsbank*, who also served as Minister of Economics between 1934 and 1937. Schacht's 'New Plan' regulated and controlled the entire foreign trade market and achieved at least a temporary relief for Germany's financial difficulties. His ingenious approach to deficit-financing enabled greater expenditure on armaments and defence-related projects, which had initially been thwarted by the falling tax revenues of the German government and the constitution of the *Reichsbank*, which placed stringent limits on the amount it could lend to the state for deficit financing. The introduction of so-called Mefo-bills of exchange (named after the newly founded company 'Metallurgischen Forschungsgesellschaft mbH' which incorporated the four biggest companies involved in armaments industry) helped finance about 50 per cent of Wehrmacht orders between 1934 and 1936.

Exercise   Study Table 17.2. What does it tell you about German military expenditure in the years prior to the outbreak of war? ■

Table 17.2 German military expenditure prior to the outbreak of war

	GNP (Rm billions)	Military expenditure	%
1929	89	0.8	1
1932	58	1.8	3
1933	59	1.9	3
1934	67	4.1	6
1935	74	6.0	8
1936	83	10.8	13
1937	93	11.7	13
1938	105	17.2	17
1939	130	30.0	23

(Source: J.Noakes and G. Pridham (eds), *Nazism, 1919–1945*, 1984, pp.297–8)

Specimen answer   Thanks to Schacht's measures, German military expenditure immediately rose rapidly both as a total sum and in proportion to the gross national product. By the eve of the Second World War, nearly a quarter of GNP was devoted to military purposes. □

Because many of the raw materials (metals, oil, rubber) for rearmament had to be purchased abroad and its export trade was stagnant, Germany was quickly faced by a severe balance of payments problem. This led in September 1934 to the imposition of exchange controls on German importers, an insistence that foreign creditors accept interest payments in *Reichsmark*, barter transactions, and the search for autarkic solutions to Germany's deficiencies. In the interests of strategic self-sufficiency, German trade was reoriented away from North America and overseas regions dominated by Britain particularly to south-east Europe where states could be persuaded to take German manufactured goods in direct exchange for foodstuffs and raw materials, and agree to payment through blocked accounts which could only be spent in Germany.

   These measures brought a temporary alleviation of the balance of payments crisis but did not permanently control the economically destabilizing consequences of rearmament. Towards the end of 1935, Germany's leaders were faced with a renewed crisis because the revival of employment had led to an increased demand for foodstuffs which German agriculture could not fulfil, and a consequent consumer pressure for more imports of food which would have used scarce foreign currency needed for imported industrial raw materials. The Nazi government was reluctant to impair its popularity by introducing rationing, but even more unwilling to slow down the rearmament programme. In this dilemma, the chemicals industry came to play a foremost part in Nazi economic and political calculations: since the 1920s, IG-Farben had been developing synthetic methods for the production of petrol and rubber – methods which were intrinsically expensive but had the signal advantage that they used raw materials Germany possessed in abundance. In 1933, IG-Farben had persuaded the Nazi government to underwrite a limited production of synthetic fuel and rubber; in 1935–36 it won important converts among the Nazi hierarchy for more extensive government support for the manufacture of synthetic materials and the company's directors began to play key roles in economic planning. The support of Hermann Göring, who needed aviation fuel for the new *Luftwaffe* (air force), was crucial to the establishment of the chemicals industry as the economic pillar of the state. In April 1936 he was appointed Commissioner of Raw Materials with wide-ranging powers over the disbursement of foreign exchange by government departments.

Exercise   During the summer of 1936, the exchange crisis intensified; munitions factories were producing much below their capacity because of the shortage of raw materials. In this situation, Hitler intervened decisively and in a way wholly uncharacteristic of his method of rule. He composed, sometime in August, a secret memorandum which is one of the most important surviving documents of the Third Reich. This is reprinted as Document I.12 in *Primary Sources 2: Interwar and World War II*. It is a fairly lengthy document that you may need to read twice before answering the following questions:

1   On what assumptions does Hitler base Germany's future political, economic and military policy, and how does he define Germany's future role?

2   How, throughout the memorandum, does Hitler view the economy and private capitalism in relation to his military-political objectives and his assessment of Germany's national needs?

3   In what way does Hitler's diagnosis of Germany's economic problems, and his proposed 'final solution', strike you as consistent with expansionist views formulated early in his political career? Does the document help settle the historiographical controversy about the meaning of *Lebensraum*?

4   What were the key practical points of his 'programme' for the preparation of Germany's 'vital needs'? ■

Specimen answers   1   In his memorandum, Hitler depicted history as a Social Darwinist struggle for survival and argued that in the present epoch Germany was at the forefront of a life and death conflict with Bolshevik Russia. Bolshevik Russia was a world menace, and only Germany and Italy, on account of their Fascist systems, would be able to meet the challenge of the inevitable clash. It is important to note that Hitler draws a direct line between this 'Bolshevik menace' and international Jewry, thus giving further justification for the regime's anti-Jewish ideology. Although he did not predict when war would actually occur, he forecast its character in truly apocalyptic terms. National Socialism had to educate and strengthen the people for this struggle which demanded that 'the military development of our resources cannot be too large, nor its pace too swift'.

2   Hitler unequivocally argued that the goal of the economy was the 'preservation of our existence'. Therefore, the economy had to cater to the military-political needs of the nation. His remarks are often contemptuous of, and even threatening towards, private capitalist interests. For example, he states that if private industry could not perform the tasks the government set it, then the government itself would undertake them and 'in that case we have no further need for private industry'. (You probably noted other examples.)

3   He maintained that Germany was overpopulated, undernourished and suffering from a lack of raw materials. He saw the 'final solution' to this problem in 'extending our living space', an argument he had been advancing since the early 1920s. The reference to 'living space' is too brief to settle conclusively the controversy over what it meant for Hitler, but the general tone of the document with its quite specific analyses of the demographic and resource problems indicates that 'living space' was a tangible reality and more than just a symbolic or metaphorical concept ('Memorandum on the Four Year Plan', J. Noakes and G. Pridham (eds), *Nazism 1919–1945*, 1984).

4   The key points were the saving of foreign exchange wherever possible, the stepping up of Germany's synthetic fuel and rubber production, and the greater use of poor-quality domestic ores in Germany's iron and steel industry in preference to high-quality foreign ores. These measures were to be taken irrespective of the economic arguments against them. □

Göring was presented with Hitler's memorandum and was made responsible for executing the tasks it set out. The 'Four Year Plan' was not intended (unlike Stalin's 'gigantic plan', in Hitler's words) to create an industrial economy in an underdeveloped society, but rather to make an already powerful industrial economy 'fit for war within four years'. Much economic activity was untouched by the planning organization, the key department of which was an Office for German Raw Materials staffed by *Luftwaffe* personnel and representatives of private industry, notably Carl Krauch of IG-Farben. Krauch was responsible for making Germany self-sufficient in about thirty major products and for allocating a huge slice of total annual industrial investment, much of it destined for IG-Farben. In fact, due to its one-sided emphasis on chemical synthesis production, the plan has been referred to as an 'IG-Farben-Plan' (Wendt, p.421). This overemphasis has inspired the charge that the private corporation was using the government agency to further its own interests, and it certainly lends colour to the characterization of the Reich as a 'monopolies' state'. A major study of the company refutes this charge; although it is true the company prospered under the Plan (P. Hayes, *Industry and Ideology*, 1987, p.178).

Economic mobilization for *Blitzkrieg* or total war?

There can be no question that from 1936 Germany mobilized economically for war, nor that from late 1937 its strategic planning switched from a defensive to an offensive posture, as an amendment to a high command directive of December makes clear:

> When Germany has achieved complete preparedness for war in all fields the military conditions will have been created for carrying out an offensive war against Czechoslovakia so that the solution of the German problem of living space can be carried to a victorious end even if one or other of the Great Powers intervene against us.

> (Quoted in W. Carr, *Arms, Autarky and Aggression*, 1972, p.80)

It is important, nevertheless, to ask for what sort of war Germany was mobilizing its economy. The conventional answer is *Blitzkrieg,* or short victorious campaigns with limited objectives, for which Germany required rearmament 'in breadth, not in depth' and which demanded only a partial mobilization of the economy. The military-economic strategy of *Blitzkrieg* was, supposedly, determined by Hitler's unwillingness to impose on the Germans the hardships they suffered on the home front during the First World War for fear that his regime would collapse internally. *Blitzkrieg,* supposedly, was the military solution to the 'internal crisis' discerned by Mason whose views we have encountered above.

Exercise   In his article in the Course Reader, Richard Overy raises some important objections to *Blitzkrieg* as an economic concept. Read the article, 'Hitler's war and the German economy', and summarize his objections to the thesis of *Blitzkrieg* economy. What explanations does Overy offer for the fact that the German economy appeared to have been only partially mobilized for war until 1942? How does he assess the part played by economic and social considerations in Hitler's foreign policy calculations? ■

Specimen answer   Overy argues that the thesis of a *Blitzkrieg* economy does not fit the facts of German economic life between 1936 and 1942. Hitler planned for a long, continental war of conquest to be fought some time after 1939, when the requirements of the army would be a 'bottomless pit'. The lesson he drew from the First World War was not the threat to his regime of 'internal crisis', but the need for a total and unrestricted use of all resources. Viewed from a prewar perspective, military expenditure was very large up to 1940, and all the plans suggest that Hitler wanted further huge increases even if war had not broken out in 1939. These plans do not at all suggest that Hitler envisaged the easy shifting of resources from normal economic needs to those of 'lightning war'. His military-economic preparations (the naval and fortifications programme, synthetic products) would only come into effect in the long term and made no sense if the prospect was a '*Blitzkrieg* economy'. The fact that Germany's economy appeared to have been only partially mobilized for war up to 1942 was because foreign policy got out of step with economic planning. Economic and social considerations, according to Overy, played only the smallest part in Hitler's foreign policy calculations.

Discussion   Historians have disagreed on whether Hitler decided on war in 1939 due to domestic policy concerns (what is known as the primacy of domestic policy), or whether he made use of favourable foreign policy constellations (primacy of foreign policy). Mason, as we have seen, was a proponent of the former view, and argued that there was a sense of domestic crisis in Germany in 1939. In a subsequent article, Overy has taken issue with this view, arguing that most of the evidence for such a 'domestic crisis' in 1938–39 originated with conservative opponents of the regime and British sources with an interest in the economic appeasement of Germany. If we discount such evidence there were few indications of a crisis, as economists understand the term. Moreover, Overy asserts that 'the working class was demoralized, powerless and fearful'. The Nazi leaders did not generally perceive a crisis, and one cannot, therefore, be invoked in explaining the outbreak of war in September 1939 (R. J. Overy, 'Germany, "domestic crisis" and war in 1939', 1987). This has provoked a lively debate between Overy and Mason (among others), in which Overy was accused of ignoring the critical problems of German trade and industry (which had lost its capacity to meet its orders because of labour and material shortages) and of putting forward a long-outmoded image of Nazi Germany as a unified monolith. Overy reemphasized the absence of any economic crisis in 1939 and argued that Hitler merely used the opportunity afforded by the diplomatic situation and had relied on the weakness of the western powers. Ideally, war with the west was to be postponed for another 4–5 years. □

CONCLUSIONS

In this unit, you have studied how the late Weimar years provided extremist parties with scope for anti-democratic propaganda, and how the economic and social misery of the Depression paved the way for Hitler and his National Socialist Party. We have traced the development of the Hitler state from the *Machtergreifung* (seizure of power) to *Gleichschaltung* (co-ordination) of every aspect of public and private life. We have seen how the lives of ordinary Germans were affected by the policies of the new regime: great improvements were experienced, for example, by those who now found employment and economic stability, or by those who were able to enjoy holidays and a limited number of consumer goods. For many Germans, however, life did not improve after 1933. German Jews suffered particularly, as we have seen, but also those members of society now considered a burden or a threat, such as homosexuals, gypsies, the 'asocial', the disabled. In a state that was motivated by a racial ideology, only those considered 'racially pure' were supposed to enjoy the benefits of the new society. We have also seen how certain sectors of society were less likely to accept or benefit from the new regime, such as the industrial workers, or Catholics. Moreover, women under National Socialism were on the whole forced into a role that encompassed allegedly 'traditional' roles, primarily that of producing children and looking after their families.

While this unit ends in 1939, the history of National Socialist Germany did not, of course, end with the outbreak of the Second World War. The '1000-Year-

Reich' would exist for almost another six years, and would end with Germany's total defeat. In the meantime, life for Germans, and especially for those considered 'undesirable', would become increasingly difficult, if not intolerable. Of course, it was the war that would provide both the opportunity and the pretext for ever more barbaric ways of dealing with the 'problem' of racially or biologically 'inferior' people.

Chronology

24 February 1920	NSDAP's 25 point party programme announced at mass meeting
8/9 November 1923	Hitler-Putsch in Munich
1 April 1924	Hitler sentenced to 5 years imprisonment (released in December 1924)
14 September 1930	NSDAP increases its mandates from 12 to 107
March/April 1932	Hitler defeated by Hindenburg as candidate for Reich President
31 July 1932	NSDAP receives 230 of 608 *Reichstag* mandates
13 August 1932	Hindenburg refuses to make Hitler Chancellor
6 November 1932	NSDAP votes decline in *Reichstag* elections (to 196)
30 January 1933	Following election victory in Lippe, Hindenburg declares Hitler Chancellor
27 February 1933	*Reichstag*-fire; beginning of anti-Communist measures
24 March 1933	'Enabling Law'
1 April 1933	Boycott of Jewish shops
19 October 1933	Germany leaves the League of Nations
June/July 1934	'Röhm Putsch'
2 August 1934	Death of Hindenburg
13 January 1935	Saarland plebiscite
7 March 1935	Remilitarization of the Rhineland
1 August 1936	Opening of Olympic Games in Berlin
18 October 1936	Announcing of Four Year-Plan
30 January 1937	'Enabling Law' renewed for four years
5 November 1937	Hitler reveals his plans for war (Hossbach Memorandum)
13 March 1938	Austria's *Anschluss*
29/30 September 1938	Munich Agreement
9 November 1938	*Reichs-Pogromnacht* – anti-Jewish pogroms throughout Germany
1 September 1939	Germany attacks Poland
3 September 1939	Western Allies declare war on Germany, the Second World War begins

Abbreviations

DAF	*Deutsche Arbeitsfront* (German Labour Front)
DKP	*Deutsche Konservative Partei* (German Conservative Party)
DNVP	*Deutschnationale Volkspartei* (German National People's Party)
HJ	*Hitler Jugend* (Hitler Youth)
KDF	*Kraft durch Freude* (Strength through Joy)
KPD	*Kommunistische Partei Deutschlands* (German Communist Party)
NPD	*Nationaldemokratische Partei Deutschlands* (National-democratic Party of Germany)
NSBO	*Nationalsozialistische Betriebszellenorganisation* (National Socialist shop-floor organization)
NSDAP	*Nationalsozialistische Deutsche Arbeiterpartei* (National Socialist German Workers' Party)
SA	*Sturmabteilung* (Storm Detachment)
SPD	*Sozialdemokratische Partei Deutschlands* (German Social Democratic Party)
SS	*Schutzstaffeln* (Elite Guard)

References

Arendt, H. (1958) *The Origins of Totalitarianism*, Allen and Unwin.

Bartov, O. (1991) *Hitler's Army, Soldiers, Nazis, and War in The Third Reich*, Oxford University Press.

Bessel, R. (1984) 'Living with the Nazis: some recent writing on the social history of the Third Reich', *European History Quarterly*, 14.

Bessel, R. (1984) *Political Violence and the Rise of Nazism. The Storm Troopers in Eastern Germany 1925–1934*, Yale.

Bracher, K. D. (1969) *The Nazi Dictatorship*, Penguin.

Broszat, M. (1981) *The Hitler State: the Foundation and Development of the Internal Structure of the Third Reich*, Longman.

Broszat, M. (1987) *Hitler and the Collapse of Weimar Germany*, Berg.

Bullock, A. (1962) *Hitler. A Study in Tyranny*, Pelican.

Burleigh, M., and Wippermann, W. (eds) (1991) *The Racial State. Germany 1933–1945*, Cambridge University Press.

Carr, W. (1972) *Arms, Autarky and Aggression: a study in German Foreign Policy, 1933–1939*, Arnold.

Czarnowski, G. (1996) 'The value of marriage for the "Volksgemeinschaft". Policies towards women and marriage under National Socialism', in R. Bessel (ed.), *Fascist Italy and Nazi Germany*, Cambridge University Press.

Eatwell, R. (1996) *Fascism. A History*, Vintage.

Fest, J. C. (1974) *Hitler*, Weidenfeld.

Friedländer, S. (1997) *Nazi Germany and the Jews. The Years of Persecution, 1933–1939*, Weidenfeld, (paperback edn 1998, Phoenix Giant).

Gillingham, J. (1982), 'Ruhr coal miners and Hitler's war', *Journal of Social History*.

Gellately, R. (1990) *The Gestapo and German Society. Enforcing Racial Policy, 1933–1945*, Oxford University Press (paperback edn 1991).

Hardach, K. (1980) *The Political Economy of Germany in the Twentieth Century*, University of California Press.

Hamburger Institut für Sozialforschung (ed.) (1996) *Vernichtungskrieg. Verbrechen der Wehrmacht 1941–1944*, Ausstellungskatalog.

Hauner, M.(1978) 'Did Hitler want a world dominion?', *Journal of Contemporary History*, 13.

Hayes, P. (1987) *Industry and Ideology: IG Farben in the Nazi Era*, Cambridge University Press.

Kershaw, I. (1983) *Popular Opinion and Political Dissent in the Third Reich. Bavaria 1933–1945*, Oxford University Press.

Kershaw, I. (1993) *The Nazi Dictatorship. Problems and Perspectives of Interpretation*, Arnold.

Kershaw, I. (1987) *The 'Hitler Myth': image and reality in the Third Reich*, Oxford University Press.

Kershaw, I. (1998) *Hitler. 1889–1936: Hubris*, Allen Lane.

Klemperer, V. (1998) Ich will Zeugnis ablegen bis zum letzten. Tagebücher 1933–1941, Berlin, 1995. English translation: I Shall Bear Witness. The Diaries of Victor Klemperer, 1933–1941, abridged and translated by Martin Chalmers, Phoenix.

Landes, D. (1969) *The Unbound Prometheus*, Cambridge University Press.

Laqueur, W. (ed.) (1976) *Fascism: a Reader's Guide: analyses, interpretations, bibliography*, Wildwood House.

Mason, T. W. (1981) 'Intention and explanation: a current controversy about the interpretation of National Socialism' in Hirschfeld, G. and Kettenacker, L. (eds), *Der 'Führerstaat': Mythos und Realität. Studien zur Struktur und Politik des Dritten Reiches*, Klett-Cotta.

Mason, T. W. (1981) 'The workers' opposition in Nazi Germany', *History Workshop Journal*, 11, Spring.

Mason, T. W. (1993) *Social Policy in the Third Reich*, Berg.

Neumann, F. (1942) *Behemoth: the Structure and Practice of National Socialism 1933 1944,*.

Noakes, J. (1978) 'The Oldenburg Crucifix Struggle of November 1936: a case study of opposition in the Third Reich', in Stachura, P. D. (ed.), *The Shaping of the Nazi State*, Croom Helm.

Noakes, J. (1980) 'The Nazi Party and the Third Reich: the myth and reality of the one-party state', in Noakes, J. (ed.), *Government, Party and People in Nazi Germany*, University of Exeter.

Noakes, J. and Pridham, G. (eds) (1984) *Nazism, 1919–1945,* 4 Vols, *Vol. 2: State, Economy and Society 1933–1939, A Documentary Reader,* 1988, University of Exeter.

Nolte, E., (1965) *Three Faces of Fascism: Action Française, Italian Fascism, National Socialism,* Weidenfeld.

Overy, R. J. (1982) *The Nazi Economic Recovery, 1932–1938,* Cambridge University Press, 2nd edn 1996.

Overy, R. J. (1987) 'Germany, "domestic crisis" and war in 1939', *Past and Present,* 116.

Payne, S. (1995) *A History of Fascism, 1914–1945,* UCL Press.

Peukert, D. (1987) *Inside Nazi Germany,* Batsford.

Roseman, M. (1996) 'National Socialism and modernization', in Bessel, R. (ed), *Fascist Italy and Nazi Germany,* Cambridge University Press.

Schoenbaum, D. (1967) *Hitler's Social Revolution: Class and Status in Nazi Germany 1933–1939,* Weidenfeld.

Stephenson, J. (1975) *Women in Nazi Society,* Croom Helm.

Stephenson, J. (1981) *The Nazi Organisation of Women,* Croom Helm.

Stephenson, J. (1997) 'The rise of the Nazis: *Sonderweg* or spanner in the works?' in M. Fulbrook (ed.) *German History since 1800,* Arnold.

Syring, E. (1990) 'Intentionalisten und Strukuralisten. Von einem noch immer ausstehenden Dialog', in Backes, U. et al. (eds), *Die Schatten der Vergangenheit,* Propyläen.

Turner Jnr, H. A. (1985) *German Big Business and the Rise of Hitler,* Oxford University Press.

Wendt, B. J. (1995) *Deutschland 1933–1945. Das "Dritte Reich". Handbuch zur Geschichte,* Fackelträger.

Further reading

The following is only a very brief list of recommendations. In addition, you could follow up the references provided in the list above.

Roger Eatwell's *Fascism. A History,* 1996, Vintage, provides a concise overview over the Nazi period, as well as other European Fascisms, and is also a useful starting point for further reading. Similarly, Stanley Payne, *A History of Fascism,* 1995, UCL Press, is an informative book to consult on Germany and Europe. Richard Bessel's edition of essays on *Fascist Italy and Nazi Germany,* 1996, CUP, provides recent updates on the main debates, and sets Germany in a comparative context. Norbert Frei's *National Socialist Rule in Germany. The Führer State 1933–1945,* 1993, Blackwell, contains documents and addresses some of the questions addressed in this unit.

On Jews in National Socialist Germany, Saul Friedländer's account *Nazi Germany and the Jews*, 1997, Weidenfeld, is an informative and moving account, soon to be added to by his second volume.

On Hitler, students are well advised to consult Ian Kershaw's masterly biography *Hitler. Vol. 1: 1889–1936: Hubris*, 1998, Penguin; *Vol. 2: 1936–1945: Nemesis*, 2000, Penguin), which also provides useful further references to the main debates among historians.

Students interested in society in Nazi Germany should turn to Michael Burleigh and Wolfgang Wippermann (eds), *The Racial State*, 1991, Cambridge, for stimulating and informative accounts of everyday life in Germany. Detlev Peukert's *Inside Nazi Germany*, 1987, Batsford, offers interesting insights. See also Jill Stephenson's *Women in Nazi Germany*, 2001, Longman, which contains more information of the gender issues explored in this unit, as well as a documents section.

To find out more about Nazi economic history, Richard Overy's account of *The Nazi Economic Recovery*, 2nd ed. 1996, Cambridge, is a good starting point.

On German resistance to the Nazi rule, see D. C. Large (ed.), *Contending with Hitler. Varieties of German resistance in the Third Reich*, 1991, Cambridge, paperback 1994. On working-class resistance in particular, see Detlev Peukert's essay 'Working Class Resistance: Problems and Options' in ibid.

Unit 18 FILM AND RADIO IN THE INTERWAR PERIOD

TONY ALDGATE AND ARTHUR MARWICK

(Section 1 by Arthur Marwick; section 2 by Tony Aldgate)

Open University students of this unit will need to refer to:

Set book: J. M. Roberts, *Europe* 1880–1945, Longman, 2001

Primary Sources 2: Interwar and World War II, eds Arthur Marwick and Wendy Simpson, Open University 2000

Secondary Sources, eds Arthur Marwick and Wendy Simpson, Open University 2000

Video 1

Audio 3

INTRODUCTION

The aims of this unit are:

To discuss film and radio in the interwar years with regard to;

1   perceptions of the First World War;

2   values and attitudes in the interwar years;

3   their place in mass society;

4   their function in national propaganda.

Throughout this unit 1 shall refer to Roberts, chapter 14 'Social and cultural change, 1918–1939', which you were instructed to read in Unit 14. I shall not be setting an exercise on this chapter here, but I should like you to remind yourself of its contents by re-reading it now. Please note what Roberts has to say on the following areas: élites and the masses (pp.382–3, 384–5, 399–401); mass communications/the social and political role of broadcasting and cinema (pp.383–4, 395); post-war 'disillusionment' (pp.392–5); and mass bombing (p.402).

Roberts deals fruitfully, if fleetingly, with film and radio during the interwar period and, inevitably, certain key aspects must be revised in the light of research appearing since he first published his account. He is somewhat inclined, for instance, to emphasize the achievements of European 'art' cinema in the 1920s and 1930s at the expense of pretty much everything else. So he singles out German 'expressionist' films, the work of the Soviet 'montage' directors, and the products of the British documentary movement, under John Grierson's leadership, instead of the ordinary everyday mainstream film programmes that constituted the usual bill of fare for cinema audiences throughout Europe. He privileges artistic merit above popular entertainment and judges films by their 'social purpose' or for advancing 'an aesthetic of the cinema'. But few, if any, of these films would have been shown at 'local' picture houses and most would only have been exhibited at cosmopolitan 'art house' venues for a relatively small discerning cultural élite.

By contrast, however, mass entertainment cinema would have comprised newsreels, feature films, and so on and it is this sort of popular culture which nowadays particularly interests historians of the media as readily as the 'high' cinematic art of the period. Like radio, moreover, where Roberts is undoubtedly stronger in highlighting political purpose and intent, it was a realm that was increasingly perceived as a powerful agent in helping to shape public attitudes within the democracies as well as the totalitarian states. Thus, in addition to the written documents that accompany this unit, we have given you a variety of film and radio extracts which are intended both to further your skills in the critical analysis of such sources and to illuminate aspects that are directly related to our study of mass persuasion and propaganda.

1   *LA GRANDE ILLUSION* AND PERCEPTIONS OF WORLD WAR I

At the end of Unit 10, James Chapman discussed (among other things) the various effects the First World War had on cinema. In my own earlier discussions of the general effects of the war I had introduced the notion of 'mass society'. The war experience did not create cinema and it did not create mass society, but it had strong repercussions (for better and for worse) in respect of both. And cinema itself, obviously, is a central feature of fully-developed mass society. In reminding you once more of that vital distinction between primary sources and secondary sources (and subsequently of the distinction between 'witting' and 'unwitting' testimony) Chapman identified the feature film *La Grande Illusion* of 1937 as *not* being a primary source for the First World War (be very clear about the distinction between, on the one side, feature films, and, on the other, documentaries and newsreels). It is a primary source for attitudes in France in the late 1930s: it also offers some perceptions of the war, particularly relating to the war's effects on social class and the aristocracy, which though, as Chapman warns, we cannot take as primary information, we can use as a stimulating introduction to discussing that topic.

A central purpose of this course is to get you to compare the changes brought about by war with those of longer-term structural, ideological and institutional circumstances. Particularly important with regard to film (and also radio) is the technological factor (an important component of structural circumstances). As you know, both basic film (and radio) technology existed before the war, though there is the crucially important point that the development of large-scale production of radio valves during the war for communication with military aircraft was an enormous stimulus to the development of peacetime radio broadcasting. With film, the great technological innovation is the introduction of sound towards the end of the 1920s – something we can't really link to the war. What we can link to the war, as again Chapman pointed out, is the way that wartime exploitation of film brought it great potential prestige; it ceased to be regarded as exclusively low-brow entertainment.

Jean Renoir (son of the famous painter, Auguste Renoir) had made a number of films in the early thirties, of definitely high-brow status and distinctly minority appeal. The appeal, in particular, was to left-wing intellectuals: Renoir was a Marxist, and a supporter of the French Communist party, though, actually it would be quite wrong to think of any of his films as in any way instruments of Communist politics. This brings me to two vital points. First, Renoir himself was interested in using the unique qualities of film to present stories which would engage audiences and to explore character – apart from a general commitment to humane and liberal values, he was not interested in making propaganda for a particular political cause. The second point is that major feature films do not usually spring from one fully worked-out blueprint, but tend to evolve, often in unexpected ways, over quite a long production period, with contributions coming from various directions (perhaps from the production company providing the funds, perhaps from individual actors, as well as from the director him or herself).

Renoir had served as an aviator during the First World War, going on reconnaissance missions. At one point his life had been saved by a fellow airman. It was a chance encounter with this former wartime comrade which provided the initial stimulus to the making of the film which eventually became *La Grande Illusion*. This other aviator had several times escaped from German prisoner-of-war camps. Renoir was greatly taken both by his stories and by the idea of creating an impression of life inside a prison camp. Thus came the original concept for the film which right up to the very last minute was titled *Les Evasions de capitaine Maréchal* (*The Escapes of Captain Maréchal*). Originally, the film was to focus entirely on a group of French characters in a German prison camp, with purely minor roles being allocated to the German airman who had shot down the eponymous Maréchal and to the commandant of the camp.

Renoir, whose previous films had not been commercially successful, had great difficulty in finding a production company willing to back this latest project. Commercial prospects often depend on the securing of well-known, or well-loved actors. The opportunity offered itself to sign up the distinguished German director Erich von Stroheim, whom Renoir greatly admired, thus launching him on a new career as an actor. Von Stroheim insisted that the two minor German parts I have just mentioned be amalgamated into one major role, that of Major von Rauffenstein. You will be looking at this character and the others in a moment: note that the neck brace, the gloves, the dress and the mannerisms are all the ideas of von Stroheim himself. For Maréchal, Renoir secured one of France's top male pin-ups, Jean Gabin, who was famous for playing rugged working-class parts. Maréchal thus became a working-class figure, and was demoted from captain to lieutenant. To match aristocratic von Rauffenstein, and to enable Renoir to present the developing idea of the First World War having dealt a fatal blow to an international European aristocracy, an aristocratic French Captain de Boeldieu came into the plot – you'll see him in a moment, played with appropriate mannerisms by a famous French *comic* actor. The other main character is the extremely rich Jew, Rosenthal. In the long final sequences of the film, Captain de Boeldieu having created a diversion and been shot and fatally wounded by von Rauffenstein, it is the rich Jew and the working-man-become-lieutenant who escape together, making their way across Germany to Switzerland. Do everything you can to see this wonderful film – if you are lucky it may be shown during your week at summer school. Meantime, you must make do with the two sequences on Video 1.

Exercise   Watch the two sequences from *La Grande Illusion,* items 21 and 22 on Video 1. What impressions do you get of the relationships between:

1   Rauffenstein and the French officers?

2   Rauffenstein and Boeldieu?

3   The different French Officers? ∎

Specimen answer   1   Obviously not harmonious since the French officers and Rauffenstein are wartime enemies and they are his captives. But Rauffenstein seems to have something of a class, and even racist, antagonism towards the French officers other than Boeldieu. They include a Greek scholar and an artist, as well as Rosenthal and Maréchal. Note Rauffenstein's close scrutiny of the scholar's features and his scorn for Rosenthal.

2   There is obviously an aristocratic bond and shared aristocratic assumptions between Rauffenstein and Boeldieu. They are both well-educated, enjoy horses, converse nearly as naturally in English as in their native languages, and in peacetime travelled abroad and frequented the same prestigious social occasions, such as a royal race meeting in England in 1909.

3   Boeldieu can easily share a joke at his own expense with the other, lower-status French officers, but he is definitely not one of them. As Maréchal and Rosenthal recognize when they chat together he is 'a good bloke', 'a fine chap', but 'you never feel completely at ease with him'. There is a 'barrier'. He had 'a different sort of education' and 'if they fell on hard times, the contrasts would be obvious. They would be beggars, he would always be addressed more formally'. However, Boeldieu is more egalitarian in his instincts than Rauffenstein. He is aware of 'the march of time' (here Renoir is sharing with us his perceptions of the effects of the First World War on class, particularly on the uppermost class), wonders whether aristocrats are superfluous, notes their former privileges are fast disappearing, and that there is a continuing process of democratization at work in society. □

What is the significance of *La Grande Illusion* for a course on total war and social change? The first question we must ask is about what it tells us of attitudes in France in the late 1930s. Since the film was the top box-office attraction in Paris and the provinces for the year 1937 and won all the major French film prizes, we can take it that the attitudes which it was taken to be representing were widely popular. Unlike almost all conventional anti-war novels and plays (and the films based on them), this film has little (directly at least) on the horrors of war. One clear meaning of the scenes between the Germans and their prisoners is that of the need, and the possibility, of reconciliation between the Germans and the French; this is driven home more strongly during the escape to Switzerland sequences when Maréchal has a love affair with a German war widow. In general terms, the textbook accounts of this film as being a film in favour of reconciliation and the pacifist cause are correct; Renoir himself spoke of his desire 'to express all my deep feelings for the cause of peace'. But do remember that it was only at the last minute that the adventure-story title was replaced by the title *The Great Illusion*. The title was lifted from the pre-war (1909) book by Sir Norman Angell, which argued that the idea that one nation could profit by defeating another in war was now a 'great illusion' – Angell argued that the nations would simply bankrupt themselves, so that war was futile, and therefore impossible. Whatever, precisely, Renoir's message is, it is very different from that. Shortly before Maréchal and Rosenthal reach safety in Switzerland, Maréchal expresses the hope that this war should be 'la dernière' ('the last'). Rosenthal replies: 'Tu te fais des illusions' ('You are giving yourself illusions'). For myself, I have always interpreted this as indicating that what, at bottom, Renoir is saying is that it is an illusion to think that wars will easily be brought to an end (for instance by the kind of romantic reconciliations which are featured in his own film) – as a Marxist he may well have believed that wars would go on as long as capitalism lasted.

But, to go back to an early point, this is not propaganda presenting one simple, insistent message. There are multiple messages and this sceptical, cynical point at the end of the film may well be taken as being swamped in the more generally reconciliationist (rather, I think than 'pacifist') tone of the whole film. But we also have to give some emphasis to the way audiences took the film. I don't think there was any doubt (from reviews and audience reactions) that the audience did take the film as a pacifist one and, from the point of view of historical significance, I think we can take the film together with its reception as indicating the strongly pacifist sentiment of the French people at this time of 'appeasement'.

What I personally find particularly interesting is the treatment of class and the war's impact on it. Rauffenstein mocks 'the legacy of the French Revolution' and laments modern warfare which brings an influx of conscript officers. (In a line cut from the final release version of the film he describes modern warfare as 'the nation in arms'.) To him the war spells 'the end of the Rauffensteins and the Boeldieux'. It does literally for Boeldieu who dies in agony with Rauffenstein apologizing with the profoundest dismay that he had actually aimed at Boeldieu's legs. Rauffenstein, who symbolically cuts the flower from the plant which he has patiently tended in the grim castle environment, is consigned, as he puts it, to 'dragging out a useless existence'. Do remember that these are fictional characters. Still, Renoir is saying something important about the effects of the First World War which is well worth thinking about.

A film is a film is a film. This was the first of a long line of prisoner-of-war escape films. When you see the whole thing you will be amazed by how many themes and ideas you are familiar with from later films have been lifted from this one.

2   MASS PERSUASION AND PROPAGANDA

Soviet Union

In Russia, after the revolutions of 1917, the Bolsheviks were faced with both external and internal threats. The external threat was posed by Britain, France and America, among others who sent in armed forces in an attempt to crush the revolutionaries. The internal threat was posed by the White forces and those among the population who continued to oppose the new regime. The immediate problems were therefore of a military nature. But in order to mobilize the masses across such a vast country and to secure the revolution generally it was necessary to disseminate the principles of Bolshevik ideology to the many peoples of Russia.

A massive propaganda programme was devised which envisaged utilizing posters and leaflets, theatre, the press and a fleet of 'agit-prop' trains, ships and lorries. The main emphasis was put on the visual media of communication to obviate the problems of differing languages and cultures and here, as Roberts states (p.383–4), the cinema was especially valuable in a country with a mainly illiterate population. All the Bolshevik leaders testified to its significance. Lenin commented that 'of all the arts for us the cinema is the most important'; Stalin called it 'the greatest means of mass agitation'; and Trotsky considered it 'the best instrument for propaganda'. Anatoli Lunacharsky, the People's Commissar for Enlightenment, set out 'The tasks of the state cinema in the RSFSR' in 1919, which you will find as Document I.13 in *Primary Sources 2: Interwar and World*

War II. Its major purpose, he stated, was to reach 'the mind and the heart' of the people with 'revolutionary propaganda'. Read this document now.

The cinema was nationalized in August 1919 and a state film school was established in the same year. Such moves, however, belied the reality of the situation and the fact that the Communist Party did not easily gain control of the cinema. For one thing, the Soviet cinema depended upon the import of foreign films (not least from America) to sustain its exhibition sector. For another, the domestic film industry, like many other realms, suffered from acute shortages as a result of wartime devastation and deprivation. Cameras, projectors, film stock, technicians, artists and money were all in short supply and desperately needed before the Soviet film-makers could begin to provide their political masters with the quantity and quality of propaganda they required.

Some areas, such as newsreels, were afforded priority and granted scarce resources to depict the struggle being waged in the civil war. Although the first newsreels were pretty perfunctory, later series, especially *Kino Pravda* ('cinema truth') which appeared in 1922, presented events in a dramatic and original fashion under the direction of talented filmmakers like Dziga Vertov. But, in fact, it was not until 1924, when the economy began to revive with the New Economic Policy (NEP), that Soviet film production really got under way. And it was only in 1928 that box-office receipts from domestic production exceeded those of imported films for the first time. In 1923, twenty-six feature films were made, but by 1928 that number had risen to 123. In 1923, the receipts from imported films exceeded those from Soviet films by 2,991,064 roubles. By 1928, when 300 million cinema tickets were sold, the income from Soviet films exceeded foreign films by 627,829 roubles.

It was during this period, furthermore, that Eisenstein, Dovzhenko, and Pudovkin, among others, produced many of the 'revolutionary epics' for which the Soviet cinema has become renowned. They served, essentially, to legitimize the revolution and the Bolshevik regime by highlighting the plight of the masses in the tsarist era.

Eisenstein's *Strike* (1925), for instance, dealt with the subject of industrial conflict in tsarist society. In this film, the workers at a factory go on strike and thereafter suffer hardship, intimidation and finally death at the hands of the police and army authorities. Throughout the factory owners are presented as fat, cigar-smoking capitalists, intent only on their own gratification and profits, who care nothing for the grievances and misery of the downtrodden workers and their children. Its emotional message was enhanced by skilful and innovative editing –'intellectual montage' – which juxtaposed disparate images so as to bring out the point being made. Thus, at a moment when police spies are introduced to the viewer, each spy is given the characteristics of an animal, such as an owl or a fox, and visually contrasted with the same, in order to emphasize the base and furtive nature of their roles. Similarly, at the climax of the film, the scenes of massacre of the workers are compared with gruesome images of bulls being slaughtered.

Eisenstein's concept of montage was put to even greater effect with his next film, *Battleship Potemkin* (1926). It was produced as part of the celebrations to commemorate the twentieth anniversary of the unsuccessful 1905 revolution and, in particular, an incident during which sailors in the tsarist fleet rebelled against their officers and sailed into the Black Sea port of Odessa. Again, great use is made of caricatures of the enemies of the working class. And once more there is a massacre of the people, this time in the course of the much praised Odessa steps sequence. Eisenstein's trilogy of films (*October,* celebrating the 1917 revolution, followed in 1927), together with Pudovkin's *Mother* (1926) and *The End of St Petersburg* (1927), and Dovzhenko's *Arsenal* (1929), these amply chronicled the development of revolutionary consciousness – albeit by resorting frequently to the creation of grandly heroic, large-scale if somewhat fictitious episodes in evoking their themes (the Odessa steps sequence, for example, was a wholly fictional and fabricated incident).

The ideological import of these Soviet epics was well recognized by censorship authorities in Britain and France who proceeded to ban them from public exhibition, though that did not always stop their exhibition in private cinema clubs, film societies and other non-theatrical outlets, where they acquired a considerable reputation. In Germany, despite attempted bans, *Potemkin* was released in 150 cinemas and proved a popular success. For all its achievements abroad during the mid- to late 1920s, however, questions were increasingly asked about the domestic relevance of the Soviet cinema and the way it was evolving.

Exercise   Read Document I.14 in *Primary Sources 2: Interwar and World War II,* 'We have no Soviet cinema', written and published in 1929 by Pavel Petrov-Bytov. In what respects did he feel the Soviet cinema was failing to achieve its objectives and why? ■

Specimen answer   It was failing because the films produced were often not watched by the people for whom they were primarily intended. They were, Petrov-Bytov considered, largely irrelevant to the current needs of the people and that is why they did not go to see them. He complained that the leading film-makers were out of touch with the mass of the population and that their films were unintelligible. While he acknowledged their films had formal qualities, he plainly believed that directors like Eisenstein were patronizing aesthetes and élitists, who displayed scant knowledge of the workers' and peasants' ways of life, and therefore could not possibly hope to engage 'the thoughts and feelings' of the masses.

Discussion   It was a scathing attack and typical of those radicals demanding 'proletarian hegemony' but unfortunately for Eisenstein and the rest, they were vulnerable to such criticism. Many of their films had not proved especially popular with Soviet audiences. *Potemkin,* for example, had been taken off less than a month after its release in Moscow on 19 January 1926. Though it was re-released on 15 June following its immense success in Germany it only lasted for a further two weeks before it was replaced by an American film. Moreover, several of their films, including Eisenstein's *October* and *The General Line* (1929), were considered to be ideologically suspect and were re-edited to make them acceptable. Finally, Petrov-Bytov's call for mass intelligibility was a call that was echoed in many important quarters of the Communist Party. □

It had emerged at the First All-Union Party Conference on the Cinema in March 1928, when A. I. Krinitsky, head of the Agitprop Department of the Central Committee urged that more films be produced which would prove 'comprehensible to the millions'. And it had been evident when the Party's

Central Committee took the first steps, on 11 January 1929, to implement that Conference's decisions. The result was that the Party determined 'to use all measures to strengthen its leadership of the work of the cinema organizations' and to aim for greater 'ideological consistency of the films produced'. Subsequently, the importing of foreign films was stopped and the Party exerted increasing control to ensure the cinema would play its full part in mobilizing society to meet the needs of the first Five Year Plan and the drive towards industrialization and collectivization. 'Socialist realism' was now the order of the day and a film like *Chapayev* (1934, S. and G. Vasiliev) was held up as a model to follow. It was, indeed, a box-office success, but most of all its plot demonstrated the superiority of Party organization over individual spontaneity. To be 'comprehensible to the millions' came, in effect, to mean 'in accordance with the Party line'. As one leading historian of the Soviet cinema has put it: 'in the 1920s Soviet film-makers had been able to portray reality as they saw it; in the 1930s they had to portray reality as the Party saw it' (Richard Taylor, *The Politics of the Soviet Cinema 1917–1929*, 1979, p.157).

Nazi Germany

Like the Communist Party in Russia, the National Socialist Party in Germany was determined not just to achieve power but also to maintain it. Thus it too was compelled to adopt a dynamic yet pragmatic approach to propaganda to meet changing needs and circumstances. One of the major charges it had to confront, at least initially, was the oft-repeated claim that Hitler only acceded to office as Chancellor by means of 'backstairs intrigue' in the wake of the collapse of first Papen's then Schleicher's governments. Given Hitler's intention at this stage to follow 'the tactic of legality', it was important to dispel the charge in order to project Hitler as the only leader capable of uniting the country and to establish the popular legitimacy of his regime.

> The way Hitler came to power by the invitation of those bourgeois and reactionaries whom Nazism was intended to supplant, was something which had to be lived down. The Nazi Dr Goebbels, minister of propaganda, understood that very well. After the Nazi accession to power, propaganda by film, wireless and newspaper treated Hitler *as if* he was the leader who had been swept to power by the crowd from outside. Goebbels used the state control of the media of mass persuasion to complete the portrait of Hitler as the kind of leader that crowd theory had always predicted. Of course, this was to a degree fraudulent, the cart having come before the horse. Crowd theory was being used not only as a means, but also as an *ex post facto* justification. This was the true sense in which the Nazis drew a technique of political persuasion out of crowd theory, but they did not thereby relinquish the rest of it, least of all the theory of crowd leadership. What Goebbels did after 1933 was to use one part of crowd theory, its techniques of persuasion, to persuade Germans that another part of crowd theory, its expectation of charismatic leadership, was realised in the person of Adolf Hitler. *Then* the Führer principle could itself be used as a technique to bind the people to its leader.
>
> (J. S. McClelland, *The Crowd and the Mob*, 1989, p.291)

Hitler outlined his opinions on the masses and propaganda in *Mein Kampf* (1925), several years before he became Chancellor. Although the book is nothing more than thinly-disguised propaganda itself, and much of what Hitler had to say about political events or his own background cannot be taken at face value, it reveals a lot about Hitler's views on propaganda and the 'psychology of the masses'. As Ian Kershaw argues, Hitler's views as expressed in *Mein Kampf* demonstrate that he considered the masses to be susceptible to 'almost boundless manipulability' (I. Kershaw, *The Hitler Myth*, 1987, p.3). Despite the book's shortcomings, Hitler's thoughts on war propaganda have been singled out for praise by some historians. Alan Bullock, for example, describes the chapter on propaganda as a 'masterly exercise', although he considers the political ideas contained within the book 'entirely unoriginal' (*Hitler*, 1962, pp.55 and 69). Similarly, James Joll agrees that the chapter demonstrates that Hitler had 'Some shrewd things to say about the value and use of propaganda' (*Europe since 1870*, 1976, p.332).

As an effective example of his propaganda once the National Socialists (NSDAP) had assumed power in 1933, one need only look at the film of the 1934 Party rally in Nuremberg, which was made 'by order of the Führer' and released with the title of the theme of the rally, *Triumph of the Will (Triumph des Willens)*. Leni Riefenstahl was credited with overall responsibility for the production (though recent research would suggest she shared the editing with Walter Ruttmann, who remained unacknowledged). No fewer than 172 people were employed in the production crew, including sixteen cameramen, each with an assistant, utilizing thirty cameras with four sound trucks and backed up by twenty-nine newsreel cameramen, with everybody dressed in uniform so as to blend into the proceedings. Far from being a literal record of the assembly, however, many scenes were rehearsed beforehand and the sequence of events in the film did not accord with their order of presentation in the course of the rally. In all, some 280,000 *Reichmarks* were spent and the result was sixty-one hours of film which, after five months' editing, ended up as a final version with a running time of two hours. The completed film was given its premiere on 28 March 1935 at the Ufa-Palast in Berlin, the city's largest cinema, before an invited audience consisting of foreign diplomats, the highest military staff, top Party officials, and Hitler himself. Few documentaries received the publicity and measure of official support that were afforded *Triumph of the Will*. But then, of course, it was a special case.

Exercise Read the chapter entitled 'War propaganda' from *Mein Kampf*, reprinted in the *Secondary Sources*. Then watch the sequence from *Triumph of the Will*, item 23 on Video 1. The translation of the speech by Hitler in this sequence can be found as Document I.15 in *Primary Sources 2: Interwar and World War II*.

1   How did Hitler view the masses?

2   What did he see as the purpose of propaganda?

3   In what ways did the film fulfil that purpose? (Analyse both the form and content.) ∎

Specimen answers 1   The simple and obvious answer is with a great deal of contempt. Their receptive powers are restricted, he asserts, and their understanding feeble and slow. They quickly forget and vacillate like children. They are ruled by sentiment rather than reason and their overall intellectual level is pretty low.

2   The purpose of propaganda is to win over the masses to serve a leader's ends. To do this it must be presented in a popular form, confined to a few bare essentials and simple themes, expressed in stereotyped formulas; it must reiterate certain basic slogans and generally be emotionally engaging. (I hope you noticed, incidentally, how successful Hitler thought British propaganda had been during World War I in achieving its objectives.)

3   Well, for a start it 'confined itself to a few themes', to borrow Hitler's words, and 'it repeated these themes with untiring perseverance'. The themes covered in this sequence, as elsewhere in the film, are: loyalty, unity, strength, German superiority and, above all, leadership. They are most evident in the course of Hitler's speech but the principal theme is reinforced throughout. The means whereby it is conveyed here, especially, have been well summarized by one scholar as follows (and I hope you spotted some of the points he mentions):

> The stage and the podium are constructed to place Hitler apart from his immediate entourage and, more important, high above the crowd. Here the people are reduced to architectural patterns, deprived of their individuality in favour of some larger communal ideal. This is accomplished through the use of flags, as if they were costumes, to cover the participants and through the distorted visual effects created by a telephoto lens. This reduction of people into masses is juxtaposed to an equally distorted elevation of the *Führer* ... From this point on, Riefenstahl continues to develop the godlike presence that began with motif and music in the early moments of the film. Now the controlling images are the recurrent shots of the huge architectural eagle and swastika and, of course, the forest of flags. Now while the canvas is crowded to the borders with men, we are given a clear picture of only one of them; the rest are supporting characters, faceless and unidentified.

> Standing behind and away from the microphones on a high platform, with hands folded in front of him, Hitler addresses the assembled crowd ...

> Moving from its position on tracks below and to the side of the high podium, the camera records Hitler's speech in a series of shots looking up at him, shots from behind, and close-ups, medium and long shots. These shots are intercut with shots of the faces of the listening audience of flag bearers; indeed, it is in these brief shots that we realize that there are actual men alive in the forest of flags. The architectural setting is severe, and the crowd seems lost in its vastness and in the murky haze which comes from the smoking torches. Although there are some 200,000 men marching in the stadium, we are aware of them only as a mass, not as individuals. At times the screen seems dark except for the spotlight on the eagle, the swastika, and Hitler, but it is only the mass of people that makes it seem dark.

Overall, it is a memorable scene. Maintaining the consistent growth of her principal theme, Riefenstahl has now advanced Hitler to yet a higher level. In his speech, he makes reference to the 'lord who has created our nation'; through the theatre and film of this spectacle, he has become that lord of creation. Now the early sequences of the film assume an added significance; here, Riefenstahl suggests that the *Führer is* the lord, that he has descended to walk among his people, to bring them food, and to receive their vows ...

In actuality, Hitler did not have many duties at the rally. He arrived by plane, observed the events, and spoke to his supporters. With music, motif, and movement, Riefenstahl creates the impression that he descended from an ethereal height, delivered sacred words, and infused the people with his spirit. The title of the film was the theme of the rally; Hitler chose it to underscore the triumph of his will over diverse party factions.

(Richard Meran Barsam, *Filmguide to 'Triumph of the Will'*, 1975, pp.49–52) ☐

Triumph of the Will, then, neatly encapsulated what Hitler expected of successful propaganda. Not surprisingly, it was shown all over Germany, particularly by means of mandatory screenings in schools, local halls and the like, and it continued to be exhibited throughout the period of the Third Reich. Although it has often been held up as a typical example of Nazi film propaganda, in fact it proved somewhat exceptional. For one thing, as we have said, it was made at the instigation of Hitler himself and enjoyed unusually lavish resources. For another, it was made outside the auspices of Goebbels's Propaganda Ministry. Indeed, Goebbels expressed misgivings about the project at its outset, though on completion he recognized its achievements and recommended it be awarded the National Film Prize for 1935 (it also won the Gold Medal at the 1935 Venice Film Festival and the Grand Prix at the 1937 Paris Film Festival). Goebbels preferred to concentrate such direct propaganda in the newsreels and, besides, he had evolved his own ideas about what constituted the best means of reaching the population through feature-length film propaganda.

Although Goebbels shared both Hitler's contempt for the masses and the conviction that 'films constitute one of the most modern and scientific means of influencing the masses', he soon came to realize that sometimes more was required than simply party propaganda. The first Nazi efforts, on assuming power, at utilizing feature film as a vehicle for this purpose – *Hans Westmar, Hitler junge Quex* and *SA-Mann Brand,* made in 1933 – were devoted to the depiction of 'heroism in the Party and the movement', and all were commercial failures. Thereafter, Goebbels was increasingly of the opinion that feature films could be of greater service if they provided 'entertainment for the masses'. Of course, this did not mean that they were wholly escapist, ideology-free or apolitical. But Goebbels was sensible enough to appreciate that cinemagoers would not be sustained on a diet of unadulterated propaganda. The German cinema in the Nazi era had more than its fair share of love stories or comedies, crime thrillers and musicals, as Table 19.1 suggests.

Table 18.1 Film genres in the Nazi era 1934–39

Year	Comedies (%)	Dramas (%)	Political (%)
1934	55	21	24
1935	50	27	23
1936	46	31	23
1937	38	34	28
1938	49	41	10
1939	42	40	18

(Extracted from David Welch, *Propaganda and the German Cinema 1933–1945*, 1983, p.43)

Goebbels was also less inclined than Hitler, incidentally, to do away altogether with American films for public exhibition, and they continued to be important to German exhibitors. However, new found censorship laws reduced the number of American films shown in Germany, and some were withheld for fear of causing disturbances in cinemas. Their numbers were almost halved within a matter of a few years.

But despite calls from more extreme Party ideologues for their total withdrawal and his own concern about the dangers that Hollywood *Unkultur* posed to the true Aryan culture, Goebbels continually refused to ban them on economic grounds, claiming that the cost of removing them was prohibitive. In fact, he did not completely ban them until the spring of 1941 and they finally disappeared from German screens around February 1942.

Table 18.2 Domestic and foreign films, 1933–38

Year	German Films	Foreign Films (total)	American films
1933	114	92	64
1934	129	81	41
1935	92	96	41
1936	112	64	28
1937	94	78	39
1938	100	62	36

(Source: M. S. Phillips, 'The Nazi control of the German film industry', 1971, p.48)

By the same token, Goebbels did not feel that state control of the cinema was economically desirable in 1933 and it was not until 1937, when the film industry was suffering from falling export revenue and increased production costs, that a state-directed reorganization took place. Alfred Hugenberg was persuaded to sell his holdings in UFA, and Tobis, the other large film company, was bought out. Along with four smaller companies, they were now told to work in co-operation rather than as business rivals. But full nationalization of the film industry did not take place until the spring of 1942, when all the film companies were placed under the control of one central administration. It has also been estimated that of the 1,097 films produced during the Third Reich, only ninety-six were commissioned directly by the Ministry of Propaganda. Few of the other films, however, escaped the eyes of the *Reichsfilmdramaturg,* a state official whose function was to vet all scripts in advance of production. He was available to advise producers whether the ideas contained in their scripts were acceptable to the regime. And at the post-production stage, films could also easily be censored or even banned from exhibition. Nothing, in short, would have been shown that the National Socialists did not want to be seen. They controlled the German cinema as comprehensively as the communists did the Soviet screen.

Britain

The new electorate contains an immense mass of very ignorant voters of both sexes whose intelligence is low ...

(Neville Chamberlain, 1923)

The modern, democratic world contains so many newly enfranchised and very slightly educated minds that it is more important than ever before to prevent their being led astray by ill-chosen ideas ...

('False values', *The Times,* 1927)

Democracy has arrived at a gallop in England and I feel all the time that it is a race for life; can we educate them before the crash comes?

(Stanley Baldwin, 1928)

Radio

Radio, as Roberts notes (p.384), provided governments with an ideal instrument of propaganda and the political use of broadcasting was very much in evidence during the interwar period, not least in Russia and Germany. By 1938, of the thirty European national broadcasting systems in existence, thirteen were state owned and run, nine were government monopolies, four were directly operated by governments, and only three were privately-owned.

   Control of wireless technologies in Britain lay with the state. The 1904 Wireless Telegraphy Act laid down that no person could establish a wireless telegraph station without a licence from the Post Office. Receivers as well as transmitters fell within the control of the Postmaster-General when they were compelled to buy a licence from the GPO. The transition to broadcasting came in 1922, when nearly 100 applications were made seeking permission to set up transmitting stations and the Postmaster-General granted a broadcasting licence to a single cartel, a combination of the six main companies. This cartel, the British Broadcasting Company, received its licence to broadcast on 18 January 1923, though transmissions had actually started in November 1922. At the end of 1922, the number of licences issued to receivers amounted to 36,000. But by 1926 the figure had increased considerably to 2,178,000.

   In 1926 the British Broadcasting Company's two-yearly broadcasting licence came up for renewal. The government, adopting in the main the Crawford Committee's conclusions, decided that henceforth broadcasting should be conducted by a public corporation, acting in the national interest and with a Board of Governors whose responsibility was to maintain broadcasting as a public service. The Company was considered the right body to perform the task and it became the British Broadcasting Corporation on 1 January 1927. John Reith, the Company's managing director, became the BBC's first Director-General and was knighted in the same month.

From the outset, public broadcasting in Britain was infused with a sense of purpose. It came, in part, as a reaction of some of the men who laid the foundations of broadcasting to their experiences of propaganda in World War I. Arthur Burrows, for example, the first Director of Programmes at the BBC, had worked for the British government in the war collecting and editing the wireless propaganda of the enemy. He was a great believer in the social potential inherent in broadcasting. So, too, was John Reith, to judge from his book *Broadcast over Britain,* which was written in 1924 and published in 1925. You will find an extract from this book, 'The best of everything', in Document I.16 in *Primary Sources 2: Interwar and World War II*. Read it now. Note in particular, Reith's emphasis on the 'educative influences' of broadcasting.

There was also a strong sense of hostility towards the popular press of the day and the generally debilitating effects it was believed to have upon the population. Against the idea of 'giving the public what it wants' was the idea that it was better that they should be given 'the best of everything'. There was a reaction, also, against anything remotely approaching the sort of commercial broadcasting that had taken hold in the United States. 'It would not have been difficult to make the service a clearing house for sensationalism', Reith commented, but he had a larger, more uplifting purpose in mind: 'Our responsibility is to carry into the greatest possible number of homes everything that is best in every human department of knowledge, endeavour and achievement, and to avoid the things which are, or may be, hurtful'. Along with such well-meaning ambitions there went a strong feeling of moral certitude, a good deal of paternalism and, last but not least, 'the brute force of monopoly'.

The General Strike of 3 May to 12 May 1926 occurred at a vitally important moment for the BBC: in the period between the publication of the Crawford Committee Report and the Postmaster-General's decision to act upon the committee's recommendations. As a result of the strike, furthermore, radio became virtually the sole means of communicating the course of events to the nation at large. Several provincial newspapers continued publication of a sort after the TUC brought out the printers, as did *The Times*. And they were joined after 5 May by the *British Gazette,* the government paper that was edited by Winston Churchill, and the TUC's official organ, the *British Worker*. But the mass newspapers in effect disappeared.

Because the radio was able to continue with a regular supply of news, it greatly assisted the government of the day. Asa Briggs suggests it did so in two ways (see his chapter on the General Strike in Volume 1 of *The History of Broadcasting in the United Kingdom,* 1961). For a start it helped to dispel rumours, doubt and uncertainty, and then, on a more positive note, it spread good cheer and boosted morale. With news bulletins at 10.00 am, 1.00 pm, 4.00 pm, 7.00 pm, and 9.30 pm each day, and a stream of programmes designed to dispel 'strike depression' while reminding listeners of the ' the cheerfulness and confidence maintained by Londoners', it is little wonder the BBC was credited by many with having a steady influence on public opinion.

But there were others at the time who felt the BBC ought more appropriately to be called BFC, or 'British Falsehood Company'. The TUC had from the first warned its members not to believe anything broadcast during the strike because it was likely to be 'just another tool in the hands of the Government'. (One section of the Cabinet, led by Churchill, had in fact wanted to take over the BBC completely and use it simply as another source of government propaganda. Baldwin did not agree to the proposal and thought it wiser to leave the BBC with a 'measure of autonomy and independence'.) The sin of omission, furthermore, sometimes rankled more than the sin of commission. It was not always what the BBC actually broadcast that caused concern but what it did not broadcast. Labour Party members agreed, for instance, that while little was said against the miners, there was certainly nothing said in their favour. Nor was anything heard of the other strikers' points of view. Briggs has examined all the news bulletins from the period of the strike and he concludes that 'there was no fabrication, no attempt to twist or to distort'. But he too makes a point of stressing that 'much news was excluded'. So, indeed, it was. And more went on besides.

Exercise   Read Document I.17 in *Primary Sources 2: Interwar and World War II,* which is a confidential memorandum that Reith sent out to his senior staff on 15 May 1926, and listen to item 1 on Audio 3, a period reconstruction of a news bulletin of 9 May 1926.

1   What would you say was the major factor governing Reith's thinking on the role of the BBC during the General Strike?

2   What does this news bulletin reveal? ■

Specimen answer   1   Reith's thinking on the matter was governed by one overriding argument: since the government was acting for the people in the crisis, and the BBC was a national institution, then the BBC was for the government. There was no feasible alternative in his eyes. As a result, Reith followed the government line and no Labour speakers, for example, were heard on the air. (He did, in fact, consider giving broadcast time to Ramsay MacDonald but a government veto settled that issue. The speeches of Labour leaders and the TUC were reported in the news but they were not allowed to broadcast for themselves.) Reith set great store, furthermore, on his reading of a High Court judgement which laid down that the strike was illegal (a point also expressed in Parliament by Sir John Simon, though the view was later challenged). Of course, as Reith well recognized, the fact was that at any time during the strike the government had the legal right to commandeer the BBC and to order it to broadcast whatever messages it chose, had it wished to do so. Thus, the 'measure of independence' which he won for the BBC was a compromise solution that suited the interests of the BBC and the government alike. Plainly, though, the paramount role, in Reith's words, had been to support 'the preservation of law and order'.

2   A bulletin like this one could do no other than aid and abet the government's cause and it was clearly chosen for broadcast because of that. Cardinal Bourne's speech lent moral force to the argument that the General Strike was 'against lawful authority'. As far as he was concerned, 'moral principles' were involved, the strike was 'a sin against obedience which we owe to God', and it therefore transgressed the laws of both God and man.

Discussion Bias, then, could be reflected in many ways, as this incident well shows. In this instance the speech by the Roman Catholic Archbishop of Westminster on 9 May was reported on the same day. By contrast, a 'peace appeal' for the resumption of negotiations to seek a compromise between the strikers and the government, which was made by the Archbishop of Canterbury and other churchmen on 5 May, was not reported until 11 May, one day before the end of the strike. The delay was caused by the fact that on reading a draft of the appeal, Reith decided to consult J. C. C. Davidson, the Deputy Chief Civil Commissioner and his 'contact man' with the government. He advised against broadcasting it 'on the ground that it would provide Churchill and his group with just the opportunity they had been wanting to take over the BBC' (Briggs, *The History of Broadcasting*, 1961, p.379). Only after consultation between Reith and the Archbishop, and when questions were asked on the matter in the Commons, was it possible to broadcast the appeal.

With the exception of item 2 and item 8 (which Antony Lentin will cover in Unit 19), the remaining items on Audio 3 have been assembled primarily to allow you to follow through the sort of issues raised here on the BBC coverage of the General Strike. Obviously the BBC continued to evolve in the period leading up to World War II. New programmes were fashioned, policies were refined, and the corporation expanded considerably. So, too, did the audience for its product. By 1939, some 8,900,000 radio licences were sold in Britain. This collection of broadcasts will enable you to pinpoint many of the changes that ensued with regard to programme format and content. One can hardly call it a representative sample, however, given the mass of material in the BBC sound archives. There are notable omissions, it must be said, such as variety and entertainment (which I shall broach on Audio 4 when we come to World War II), music, and regional programmes. For the most part, my selection draws upon current affairs sources such as talks, news and the like. It was made on the basis of highlighting topics, issues and presentation. The items chosen are relevant to several units in this part of the course but, as will be evident, all are related to this unit and to this section in particular. Bear in mind the general questions raised so far – not least the matter of the relationship between the BBC and government – and address them to the material you hear. I have posed one or two more specific questions and, to help contextualize the individual broadcasts, have appended some commentaries that bear directly upon them. □

Exercise Listen to the remaining items on Audio 3, from item 3 onwards. Refer to the notes which follow before you listen to the appropriate item.

Items 3 and 4: 'General Election speech' by David Lloyd George (15 October 1931*),* and 'General Election broadcast' by Ramsay MacDonald (24 October 1931).

> ... the General Strike was not the only cause of bitterness between the wars. Anger at obvious bias was powerfully reinforced during the 1931 election, which ended in Labour's catastrophic defeat. If the exploitation of the fraudulent Zinoviev letter by the press was often blamed for Labour's loss of office in 1924, a broadcast allegation by the turncoat Chancellor, Philip Snowden, that Labour's programme was 'bolshevism run mad', was widely taken as a cause of the 1931 calamity. Clement Attlee, one of the few survivors, later described the

1931 election as 'the most unscrupulous in my recollection'. The complaint against the BBC was that Labour had been denied a right of reply. It seemed that in this most one-sided of contests, the Corporation abandoned all pretence at neutrality, arbitrarily weighting the scales to the benefit of the 'National' coalition.

One issue concerned an interpretation of the rules: the BBC decision to treat each of the three elements in the government – Conservative, 'National' Liberal and 'National' Labour -as if they were separate and independent bodies, when, in reality, all were dependent on the National ticket and did not compete electorally among themselves. On this basis, eight out of eleven pre-election broadcasts went to government speakers, and only three to the official Labour Party. A second grievance, after the campaign, concerned the broadcast of speeches by the Prime Minister and the Chancellor during the gold crisis which preceded the election. 'Under the guise of national appeals and statements on the financial emergency', protested the Labour Executive, 'Ministers and their supporters had a complete monopoly of broadcasts'. A third accusation was that the BBC presented National Government slogans as though they were the Corporation's own moralisms. 'On your action or failure to act', the BBC had admonished listeners just before polling began, 'may depend your own and your children's future and the security and prosperity of the country'. These were almost precisely the terms in which the 'National' parties had pushed their 'national unity' platform.

(Jean Seaton and Ben Pimlott (eds) *The Media in British Politics*, 1987, p.135)

Why do you think the BBC permitted these two speeches to be broadcast? Notice the basis of Lloyd George's appeal to the voters and the arguments (and tone) used by MacDonald to condemn the last Labour government.

Items 5, 6 and 13: 'Whither Britain? No. 1 "Taking stock" ' – by H. G. Wells (9 January 1934), and 'No.7' by Quintin Hogg (20 February 1934); 'Rearmament and unemployment' by John Maynard Keynes (23 May 1939).

That the BBC sought to establish itself as a national institution we have already seen. The ease and speed with which it was recognized and accepted as such was due to a number of factors. In the first place it had no competition. Moreover it was in the nature of the programme service itself to fuse together social needs and interests which had previously been separated and unconnected. Sport, music, drama, news – social needs and pleasures which became so rapidly taken for granted as programme categories – entered into new relationships and were transformed by radio. This was especially true of such things as the Cup Final, the Boat Race and the Grand National. These, through the running commentaries broadcast as they happened, became for the first time truly national events to which the whole country could listen. The Monarchy, too, through the microphone, became accessible to the people in a wholly new way. There is no doubt that such programmes along with the Christmas and New York specials were widely regarded as the outstanding achievements of broadcasting before the war. More than anything else they established the popularity of the medium with a public which grew each year. They were ritual expressions of a corporate national life. But the legitimation of the BBC's enterprise, of its service to the nation, came not from the majority audience but from the great and the good who trooped into the studios to educate and inform on every subject, from unemployment to the origin of species: Shaw, Wells, the Webbs, Beveridge, Keynes, Huxley – the roll call is endless. These accredited spokesmen, not merely in the areas of their particular expertise, were endorsed in their public personas by the microphone, and *quid pro quo* endorsed the BBC as an agent and institution of the educational and cultural life of the nation.

(Open University, DE353 *Mass Communication and Society,* Offprint, 1977, p.10)

In broad cultural terms, the BBC was far from conservative. Even in the field of economic or social ideas (when detached from immediate events) the accusation of rightward bias could scarcely be maintained. Maynard Keynes, still officially out of favour, was a frequent speaker, so was William Beveridge. Indeed, the list of pre-war broadcasters, which included many of the most fertile and imaginative speakers of the day, has led some historians to suggest that the spirit of reform of the 1940s had been nurtured by radio during the previous decade. Party or organisational politics, on the other hand, were another matter. The BBC would only countenance reform in the terms of which it approved: 'non-partisan', advocated by speakers talking in an individual capacity, who had been invited on the basis of their particular achievement or of personal friendship with somebody at the BBC. 'Contacts' was a key word in Corporation circles. Trade unionists did not count as 'contacts'.

(Seaton and Pimlott, p.135)

Wells's talk is especially rich in ideas and illuminates many of the aspects I have been talking about with regard to mass society. Notice the distinctly pessimistic note, the patronizing tone, the feeling that World War I was a great watershed, and the fear that Europe is drifting towards another war. Interestingly, later in the same year, Wells set about adapting his book, *The Shape of Things to Come* (1933), as a film treatment for producer Alexander Korda. He initially called it *Whither Mankind?* and we shall see an extract from the completed film, *Things to Come* (1936), towards the end of this unit. Keynes, you will note, ties war in with the tantalizing prospect of increased employment – a link also forcefully made by the cinema newsreels which, once again, you will encounter later. (Keep these two items in mind for future use.) Hogg, later Lord Hailsham, hardly qualified at the time he was delivering this talk as the sort of 'expert' cited in the passages above, though he was certainly 'up-and-coming': 26 years old, Eton and Christ Church, former President of the Oxford Union, Fellow of All Souls, son of a peer and cabinet minister, he stood as a candidate in the 1938 Oxford by-election and retained it for the Conservatives.

Items 7 and 12: '2nd General News: German conscription' (16 March 1935), and 'Sudeten dispute' (7 September 1938), both by F. A. Voigt.

> As for news, it is true that the BBC was in the beginning forbidden to broadcast news, and won the right from the national press to transmit news bulletins only after protracted negotiations. By 1932 it had won the right to run commentaries on events by its own reporters, and to recruit journalists onto its new production staff; yet it did very little with these new freedoms. As Francis Williams observes, 'It is remarkable how little radio reporting contributed to the serious reporting of current affairs ... Right up to the Second World War the BBC was astonishingly unconcerned with radio as journalism'. Undoubtedly the major inhibiting factor in the development of live actuality in news and documentary programmes was the BBC's self-imposed censorship system, whereby *all* material broadcast over the air had to be written down and checked before it could be transmitted. Only in rare and exceptional cases were people allowed to speak spontaneously into the microphone in the pre-war period; in, for instance, occasional live studio debates on carefully selected topics, with carefully selected speakers. The live news interview appears to have been unknown or unthought of in the thirties.

> (Open University, DE353 *Mass Communication and Society*, Offprint, 1977, p.11)

Although his [Voigt's] relations with the Foreign Office were good and his attitude from their point of view sound, the medium of radio itself posed a problem. There was a considerable difference between the reactions to a responsible newspaper and to a popular broadcast. A report on German rearmament in March 1935 [the first of the two broadcasts you hear now] caused considerable press comment and prompted the editor of the *Manchester Guardian, W.* Crozier, to question Voigt's use of material not previously submitted to the paper. (A condition of employment by the BBC had been that Voigt should not broadcast anything not previously contained in his press reports.) He replied that all the information in the talk had in fact been published and he was surprised 'that the particular passage (on the scale of rearmament) should be lifted out'. What to the leader of the serious press should have been familiar knowledge was, apparently, sensational revelation to radio listeners. The very impact of the wireless, as Sir John Simon had earlier pointed out to the cabinet, was the important factor, rather than the content of the disclosure ... Undoubtedly, for the BBC, such incidents reinforced the wisdom of using known and 'safe' people. Journalists had divided loyalties and were subject both to unpredictable pressures and independent thought.

> (Bryan Haworth, 'The BBC, Nazi Germany and the Foreign Office, 1933–1939', 1981, pp.53–4)

The extracts above describe succinctly the constraints on BBC news reporting. But, clearly, Voigt at least continued to broadcast despite the difficult circumstances. Some officials welcomed his engagement by the BBC as a step towards informing the public of 'how serious the European situation is'.

Items 9 and 10: 'Radio Gazette No. 1 – review of events at home and abroad' (10 October 1936), and 'Children's Hour talk' by Stephen King-Hall (9 July 1937).

The first broadcast here is a fascinating example of the kind of compendium news review the BBC experimented with at various points during the late 1930s. As you will hear, it contains dramatized re-enactments of topical events, a lot of sound effects to lend substance to the proceedings, some more lighthearted items, and the announcer adopts an altogether different and jokey tone from that normally employed – this was the era, remember, when announcers invariably donned formal evening wear to read the news. Notice, in particular, the use of an American (supposedly more disinterested?) to report upon 'The Battle of Cable Street', though it is not described in such emotive terms. Notice, also, the commentator's emphasis upon 'the crowd' and 'the mob' which gets out of hand only to be put firmly in its place by the valiant 'cops'. The report, in short, ends up as a fulsome tribute to the British police and the events are presented solely as a matter relating to the question of 'law and order' – an interpretation which was reinforced constantly in many a newsreel story of the day, regardless of the event being covered. The political ramifications of Mosley's march through the East End are completely ignored. Then, the BBC announcer proceeds to mock the American's accent as he leads into the lightweight report on a dog show. This, in itself, proves very revealing. Note the patronizing and pompous air he adopts as he proceeds to spell out the names of the more exotic dogs (quiz shows called 'spelling bees' were quite common on the radio at the time and they generally manifested the same condescending tone). This is a rich and rewarding item which deserves repeated scrutiny for the insight it gives on British broadcasting of the period – the values it represented and the view it took of the audience. Though by no means as rich, the King-Hall talk is interesting because of the way it inserts reference to pressing current affairs into the midst of a 'Children's Hour' broadcast; only to end, as you might expect, with some fatherly advice and a reading from the Bible.

Item 11: 'The cinema and censorship' by Lord Tyrrell (21 March 1938).

I have included this for two reasons. First, Lord Tyrrell, the President of the British Board of Film Censors, was yet another 'expert' of the sort so often used by the BBC. Second, his talk serves usefully to summarize the bounds which the BBC (British Board of Film Censors) set for the mainstream British cinema. Although established by the film industry in 1912 as a self-regulating body, the BBFC's president was in practice appointed by the Home Secretary. And it worked according to a fairly comprehensive list of censorship rules covering religious, moral, social and political matters, among many others. These rules were rigorously applied to feature films throughout the period at both the pre-production stage (with the submission of scripts and scenarios for scrutiny in advance of going into production), and post-production stage (when a film was completed and awaiting the award of a BBFC certificate, without which it could not be shown in a cinema). The rules did not apply, however, to the cinema newsreels, but other means were employed there to achieve the desired effect, as you will learn.

Thus, for example, in one of the better known and well-documented cases, the BBFC suggested to the Gaumont British company on 15 March 1936 that it would not be a good idea if they proceeded with the filming of Walter Greenwood's best-selling Depression novel, *Love on the Dole* (1933). One BBFC criticism was that it contained 'too much of the tragic and sordid side of poverty' and so it 'would be very undesirable as a film'. In contrast they were happy to allow director John Baxter to proceed with his proposed film of A *Real Bloke* (1935). Although it also told the story of an unemployed labourer and 'the pathetic side of life is well shown', the BBFC were heartened by the fact it depicted a character who 'doesn't whine and whimper but tries to keep his chin up bravely'. Spirit and fortitude in the face of adversity were what the BBFC wanted to see on the screen.

The talk here by Lord Tyrrell explains broadly why the BBFC took the line it did. Note, in particular, his concluding remarks that 'The cinema caters for millions whereas other forms of art cater only for thousands' and that 'To a degree which has not been reached by any other form of entertainment, the cinema is the resort of the family'. He appears to have forgotten the existence of radio, it is true. But given that there were between 18 and 20 million people frequenting the cinema each and every week in Britain at the time, he was right to single out the cinema as the mass medium *par excellence.* ■

Newsreels

For this section, I would like you to begin immediately with an analysis of the film evidence I have assembled, without any preamble from myself. We shall then discuss the background to these documents. Once again, my selection of source material cannot claim to be either representative or comprehensive. The newsreel libraries for the period contain many millions of feet of film. My choice was made this time in order to highlight certain themes, some of which I have already broached, some of which are new. Please watch the items in the order I specify. There are only a couple of occasions, in fact, when my preferred viewing order differs from the running order you will find on Video 1.

Exercise   Watch the following items on Video 1:

Item 14: 'Hunger trek ends', British Paramount News, Issue No.175, 31 October 1932.

Item 11: 'Jarrow unemployed march to London', British Movietone News, Issue Vol. 8 No. 383A, 8 October 1936.

Item 12: 'Jarrow marchers reach London', British Movietone News, Issue Vol.8 No.387, 2 November 1936.

Item 13: 'Demonstration – police kept busy by street clashes in a tale of two cities', British Movietone News, Issue Vol.8 No.383A, 8 October 1936.

1   What obvious points of contrast do you detect in the newsreel presentation of the NUWM Hunger March story and the two stories on the Jarrow March?

2   What contrasts, once again, are being drawn in the depiction of the East End street clashes (remember, here, the BBC sound coverage of the same event, 'The Battle of Cable Street') and the Paris demonstrations?

3   What would you say was the overall purpose behind the newsreel characterization of the NUWM story and the East End story? ■

Specimen answers   1   Well, I trust you noticed straight away that the Jarrow march received sympathetic and favourable treatment in a way that the earlier NUWM march did not. The coverage of the first march, in 1932, makes reference to 'extremist speeches', it stresses that the Hyde Park meeting was 'completely disorganized' and got out of hand when 'the hooligan element' took over. Although it concedes that 'ruffians unconnected with the marchers' caused the bother, nevertheless 'mob' violence ensues and rioting is brought to an end only by the timely intervention of the police.

By contrast, as you see, the 1936 Jarrow 'crusade' was greeted by the newsreels, as indeed it was by much of the news media, in terms of positive approval. It was 'an orderly demonstration' with 'a deserving object', later, in the second report, reiterated as 'most orderly' and 'their object ... a worthy one'. Mind you, the newsreels are still selective in their treatment. They minimize many of the larger issues at stake by concentrating upon the plight of one town – a notorious 'black spot' – and they personalize the story by highlighting some of the individuals involved, notably the MP, Ellen Wilkinson. Notice we are not told that she was an MP for the Labour Party. (But then this was an unsurprising omission, really, given the supposedly non-partisan nature of the march and the fact that it was not overtly anti-government. The local Conservative agent also accompanied it for part of the way.) In short, this was considered to be a respectable march conducted by responsible people. Thus, the newsreel's sympathies were clear, their approbation obvious, the march was sanctioned, space was found to mention such comforting features as the presence of a dog 'that joined the crusade', and, in all, the event merited, as you hear, a constant stream of good wishes for 'a happy march' and 'the very best of luck'.

2   The immediate point being made is that the riots in France 'appear' more violent than they do in Britain. And this was a common enough feature in British newsreels of the day – the current situation was always presented as being worse abroad than in Britain. They were nothing if not patriotic and nationalistic, as you would expect, and we shall see more examples of this trait shortly. In the final analysis, however, I hope you spotted just how comforting and reassuring this story was, whether dealing with France or Britain. Indeed, the commentary goes out of its way to stress that these pictures should not lead one to infer there is profound 'political upheaval' in either country. The implication is that these are only rare and unusual outbursts and are easily contained. How could things be otherwise when there is always a French gendarme or British bobby on hand, to restore law and order? 'It's not a riot. It's a policeman's holiday' the commentary states. Which reminds me of the interpretation forthcoming in the BBC coverage of Mosley's British Union of Fascists march through the East End, and leads on to the final point.

3   Once again, as with the BBC, the newsreels were especially prone to present issues like the NUWM march and the BUF demonstration without adequate contextualization or analysis. They were incorporated within the framework largely of one specific debate, that of 'law and order' news, and served, quite simply, as an excuse for a panegyric on the British police.

Discussion   Where, though, did the newsreel companies find the inspiration for the line they took? Well, the agenda for the media coverage of the NUWM marches, for instance, was very much set by the government response to them. It viewed them with hostility and, as J. Stevenson and C. Cook have argued, sought 'to give a lead to public opinion by suggesting that the [NUWM] hunger marches were a major threat to public order' (*The Slump*, 1977, p.222). Sir John Gilmour, the Home Secretary of the day, vehemently condemned the first of the NUWM marches in the House of Commons on 19 October 1932, even before it arrived in London. (It was also disowned by the Labour Party, incidentally.) He pointed out that the NUWM had close connections with the Communist Party of Great Britain and cited an article in the *Daily Worker* which called for 'mass struggle in the streets'. Subsequently, the bulk of the British news media took up the same line, adopted an antagonistic stance, and denounced them accordingly. The newsreels were little different, as we have seen, except that they tended to ignore most of the political connotations and their reportage, such as it was, rested solely on emphasizing the general threat to public order.

The Jarrow march escaped this sort of vilification, basically because it was considered to be of a 'non-political' nature and because its organizers consciously disavowed any sort of connection with the NUWM or the Communist Party. They rejected the former's offer of co-operation and carefully followed the stringent conditions laid down by the police for their march.

Still, the government view on law and order provided a ready-made mould into which any such story could be cast. And the newsreel depiction of the marches by the BUF showed, once again, much the same sort of emphasis and reassurance. Indeed, if anything, it revealed even less inclination to delve into the issues at stake. To add to the BBC and newsreel stories I have given you, take a look finally at the script for the Universal Talking News report on 'The Battle of Cable Street'. Unfortunately, in this case I do not have the film which accompanied the report but the script for the commentary alone is revealing enough and bears out the points I have been making. In view of what you have already seen and heard, I think you will agree. Anyway, the story in Universal Issue No. 652 for 8 October 1936 read as follows:

> All this shemozzle arose because one man in whom a lot of people placed faith said 'We'll take a walk through the East End of London'. Then several other men, in whom a lot of people placed faith, said 'Not on your ———— life, you don't.' Then the police said 'Now, now, you children, you can't do that there 'ere', and started sorting them out. It wasn't easy but they did it because if you want to place faith anywhere safe, put your money on the police.

> Batons and truncheons were drawn, exhibited quite a lot, but used comparatively little. A look was usually sufficient. A hundred arrests were made and, while watching, I realised how right film stars don't know they are when they say, 'I think your police are wonderful.' The way they kept their heads in the middle of a mob which had lost theirs, was an object lesson. Watch how this baton doesn't hit! You've read all about the whys and wherefores of the riot, so I needn't go into that ... it's been written about enough, or too much, already. But

whatever colour of political roulette you back, pink, red or black, every perfervid party punter will, I think, agree that blue is a wonderful saver.

The fact that the clashes on Sunday 4 October proved the final straw before the government set about legislating for its Public Order Act was subsequently acknowledged by Universal, albeit briefly and in the same lighthearted, punning vein. Its Issue No.675 for 28 December 1936 contained a short item looking back on the events in October, which stated:

> Disorderly scenes in London's East End, caused by the clashing of political factions, took place and gave rise to a few new laws regulating or banning the use of uniforms for political bodies ... Arthur and Ernest didn't want them – it was Oswald Mosley.

Beyond that Universal was not prepared to comment. But then that was virtually as far as any newsreel was prepared to go in reporting upon these matters. □

Exercise   Now watch the following items on Video 1:

Item 15: 'General Election section', Gaumont British News, Issue No.192, 31 October 1935.

Item 16: 'National Government returned', Gaumont British News, Issue No.197, 18 November 1935.

Item 10: 'The Prime Minister speaks out', Gaumont British News, Issue No.303, 23 November 1936.

Item 24: 'The world today', Gaumont British News, Issue No.278, 27 August 1936.

1   Compare the treatment of Attlee's speech with that afforded to Baldwin in the first item. Which one, would you say, did the newsreel favour and in what ways does the report on the election results further substantiate the newsreel producer's attitude?

2   To judge from the last two stories, in particular, what picture did the newsreels present of the state and condition of Britain, and how did they seek to convey it? ■

Specimen answers   1   The opening title to this story, of course, insists that Gaumont British is 'non-party' in regard to the forthcoming general election. Yet despite that fact, and the obvious attempt to achieve a balance of sorts by including speeches from the Labour leader and the Prime Minister, it is pretty obvious the newsreel favours Baldwin. Attlee looks distinctly uncomfortable, being precariously perched on the edge of an armchair with his notes balanced on his knees. He is hardly very convincing when delivering his speech and altogether looks ill at ease. By contrast, Baldwin is set in what appears to be typical prime ministerial splendour and talks with authority, as befitting a man who has already accumulated considerable experience in office. The partisan attitude of the newsreel company is reinforced, furthermore, with its coverage of the election results where it clearly contrives to emphasize that the country took the right and proper course in electing Baldwin's national government – did you notice the way in which Baldwin's speech was selectively re-edited and re-used, with captions added to spotlight the measure of agreement between Baldwin and the electorate, between the leader and the led?

2 Both stories obviously stress that Britain is best, not least when compared with conditions abroad. In both instances there is a cursory review of the turbulent state of affairs existing in other countries accompanied by a heartening and reassuring report upon the situation obtaining in Britain. In the first example, of course, the message is self-evident and the country's case is plainly outlined in glowing terms by the Prime Minister. It is a pretty straightforward state of the nation speech and all very predictable, you might say, with the newsreels simply presenting the Prime Minister's assessment for endorsement. (All five of the newsreel companies, incidentally, carried exactly the same story on the same release date though Paramount entitled it, 'Premier takes stock, finds Britain best'.)

But the last story goes further and illustrates the way in which the newsreels utilized the full array of cinematographic effects to achieve their purpose. It is especially well constructed with its literary turn of phrase ('fortunate Britain ... the rock of steadying influence amid the eddying stream of world affairs'; 'Britain's industries ... have arisen from the slough of despond which clogged the wheels of progress in the depression of the last decade'), some neat visual touches (notice the wipe from foreign to home affairs), and the calculated use of comforting imagery and symbols (everything from rural idyllic country cottages to the Queen Mary – 'unquestionably supreme upon the mercantile lanes of the sea', from 'the vital factor of British justice' to the power and might of the armed forces, then, at the end, the royal family is dutifully and patriotically trooped out to bring the proceedings to a suitable climax and to reinforce the overall message that Britain is definitely best).

Discussion The newsreels, then, as you have seen, were nothing if not highly partisan in their approach to political issues, politicians and current affairs. For all that they consciously invoked the neutral ideology of the contemporary news media and supposedly sought to manifest the professional goals of balance, fairness and impartiality, in fact they invariably selected and interpreted the news within a framework which supported the government of the day. Indeed, they went even further than these film reports might suggest in ensuring that the 'correct' views and opinions came across in the manner that was intended.

The historian, John Ramsden, tells us that in the case of the Baldwin pre-general election story, a special set was constructed so that he would appear convincingly as in a prime minister's study, with the solid looking desk, imposing columns, and all the other trappings of authority you see. By contrast, as Ramsden points out, Attlee looks as if he has been placed in a traditional suburban sitting room. There again, Baldwin was provided with a roller mechanism carrying his speech, which was attached to the camera and allowed him to talk comfortably. Attlee, of course, looks down constantly to read from his notes. Last, but not least, Baldwin had a distinct advantage over Attlee in that he had been shown a copy of the latter's speech in advance of it being recorded and so could amend his own speech to anticipate his opponent's arguments – though this bit of sharp practice owed more to Conservative Central Office than the newsreel companies (see John Ramsden, 'Baldwin and film', 1982, pp.126–43)

The Baldwin speech on the state of the nation is perhaps less impressively rendered. But then that was actually filmed in Downing Street, under less favourable and controlled conditions, and in something of a rush. Notice the date of the release, 23 November 1936 – barely a week or so before the Abdication Crisis became public knowledge. (Three newsreel stories of the Abdication crisis are included on Video 1, items 17–19, for you to follow through coverage of the matter.) The newsreel reaction to the constitutional crisis, like much of the rest of the British media, was to follow the line dictated by Baldwin, which was to say nothing at all until they had something positive to report, namely the advent of a new king in George VI. Then, as with so many other matters, the newsreels largely ignored the controversial and potentially divisive aspects surrounding the issue. After all, they had spent so much time glorying in the image of the monarchy in earlier stories – such as 'The World Today' which was, by the way, originally meant to be titled 'Wonderful Britain' – that to do otherwise would have undermined their point about the essentially stable nature of the country, and the idea they had conjured of the nation as one great family with the monarchy at its head. Hence they settled for the course of action they followed when the story of Edward VIII's intention to abdicate became public knowledge. But the timing of release to the cinemas of this particular speech by Baldwin, a week before the crisis story broke, shows it was clearly intended to prepare the way and to reassure the country at large about the state of the nation in anticipation of the dramatic events that were to follow. □

There were, however, some matters the newsreels did not wish to play down or defuse in the manner they employed over the abdication crisis. Rearmament was one such issue. It was given increasing prominence as the European situation gradually worsened throughout the latter half of the 1930s and here, it is evident, the newsreels felt they had an important job to do in 'educating the public'. Once again, though, it is interesting to note how closely this process of 'psychological rearmament', as it has been described, linked with the official government view of the matter. The final selection of newsreel items in this section has been chosen to highlight the process at work.

Watch the following items on Video 1, referring to the notes below in advance of the appropriate report:

Item 25: 'Is there to be an armaments race?', British Movietone News, Issue Vol.6 No. 300A, 7 March 1935.

Item 26: 'Where stands peace?', British Paramount News, Issue No.597, 16 November 1936.

Item 27: 'Britain's re-armament plan', Gaumont British News, Issue No.328, 18 February 1937.

Item 28: 'Austria abolished', Gaumont British News, Issue No.440, 17 March 1938.

Item 29: 'Britain's reply – re-arm on a war basis', Gaumont British News, Issue No.440, 17 March 1938.

Item 20: 'Armistice 1918–1938', Gaumont British News, Issue No.509, 14 November 1938.

Item 25, from Movietone, was released three days after the government's 'Statement Relating to Defence' had been issued as a White Paper. Though the latter was somewhat watered down by the time of publication, for fear of offending Hitler, A. J. P. Taylor considers it 'a remarkable innovation' since 'it announced that the British government had ceased to rely on collective security and were now going to rely on the older security of armed force' (*English History 1914–1945*, 1965, p.464). As you see, Movietone's report was unequivocal in vindicating the government's standpoint with regard to rearmament. The opening lines to the commentary suggest that Britain was being compelled to prepare itself militarily because other nations were now rearming (though subsequent stories made it clear that Germany was the major source of concern – see, for instance, Movietone's report of exactly two weeks later, 'Germany asserts right to re-arm', Video 1, item 35, which Antony Lentin mentions in the next unit).

The use of the terms 'imperial defence' and 'defensive ratio' emphasizes, however, that Britain should not be seen as a potential aggressor. And the review which scans the rearmament by the world powers leads quite logically, albeit somewhat apologetically, into a final rejoinder stating Britain's case. The spirit of peace exists by implication, although throughout the visual accompaniment is of a decidedly aggressive nature, not resting simply within the realms of military preparedness but pointing most of all to armaments in action. The same mixture of peaceful intent and military power is to be found in the Paramount story, 'Where stands peace?'. It culminated, of course, in the Gaumont report on the 1938 Armistice Day ceremony which shows yet again, the message of 'peace through strength', even in a story given over to commemorating the dead of the Great War.

The item on 'Britain's rearmament plan' has been described by the historian, Nicholas Pronay, as 'one of the most brutally effective pieces of screen propaganda of the interwar years'. He elaborates as follows:

> The running refrain of 'every aeroplane' (or tank or ship, or training establishment or storage depot) 'means more work; more wages; for more men' on the soundtrack was rammed in by the use of some really dubious cinematic devices, some of which in later times came to be banned in screen advertising as psychologically damaging. One such was cutting in at the refrain point a close up shot of a steam hammer striking towards the audience, over which for just a couple of seconds was superimposed in huge white letters *Men Wanted*. The combined impact of the steam hammer rushing at the viewer as if he were right under it and the sudden blinding of his eyes by large white areas on the screen is really overwhelming. This was classic, brainwashing, 'forced association' technique; for a generation for whom the sign 'Men Wanted' became the symbol of hope, cruelly effective too.
>
> (N. Pronay, 'Re-armament and the British public: policy and propaganda', 1987, p.83–4)

Notice, also, that the forced association of rearmament with the prospect of new-found employment recurred in the BBC talk by Keynes which you have already heard. It was by no means confined to one medium alone. As you see here, however, the technique was put to best effect in the cinema newsreels.

Items number 28 and 29 were released in the same newsreel issue (indeed, the last one followed immediately upon the former and consciously sought to capitalize on it, as the captions indicate). By now the message is all too evident, though, with little need to resort to extraneous cinematic devices to reinforce it. The point being made, quite simply, is that rearmament is necessary to guarantee 'security' and 'the safety of our homes and our own people' – 'Your safety'.

In the vast majority of cases, then, the newsreel companies adhered to the government view on whatever issues were considered to be significant throughout the period of the 1930s. And it showed in their coverage of events. You have seen enough film evidence to bear out this point. On one notable occasion, however, the British Paramount News chose to depart from the agreed consensus in their coverage of a story related to the Czechoslovak crisis in September 1938. So, to conclude this section, let us look now at what happened to bring the offending company back into line in that instance, bearing in mind, as I have already indicated, that the newsreels were not subject to the censorship generally exercised over the cinema by the British Board of Film Censors. The incident did not go unnoticed, as you would expect, and it was cited in some quarters, not least in the House of Commons, as an obvious case of government interference with a supposedly free medium of communication. The means whereby the government achieved the effect it desired, however, demonstrates all too clearly how pressure was brought to bear on the news media without recourse to any sort of overt control.

Exercise   Read Document I.18 in *Primary Sources 2: Interwar and World War II*. It is extracted from the Commons proceedings of 7 December 1938, and relates to the debate on the motion which was put by Geoffrey Mander, Liberal MP for East Wolverhampton, that:

> This House, attaching the utmost importance to the maintenance undiminished of British democratic traditions of the liberty of expression of opinion, both in the Press and in public meetings and also in other media such as cinema films, would greatly deplore any action by the Government of the day which tended to set up any form of political censorship or which exercised pressure direct or indirect.

1   Why does Mander believe the government wanted to cut Paramount's story on the Czechoslovak crisis?

2   How did the government effect the cut? ■

Specimen answers   1   For the obvious reason that it gave vent to feelings which were highly critical of Chamberlain's policy in his dealings with Hitler over the Czech crisis. Although the newsreel was ostensibly expressing the personal opinions of Wickham Steed, A. J. Cummings and Herbert Hodge, they were plainly being put in the position of political commentators. Steed and Cummings were intended to represent informed and independent 'expert' opinion, while Hodge was meant to convey the ordinary man-in-the-street's viewpoint.

2   By the simple expedient of letting the American Ambassador know of the British government's misgivings and concern. The argument being used here was perfectly precise if, Mander felt, somewhat difficult to credit: the newsreel report might prejudice the negotiations taking place in Godesberg between Chamberlain and Hitler. The American Ambassador, Joseph P.

Kennedy, then proceeded to contact the Hays organization (the American equivalent of the BBFC). They got through in turn to the head of Paramount News. Clearly, as a result of the right word being dropped in the right place, the story was excised. And I hope you noticed how speedily this process of contacts worked: the newsreel was withdrawn within twenty-four hours of its release.

Discussion   Mander was well-informed and his deductions were essentially correct. Moreover, his allegation that 'the Conservative Central Office is not wholly disinterested in or without knowledge of what is going on' was right on the mark. As recent research has confirmed, it was Sir Patrick Gower of Conservative Central Office who started the ball rolling by writing to the Foreign Office demanding the newsreel's withdrawal. Thereafter, Halifax requested Kennedy to intervene with the American parent company of British Paramount News. Kennedy, it transpires, wisely advised caution on the grounds that censorship would raise an inevitable storm of protest and, after all, Steed and Cummings were well-known and much respected journalists. But Samuel Hoare was consulted and provided the winning argument. He considered 'it was definitely undesirable that such speeches should be heard in the cinemas while the talks at Godesberg were actually in progress. Whilst he did not wish to apply any pressure and there was no question of censorship, he would prefer that the speeches should be taken out on these grounds'. 'This clinched the matter', as Anthony Adamthwaite puts it, 'and Kennedy secured the withdrawal of the offending reel' ('The British government and the media, 1937–1938', 1983, pp.288–9). □

In the event Mander lost the debate when, as you see, a Conservative MP amended his motion to read that the House 'is fully satisfied that His Majesty's Government have maintained these traditions unimpaired', and the newly formulated motion won the vote. Furthermore, British Paramount quickly atoned for its sin and rejoined the ranks of those for whom, to borrow Mander's words, 'nothing anti-Government, nothing anti-fascist is permitted, but anything that is favourable to the policy that the Government are pursuing is allowed to go forward'. The three speakers were replaced by a new story entitled 'Premier flies for peace' in which Neville Chamberlain appeared and talked of 'A peaceful solution to the Czechoslovak problem', of seeking 'a better understanding between the British and the German peoples', and in which he promised: 'European peace is what I am aiming at'. Appeasement was definitely the order of the day as far as a contrite Paramount News was concerned and subsequently, with Chamberlain's return from Munich, it proved only too happy to go along with the other newsreels in stating that he had secured 'peace in our time'.

Obviously, for all that the newsreels fell outside the remit of the BBFC, it was a relatively simple job to ensure they did not step out of line. But then, of course, they rarely wished to do so. The Paramount case was exceptional and, in my opinion, born of a maverick news editor's attempt to try his hand at something new, to scoop the rest. Tom Cummins was an independent-minded newshound who clearly fancied experimenting with the novel idea of political commentators. But he was not a political radical. Moreover, it was hardly as though the newsreel companies in general were seething with radical intent and only contained or kept in their place by extreme and repressive measures. Far from it, as we have witnessed from the film evidence. To judge from remarks made in 1938, furthermore, emanating from the highest echelons of both the Newsreel Association of Great Britain and the Conservative Central Office, it is abundantly clear that the newsreel companies were motivated, for the most part, by feelings of loyalty towards the national government.

In June of 1938, for instance, the executives of the Newsreel Association invited Sir Albert Clavering of the Conservative and Unionist Films Association along to one of their council meetings. It was not the first such meeting, nor indeed the last, at which they 'emphasised the readiness of all the newsreel companies to assist the government and public departments on all suitable occasions in reproducing items deemed to be of public interest, although not necessarily of great news value'. In that same month, Sir Joseph Ball, director of the Conservative Research Department, confided to Neville Chamberlain that he had cultivated close personal contacts with the leaders of the British film industry, including the chairmen of the five newsreel companies and certain key producers like Alexander Korda. And he felt satisfied that he could 'count upon most of them for their full support to any reasonable degree'. It is little wonder the government did not need to resort to overt control when the newsreels, plainly, were such natural allies in helping to 'educate' the masses.

Mass bombing

I think it well ... for the man in the street to realise that there is no power on earth that can protect him from being bombed. Whatever people may tell him, the bomber will always get through.

(Stanley Baldwin to the House of Commons, 19 November 1932)

Exercise Read what Roberts has to say about the bombing of Guernica (p.418–19), and then watch the following items on Video 1.

Item 30: Extract from *Things to Come* (1936).

Item 31: 'Guernica wiped out by air-raid', Gaumont British News,, Issue No.350, 6 May 1937.

Item 32: 'Die Ruinen von Guernica', UFA Ton-Woche, Issue No.349, May 1937.

Item 33: 'Espagne dans les villes en ruines de Guernica et Durango', France Actualités Gaumont, Issue No.19, 7 May 1937.

Item 34: Soviet display of air strength' Gaumont British News, Issue No.419, 3 January 1938.

1   What according to the British, German and French newsreels caused the destruction of Guernica and who was responsible for it?

2   To judge from this extract, what would you say was the major purpose of *Things to Come?*■

Specimen answers 1   The British newsreel plainly states that Guernica was destroyed by aerial bombardment, though it does not say who did the bombing; the German newsreel states it was destroyed by retreating Bolshevist incendiarists and categorically denies the claim that it was bombed by German planes; while the French newsreel states simply that Guernica was destroyed but it does not say how or by whom.

2   *Things to Come* was clearly intended to warn against the horrors of aerial bombardment and vividly highlights, in particular, the consequences of mass bombing for the civilian population and the havoc and devastation it would cause. One might almost see this extract as a graphic illustration of Baldwin's maxim 'The bomber will always get through'.

Discussion   I hope you also noticed, in regard to the three Guernica newsreels, that the newsreel companies were using the same source of film. It was shot by a French cameraman, Raymond Méjat, who was working for Hearst Metrotone News and who arrived in Guernica on Thursday 29 April, three days after it had been destroyed. His film was syndicated, picked up by Gaumont British, UFA Ton-Woche and Gaumont Actualités, and put to use in the manner you see.

As is clear, however, it was used for varying ideological purposes, all of which reveal the immense potential for manipulation of the image. The manipulation by the German newsreel is the most blatant since it used the original film to fabricate a story which best suited the German (and Franco's) propaganda machine. In view of the immediate and widespread public condemnation of Guernica's destruction, the Germans and Spanish Nationalists acted quickly to try to scotch the argument that German planes had been responsible for it and, it should be noted, their story about Bolshevist incendiarists attracted a measure of support, in some quarters, for a considerable time.

The French report is the least informative. It apportions no blame for the incident, there is no mention of what caused the destruction, and it settles instead upon emphasizing the tragedy, in human terms, comparing it with the devastation which befell French villages in World War I (though because the latter had been caused by German forces the audience may just have been intended to infer who was responsible for Guernica). The British newsreel, of course, carefully treads a path which highlights all the features they wanted, while at the same time making the appropriate compromises. Thus there is no mention of the controversial aspects surrounding Guernica's destruction – no less a paper than *The Times* admitted initially that Guernica had been bombed by German planes, though it later claimed it may have been over-hasty in reaching that conclusion and afforded space and credence to the Basque incendiarists argument. To that extent, Gaumont British was of the same mind as those who wished to appease Hitler's Germany. It joined the ranks of those for whom responsibility for the bombing was never definitely apportioned. In fact, like the rest of the British newsreels, it did not even acknowledge that any Germans were fighting in Spain.

Yet at least Gaumont British acknowledged that Guernica had been bombed. The reasons why it did so are not difficult to fathom and are revealed, most of all, in the final sentence of the newsreel commentary: 'This was a city and these were homes, like yours.' The fact of the matter is that, as we have seen, the newsreels at this point were conducting a campaign to bolster the government line on rearmament. This report fitted neatly into that campaign. At the same time it emphasized the importance that the government now attached to the power of aerial bombardment. □

After Guernica, not surprisingly, stories on air power proliferated. Gaumont's Issue No.363 of 21 June 1937, for example, showed that 'Flying over Henlow, our cameraman with the Royal Air Force secured pictures of parachute training' and went on to reveal: 'The most spectacular of all exercises, a mass formation of flight. Two hundred and fifty planes darkened the sky and the roar of engines set the earth athrob. It was the biggest mass flight ever attempted'. Gaumont's Issue No.378, for 12 August, also centred on Britain and showed how '398 planes test London's air defence plan' in a story noting that the mock raiders were foiled and that the plan 'claims 80 per cent success'.

Shortly after that occasion, Gaumont spotlighted Air Ministry and War Office representatives at a mock air-raid during the rush hour in Berlin. 'At the first warning', the story ran, 'houses, offices, shops, buses, cars and trams were all deserted for bomb and gas-proof shelters'. It concluded by stating: 'Overhead, squadron after squadron of bombers darkened the sky, playing a duet of death with defending anti-aircraft guns. This is peacetime make-believe, in war it would be worse than this.' The same issue, No.390 for 23 September, complemented Germany's show of strength by observing Hore-Belisha, the British War Minister, as a representative at French army manoeuvres. The filming of aerial power continued into the following year with such stories as the one you have seen as item 34 on Video 1, the mass parachute descent near Moscow. (Did you notice, incidentally, how similar the concluding images on this report were to some of the shots in *Things to Come?*)

On the general question of aerial power and warfare the other newsreels were not lacking in stories either. Indeed, it was British Movietone News which, in effect, had started these reports, drawing parallels with Spain in its Issue No.394 on 12 December 1936. There Sir Malcolm Campbell had made one of his occasional appearances before the Movietone cameras with an item entitled 'Preparedness: the grim face of Madrid brings home the moral of air-raid danger'. He proceeded to recount how he had made an air-raid shelter in his back garden, to see what it would take to construct. He concluded by commenting: 'I hope these pictures will not mar your Christmas festivities, but we shall have to take real steps to grapple with this menace from the skies in the immediate future.' Campbell reappeared again on 14 January 1937 in a Movietone report entitled 'Gas respirators for all is a timely answer to the danger of air-raids'.

Clearly, as far as the newsreels were concerned, aerial warfare had become an awesome reality and mass bombing was the likely prospect of any future war. But then, as we have seen, Alexander Korda had already speculated upon the effects of this force. What his film had demonstrated most of all was an élitist fear about the collapse of morale and the likelihood of social unrest as a consequence of the mass bombing of the civilian population. His film predicted panic, anarchy and the breakdown of civilization. This did not materialize, even under the testing conditions of the total war that followed.

References

Adamthwaite, A. (1983) 'The British government and the media, 1937–1938', *Journal of Contemporary History,* vol.18, no.2, April.

Barsam, R. M. (1975) *Filmguide to 'Triumph of the Will',* Indiana University Press.

Briggs, A. (1961) *The History of Broadcasting in the United Kingdom. Volume 1. The Birth of Broadcasting,* Oxford University Press.

Bullock, A. (1962) *Hitler,* Penguin.

Curran, J., Smith, A. and Wingate, P. (eds) (1987) *Impacts and Influences. Essays on Media Power in the Twentieth Century,* Methuen.

Haworth, B. (1981) 'The BBC, Nazi Germany and the Foreign Office, 1933–1939', *Historical Journal of Film, Radio and Television,* vol. 1, no. 1, March.

Joll, J. (1976) *Europe since 1870,* Penguin.

Kershaw, I. (1987) *The Hitler Myth,* Oxford University Press.

McClelland, J. S. (1989) *The Crowd and the Mob,* Unwin Hyman.

Open University (1977) DE353 *Mass Communication and Society,* Offprint, Scannell, P. and Cardiff, D. 'The social foundations of British broadcasting', The Open University.

Phillips, M. S. (1971) 'The Nazi control of the German film industry', *Journal of European Studies,* vol. 1, March.

Pronay, N. (1987) 'Re-armament and the British public: policy and propaganda' in Curran, J., Smith, A. and Wingate, P. (eds) (1987).

Ramsden, J. (1982) 'Baldwin and film' in Pronay, N. and Spring, D. W. (eds) *Propaganda, Politics and Film 1918–45,* Macmillan.

Seaton, J. and Pimlott, B. (eds) (1987) *The Media in British Politics,* Gower.

Stevenson, J. and Cook, C. (1977) *The Slump,* Cape. (Chapter XIV is reproduced in the *Secondary Sources.*)

Taylor, A. J. P. (1965) *English History 1914–1945,* Clarendon Press.

Taylor, R. (1998) *Film Propaganda, Soviet Russia and Nazi Germany,* I. B. Tauris (second edition).

Taylor, R. (1979) *The Politics of the Soviet Cinema 1917–1929,* Cambridge University Press.

Welch, D. (1983) *Propaganda and the German Cinema 1933–1945,* Clarendon Press.

Further reading

Aldgate, A. (1979) *Cinema and History. British Newsreels and the Spanish Civil War,* Scolar.

Aldgate, A. and Richards, J. (1999), *Best of British. Cinema and Society from 1930 to the Present,* I. B. Tauris.

Armes, R. (1985) *French Cinema,* Secker and Warburg.

Bergan, R. (1992) *Jean Renoir: Projections of Paradise. A Biography,* London, Bloomsbury.

Biddiss, M. (1977) *The Age of the Masses. Ideas and Society in Europe since 1870,* Penguin.

Carey, J. (1992), *The Intellectuals and the Masses,* Faber and Faber.

Cunningham, V. (1988) *British Writers of the Thirties,* Oxford University Press.

Curchod, O. (1994) *La Grande Illusion (Jean Renoir): Étude Critique,* Paris, Nathan.

Curran, J. and Porter, V. (eds) (1983) *British Cinema History,* Weidenfeld and Nicholson.

Kenez, P. (1985) *The Birth of the Propaganda State. Soviet Methods of Mass Mobilization 1917–1929,* Cambridge University Press.

LeMahieu, D. L. (1988) *A Culture for Democracy. Mass Communication and the Cultivated Mind in Britain Between the Wars,* Clarendon Press.

Ortega y Gasset, I. (1932) *The Revolt of the Masses,* Norton.

Paris, M. (ed.) (1999), *The First World War and Popular Cinema,* Edinburgh University Press.

Richards, J. (1984) *The Age of the Dream Palace,* Routledge and Kegan Paul.

Short, K. R. M. (ed.) (1981) *Feature Films as History,* Croom Helm.

Smith, A. (1976) *The Shadow in the Cave. The Broadcaster, the Audience and the State,* Quartet.

Taylor, R. and Christie, 1. (eds.) (1988) *The Film Factory. Russian and Soviet Cinema in Documents 1896–1939,* Routledge and Kegan Paul.

Vincendeau, G. and Reader, K. (eds) (1986) *La Vie est à Nous. French Cinema of the Popular Front 1935–1938,* British Film Institute.

Ward, K. (1989) *Mass Communications and the Modern World,* Macmillan.

Williams, K. (1996), *British Writers and the Media, 1930–45,* Macmillan.

Unit 19 THE ORIGINS OF WORLD WAR II

ANTONY LENTIN

Open University students of this unit will need to refer to:

Set book: J. M. Roberts, *Europe 1880–1945*, Longman, 2001

Primary Sources 1: World War I, eds Arthur Marwick and Wendy Simpson, Open University, 2000

Primary Sources 2: Interwar and World War II, eds Arthur Marwick and Wendy Simpson, Open University, 2000

Course Reader: *Total War and Historical Change: Europe 1914–1955*, eds Clive Emsley, Arthur Marwick and Wendy Simpson, Open University Press, 2000

Secondary Sources, eds Arthur Marwick and Wendy Simpson, Open University, 2000

Maps Booklet

Video 1

Audio 3

The author would like to thank Richard Bessel, Arthur Marwick, Peter Neville and Bill Purdue for comments made on this unit.

INTRODUCTION

A Thirty Years' War 1914–1945?

In 1919 the Allied Commander-in-Chief, Marshal Foch, described the Treaty of Versailles as 'the twenty-year armistice', implying that it would not be adequate to contain Germany for more than twenty years and that a second German bid to dominate Europe by force of arms would be the consequence. His remark presupposed the existence of a 'German problem', 'the problem of fitting Germany into the European political system without endangering the independence of other states and the self-determination of other peoples' (H. Bull, *The Challenge of the Third Reich*, 1986, p.10).

It is common ground among historians that there *was* a 'German problem' which had been in existence at least since 1900, perhaps since 1870, and that this was the overriding international problem in Europe in the first half of the twentieth century. Failure by the First World War victors to solve it – failure for that matter by the Germans themselves to solve it – resulted in a Second World War. Outside attempts to solve it included the use of military force (Allied victory in 1918, French occupation of the Ruhr in 1923), or treaties and diplomacy (controls imposed on Germany under the Treaty of Versailles (1919), conciliation and compromise under the Treaty of Locarno (1925) and Germany's admission to the League of Nations (1926)), 'appeasement' in the Munich agreement (1938) – or in Russia's case in the Molotov-Ribbentrop pact (1939). In the words of the Prime Minister, Neville Chamberlain, who had done his utmost to avoid the conflict, Britain went to war in 1939 'to put an end to the successive acts of German aggression which menaced the freedom and the very security of all the nations of Europe' (speech to House of Commons, 3 October 1939, *Parliamentary Debates*, 351 HC Deb5s, p.1856).

Was there across the period 1914–1945 the equivalent of a Thirty Years' War? Was World War II essentially a replay of World War I, the second round of a *continuous* struggle for German hegemony in Europe? Some historians (notably Fritz Fischer, whose views were discussed in Unit 5, and A. J. P. Taylor, whose views are discussed in this unit) assert an underlying continuity in German history, an aggressive annexationism (dating back in the case of Prussia to the mid-seventeenth century, and featuring Frederick the Great in the eighteenth century and Bismarck in the nineteenth). World War II, Arno Mayer agrees, was 'umbilically tied to' World War I (Course Reader, p.42). Such historians also stress the similarity of war-aims evolved in both wars, German conquests in World War II apparently mirroring an 'almost megalomaniac annexationism of the German leadership, civilian as well as military' in World War I (S. A. Shuker in G. Martel, *The Origins of the Second World War Reconsidered*, 1986, p.57). Are these parallels valid? And if so, how does the foreign policy of Weimar Germany fit into the pattern? As an interval? Or as a connecting link?

Other historians see the two wars as basically separate and unconnected. The second did not flow inevitably from the first. The peace of 1919 was not doomed to be a mere truce. While Arno Mayer sees both wars flowing directly from an underlying chronic European crisis, the '*causa causans*' (ultimate cause) of both wars (Course Reader, p.42), others (such as Gerhard Weinberg and Norman

Rich) see World War II as the result of a *novus actus interveniens*, a new supervening element, which was itself the real, substantial cause of World War II. This was the advent of Hitler and Nazism, which, while building on existing trends towards German expansionism, added, it is said, a wholly new impetus and ideology, going far beyond those of Weimar or Imperial Germany.

The objectives of this unit are to enable you:

1   to identify the main events and developments in European international relations 1919–1939, geopolitical, diplomatic and ideological;

2   to examine and evaluate a variety of primary sources (mostly documentary but also pictorial and audio-visual) as evidence of the origins of World War II;

3   to engage in some of the main historiographical debates on the origins of World War II and to reach your own informed conclusions.

In particular, you are asked to consider the following five questions, discussed in the corresponding sections of the unit:

1   How far did the authors of the Versailles settlement and the Locarno agreements address the 'German problem' in the 1920s?

2   Did German foreign policy under the Nazis differ materially from its predecessors?

3   In what ways can the Rhineland crisis of 1936 be seen as a crucial turning-point to war?

4   Was the 'Appeasement' policy of Neville Chamberlain a contributory cause of war?

5   How far were German designs on Russia an underlying cause of World War II?

You should be well equipped to consider these questions (and the specific 'exercises' in the unit) from the information supplied in the unit, in Roberts, and in the associated material listed at the beginning of the unit. Note, however, that some of the 'specimen answers' and 'discussions' also contain additional information and lines of thought, intended to enhance your knowledge and to prompt further reflection.

1   THE TREATY OF VERSAILLES AND THE 'GERMAN PROBLEM' 1919–33

Versailles: a *'Carthaginian peace'*?

The Treaty of Versailles cast a long shadow across the interwar period (and for historians, far beyond). Many have argued that the entire European peace (the Treaty of Versailles with Germany and the associated treaties with the other defeated central powers) itself contained the seeds of war or was itself the root cause of World War II.

Exercise   Please re-read A.W. Purdue's analysis in Book 2, Units 7–10, and/or Roberts, pp.256–62, and consult the map 'Germany 1919–38' in the *Maps Booklet*. Then make brief notes on the impact on Germany of the Treaty of Versailles.

Now please consider the following, and use them to flesh out your notes on the impact of Versailles on Germany:

- 'Article 231' of the treaty of Versailles, the so-called 'war-guilt clause' (Document I.13 in *Primary Sources 1: World War I*) and Document I.19 in *Primary Sources 2: Interwar and World War II* (from the 'reply of the Allied and Associated Powers to the Observations of the German Delegation on the Conditions of Peace', 16 June 1919).

- A cartoon from the German satirical magazine *Simplicissimus*, 1919, reproduced below.

Is the description of the treaty of Versailles as a *Diktat*, or dictated settlement, a fair one? ■

Specimen answer   Individually and cumulatively, the 440 terms of Versailles do seem to represent a
and discussion   harsh and crushing imposition. General Jan Christian Smuts, a member of the British delegation at the peace conference and an early revisionist, described it as 'this reactionary peace, the most reactionary since Scipio Africanus dealt with Carthage' (quoted in A. Lentin *Guilt at Versailles*, 1985, p.132. The reference was to the peace imposed on Carthage in 146 BC, when the Romans razed it to the ground). The phrase 'the Carthaginian peace' was given wide currency by another British delegate, John Maynard Keynes, in his book *The Economic Consequences of the Peace* (1919). Hitler was famously to denounce Versailles as the *Diktat*. When, in *Mein Kampf* (1925) he lambasted it as 'this instrument of unlimited blackmail and shameful humiliation' (Document I.22(a) in *Primary Sources 2: Interwar and World War II*), he echoed a verdict widely shared in Germany. Almost every aspect of Versailles offended German opinion: the territorial amputations (especially the territories and nationals lost to Poland), the loss of raw materials (iron and coal) in Alsace-Lorraine and Upper Silesia; the loss (albeit temporary) of the Saar, with its coal-mines; occupation of the Rhineland by allied troops (albeit for a maximum fifteen years); confiscation of all German colonies; exclusion (albeit temporary) from the League of Nations; disarmament and massive cuts in Germany's armed forces.

The treaty was certainly a *Diktat* in the sense that its terms were settled between the Allies and imposed unilaterally on the Germans without face-to-face negotiations and with few amendments, under threat of a renewal of hostilities. The blockade of Germany was not fully lifted until the treaty was signed.

To add insult to injury in German eyes was Article 231, the notorious 'war-guilt' clause, which imposed historical, moral and financial responsibility on Germany for causing the war and for the losses brought about by 'the aggression of Germany and her allies'. □

Document I.19 shows the thinking of the 'Big Three' Allied peacemakers (Wilson, Clemenceau and Lloyd George) and reveals why reparations, war-guilt and the trial of Kaiser Wilhelm II were felt to be integral parts of the treaty as a 'settlement of the accounts of this terrible war'. It constituted the Allies' 'reply' and final word to the German delegation in answer to the latter's objections, and an explanation and justification of the treaty overall as inspired by considerations of 'justice' and 'reparation'. The document formed an introductory covering-note to the treaty; and its purpose, and that of the treaty, was emphasized by Lord Curzon when presenting the treaty to the House of Lords: 'The bringing home to Germany and its rulers of their responsibility for having inflicted on the world the sufferings and calamities of the last five years fundamentally distinguishes the Treaty of Versailles from any previous peace treaty' (quoted in Lentin, 1985, p. xi). Language like that of Article 231 and Document I.19 was unprecedented in a treaty of peace. Was it likely to conciliate German opinion?

*'Even you have one right to self-determination: do you want your pockets emptied before or after execution?' (*Simplicissimus, *3 June 1919. Bildarchiv Preussischer Kulturbesitz, Berlin)*

At the time of the armistice, Wilson and the Allies had promised Germany 'a peace of justice' on the basis of the Fourteen Points (Roberts, p.248), especially if Germany got rid of the Kaiser and adopted a democratic form of government. Germany had duly declared itself a Republic and the Kaiser fled to Holland. But under the treaty not only was the new Germany saddled with moral and financial responsibility for the war as 'a crime against humanity and right' (Document I.19), but there were numerous and obvious violations of the Fourteen Points (for example, the principle of open diplomacy and the refusal to negotiate; the principle of national self-determination and the prohibition on Austro-German union; the principle of fair arbitration of colonial questions and the wholesale confiscation of Germany's overseas possessions). The German delegation protested that Versailles was 'a peace of violence and not of justice' (Document I.19).

In Germany, the suspicion gained currency that Wilson's promises had been no more than a *ruse de guerre* to trick Germany into armistice; and even that the German army had not been defeated in the war, but betrayed by left-wing politicians and revolutionaries at home – the notorious *Dolchstosslegende,* the legend of the 'stab in the back' by the 'November criminals' who signed the armistice. There were few visible symbols of military defeat; negligible war damage; no Allied invasion of Germany or march to Berlin in 1918; only the post-armistice occupation of the Rhineland. The psychological shock of Versailles was all the greater to a nation which had felt assured of victory almost until the last moment, which had dictated crushing terms to Russia in March 1918, and which now felt bewildered, deceived and betrayed.

No one in Germany had, or could be expected to have, a good word for Versailles. The first Weimar government refused to sign it and resigned, protesting that 'the hand that signed would wither'. A German signature was extorted under threat of a resumption of hostilities, the Social Democrat President Ebert complaining of the Treaty's 'unheard-of injustice'. German perceptions of Versailles were at least as important as Allied ones when it came to willingness to comply with it, and all German governments after 1919 were revisionist. In the politically fragmented Weimar Republic, the perceived iniquity of Versailles was the one issue on which Germans were united.

The cartoon from the left-wing satirical magazine, *Simplicissimus,* shows Versailles from a German point of view: the young Weimar Republic is depicted stripped and bound, ready for execution. Lloyd George brandishes the death sentence; Clemenceau is the executioner and Wilson, the chaplain, vindictive and pharisaical. Germany is the innocent victim of 'unheard-of injustice'. Again, while the Allies agreed that a democratic Germany was 'a great hope for peace' (Document I.19) they did nothing to conciliate it at Versailles.

Wilson, Clemenceau, Lloyd George and the 'German problem'

Exercise   Do you agree – the Germans, Smuts and Keynes certainly did – that the conditions imposed on Germany at Versailles suggest extraordinary vindictiveness or irresponsibility on the part of the victors? ∎

Specimen answer   A glance at Article 231 or the cartoon from *Simplicissimus* certainly bears out such an interpretation, which remains the popular view of Versailles and a sufficient explanation of what followed. □

An alternative view is that the treaty stemmed from serious but conflicting and often contradictory attempts to deal with the 'German problem'. The 'Big Three' all agreed that Imperial Germany had come close to pulling off a bid for military domination of the European continent: at the height of its military success in Spring 1918, German troops were entrenched from the Belgian coast to the Black Sea and from Riga on the Baltic to Baku on the Caspian. They held these positions until the armistice (see *Maps Booklet*, map of 'The First World War' or Roberts, Map 5, p.xviii). Only American intervention had turned the scales. How to prevent the catastrophe of the world war from repeating itself was foremost in the victors' thoughts. Whatever their views on a solution, however, their freedom of action was crucially predetermined by their acceptance and recognition, at the armistice and in the treaty, of a sovereign, united Germany. As Wilson said, 'we do not want to destroy her, and we could not do so' (quoted in Lentin,1991, p.20). There was no intention – despite frantic French attempts to secure the detachment of the Rhineland from the Reich – of partitioning Germany in order to solve the 'German problem' (as happened after the Second World War). It therefore followed, as Smuts pointed out to Lloyd George, that 'the Germans are, have been, and will continue to be the *dominant factor* on the Continent of Europe, and no permanent peace is possible which is not based on that fact' (*Primary Sources 2: Interwar and World War II*, Document I.20). Each of the 'Big Three' agreed with Smuts's proposition.

Wilson and national self-determination

Wilson (and, indeed, Lloyd George) sought to accommodate legitimate French desires for security within a more liberal and lasting system of international relations based on national self-determination, the denial of which he believed to have been an underlying cause of the war. Hence his insistence on the return of Alsace-Lorraine to France. Hence his encouragement of the new nation states, on the principle that 'no people must be forced under sovereignty under which it does not wish to live' (quoted in Lentin, 1985, p.5). The application of national self-determination he described as 'an imperative principle of action' (ibid., p.3). What, indeed, was the alternative?

The problem, however, as Wilson soon discovered, was that the rights of different nationalities (including Germans) could not always be reconciled, especially in areas of mixed population (such as Upper Silesia and the Polish Corridor). Any settlement which discriminated against Germans was bound to stir German national resentment, notably in the areas ceded to Poland, but also among ethnic Germans in the former Austro-Hungarian Empire who sought unification with the Reich, such as the Austrians (unification, *Anschluss*, between Austria and Germany was forbidden under the treaty) or the Sudeten Germans of Czechoslovakia. Wilson looked to his 'brain-child', the League of Nations, for 'reconciliation and appeasement' (Document I.19), once the atmosphere of war hatred had died away, and even, where necessary, for revision of the peace treaties. However, America repudiated both the treaty and the League, leaving Europe to sort out its own problems. This left Britain and France with effective responsibility for Versailles.

France and security

France's basic concern was not so much punitive as for compensation and security. Clemenceau knew that in the long run time was on Germany's side. Its territory, population and resources, even after Versailles, were superior to France's. Its birth-rate was higher (see the demographic and economic analysis in Book 2, Units 7–10.) The war seemed to have left France with old men, widows and cripples. Furthermore, Germany was by far the leading industrial power on the continent.

France sought first to weaken German power and hold it down, and second to make Germany contribute towards making good in payments and in kind the devastation inflicted on war-ravaged north-eastern France. Scores of French towns and villages had been destroyed, and mines and key industries wrecked and pillaged, while (outside East Prussia) Germany suffered no physical war damage and its industries were unimpaired despite serious losses of raw material. Germany was bound to recover much of its natural strength in Europe. France also hoped to contain Germany by means of alliances with the 'succession states' to the east and south of Germany (Poland and Czechoslovakia in particular), which France saw as an 'eastern barrier' against Germany and at the same time as a *cordon sanitaire* against Russian bolshevism. Thus France, said Clemenceau's Foreign Minister, Pichon, wanted a Poland *'grande et forte – très forte'*.

For France, the key to enforcement of the treaty was the permanent demilitarization by Germany of the Rhineland and its occupation by allied forces for a fifteen-year period (theoretically extendible). Clemenceau saw occupation of the Rhineland (a) as a general security against German aggression and (b) as a sanction and means of retaliation and enforcement in case of other breaches of the treaty (for example, default in payment of reparations).

Clemenceau also secured from Wilson and Lloyd George a pledge to come to France's aid in the event of a future unprovoked attack by Germany. America, however, refused to ratify Versailles, whereupon Britain withdrew its military commitment to France. For France, the Anglo-American guarantee underpinned the entire settlement. Its failure to materialize added to French fears of Germany (Lentin, in Stone and Sharp (eds) *Anglo-French Relations in the Twentieth Century*, 1999, pp.104–19).

Britain

Britain secured most of its objectives at the armistice. British policy was essentially satisfied with the disappearance of the German navy and the confiscation of the German colonies. Additionally Britain was committed to exacting reparations, which Lloyd George had made a main plank of his election platform in December 1918. By 1920, however, Lloyd George, while still intent on recouping Britain's financial losses from Germany, was anxious not to 'kill the goose that laid the golden egg,' and was ready to sponsor the reduction of reparations to a level acceptable to Germany. While hoping that implementation of national self-determination would bring lasting peace, Britain worried about new trouble-spots, especially in a volatile eastern Europe. Once the treaty was signed, Britain was not wholeheartedly committed either to the full exaction of reparations or to the immutability of the settlement in eastern Europe. There were misgivings among the British delegates at Versailles about the harshness of Versailles. Such qualms were crystallized in Keynes's, *The Economic Consequences of the Peace* (1919), which profoundly influenced British attitudes to Germany between the wars, with its denunciation of alleged Allied bad faith and its critique of the dislocation caused to the European economic system by reparations and by the peacemakers' emphasis on the principle of nationality. After 1919 Britain backed away from commitment to the treaty. It was unwilling and unable to enforce militarily the peace settlement by continuing to act as the 'policeman of the world' (as the conservative leader, Andrew Bonar Law, protested in 1922). Andrew Crozier states that 'from the moment the treaty of Versailles was signed, British policy was revisionist' (A. J. Crozier, *The Causes of the Second World War*, 1997, p.90). The generalization is broadly true.

Versailles: 'an impossible peace' (Smuts)?

Exercise   Please (re-)read Roberts, pp.258–62. Then read Document I.20 in *Primary Sources 2: Interwar and World War II* (Jan Smuts' letter to Lloyd George, 26 March 1919 and see the *Maps Booklet*, 'Germany 1919–38'). Identify the particular proposals criticized by Smuts, and their authors, if possible. Outline the relevant provisions of the treaty. ■

Discussion   1   *Danzig.* America and France wanted to transfer the German port of Danzig to Poland outright, Wilson having, in the Fourteen Points, promised Poland 'free and secure access to the sea' and Clemenceau wishing to strengthen Poland. A compromise was imposed at Lloyd George's suggestion, whereby Danzig became an autonomous 'Free City' under League of Nations' sovereignty and Poland was granted the right to use the port.

2   *The Polish Corridor.* Wilson and Clemenceau wanted to make Poland viable by granting a territorial corridor through West Prussia between Danzig and the Polish hinterland. The corridor cut off East Prussia from the rest of Germany. The corridor and Poznania also included half a million Germans and remained a running sore between Germany and Poland between the wars. Again at the promptings of Lloyd George, plebiscites were held in the contested areas of Marienwerder and Allenstein, in East Prussia, and in Upper Silesia. Eastern Silesia, Marienwerder and Allenstein voted to remain with Germany (1921), but neither Germany nor Poland was satisfied.

3   *The Saar Valley.* Clemenceau wished to annex the Saarland (which had last belonged to France in 1814) in part to compensate France for the wartime destruction of its coal mines. Wilson and Lloyd George opposed this as a clear violation of self-determination. Lloyd George again came up with a solution: France should occupy and use the mines, but sovereignty of the Saar should go to the League of Nations for fifteen years, after which its future would be decided by plebiscite.

4   *Separation of the Rhineland.* Clemenceau held out for the detachment of the Left Bank of the Rhine from Germany as a buffer-state under French tutelage; but this was vetoed by Wilson and Lloyd George, who warned against creating an 'Alsace-Lorraine in reverse'. In 1919 and 1923 there were abortive French attempts to foment Rhineland separatism.

5   *Trial of the Kaiser* and others held responsible for 'crimes against humanity';
     and payment of reparations by Germany. Lloyd George was closely tied to
     both policies. Clemenceau was equally anxious to exact reparations and
     claimed the lion's share for France as the country most severely damaged by
     the war. The trial of the Kaiser was abandoned in 1920 when the Dutch
     refused to surrender him. A few named war criminals were formally tried by
     the German high court at the Allies' request, and let off with derisory
     sentences in 1922. Wilson strove to moderate the sums being canvassed by
     way of reparations and (like Smuts) to persuade Lloyd George to agree to a
     fixed figure; but a final sum was not laid down until 1921. Both the amounts
     demanded and the obligation to pay at all were fiercely resented in
     Germany, linked as they were with Article 231, the offensive 'war-guilt'
     clause. Throughout the 1920s reparations remained a constant source of
     difficulties and friction between Germany and the Allies.

6   *The League of Nations and Germany.* Wilson and Lloyd George wanted
     Germany to enter the League from the start. Clemenceau opposed German
     membership so soon after the horrors of the war. The 'Big Three' agreed that
     Germany should join the League after a few years' probation. Germany
     became a member in 1926. □

Versailles: a compromise peace?

Few of the 'solutions' imposed at Versailles were clear-cut. They were the fruits
of agonizing political compromise between the 'Big Three' who, united in their
desire for a lasting settlement, had very different ideas of how best to bring it
about. Wilson's closest aide had rightly predicted: 'It took many of us to win the
war, and each of the powers will have to be consulted in winning the peace. In
adjusting these different points of view, our principal difficulty will lie' (E. M.
House quoted in Lentin, 1991, p.5). Without such compromises, the Peace
Conference would probably have broken up. Versailles was largely a
compromise between French and American policies. It was not a happy
compromise. Above all, it was not a compromise with Germany, whose
counterproposals were almost entirely rejected.

'What has become of Wilson's Fourteen Points?' Smuts (and the Germans)
quite reasonably complained.

A literal application of national self-determination, enclosing within the Reich
those outside it who (like the 7 million Germans of Austria and the 3½ million
Germans in Czechoslovakia, see *Maps Booklet*, 'Germany 1919–38') thought of
themselves as German by race, language and culture, would have made
Germany even larger and more preponderant in Europe than in 1914. The
outcome of the war would have meant 'solving' the 'German problem' by
creating a 'Greater Germany' (*Grossdeutschland*). Such a solution might have
satisfied German aspirations; but its effects on the balance of power in Europe
would have been awesome: an acquisition of territory 'more extensive than the
vast terrain acquired by Hitler through intimidation by the beginning of 1939'
(William R. Keylor in M. Boemeke, G. Feldman and E. Glaser (eds) *The Treaty of
Versailles*, 1998, p.492. See *Maps Booklet*, 'Germany 1919–38'). For that reason it
was ruled out, at Clemenceau's particular instigation; but the promotion of self-
determination at Versailles unwittingly gave fresh impetus to Pan-Germanism.

As Roberts points out (p.261–2) the demand for the union of all ethnic Germans in a 'Greater Germany' headed the programme of the emergent Nazi Party in 1920. Even the moderate President Ebert claimed 'the right of self-determination for all Germans (even for those beyond the old borders of the Reich)' (K. Schwabe, *Woodrow Wilson*, 1985, p. 189). Hence, at Clemenceau's insistence, the treaty forbade union between Germany and the new Austrian state. A strict application of self-determination would likewise have assigned the Sudeten Germans to Germany. Again, this would have deprived the new Czechoslovakia of vital industries and a defensible frontier, as well as enlarging Germany.

Such compromises were not consciously cynical violations of the Fourteen Points, though they often seemed so to German opinion; but they served to make the treaty seem inconsistent and unjust at Germany's expense.

At the last moment, the revisionist arguments of Smuts began to find favour in the British delegation; and Lloyd George, having secured Britain's main objectives, argued for some measure of leniency. The most he could secure were the plebiscites in East Prussia and Upper Silesia. Clemenceau refused further concessions; and he was supported by Wilson, anxious not to unravel the series of hard-won inter-allied compromises, and looking to the League of Nations to settle outstanding grievances.

As an attempt to come to grips with the 'German problem', however, the treaty, a collection of improvizations designed to suit the victors, was a failure. It wrested a German signature; it did not win German acceptance. Versailles neither destroyed Germany, nor did it pacify it. It left Germany with numerous causes for resentment, without rendering it permanently harmless. It was, a French observer, Jacques Bainville, commented in 1919, 'too mild for its severity' (*Les conséquences politiques de la paix*, p.35).

Versailles not self-enforcing

Moreover the 1919 settlement was not self-enforcing. As events showed, Germany would comply only reluctantly and under protest, not feeling morally bound by it. America refused to ratify the treaty, and repudiated most of its responsibilities under it. This left Britain and France as guardians of the peace. Italy, disappointed with its gains, was half-hearted in its attitude towards the settlements and periodically sided with other discontented defeated states, such as Hungary (which lost two-thirds of its territory and one-third of its population).

Once the treaty was signed, Britain, soon beset by economic recession, looked to a revival of international trade in which Germany would resume its pre-war role as a leading purchaser of British goods. British opinion thus favoured a peaceful German recovery. Keynes's *The Economic Consequences of the Peace* helped to sway public opinion; and successive British governments spoke of peaceful treaty revision, or 'appeasement' – the word did not take on pejorative connotations until 1939. Apart from the occupation forces in the Rhineland, Britain and America withdrew their armies from the continent. France alone, fearful of German recovery, sought to enforce Versailles to the letter, particularly after the collapse of the Anglo-American guarantee.

Exercise   Please compare in the *Maps Booklet* 'Europe 1914' with 'The Settlement of Europe after World War I (1919–1926)' (or Roberts, Map 6, p.xix), read Roberts, pp.259–61 and consider the proposition that Germany was actually *stronger* after Versailles. ■

Discussion   To suggest that Germany's position in Europe after Versailles was relative to its neighbours, more preponderant than in 1914, may seem paradoxical. Yet so it was. France, Britain, Russia and Italy together had been unable to break Germany in the war; and as well as holding off the three western powers, Germany had overrun the Balkans and defeated Russia. It required American intervention to turn the scales in 1918. After Versailles, America withdrew into two decades of political isolationism. So, in effect, did Bolshevik Russia.

The 'succession states' of central and eastern Europe (carved out of or enlarged from the former Austro-Hungarian and Russian empires) were either small, relative to Germany (Austria, Hungary, the Baltic states); or, if large, contained sizeable dissident minorities (Poland, Romania, Yugoslavia; Czechoslovakia was both relatively small and contained several minorities including the 3½ million Sudeten Germans). They were often economically and politically unstable, and commonly rivals for disputed territories or even (in the first few years immediately after the war) actually embattled. This fragmentation (or 'balkanization') and mutual hostility across the power-vacuum in central and eastern Europe and the Balkans themselves underscores the overall predominance of Germany as the one state in the region that was truly nationally homogeneous (shorn at Versailles of its French, Polish and Danish minorities). Economically too Germany was the dominant power, and its economic influence in the region was paramount.

Even counting its losses at Versailles, then, Germany remained, as Smuts pointed out, by virtue of its size, population, resources and geopolitical situation, 'the *dominant factor* on the Continent of Europe' (*Primary Sources 2: Interwar and World War II*, Document I.20). The war had damaged Germany far less than its neighbours. The combined result of the war and the peace settlement was to destroy the 1914 balance of power and in a relatively weakened Europe, to shift the balance of power in Germany's favour. What does this suggest about the 'German problem' after Versailles? □

'Enforcing' Versailles

It was acknowledged that by the early 1930s Germany would have recovered from the war; yet 1935 at the latest was the time fixed by the treaty for withdrawing the allied armies of occupation. That was why, as Roberts says (p.257), France sought in the meantime 'to wound Germany as deeply and as permanently as possible' by supporting Poland and Czechoslovakia and by insisting on punctilious payment by Germany of reparation instalments as they fell due, in the hope that rigorous enforcement of the treaty and the maintenance of a system of alliances encircling Germany would keep Germany in check. Hence alliance with Belgium (1920), Poland (1921), Czechoslovakia (1924), Romania (1926) and Yugoslavia (1927). Hence French support for Poland against Russia (1920–21) and for the Little Entente (Czechoslovakia, Yugoslavia, Rumania) against Hungary. Hence French military intervention (with British and Belgian military assistance) in 1921 when Germany defaulted on reparations, culminating in the invasion of the Ruhr in 1923 (in the face of British disapproval). Roberts refers to the years 1919–23 as France's 'brief Indian summer as a great power' (p.278). In reality the 'Indian summer' was mainly the reflection of temporary German weakness, and France's apparent 'belligerence' – the reflection of its realization of the fragility of Versailles as a shield against German resurgence. The British elder statesman, Balfour, commented in 1925 that the French 'are so dreadfully afraid of being swallowed up by the tiger, yet they spend their time poking it'. To which the Foreign Secretary, Lord Curzon, added, 'And the tiger is not a tiger for the moment' (Public Record office, 195C.I.D. 13 February 1925, CAB/2/4).[1]

Britain accepted that Germany remained 'the dominant factor' in Europe, but felt that now that it was no longer a colonial or naval rival, but disarmed and a democracy, there was no longer a 'German problem'.

Occupation of the Ruhr 1923

Of the Allies only France was really willing to attempt to enforce Versailles by military force. In 1922, Germany surprised the Allies by recognizing Soviet Russia in the treaty of Rapallo. France saw this as a threat to Poland and as a challenge to the Versailles settlement generally, to which France must either react or face further defiance. In 1923, when Germany defaulted on reparations and requested a moratorium, Prime Minister Poincaré insisted on action; and French and Belgian troops were sent to occupy Germany's industrial heartland in the Ruhr (see Map 7) and to attempt to ensure the delivery of reparations in kind by taking control of the coal-mines.

Exercise   Please read Roberts, pages 279–81, on the invasion of the Ruhr, and also note the inflationary consequences in France and especially in Germany. How effective was the occupation of the Ruhr in enforcing Versailles? ∎

Discussion   The use of force eventually persuaded the German government to abandon passive resistance and to acknowledge its reparations obligations, but these were soon rescheduled and scaled down in the Dawes Plan of 1924, under pressure from American bankers who now intervened to finance loans both to France and Germany. The United States, while continuing to eschew direct political involvement in Europe, and insisting on the repayment of allied war loans, favoured granting further loans in Europe, especially to Germany, both as a profitable mode of investment and with a view to restoring political stability. As the world's greatest creditor-state, America imposed its terms on the borrowers and made its own assessment of their capacity to pay. As the central economic pivot in Europe, a liberal democratic Germany seemed the best prospect for American investors. Loans to France were conditional on French 'good behaviour' towards Germany over reparations: withdrawal from the Ruhr and no more military intervention. Meanwhile, the Ruhr invasion profoundly alienated British opinion, and while the British government did not hinder it, it questioned the legality of the invasion and in particular condemned renewed French encouragement of Rhineland separatism (by which Poincaré had hoped to compensate for the dishonoured Anglo-American guarantees of 1919).

[1] I am grateful for these references to Professor Alan Sharp and Dr Peter Yearwood.

France was forced (as much by American financial pressure as by British political pressure) to accept a promissory note from Germany for considerably less by way of reparations under the Dawes plan than its entitlement under Versailles. More important still, France accepted that it could not single-handedly prevent the withering-away of the treaty. Armed force in the Ruhr had won a pyrrhic victory. It was the last attempt of its kind to enforce Versailles and it left a deep impression on French policy-making. If military force under 'Poincaré-la-guerre' could not make Versailles work, how should France approach the 'German problem' in future? □

Modifying Versailles: 'the spirit of Locarno' 1925

A new policy of concerted conciliation was entered into very largely as a result of the efforts of the foreign ministers of France, Germany and Britain, whose strategies (though not their objectives) happened to coincide. France's foreign minister, Aristide Briand, abandoned the policy of attempting to *force* German compliance with Versailles, and sought to bind Germany to a modified version of the settlement through voluntary agreement. Germany's foreign minister, Gustav Stresemann, accepting the futility of resistance, whether military or passive, to overwhelming armed force applied against a disarmed Germany, sought, ostensibly in the name of a policy of understanding with France (*Verständigungspolitik*), to achieve radical revision of Versailles by consensus. Austen Chamberlain sought to mediate between Briand and Stresemann and to assist in a general European 'appeasement'. All three were thought to embody 'the spirit of Locarno', the Swiss resort where far-reaching agreement was reached in 1925. Both at Locarno and at the League of Nations at Geneva (which Germany, sponsored by France, joined in 1926 as a permanent member of the Council) the three statesmen were given to euphoric expressions of international amity and of hopes of Locarno as 'an arrangement which would close the war chapter and start Europe afresh' (Austen Chamberlain, quoted in Lentin, 1991, p.24), and of the League as an even-handed instrument of pacification. 'Away with rifles, machine-guns, cannons,' exclaimed Briand, welcoming Germany to the League. 'Make way for conciliation, arbitration, peace' (V. Margueritte, *Briand*, 1932, p.283).

   The three were jointly honoured as the architects of Locarno by the award of the Nobel Peace Prize. 'The spirit of Locarno' was hailed as a symbol of lasting stability and even cordiality in relations between France, Germany and Britain, and as a harbinger of still better things to come. Marked by American investment, general economic recovery and the surpassing of pre-war levels of production in France, Germany and Britain, the years 1925–29, as Roberts says, were years of 'optimism and confidence' (p.283), symbolized in 1928 by the adherence of the three states to the Kellogg-Briand Pact, renouncing war as an instrument of national policy.

Exercise   Please read Roberts, pp.280–3. Outline the main features of the Treaty of Locarno and assess how far it advanced a solution of the 'German problem'. ■

Specimen answer and discussion   Locarno laid down guarantees of mutual security in a 'Rhineland Pact' underwritten by Britain and Italy, which upheld the 1919 frontiers between Germany and France, and Germany and Belgium and confirmed the permanent demilitarization of the Rhineland (the first allied zone of occupation was duly evacuated in December 1925). Coupled with Locarno were sets of arbitration treaties between Germany and France, Germany and Belgium, and Germany, Poland and Czechoslovakia. Thus Locarno seemed to bring about the objective which had eluded the Allies since Versailles: a *voluntary* acceptance by Germany of the Versailles framework and the permanent integration of Germany within the post-war European system. Unlike Versailles, Locarno was freely negotiated and freely accepted by Germany as an equal and recognized as such by Britain and France. □

'Locarny-blarney' and the dismantling of Versailles 1925–30

Beneath the optimism of what the humorist A. P. Herbert called 'Locarny-blarney', however, Locarno should also be understood as the expression of a new balance of power: a French retreat, a German advance. It was a radically modified version of Versailles that Germany assented to. Under the Dawes Plan reparations were sharply scaled down, to France's detriment.

Moreover, Locarno guaranteed only the *western* frontiers laid down at Versailles. Stresemann rejected French proposals for an 'eastern Locarno', and while Germany signed arbitration treaties with Poland and Czechoslovakia, Stresemann declined to recognize its 1919 frontiers with them as final; and these frontiers, though guaranteed by France by virtue of its treaties of alliance, were not guaranteed by Britain and Italy. Austen Chamberlain pointedly dissociated Britain from any underwriting of the Polish Corridor as an issue 'for which no British Government ever will or ever can risk the bones of a British grenadier' (quoted in Lentin, 1991, p.25).[2] Britain would fight for France or Belgium against German aggression, but declared its unwillingness to do anything for Poland or Czechoslovakia. Under Locarno, as Roberts says, 'certain sections of the Versailles settlement were given a privileged status: that very fact weakened the rest of it' (pp.282).

Locarno thus implicitly relegated Poland and Czechoslovakia to the status of second-class powers, whose very territorial integrity was put in question. From French client states, to be rallied against Germany at France's behest, Poland and Czechoslovakia now seemed more likely to drag France into conflict with Germany on their own account over some such trouble-spot as the Polish Corridor. And if France went to war for Poland, it risked fighting without Britain, whose commitment to assist France under Locarno operated only in the event of an unprovoked German invasion of France, but not if Poland were the *casus belli*. But for France to fight Germany without Britain was unthinkable. Here was a circle that could not be squared. Stresemann boasted justifiably that Locarno broke the back of the Franco-Polish alliance. It did more: the British guarantee of the Franco-German frontier benefited Germany more than France; it signified that France had finally abandoned all hope of detaching the Rhineland and renounced the option of any future invasion of the Ruhr. Once the British and French finally evacuated the Rhineland, Locarno left France without effective means of enforcing what was left of Versailles, and increasingly reliant on German goodwill, the price of which was continually rising. France was the

---

[2] This echoes a remark by Bismarck that the Balkans were 'not worth the bones of a Pomeranian grenadier'.

loser at Locarno: that treaty was the price it had to pay for the British commitment. After Locarno France retreated into the 'Maginot' mentality: it would not take the offensive, if attacked by Germany; its troops would remain on the defensive behind the Maginot Line (a chain of fortifications along the Franco-German border, completed 1930–36).

For Britain, Locarno offered the prospect of ongoing 'appeasement', a continuing search for settlements of the 'German problem' whereby alleviation of further provisions of Versailles was granted in return for German undertakings to fulfil successively less. Since the Ruhr crisis, Britain had moved from ostensible solidarity with its ex-ally France to a position of 'honest broker' between France and Germany. Objectively this represented a weakening and isolation of France and a corresponding strengthening of Germany's weight in the balance of power.

For Stresemann, Locarno was a starting-post for revisionism and for Germany's rapid recovery as a great power. An admirer of Ludendorff and an extreme annexationist in World War I, Stresemann, as Chancellor during the Ruhr crisis, 1923, and Foreign Minister in most cabinets thereafter until his death in 1929, adopted Bismarck and Metternich as his models. His policy of 'understanding' was a means to an end: the piecemeal dismantling of Versailles; privately he described his aim as being 'to push France back trench by trench' (quoted in W. Mommsen, *The Rise and Fall of Weimar Germany*, 1996, p.206), and his method as one of 'finessing' (*finassieren*). For Stresemann 'the spirit of Locarno' was a process of continually pressing further demands: for further downgrading of reparations, for reductions in the size of the occupation forces and for accelerated evacuation of the Rhineland,[3] for the withdrawal of the Inter-Allied Military Control Commission and for recognition of Germany's right to parity of armaments with France (which meant German rearmament). He regularly threw in demands for the revocation of the war-guilt clause, the return of the Saar, and of Eupen-Malmédy from Belgium, the restoration of the German colonies and even *Anschluss* with Austria. In the League he championed the German minority in Poland. In 1927 Germany roundly informed the League that 'Germany could neither accept her frontiers in their present form, nor could she support treaties which would not permit the eventual revision of her frontiers' (M. M. Lee and W. Michalka, *German Foreign Policy 1917–1933*, 1987, p.101).

Exercise   How successful was Weimar Germany's revisionist policy after Locarno in undermining the Versailles settlement? ■

Specimen answer and discussion   Extremely successful:

- Reparations were reduced and regulated by the Dawes Plan (1924) and again under the Young Plan (1929), whereby Germany's total capital debt was reduced to less than one-third of the amount fixed in 1921. The annual instalments were sharply revised, and a final date for payment (1988) was fixed. In 1931, in the face of the world economic crisis, payment of reparations was suspended by international agreement (the Hoover moratorium) and terminated in 1932.

---

[3] 'If the spirit of Locarno was to be a symbol of future European policy, then its final and visible expression must be the withdrawal of troops from the Rhineland' (speech of 21 February, 1926, quoted in D. G. Williamson, *The British in Germany*, 1991, p.305).

- The Inter-Allied Military Control Commission was withdrawn in 1927.

- The Allied armies of occupation completed a phased withdrawal from the Rhineland by 1930, five years ahead of time.

- From pariah nation of 1919 and the Ruhr occupation of 1923, Germany had regained international recognition and respect as one of the great powers with equal rights (*Gleichberechtigung*). At the Geneva Disarmament Conference of 1932, Germany won approval in principle to military parity with France.

- Furthermore, while Weimar Germany was never in a position to contemplate a war with France, the prohibitions on rearmament laid down at Versailles were notoriously defied, both by secret agreements with neutral states, and in particular with Russia dating from before Rapallo (1922), permitting German rearmament and training on Russian soil, and by continual flouting of Versailles inside Germany, evidenced in damning reports by the Inter-Allied Military Control Commission. (These made it clear that 'Germany never was disarmed, never intended to disarm, and for seven years did everything in her power to obstruct, deceive and "counter-control" the Commission' (General J. H. Morgan, quoted in E. Eyck, *A History of the Weimar Republic*, 1967, p.47). □

Versailles limited the German army to 100,000 men. Plans were laid in the 1920s to treble this, and were put in motion in 1932. In 1931, during the Slump, the German army budget was nearly three times that of Britain (S. Marks, *The Illusion of Peace*, 1976, p.117) and the pocket battleship *Deutschland* was launched, with plans for more to follow. 'We are again masters in our house,' Stresemann declared just before his death in 1929 (J. Hiden, *Republican and Fascist Germany*, 1996, p.27). The controls of Versailles having been shaken off by 1930, Germany was poised to resume its position as the leading military power in Europe, if it chose.

Exercise   Please read Roberts, pp.404–7.

How far (if at all) do you consider that the resurgence of German power by 1930 was a threat to peace? ■

Discussion   Perceptions at the time differed according to national viewpoints. Austen Chamberlain, exhilarated by the 'spirit of Locarno', did not object to the shifting balance of power, and regarded Germany's recovery of its 'rightful' place as natural and beneficial to peace, so long as it evolved consensually in co-operation with Britain and France. Briand, powerless to prevent that recovery, sought at Locarno and after to keep Germany peaceful by multilateral treaty engagements and by offers of economic and even political ties, including, in 1930, a desperate but abortive bid for European federal integration. German nationalist opinion, by contrast, represented by the parties of the right, denounced Locarno and each subsequent allied concession as inadequate, and seriously underestimated the magnitude of Stresemann's achievement. In Roberts' words, 'German revisionism had been appeased at Locarno but remained as alive as that of Hungary or Italy' (p.404).

The basic answer to the question depends on how far Germany intended revisionism to go and how far it was prepared to go in pursuit of it. The traditional surviving power élites in Weimar Germany – the army, the foreign office, the civil service, the universities, big business – looked back with nostalgia to the pre-war Reich and to the victories of World War I. The evidence does not suggest that they were satisfied with the radical revisions of Versailles achieved with the consent of Britain and France in the 'spirit' of Locarno. □

Exercise Consider Document I.21 in *Primary Sources 2: Interwar and World War II* as evidence of German opinion about Versailles in the Locarno era. ∎

Discussion This document was an official government manifesto, published in June 1929 while Stresemann was still in power and *before* the onset of the Great Depression in October. It suggests that ten years after Versailles, despite Locarno, the treaty of Versailles (including the war-guilt clause) continued to rankle and to unite German resentment. It was seen as the cause of all Germany's ills. □

The early completion of the evacuation of the Rhineland by the armies of occupation in 1930, far from being appreciated as a remarkable gesture of 'appeasement', ignited an explosion of pent-up German nationalism and demands for more. Six million signed a petition of protest against the Young Plan. Foreign policy dominated the election of 1930, in which Nazi representation in the *Reichstag*, boosted by 6.5 million voters, rose from 12 seats in 1928 to 107, making the party the second largest. In July 1932, the Nazi vote soared to nearly 14 million, and the Nazis became the largest party with 230 seats. As you may recall, the programme of the Nazi (National Socialist German Workers') Party, drawn up in 1920, called for rejection of the Versailles settlement and the creation of a 'Greater Germany' (*Grossdeutschland*) 'on the basis of the right of self-determination.' The last governments of the Republic tried to outbid the Nazis in revisionist demands, clamouring for an end to reparations, for the right to rearm to a level with Britain and France and for an economic customs-union with Austria (1931), no doubt as a prelude to *Anschluss*.

How far, then, did German aims extend? And did Weimar Germany seriously contemplate war to achieve them?

Germany could probably have gone to war with Poland to modify its eastern frontiers without involving Britain and France, since Britain had expressly and France had by implication written off Poland at Locarno, and Russia's benevolent neutrality (to say the least) was secured by Stresemann at the Treaty of Berlin (1926) which reaffirmed Rapallo, isolated Poland, and reminded Britain and France that Germany could invoke Russian support for revisionism. 'Naturally,' Stresemann informed his Russian opposite number, 'we refuse to see any justification for the continued existence of the present Polish state' (quoted in Eyck, p.25). Even at Locarno he explicitly refused to renounce the use of force against Poland (Lee and Michalka, p.145), and the *Reichswehr* drew up plans for a limited war with Poland. In 1925 he secretly informed his cabinet that his policy was to create a 'Greater Germany' in central Europe, such a state to include non-Germans 'under German suzerainty' (F. Fischer, *From Kaiserreich to Third Reich*, 1986, p.84). He told his own party, the German People's Party, that once Germany was rearmed he would seek to recover Alsace-Lorraine. Recent research suggests that 'Stresemann's ultimate goal ... went considerably beyond simple revision of the Versailles system: he intended on the ruins of Versailles to reconstruct and even to expand the pre-war Great Power position of the German Reich' (Lee and Michalka, p.98). Would this, if true, necessarily have led to war? Or could the re-establishment of German hegemony in Europe have continued to evolve peacefully? We can only speculate about this, since Stresemann died in 1929, and the Weimar Republic came to an end soon after. The important point is that whatever Germany's political complexion after 1930, Stresemann's achievements would soon enable it to make wide-ranging foreign policy choices in defiance of what remained of Versailles.

In considering the increasing pressure in Germany after Stresemann for further revision of Versailles, attention should be paid to the Great Depression, whose effects in Germany were particularly marked. The rise in unemployment from 2 million in 1929 to 6 million in 1932 was undoubtedly reflected in the electoral triumphs which made the Nazis the largest party in the *Reichstag*. While, as A. W. Purdue states 'it is difficult to argue that the Depression caused the Second World War in any straightforward sense' (*The Second World War*, 1999, p.18), its effects in Germany provoked mounting despair and alienation from the Weimar Republic and a readiness to embrace political extremism; and they rekindled and refocused resentment at the Versailles settlement (on which Germany's latest economic catastrophe was also questionably but universally blamed). The Depression, then, was crucial: it 'gave Nazism its opportunity' (Roberts, p.467, and see I. Kershaw, excerpt from *Hitler 1889–1936. Hubris, Secondary Sources*, pp. 72–8).

2   THE CHALLENGE OF NAZI FOREIGN POLICY: (a) THE TAYLOR THESIS

Exercise: the disintegration of Versailles to 1933

By the end of the Weimar Republic, the Versailles settlement lay in tatters so far as its constraints on Germany were concerned. What was left of the treaty in this respect at the time Hitler became Chancellor in 1933? (See 'Germany 1919–38' in the *Maps Booklet* and Roberts, Map 7, p.xx and please read Roberts, pp.413– 17 and 425–38.) ■

Specimen answer

1   German inequality of armaments, despite acceptance in principle of *Gleichberechtigung* by Britain and France, and continuous breaches of the disarmament provisions of Versailles. In 1933 Germany's armed forces were in no condition to fight a major war.

2   Control of the Saar by the League of Nations, the future of the territory to be decided by plebiscite in 1935.

3   Demilitarization of the Rhineland (freely accepted by Germany at Locarno).

4   Prohibition on *Anschluss* with Austria (an attempt to establish an Austro-German customs union in 1931, vociferously opposed by the French, was narrowly vetoed by the International Court as contrary to Versailles).

5   Inclusion of 3½ million Germans in the Czech Sudetenland, though neither this territory nor its German minority had ever formed part of the Reich.

6   Inclusion of former German territory and half-a-million former German nationals in the Polish Corridor and Poznania and control of Danzig by the League.

7   Grievances such as the loss of Memel to Lithuania, the loss of the former German colonies and the long-standing stigma of the war-guilt clause. □

Exercise: the reversal of Versailles after 1933 Specimen answer

Taking the same items, what was left of Versailles by the end of 1939? ■

Little or nothing: the peace settlement was destroyed.

1   The prohibition on German rearmament was a dead letter. Germany withdrew from the Disarmament Conference in 1933 and began rearming in earnest. By 1939, the *Reichswehr* of 100,000 had become the 3 million-strong *Wehrmacht*, ready for war, supported by the *Luftwaffe*, with over 4,000 front-line aircraft, and a growing Atlantic fleet, including submarines.

2   The Saar was restored to Germany after a plebiscite (1935) in accordance with the treaty.

3   German troops reoccupied the Rhineland (1936) in violation of the treaty.

4   Austria was united with Germany (*Anschluss*) (March 1938) in violation of Versailles and Locarno.

5   The Sudetenland was voluntarily ceded to Germany by Britain and France (September 1938), which then took over Bohemia-Moravia as a 'protectorate', Slovakia becoming a satellite state (March 1939).

6/7   Germany re-took Memel (March 1939) in violation of the treaty. Germany invaded and defeated Poland and re-took the territories lost in 1919 (September 1939). Hitler had repudiated the war-guilt clause in 1937. On 6 October 1939 he declared that (apart from the recovery of Germany's colonies) 'we consider the treaty of Versailles extinct'. □

By March 1939 Hitler had, without war, propelled the balance of power in Europe still further in Germany's favour by annexing Austria and partitioning Czechoslovakia. By October 1939 he had conquered and partitioned Poland.

The traditional interpretation of World War II: Hitler's war

In contrast to the controversy over the origins of the 1914 war, the origins of World War II seemed obvious to contemporaries and could largely be put down to one man's limitless megalomania: 'the policy of a fanatic ideologue who ignored sober calculations of national interest in order to put his manic ideas into practice' (Norman Rich, Course Reader, p.129). For twenty years after 1939, few doubted the explanation that World War II was intended, planned and ignited by Hitler, at the head of a Germany that by the time he came to power was already manifestly the 'dominant factor' in Europe. To this was added contributory negligence by Britain and France: their failure to counter Germany's growing challenge for mastery in Europe after 1933. Failure to act in 1935, when Germany began *openly* rearming, or in 1936, when German troops reoccupied the Rhineland, meant inevitable European war and an uncertain outcome if resistance was finally offered.

The Taylor thesis: World War II – the result of 'diplomatic blunders' and German history

In 1961 this thesis was challenged by A. J. P. Taylor (1906–1990) in *The Origins of the Second World War*. Taylor's views were radical, cogently put and argued with point and wit. His book remains full of illuminating insights. But his fundamental thesis flouted conventional wisdom, aroused passionate controversy at the time and continues, forty years on to stimulate debate. (See E. M. Robertson (ed.) *The Origins of the Second World War. Historical Interpretations*, 1971; G. Martel (ed.) *The Origins of the Second World War Reconsidered. The A. J. P. Taylor Debate after Twenty-five Years*, 1986; R. Boyce and E. M. Robertson (eds.) *Paths to War. New Essays on the Origins of the Second World War*, 1989, Andrew Crozier, *The Causes of the Second World War*, 1997, pp.226–32; A.W. Purdue, *The Second World War* (1999), pp.7–41). Taylor rejected the explanation accepted by the Allies at the post-war Nuremberg trials in 1946, just as historians between the wars rejected the Allies' thesis of German 'war-guilt' laid down at Versailles. He denied that Hitler sought a war of territorial conquest for 'living-space' (*Lebensraum*) at the expense of Poland and Russia, or that he intended war with Britain and France.

According to Taylor, an expert in nineteenth and early twentieth-century diplomatic history, Hitler, like most modern statesmen, was a tactician and an opportunist, not a warmonger: 'He exploited events far more then he followed precise coherent plans' (*The Origins of the Second World War*, 1964, p.10). Like most Germans, and like Stresemann before him, he wished to undo what was left of Versailles and to reverse the verdict of November 1918 by continuing to increase German influence in central and eastern Europe. Again like Stresemann, he sought to do so by 'finesse', by a game of diplomatic poker, backed by bluff, by out-manoeuvring western statesmen in a war of nerves. Since he was far better at this game than they were, he was continually more successful, and played for ever higher stakes: reintroduction of conscription 1935, remilitarization of the Rhineland 1936, annexation of Austria and the Sudetenland 1938, occupation of Bohemia-Moravia 1939. At most, he contemplated making limited gains by means of short, localized campaigns of the *Blitzkrieg* variety, and it was such a war with Poland for the recovery of Danzig that he intended in September 1939, not the general European war which actually broke out when, much to his surprise, Britain and France declared war on Germany. 'Far from wanting war', says Taylor, 'a general war was the last thing he wanted' (ibid., p.16). 'The war of 1939, far from being premeditated, was a mistake, the result on both sides of diplomatic blunders' (ibid., p.269).

Taylor denies that Hitler had any serious long-term plans for conquest in Russia, still less for world domination. His utterances about *Lebensraum* were coffee-house babble or table-talk, without any effect on his actual pre-war foreign policy. We should not, Taylor urges, judge that policy as the judges at Nuremberg allegedly did, with benefit of post-war hindsight. We should not conclude that Hitler always intended to dominate Europe by force and bring Western Russia under German sway simply because that was what he temporarily achieved, or that his rearmament policy meant that he was set on war, any more than rearmament in Britain meant that Neville Chamberlain wanted war.

Taylor draws a clear distinction between Hitler's domestic and foreign policy. At home, Taylor agrees, Hitler destroyed democracy and instituted a ruthless dictatorship. But his foreign policy, according to Taylor, followed traditional lines. 'His foreign policy,' Taylor writes, 'was that of his predecessors, of the professional diplomats at the foreign ministry, and indeed of virtually all Germans' (quoted in the Course Reader, p.126). Taylor makes the paradox that in some respects Hitler was more moderate in his foreign policy than his predecessors. Unlike Stresemann, he was willing to conclude a non-aggression pact with Poland in 1934, despite Danzig and the Corridor; and he renounced any claim to Alsace-Lorraine. Unlike the Pan-Germanists, he wrote off the South Tyrol in order to keep on good terms with Mussolini. He never showed any real interest in recovering the German colonies, except to embarrass the British. Unlike the Wilhelminian Imperialists, he was not interested in the Middle East, nor did he aspire to naval rivalry with Britain. 'Hitler,' Taylor argues sardonically, 'was treading, rather cautiously, in Bethmann Hollweg's footsteps. There was nothing new or unusual in his aims or outlook' (quoted in Course Reader, p.131).

In both aims and methods, therefore, Hitler's foreign policy, according to Taylor, was conventional. Whoever had been in charge of German foreign policy in the 1930s would have continued in the tradition of Stresemann to exploit the international situation to Germany's advantage as its natural preponderance in Europe continued to reassert itself. The Nuremberg explanation of Hitler as the author of long-premeditated plans for step-by-step aggression, by placing responsibility for World War II on Hitler and his henchmen, absolves the German people. It also relieves historians of the task of explaining World War II in the context of German history, of which, in Taylor's view, it was the logical outcome. For all his insistence on the accidental and the contingent – 'diplomatic blunders' as the immediate causes of the war – at a deeper level Taylor sees the fundamental long-term cause of the war in the persistence of the 'German problem', which the Allies had failed to solve in 1919. The 'German problem' was not Hitler, but the existence of Germany as the 'dominant factor' in Europe. Since 1870 a united Germany had proved incapable of peaceful integration within Europe, and the 'German problem' remained unsolved until the intervention of Russia and America and the partition of Germany in 1945. Hitler was not an aberration, but the culmination of German history.

Such is Taylor's thesis, argued both in *The Origins of the Second World War* and in his earlier book, *The Course of German History* (1945).

Taylor continues to make us rethink several basic aspects of Hitler's foreign policy and their relation to the causes of World War II. First and foremost, what *were* Hitler's foreign policy objectives? Was there anything to distinguish them from those of Stresemann? The question is not merely academic. If Hitler's ambitions were limited to a *Grossdeutsch* programme in accordance with German self-determination, (as stated in point 1 of the Nazi party programme) then 'appeasement' of Germany might have worked. If Germany would have been satisfied with the incorporation of Austria, the Sudetenland, Danzig and the Corridor, then 'appeasement' made sense, and British and French intervention in 1939 was a fatal error, leading to world war on an issue in which Germany was in the right.

Exercise Let us now consider a critique of Taylor's thesis by Norman Rich, formerly Professor of History at Brown University. Please read his article entitled 'Hitler's foreign policy' in the Course Reader, pp.125-41. What, in general terms, is Rich's basic objection to Taylor's approach to the evidence? ■

Specimen answer Any historical thesis must be based on *fact,* and its validity depends not on its 'brilliance' (which Rich concedes in Taylor's case), but on its relationship to the evidence; that is, it must be judged on the historian's treatment of the primary sources and on the inferences which he or she draws from them.

Rich complains that Taylor's basic thesis is flawed by unsound treatment of primary sources, which Taylor either ignores or recklessly dismisses. □

Hitler's *Mein Kampf*: day-dreams or foreign policy objectives?

Exercise Let us put Rich's criticism to the test. Please examine for yourself the excerpt from Hitler's *Mein Kampf* (Document I.22(b) in *Primary Sources 2: Interwar and World War II*) and consider it as evidence of Hitler's ideas on foreign policy. ■

Discussion The passage is a clear, open rejection of the restoration of Germany's 1914 frontiers as a foreign policy objective. Revision of the frontiers laid down at Versailles would not be worth a war. Hitler rejects the 1914 frontiers as arbitrary, strategically weak and in any case inadequate. Not only would they still not include all Germans within the Reich (a *Grossdeutsch* aim), but they would not sufficiently enhance Germany's 'world power' status *vis-à-vis* Britain, America and France. The aim of Nazi foreign policy must by contrast be the forcible acquisition of *Lebensraum* (living-space) – not as client-states but by outright annexation for resettlement by Germans, as a prerequisite to Germany's becoming a 'world power'. *Lebensraum* will involve war with France, but this will be a secondary war: its purpose will be to protect German gains in the east. *Lebensraum* is the only achievement that will justify war.

The aim of *Lebensraum* thus went far beyond a policy of the 1914 frontiers and a *Grossdeutsch* policy. Explicitly it involved territorial conquest in Russia. □

Taylor on *Mein Kampf*

According to Taylor, far too much has been read into *Mein Kampf*. He points out that Hitler at the time he wrote the book, in 1924, was a nobody, an obscure failed street politician who could not seriously expect ever to come to power. Writing *Mein Kampf* from his prison cell, Hitler was indulging in fantasy, regurgitating ideas about *Lebensraum* current in right-wing circles since before World War I. To Hitler, in Taylor's view, 'these were no more than day-dreams concocted in his spare time' (Course Reader, p.127). Hitler did not take them seriously and neither should historians. We should judge his foreign policy after 1933 in the light of circumstances at the time he directed it, and disconnect it from its supposed origins in *Mein Kampf*. Just because after 1939 Hitler went on to attempt much of what he described as his aims in *Mein Kampf,* it does not follow that that was his intention all along. We should beware, says Taylor, of judging Hitler's pre-war policy with post-war hindsight, and extrapolating from *Mein Kampf* an illusory common origin, linking pre-war policy with policy in wartime. Before 1939, Taylor insists, Hitler did no more in foreign policy than any other successful German statesman would have done. *Mein Kampf* and *Lebensraum* are red herrings.

Yet however unlikely it was in 1924 that Hitler would be Chancellor of Germany nine years later, it does not follow either that he did not mean what he said in *Mein Kampf* or that what he wrote bore no relation to his subsequent foreign policy. Repeatedly in the years after *Mein Kampf,* both before and, more significantly, after 1933, he reverted openly to the acquisition of *Lebensraum* as his ultimate objective.[4] Evidence of this appears, for example: (a) in a speech to industrialists at Düsseldorf in January 1932 (G. L. Weinberg, *The Foreign Policy of Hitler's Germany,* 1970, p.25); (b) in a speech to high-ranking generals and admirals, including the Commander-in-Chief of the army, in February 1933, immediately after becoming Chancellor, when he stated as the goal of his foreign policy the 'conquest of *Lebensraum* in the east and its ruthless Germanisation' (ibid., p.27); (c) in February 1934, when he told his new Commander-in-Chief and Chief of Staff to prepare for an eventual pre-emptive strike in the west, followed by an offensive war in the east, a strategy identical to that set out in *Mein Kampf* (ibid., p. 178); (d) in March 1935, in conference with Goering, when he stressed that whatever interim stratagems he might adopt, his ultimate aim remained expansion eastward (ibid., p.226); (e) in August 1936, in a memorandum for a four-year plan, which defined his ultimate objective as *Lebensraum* (Document I.12 in *Primary Sources 2: Interwar and World War II*); and (f) in September 1936 in a speech at the Nuremberg rally.

If Hitler meant what he said in 1932, 1933, 1934, 1935 and 1936, why not in 1924? Taylor, though he does not refer to these later instances, maintains that even in the 1930s Hitler was merely day-dreaming or talking for effect when he spoke of war for *Lebensraum.* Paradoxically, however, as Rich points out, Taylor also agrees that 'the driving force in him [Hitler] was a terrifying literalism' (Course Reader, p.127). In other words, there were occasions when Hitler did mean what he said. The question, then, is did he mean what he said about *Lebensraum?* Taylor denies it, though his point that Hitler was merely repeating 'the conversation of any Austrian cafe or German beer-house' does not undermine but could corroborate his attribution to Hitler of 'a terrifying literalism'. There is no necessary incompatibility between short-term tactical aims (liquidation of Versailles) and long-term, strategic objectives (*Grossdeutschland/Lebensraum*). There seems therefore no good reason to dissociate *Mein Kampf* from Hitler's subsequent pronouncements and actions. On the contrary: Hitler's book, as Rich says, provides 'an exposition of the ideas which he proposed to translate into action' (ibid.).

---

[4] This is also evidenced in Hitler's so-called *Second Book* (1928), first published in 1961 by Gerhard Weinberg. See *Hitler's Second Book* (1961) intr. T. Taylor, New York.

The Hossbach Memorandum

Let us pursue this theme and test Taylor's interpretation against another primary source, this time relating to Hitler's intentions in late 1937.

Exercise   Please read Document I.23 in *Primary Sources 2: Interwar and World War II*, an excerpt from the Hossbach Memorandum, 5 November 1937. What does it suggest about Hitler's foreign policy objectives and responsibility for World War II? ■

Specimen answer and discussion   It seems clear proof, consistent with *Mein Kampf* and Hitler's annual pronouncements between 1932 and 1936 noted earlier, of his unabated determination to realize the goal of *Lebensraum* ('Germany's problem of space'). He posits the opposition of Britain and France to 'any further strengthening of Germany's position' in Europe by way of territorial expansion, concluding that such expansion 'could only be solved by means of force'. War was inevitable. The only questions were 'when and how'. Hitler stressed the need for a showdown by 1943/45 'at the latest', before German rearmament became obsolescent and while 'the rest of the world was still preparing its defences'. Expansion would begin with the 'elimination' of Austria and Czechoslovakia as independent states, the expulsion of their non-German inhabitants and their incorporation within Germany as a starting-point for further action. □

Taylor on the Hossbach Memorandum

Taylor was at pains to deny the significance of this document, both in his book and in the Foreword which he added in 1963. In the Foreword he queried the memorandum's authenticity. He stressed that it was put in evidence after the war at Nuremberg, implying that this in itself makes it suspect ('those who believe the evidence in political trials may go on quoting the Hossbach Memorandum', Taylor, 1964, p.22). In his book, describing the memorandum as 'this rambling disquisition' (ibid., p.170), he argued, as he did about *Mein Kampf*, that 'Hitler's exposition was in large part day-dreaming', and that in any case Hitler's point was that 'Germany would gain her aims without a great war; "force" apparently meant to him the threat of war, not necessarily war itself' (ibid., p.169). Taylor also advanced the hypothesis that Hitler's address was designed as an internal political manoeuvre; and while he withdrew this suggestion in an article in 1965, he continued to dismiss the memorandum as another example of Hitler 'ranting in his usual fashion' (quoted in Robertson (ed.), p.136). Taylor insisted that no one took much notice of it at the time.

   All these assertions are open to question.

1   It is one thing to question the memorandum's authenticity (as to which there is room for argument, the document being a copy of a copy); but to deny its evidential value simply on the grounds that it was accepted as proof by a tribunal of which Taylor disapproves is illogical.

2   Taylor offers nothing to support his suggestion that by 'force' Hitler only meant the threat of force. Hitler's own examples ('the campaigns of Frederick the Great for Silesia, and Bismarck's wars against Austria and France') are examples of war, not the threat of war; and, by the 'risks'

attendant on 'the resort to force', Hitler surely meant defeat rather than war. Hitler himself speaks of 'the resort to force' (not 'the threat of force'), and of 'our attack' and 'take the offensive'.

3   As for its being a 'rambling disquisition', the memorandum is not a precise timetable, but it does restate a long-term objective of *Lebensraum,* interim aims regarding the conquest of Austria and Czechoslovakia, and the contingent questions of how and when to deal with Britain and France (who, Hitler rightly predicted, would not in fact intervene).

4   As for not taking himself seriously, why should Hitler stress that the speech be regarded as 'his last will and testament' and summon his Foreign Minister, Minister of War and the three service chiefs to hear it, if he did not mean what he said? In fact, there is ample evidence both that he was in deadly earnest and that they took him seriously. Far from Taylor's claim that none of those present 'gave it another thought' (p.171), later the same month Hitler himself told pupils at a Nazi training centre that his aim was *Lebensraum* in the east. In December 1937 the armed forces were ordered to prepare for an attack on Austria and Czechoslovakia, even at the risk of intervention by Britain and France, with a view to realizing the explicit goal of *Lebensraum*. Goering gave orders to this effect to the *Luftwaffe* immediately after the 5 November meeting.

Early in 1938 Hitler dismissed the relatively cautious Minister of War, Blomberg and military Commander-in-Chief Fritsch, and replaced Neurath by Ribbentrop as Foreign Minister. He set Neurath (as 'Protector' of Bohemia-Moravia) the task of drawing up plans for the 'compulsory emigration of 2 million people from Czechoslovakia' (Document I.23 in *Primary Sources 2: Interwar and World War II*). He abolished the Ministry of War, replacing it by a High Command of the Armed Forces *(Oberkommando der Wehrmacht)* responsible to himself as Supreme Commander. In March, he ordered his troops into Austria. In May, he gave orders for the invasion of Czechoslovakia.

Unbiased consideration of the evidence, direct and circumstantial, therefore suggests that Taylor's basic thesis is untenable. His interpretation of some of the primary sources does not always stand scrutiny, and, as Rich complains, 'he cavalierly disregarded a great deal of other evidence which did not happen to fit with his own theories' (Course Reader, p.126). Instead of 'rubbishing' the Hossbach Memorandum because it did not match his interpretation of Hitler, he might tellingly have compared it with Wilhelminian plans for eastward expansion (for example, the War Council of 8 December 1912 and the 'September Programme' 1914, see Book 1, Unit 5, p.182–4 and Book 2, Unit 6, pp.21–2) in support of his underlying thesis of continuity in German foreign policy. If war for *Lebensraum*, as Rich emphasizes (Course Reader, p.129), was 'the policy of a fanatic ideologue', how do we explain its acceptance and ultimate implementation by the military and Foreign Office if not in terms of at least *some* degree of continuity of aims?

Continuity and change in German foreign policy after 1933

Roberts, discussing Hitler's foreign policy aims (p.415), more or less follows Taylor's view of a continuity of aims in German foreign policy. Hitler's demands 'did not seem very unusual': the destruction of Versailles, the recovery of 1914 *irredenta,* Germany's re-emergence as a great military power – '*Grossdeutsch* themes'. The aims outlined in *Mein Kampf* and the Hossbach Memorandum Roberts too dismisses as 'only a vague dream of a racialist policy of "living space" in the east' (Roberts, p.415), rather than Hitler's ultimate objective and the mainspring of his foreign policy. Essentially, Roberts argues, Hitler's contribution to German diplomacy was 'not one of content, but of technique'. Even then, Roberts, like Taylor, sees Hitler's methods in terms only of 'great daring and dexterity', of opportunism and bluff (ibid.).

Leaving aside for the moment the central issue of the objectives of Nazi foreign policy, let us turn to Nazi *methods* in foreign policy. While Stresemann as Foreign Minister had been responsible to the cabinet and to the *Reichstag,* Hitler as Führer (leader), was constitutionally accountable to no-one. After President Hindenburg's death in 1934, Hitler made himself Head of State and Führer as well as Chancellor, and bound the armed forces to himself (rather than to the state) by exacting a personal oath of unconditional obedience. In 1936, the year of his Rhineland *coup,* he summoned his cabinet only four times. He conducted his own foreign policy, both in regard to long-term strategy and to immediate timing and method, in accordance with his own perceptions, unrestrained by institutional pressures, which he bypassed by submitting each successful *fait accompli* to the suffrage of a general election or plebiscite (or both simultaneously): on quitting the League of Nations, 1933 (plebiscite and *Reichstag* elections); on the reoccupation of the Rhineland, 1936 (election); on the *Anschluss* with Austria, April 1938 (plebiscite and election); on the incorporation of the Sudetenland, December 1938 (plebiscite and election).

Increasingly he distanced himself from the Foreign Office, whose cautious gradualism he despised. In March 1935, he informed the Foreign Office only at the last moment of his decision to announce the reintroduction of conscription. The professional diplomats of Imperial and Weimar Germany found their influence superseded by that of Nazi adventurers contemptuous of aristocratic gentility or bourgeois inhibitions – 'men who, having taken an active part in the Nazi revolution, have a certain obduracy and a certain very characteristic preference for actions that might be interpreted as being rather defiant' (F. A. Voigt, *Manchester Guardian* Central Europe correspondent, in a broadcast of March 1935, Audio 3, item 7). Chief of these was Ribbentrop, formerly a travelling champagne salesman, after 1933 Hitler's chief foreign policy adviser and roving ambassador at large. By 1937 Ribbentrop's own organization (*Dienststelle Ribbentrop*) of party contacts inside and outside Germany had greater influence on foreign policy than the Foreign Office. Convinced of Ribbentrop's superior expertise, especially in Anglo-German relations, Hitler in 1936 appointed him Ambassador in London (where he won the nickname 'von Brickendrop'), and in 1938 Foreign Minister. Ribbentrop, a fanatical Nazi and a vain and dangerous amateur, persuaded Hitler that Britain was a 'hate-inspired antagonist' (*Primary Sources 2: Interwar and World War II*, Document I.23), and egged him on in his increasingly reckless foreign policy.

The Weimar Foreign Office, despite its desire for frontier revision, had not actively interfered in the internal affairs of neighbouring states. After 1933 a special Nazi Foreign Organization *(Auslandsorganisation)* was set up for the purpose of fomenting dissent among Germans domiciled outside the Reich, particularly in Austria, Poland and Czechoslovakia (for example, through the

Sudeten agitator, Konrad Henlein) and to destabilize the host countries. In 1937 this body was made part of the Foreign Office, but took its orders from Hitler's deputy, Rudolf Hess.

The downgrading of the Foreign Office was compounded by the fact that the permanent officials, however much they feared Hitler's methods, were delighted at his revisionist achievements. Each foreign policy success, flouting their cautious fears, seemed to suggest that Hitler's bold instincts were surer than the measured judgements of professional diplomats.

Nazi methods in foreign policy

Nazi methods exemplify what Karl Dietrich Bracher calls 'the change from traditional diplomacy to the strategy of surprise' (*The German Dictatorship*, 1973, p.364), freedom from traditional constraints, ruthlessness, speed, suddenness and the presentation of the *fait accompli* (often at the weekend) accompanied by expressions of peaceful intentions, all of which dazzled, disoriented and divided the other powers.

To take the main examples between 1933 and 1936:

1   October 1933: Germany ostentatiously withdraws not only from the Disarmament Conference (repeating a similar walk-out the year before) but also from the League of Nations, which it had joined only seven years before.

2   January 1934: Germany signs a non-aggression pact with Poland. This *apparent* retreat from Weimar's intransigence over the eastern frontiers illustrates Hitler's flexibility and short-term opportunism: by this tactical *démarche*, designed to gain time for German rearmament, he neutralized the possibility of Franco-Polish action against Germany.

3   July 1934: assassination of the Austrian Chancellor, Dollfuss, in an attempted Nazi *coup*, to which (as Weinberg argues (*Germany, Hitler and World War II*, 1995, pp.96–7) Hitler was unquestionably privy, intended to lead to *Anschluss*.

4   March 1935: while Weimar Germany had rearmed in secret, Hitler publicly announces and triumphantly celebrates the reintroduction of conscription and the creation of the *Luftwaffe*, both in violation of Versailles. (Please see Video 1, item 35, 'Germany asserts the right to re-arm', 21 March 1935. Note how the 'formidable demonstration of German armed discipline' is preceded by War Minister Blomberg's reassuring reference to 'a Germany at peace in a Europe appeased' and followed by the commentator's 'hope that Germany's aims are as pacific as her leaders' utterances declare them to be'.)

5   June 1935: Anglo-German naval agreement. While Weimar's pocket battleship, the *Deutschland*, was within the letter of Versailles, Hitler determined to build up German naval power. In a diplomatic *coup* carried through by Ribbentrop, he secured Britain's consent to the radical amendment of Versailles by undertaking, for the time being, to restrict the German navy to one-third of Britain's naval strength.

6   March 1936: German troops reoccupy the Rhineland, in violation both of
     Versailles and of Locarno. (Note the revealing newsreel title - Video 1, item
     36 – 'Hitler staggers Europe', 9 March 1936.)

Leaving aside the question of Hitler's ultimate objectives, then, Nazi *methods*
in themselves introduced a disturbing new element to European relations: a
new dynamism, characterized by open defiance not merely of Versailles, but
also of Locarno and, by implication, of the existing European order.

Nazi methods in foreign policy – 'a kind of *Blitzkrieg* diplomatic offensive'
(R. Boyce and E. M. Robertson (eds), 1989, p.6) – accentuated as never
before the 'German problem', increased international tensions and made
war more likely.

3   THE CHALLENGE OF NAZI FOREIGN POLICY: (b) THE RHINELAND CRISIS 1936

The Rhineland crisis of 1936 provides a clear example of Nazi foreign policy in
action.
Please read Roberts, pages 416–17, and consult Map 7 in the *Maps Booklet*.

Hitler's challenge

In March 1936, overriding the fears of his War Minister and Foreign Minister,
Blomberg and Neurath, Hitler ordered some 30,000 troops into the Rhineland
zone – all that territory on the left bank of the Rhine and a fifty-kilometre wide
strip on the right bank which had been declared a permanent demilitarized zone
at Versailles and Locarno.

The troops marched in on Saturday 7 March – one of Hitler's 'Saturday
surprises'. As they did, Hitler delivered a broadcast speech in the *Reichstag*,
repudiating the Treaty of Locarno as incompatible with the Franco-Soviet pact of
1935 and justifying the reoccupation of the Rhineland as a defensive measure
against the danger to Germany of encirclement by France, Russia and
Czechoslovakia. (The pretext of the Franco-Soviet pact was rightly derided in
Punch as a 'cock-and-bear story' 25 March, 1936.)

At the same time, Hitler offered to negotiate a set of 'new agreements for the
establishment of a system of European security' (Document I.24 in *Primary
Sources 2: Interwar and World War II*) and announced an immediate general
election to approve the occupation.

The remilitarization of the Rhineland destroyed the basis of the post-war
system of European security. Demilitarization was the key to strategic control of
the 'German problem': with the gradual and now increasingly defiant reassertion
of Germany's natural preponderance, the Rhineland zone served to contain and
block German military aggression. As long as the zone remained demilitarized,
Germany could not invade France, Belgium or Holland; and since the zone left
Germany's industrial heartland open to invasion from the west, Germany could
not advance in any other direction without risking retaliation by France. The

independence of Austria, Czechoslovakia and Poland was thus directly linked with the maintenance of the zone's demilitarized status.

Responsibility for enforcing Locarno lay with its other signatories: France, Britain, Italy and Belgium. Mussolini, rebuffed by Britain and France over Abyssinia (Roberts, pp.409–13), stood aside. Britain, France and Belgium took no counter-measures.

Nazi foreign policy techniques in the Rhineland crisis

1   *Timing.* While remilitarization in itself was not unexpected by the British and French governments, its timing took them unawares, particularly since Hitler, Neurath and the German Foreign Office had given repeated assurances of loyalty to Locarno, including demilitarization. As with most of his foreign policy *coups* since 1933, Hitler enjoyed the psychological advantage of surprise, shock and the *fait accompli.* (See Video 1, item 36, 'Hitler staggers Europe' for immediate British reaction. The commentator ends on a bewildered note: 'Where does it all lead? To a new war, or to a surer peace?')

2   *Presentation.* Hitler's speech to the *Reichstag* (part of which can be heard on Audio 3, item 8) brings out his quite extraordinary effectiveness as a manipulator of opinion, domestic and foreign. He presented 'the motivating forces in the foreign policy of National Socialism' (quoted in F. J. Berber (ed.), *Locarno*, 1936, p.204) as moderate and rational. He alternated themes that appealed to all shades of German opinion (contrasting Germany's humiliation under Versailles and the recovery of German honour since 1933) with themes designed to conciliate foreign opinion. He made friendly references to Britain, France and Poland. He invoked the Anglo-German Naval agreement of 1935 and the non-aggression pact of 1934 with Poland. He spoke of Germany as a bastion against Bolshevism and as a contributor to 'European culture and European civilization'. He posed, not as a rabid nationalist, but as a responsible and moderate statesman, who professedly did not even aim at Germany's 1914 frontiers, let alone at a *Grossdeutsch* policy, still less at *Lebensraum* – a good European, albeit a patriot, who sought to co-operate 'in lessening the strained tensions by means of a slow evolutionary development in peaceful collaboration' (Berber, p.226), (a brilliant evocation of the 'Spirit of Locarno' and an excellent definition of 'appeasement'). He denied hostile intentions against Poland or Czechoslovakia, deprecated any idea of war, and while stating that he expected eventual colonial concessions, declared (not for the first or last time) that 'in Europe we have no territorial claims to put forward' (Berber, p.226).

Exercise   Please read Document I.24 in *Primary Sources 2: Interwar and World War II,* which contains what Hitler called his 'concrete proposals' for peace. Summarize and assess them. What do you suppose was their purpose? ∎

Specimen answer and discussion

To replace Locarno, Hitler proposed a demilitarized zone on *both* sides of the Franco-German border, non-aggression pacts with France and Belgium, guaranteed by Britain and Italy; an air pact with the Western powers, non-aggression pacts with the states to Germany's east, and Germany's re-entry to the League of Nations.

These offers were brilliantly designed in that: (a) they appeared to correspond with what Britain in particular had long been seeking; (b) they softened the sting of the occupation; (c) they gave Germany time to consolidate the occupation by sending in more troops, while Britain and France considered how to respond to the offers. □

But were they seriously meant?

1   Hitler can hardly have been serious about the bilateral demilitarized zone with France. Such a zone would have rendered useless the Maginot Line which, as he knew, was built only for defence.

2   What could be the value of Hitler's commitment to a new Locarno, when he had just repudiated his obligations under the existing treaty?

3   When Britain and France attempted to follow up Hitler's 'concrete proposals' with detailed requests for clarification, they were fobbed off. The questions went unanswered. The proposals came to nothing. This suggests that they were never seriously intended except as a ruse.

Why did France and Britain not act?

The remilitarization of the Rhineland was an open challenge to France, its domestic security and its alliance-system. German troops now stood on the French frontier and began work on their own defences. France could no longer 'intervene effectively in order to assist our eastern allies,' the Prime Minister Sarraut pointed out (A. Adamthwaite, *Grandeur and Misery*, 1995, p.205). But this was as much a statement of fact as a complaint. Ever since the Ruhr debacle of 1923, it had been the cardinal principle of French foreign policy that no military action against Germany could be contemplated without British support. The consensus among recent historians is that calls by the French government for such support in 1936 were largely shadow-boxing. French military thinking, strategic and tactical, was exclusively defensive. No plans existed for operations east of the Maginot line (completed in 1936). There was no rapid reaction force to respond to the emergency, and the Chief of Staff, General Gamelin, advised that French entry into the Rhineland would unleash full-scale war. The 'Maginot mentality' reflected the reality that France lacked the political will to take offensive military action. This is corroborated by opinion across the political spectrum in the Chamber of Deputies and the press. The Rhineland had already been tacitly written off (Adamthwaite, pp.202–5; P. M. H. Bell, *The Origins of the Second World War in Europe*, 1997, pp.204–7).

Baldwin's National government had been re-elected with a huge majority in November 1935. It was committed to *limited* rearmament and to 'collective security' through the League of Nations, at that time preoccupied with Italy's aggression against Abyssinia. Far from contemplating military action over the Rhineland, the government had already agreed in 1935 that the Rhineland was not a vital British interest, and had indeed hoped to 'trade' remilitarization in return for 'a new Locarno'. This was precisely what Hitler seemed to offer in his speech of 7 March. Given Germany's enhanced 'power of mischief in Europe', Anthony Eden, the Foreign Secretary, told the Cabinet on 8 March, 'it is in our interest to conclude with her as far-reaching and enduring a settlement as possible while Herr Hitler is still in the mood to do so' (E. H. Haraszti, *The Invaders*, 1983, p.149).

British policy was to follow up Hitler's offers and to restrain France from taking any counter-measures against Germany which might drag Britain into war. The Chiefs of Staff warned that Britain was in no condition to fight. Britain's dispositions in 1936 were directed against Italy, not Germany, with a possible Mediterranean conflict in view. Its other naval and military resources were distracted by imperial commitments in India, Egypt and Palestine: the Empire, not Europe, remained central to defence planning between the wars. The most that Britain could offer France was two divisions. Naval and air forces at home were 'denuded to an extent almost unparalleled in the past', and Britain was 'perilously exposed in the air and completely open to attack by sea' (quoted in J. T. Emmerson, *The Rhineland Crisis, 7 March 1936* p.136).

While Eden made it clear in the Commons on 9 March that a German attack on France or Belgium would be a *casus belli* for Britain, it was clear that Hitler had no intention of attacking east or west in 1936.

There was much expression of public sympathy for Germany, or at any rate of opposition to military action. Even critics of Nazi Germany tended to be pro-German on the merits of the Rhineland case. The Labour opposition was adamant against retaliation. 'Certainly the Labour Party', Dalton told the Commons, 'would not support the taking of military sanctions or even economic sanctions against Germany' (quoted in A. Lentin, *Guilt at Versailles*, 1985, p.149). For the Liberals, Sir Archibald Sinclair and even Lloyd George appealed for understanding of German national feeling. Many continued to approve of Germany as a bastion against communism. Overt pro-Germans included a former Air Minister, Lord Londonderry, and Lord Lothian, formerly Philip Kerr, who, as secretary to Lloyd George, had written the vitriolic reply to the German delegation at Versailles – (see Document I.19 in *Primary Sources 2: Interwar and World War II*). Lothian, now a convert to the view of Versailles as the root cause of Europe's current instability, summed up popular reaction to the reoccupation of the Rhineland: 'After all', he said, 'they are only going into their own back garden' (quoted in Lentin, 1985, p.147). 'The only way to peace', he told Lloyd George, 'is justice for Germany; and justice for Germany means dropping encirclement and letting Germany become the leading power in Central Europe' (quoted in Lentin, 1985, p.148). Baldwin himself, addressing the House of Commons, excused Hitler's action as 'the breaking of a treaty which has shocked our conscience' (R.A.C. Parker, *Chamberlain and Appeasement*, 1995, p.63).

The only British statesmen of influence to call for counter-measures were Austen Chamberlain (who distinguished between 'appeasement' of Weimar Germany and of Nazi Germany) and Churchill. Both were out of office.[5]

---

[5] Churchill's reaction at the time was less clear-cut than he implied in his *The Second World War* (R.A.C. Parker, *Churchill and Appeasement*, 2000, pp.85–91).

Exercise   Please read Document I.25 in *Primary Sources 2: Interwar and World War II*, an editorial in *The Times*, 9 March 1936, and note the writer's reactions. ∎

Specimen answer   While not denying that reoccupation of the Rhineland constituted a flagrant violation of Locarno, the writer (the deputy editor, Barrington-Ward) extenuates and accepts it. He:

1   takes an even-handed attitude between France and Germany (Britain's official attitude since at least 1923);

2   criticizes Locarno as 'one-sided and unbalanced' (Hitler's argument);

3   stresses that Locarno was objectionable because 'it embodied the clauses of the Versailles Treaty which imposed demilitarization upon the German side only' (Hitler's argument);

4   argues that demilitarization could not last forever and that Germany was entitled to protect itself against the possibility of attack by France and Russia (Hitler's argument);

5   denies that German reoccupation of German territory constitutes 'aggression' (the 'back garden' argument);

6   urges Britain and France to accept the *fait accompli*, and to take up Hitler's offers. ☐

Exercise   Please read Document I.26 in *Primary Sources 2: Interwar and World War II* (Eric Dunstan's commentary to *The Rhine*, newsreel item, 12 March 1936). Compare Dunstan's reaction with Barrington Ward's. ∎

Specimen answer and discussion   Both commentators take a similarly passive view. Dunstan stresses the seriousness of the crisis in terms of the entry of German troops and the repudiation of Versailles and Locarno; at the same time he explains the event's symbolic significance for Germany and echoes Barrington-Ward's hopes of Hitler's offers of 'a new peace system on a surer foundation' (p.67). Note that neither Barrington-Ward nor Dunstan even hints at the possibility of counter-measures. ☐

In this they were typical of the British press and media. The Labour *Daily Herald* said that the only alternatives were 'a new settlement' or war. 'Certainly the people of this country would not stand for such a war.' 'As to British opinion generally', wrote Barrington-Ward of the readers' letters to *The Times*, 'our difficulty has been to find enough letters stating what might be crudely called the anti-German view to balance the correspondence' (quoted in Lentin, p.149. On *The Times* see Roberts, p.414, footnote 12.)

Documents I.25 and I.26 suggest little understanding in the media of the wider geopolitical and strategic significance of the *coup* as a fundamental disturbance to the European security system. The objections are of a moralistic nature, noting the violation of Locarno, but offset by expressions of sympathy for German national sensibilities. From this viewpoint, German reoccupation of the Rhineland appeared venial compared to Italian aggression against Abyssinia. Thus public opinion reacted in inverse proportion to the gravity of the crises: Mussolini's aggression, however deplorable, represented no threat to European security; Hitler's action struck at its very heart.

The Rhineland crisis 1936: last chance to stop Hitler?

Could Hitler have been stopped without war in 1936, as Churchill, among others, argued later?

Hitler later said that had the French gone into the Rhineland, he would have had to order an ignominious German withdrawal. But this may have been mere boasting of his nerve and audacity at the time; and in any case a tactical withdrawal to a defensive line would have been perfectly consistent with armed resistance and with 'the *Wehrmacht's* actual orders on 7 March to fall back, but not flee' (Nicole Jordan in Boyce and Robertson, p.142). The language of his speech to the *Reichstag* on 7 March and of his subsequent election speeches strongly suggests that Germany would have fought. The point is that no one dared to put it to the test. Baldwin told the French foreign minister, Pierre-Etienne Flandin that because of the state of British defences, if the chance of war was only one in 100, he could not risk it. Even if Germany were beaten, the British government asked, would war solve the 'German problem'? Harold Nicolson put the dilemma well (though perhaps he was over-optimistic about the chances of easy victory):

> If we send an ultimatum to Germany, she ought in all reason to climb down. But then she will not climb down and we shall have war. Naturally we shall win and enter Berlin. But what is the good of that? It would only mean communism in Germany and France, and that is why the Russians are so keen on it. Moreover the people of this country absolutely refuse to have a war. We should be faced by a general strike if we even suggest such a thing. We shall therefore have to climb down ignominiously and Hitler will have scored.
>
> (H. Nicolson to Vita Sackville-West, 12 March 1936, *Diaries and Letters 1930–1939*, 1966, pp.249–50)

Hitler's success dealt a death-blow to Versailles and Locarno. This was his first open challenge to the territorial settlement of 1919, even though it took place on German soil. Henceforth the balance of power and the diplomatic initiative shifted visibly from France and Britain to Germany. K. D. Bracher writes: 'the European peace order had collapsed even though the facade continued to stand for another three years' (*The German Dictatorship*, 1973, p.375).

Popularity of Nazi foreign policy in Germany

Remilitarization had been contemplated in Weimar Germany since at least the allied evacuation in 1930. But Hitler rightly took the credit for its implementation – 'the achievement, at last, of Germany's equality of rights (*Gleichberechtigung*) and the restoration of full sovereignty over the whole territory of the German *Reich*' (Document I.24). His speeches to the *Reichstag* on 7 March and at German Remembrance Day ceremonies on 8 March were tremendous propaganda successes for Nazi foreign policy.

Exercise   Please listen to the recording of Hitler's peace offers from the broadcast speech (Audio 3, item 8), the script of which you have already examined (Document I.24). What evidence does it afford of opinion in the *Reichstag*? ∎

Discussion   There is much loud cheering and applause following each of Hitler's proposals for peace. Since all political parties other than the Nazis had been banned since 1933, one would expect the deputies, all Nazis, to applaud what Hitler had to say. It may be that they would have cheered even if he had made a declaration of war, such, it may be argued, was his hold on his audience (which can certainly be felt in the recording). But the fact is that, whatever may have been Hitler's own lack of seriousness about a 'new Locarno', the only inference that can legitimately be drawn from the recording is that *prima facie* the *Reichstag* in 1936 expressed its overwhelming support for a policy of *peaceful* revisionism. ☐

Exercise   Please consider Video 1, item 37, 'The Rhine' 12 March 1936 (the script of which you have already examined) as evidence of internal support for the remilitarization of the Rhineland. ■

Discussion   1   It is clear that the re-entry of troops into the Rhineland zone is popular with the local civilians. There is positive, active enthusiasm: waving of handkerchiefs and hats, offerings of flowers, cheering, taking of photographs. Note that few civilians give the Nazi salute: they welcome the event as Germans.

2   In the crowd scenes outside the temporary *Reichstag* and the chancellery in Berlin, by contrast, after Hitler's announcement of the remilitarization, nearly everyone is giving the Nazi salute. There is pleasure and excitement at the achievement *and* a mass expression of solidarity with the Nazi government which has brought it about. This identification of Nazi rule with the gratification of national feeling is further evidenced in the footage where the Berlin crowd both salutes and sings *Deutschland über Alles*.

3   In the Remembrance Day ceremonies in the Opera House (as in 1935 – see Video 1, item 35), brilliantly stage-managed by Goebbels with dramatic use of lighting, music and symbol, the theme is of continuity of military tradition between Nazi and Imperial Germany. The solidarity of the army with the new regime (underlined in a fulsome speech from War Minister Blomberg on stage) is brought out by the lowering of the imperial banners and the joint singing of the national anthem and Nazi salutes. (The theme of continuity is personified in the presence of Hitler with August von Mackensen, veteran Field Marshal of the Great War, on his right and Neurath, Foreign Minister since 1932, aristocrat and conservative, on his left). Other ex-servicemen include Goering, head of the *Luftwaffe* (at the end of Hitler's box on the right), Fritsch, the army chief, Erich Raeder, the navy chief, and Hans von Seeckt, creator of the *Reichswehr* under Weimar).
      Visual and aural evidence thus suggests overwhelming popular support, genuine and spontaneous, for Hitler's foreign policy in 1936, in so far as the remilitarization of the Rhineland was understood as the triumphant but peaceful vindication of national honour. ☐

In the snap general election which Hitler called for the end of March to give the seal of public approval to himself and what he had done, his campaign theme was 'peace'. His slogan was 'international peace, reconciliation and understanding'; and in an eve-of-election speech, he declared: 'I do not believe there is a man in the world who has done more than I have to speak and

fight for peace' (*Germany and the Second World War. Volume I*, pp.111–12).
Martin Broszat stresses that much of German society supported Hitler's active
revisionism as long as it was accomplished without war: Hitler enjoyed 'support
not only from the German middle class but also from the old political élite, from
those sharing influence and power during the Nazi regime in the armed forces
and the diplomatic and bureaucratic services, and even from most of the leading
representatives of the Protestant and Catholic Churches' (in H. Bull, *The
Challenge of the Third Reich*, 1986, p.77).

The Rhineland *coup* consolidated Hitler's personal ascendancy. The electorate
(minus the now disenfranchised German Jews), invited by him 'to give their
verdict as to my leadership' (quoted in Berber, p.227), responded
enthusiastically: if published figures can be relied on, 98.9 per cent voted in
his favour.

Remilitarization greatly enhanced Hitler's self-confidence and the confidence
of others in his judgement after what he privately admitted was the most nerve-
racking crisis of his career. 'The world belongs to the man with guts!' he
exclaimed after the *coup* (quoted in J. C. Fest, *Hitler*, 1977, p.683). He had taken
the measure of western statesmen and correctly foresaw that Britain and France
would do nothing. Henceforth he would be still more daring and reckless in his
defiance of the European *status quo*, advancing, as he boasted, 'with the
certainty of a sleepwalker' (quoted in I. Kershaw, *Hitler, 1980–1936: Hubris*,
1998, p.591). His standing rising far above that of the Foreign Office and General
Staff, he succumbed increasingly to the extremist advice of Ribbentrop,
Goebbels and Goering. Together with the habitual protestations of peaceful
intent, an increasingly strident note of triumphalism, sabre-rattling and menace
enters German propaganda. In July 1936 Hitler decided to intervene on Franco's
side in the Spanish Civil War. In August he drew up a memorandum directing the
army and economy to prepare for general war by 1940 (*Primary Sources 2:
Interwar and World War II*, Document I.12). At the Nuremberg rally in
September, he announced the extension of conscription from one year to two
and openly championed the cause of the German minority in Czechoslovakia.
Hitler's success – and the passivity of Britain and France – helped to persuade
Mussolini to come over to his side. Mussolini too intervened on Franco's side. In
November he openly aligned himself with Germany in what he called 'the
Rome-Berlin axis'. Having mobilized to protect Austria in 1934 (Roberts, p.426),
he now abandoned the cause of Austrian independence.

4   NEVILLE CHAMBERLAIN, 'APPEASEMENT' AND THE SLIDE TO WAR 1937–39

The policy of appeasement associated with Prime Minister Neville Chamberlain
was and remains the subject of intense controversy. Critics denounce it as craven
and naïve, as acquiescence in aggression and a cause of World War II in itself;
apologists see it as a brave, radical and rational attempt to prevent war
altogether by tackling its causes, or at least to stave off war until Britain was in a
position adequately to defend itself. Chamberlain himself was unrepentant. On

his deathbed he wrote: 'I regret nothing' (quoted in S. Aster, 'Guilty men' 1989, p.260). Whatever view one takes, in the words of D. C. Watt 'Chamberlain's character and personality are central to the story of how war came to Europe in 1939' (*How War Came*, 1990, p.76).

Exercise   Please read Roberts, pp.429-34 and P. M. H. Bell's chapter on 'Appeasement' (*Secondary Sources*, pp.84–102), consulting 'Germany 1919–38' in the *Maps Booklet*, and Document I.27 in *Primary Sources 2: Interwar and World War II*, Chamberlain's speech to the House of Commons, 24 March 1938, encapsulating his appeasement policy. Was Appeasement a new policy? What were its characteristics? ■

Discussion   'Appeasement' was not new in itself. It had its origins at Locarno and even, in embryo, among the British delegation at Versailles (see *Primary Sources 2: Interwar and World War II*, Document, I.20 and Lentin, *Lloyd George and the Lost Peace*, 2001, pp.67–88). Ever since the Ruhr crisis (1923), British governments had sought, in some degree, to accommodate German national feeling by gradual, limited, agreed revisions of Versailles. As late as February 1939, Chamberlain continued to insist that Versailles had given the Germans 'good cause to ask for consideration of their grievances' (quoted in Aster, p.243). As we have seen from British reactions to the Rhineland crisis, there was some sympathy with these grievances, a desire to bring stability to Europe by coming to terms with them, and a willingness to accept the fact of increasing German predominance in Europe. Above all, there was abiding revulsion, fully shared by Chamberlain, at the terrible carnage and waste of 1914–18, and universal anxiety to avoid a repetition, by reaching an 'understanding' with Germany (see McDonough, *Neville Chamberlain*, 1998, p.95–101). □

Contrary to a popular image of weakness, Chamberlain was a strong and tenacious prime minister. If his policy was misconceived, he may be faulted for obstinacy, but not for cowardice. He dominated his cabinet and his party. He took personal charge of foreign policy. He overruled Foreign Office advice. He influenced the presentation of his policy by the BBC and cinema (see McDonough, pp.114–32)'. Above all, he added a sense of urgency, vigour and personal commitment to 'appeasement', a conviction that he could 'do business' with Hitler direct. 'If we could sit with the Germans at the same table', he observed in June 1937, 'and, pencil in hand, run through all their complaints and claims, then this would to a significant extent facilitate a clearing of the atmosphere' (quoted in J. Haslam, *The Soviet Union and the Struggle for Collective Security in Europe 1933–39*, 1984, p.150). He spurned the League of Nations, which he saw as a time-wasting talkshop which had alienated but not stopped Mussolini (whom Chamberlain continued, unsuccessfully, to try to isolate from Hitler. Eden, who disagreed with appeasement of Mussolini, resigned in February 1938, and was replaced by Halifax.) Even if it could be organized, Chamberlain believed that 'collective security' against Germany, especially with Soviet participation, was more likely to provoke war than to prevent it. Chamberlain wanted direct bilateral discussions with Germany, cut-and-dried solutions, and an end to drift, while rearmament, begun under Baldwin, continued apace.

Chamberlain felt that Britain had been in danger of sliding into war over the Rhineland in 1936 through muddle and failing to make its intentions clear. Hence his explicit refusal to commit Britain to defend Czechoslovakia, accompanied by expressions of British readiness to mediate between Berlin and Prague (*Primary Sources 2: Interwar and World War II*, Document I.27).

Under Chamberlain, appeasement became a policy of actively seeking to pre-empt Hitler by offering Britain's good offices in settling his grievances and thus to prevent further unilateral *faits accomplis*. Changes in the 1919 settlement in the east, including *Anschluss* with Austria and the transfer of the Sudetenland from Czechoslovakia to Germany, were not objectionable to Chamberlain, provided that they were brought about peacefully and with the consent of the four western European great powers (Britain, France, Germany and Italy). Hence the visit to Hitler by Halifax in 1937 to find out, in effect, what Hitler wanted (and indeed to hint at specific concessions over Austria, Czechoslovakia and Poland).

The Munich crisis 1938

Chamberlain was keenly alive to the danger of Britain's being dragged into war with Germany as a result of France's commitment to defend Czechoslovakia through alliances of 1924 and 1935.[6] The crisis over the Sudeten German minority in Czechoslovakia was accentuated by the *Anschluss* with Austria on 12 March 1938. Determined to forestall the very real danger of imminent war, Chamberlain immediately formulated his policy, presented it to the Commons on 24 March (*Primary Sources2: Interwar and World War II*, Document I.27), and followed it up with vigour, intervening directly in the Czech crisis:

- He pressed the Czech government to concede greater autonomy to the Sudeten Germans.

- Bypassing the Foreign Office, he sent the ex-Cabinet minister, Lord Runciman, to Prague in August to attempt to mediate over the Sudetenlanders' grievances. (For the extent of Czech willingness to concede, listen to Audio 3, item 12.)

- When mediation failed because Henlein (on Hitler's instructions) stepped up the Sudetenlanders' demands and asked for outright incorporation within the *Reich*, Chamberlain himself made three successive flights to Germany within a fortnight to see Hitler at Berchtesgaden (15 September), at Bad Godesberg (22–24 September) and at Munich (29 September), where he agreed to Hitler's maximum demands for the immediate secession of the Sudetenland wherever there was a bare German majority.

---

[6] Russia was also pledged under a treaty of 1935 to come to Czechoslovakia's defence, *but only if France did so first*. The much debated proposition that Russia was ready to intervene in 1938, even without France, and was frustrated by the Munich agreement, is convincingly rebutted by Igor Lukes (in I. Lukes and E. Goldstein, *The Munich Crisis, 1938*, 1999, pp. 13–47).

The Munich Agreement (29/30 September 1938)[7] achieved what Chamberlain sought:

1   a peaceful settlement of a European crisis by the four western great powers (Britain, France, Germany and Italy) and the exclusion of Russia;

2   the 'appeasement' of a German grievance by the revision of Czechoslovakia's 1919 frontiers in accordance with the principle of self-determination denied to the Sudeten Germans at Versailles.

Appeasement averted almost certain war, and gave Britain and France time to press on with rearmament (though it gave Germany time to do the same). But Chamberlain wanted permanent peace, not postponement of war; and that was what he thought Munich had brought when he returned waving the famous 'piece of paper' signed by himself and Hitler, which pledged 'the method of consultation' in any dispute between Britain and Germany, and the two countries' resolve 'never to go to war with one another again'. Hitler had assured him that 'this was the last of his territorial ambitions in Europe' (speech to the Commons, 28 September 1938) and, as Chamberlain told the Cabinet, 'he was satisfied that Herr Hitler would not go back on his word, once he had given it to him' (quoted in K. Middlemas, *Diplomacy of Illusion*, 1972, p.375).

Contemporaries and recent historians have asked: did Chamberlain have any effective choice of policy and did he not indeed make the best of a bad job? (See, for example, Sir Patrick Donner, *Crusade*, 1984, pp.232–46; Roy Douglas, 'Chamberlain and appeasement' in W. Mommsen and L. Kettenacker (eds) *The Fascist Challenge and the Policy of Appeasement*, 1983, pp.79–88; Paul Kennedy, 'Appeasement' in G. Martel (ed.) *The Origins of the Second World War Reconsidered*, 1986, pp.140–61 and *The Realities behind Diplomacy*, 1985, pp.223–312; and John Charmley, who argues that 'this was the only policy which offered any hope of avoiding war' (*Chamberlain and the Lost Peace*, 1989 p.212). Chamberlain's decision in March 1938 not to guarantee Czechoslovakia was based on rational and convincing arguments supported by Halifax and by Britain's ambassadors in Prague and Berlin. Under pressure to stand by the Czech state, he complained: 'to be badgered and pressed to come out and give a clear, decided, bold, and unmistakable lead, show 'ordinary courage,' and all the rest of the twaddle, is calculated to vex a man who has to take responsibility for the consequences' (20 March 1938, letter to his sister, quoted in R. J. Q. Adams (ed.) *British Appeasement and the Origins of World War II*, 1995, p.87).

1   Both France and Britain accepted that no military action could save Czechoslovakia in the short term, and that to plunge Europe into war (and world war at that, if, as was likely, Japan and Italy joined in) for the sake of preventing the Sudeten Germans from joining the *Reich* would not be understood or accepted by public opinion. It was certainly opposed by the Dominions.

2   Britain's military resources were limited and over-stretched. Overseas areas requiring a British military and naval presence included the Far East and

---

[7] Richard Overy argues that Hitler's last-minute agreement on 27 September to meet Chamberlain at Munich for a negotiated settlement was in fact dictated by the risk of war with Britain and France. Hitler bitterly regretted his decision and took care not to repeat it in 1939 (in Lukes and Goldstein, p.191–215).

Australasia, threatened by Japan, and the Middle East and Mediterranean, threatened by Italy. In December 1937 the cabinet approved a policy document which listed strategic objectives in the following order of priority, reflecting the primacy of imperial defence:

(a) protection of the United Kingdom against air attack;

(b) protection of trade routes;

(c) defence of British territories overseas;

(d) co-operation in defending the territories of wartime allies.

Chamberlain was warned by the Chiefs of Staff that Britain could not simultaneously take on Japan, Italy and Germany. It was accepted that Germany was the most dangerous; but only two divisions were envisaged for action on the continent.

3   British rearmament was not ready for war. Spitfires, Hurricanes, radar and anti-aircraft artillery were still only in production. The Committee of Imperial Defence advised Chamberlain that 'if war with Germany has to come, it would be better to fight her in say six to twelve months' time than to accept the present challenge' (quoted by Douglas, in Mommsen and Kettenacker (eds), p.86). Both Chamberlain and Daladier were advised that immediate war could lead to rapid defeat in the air by a 'knock-out blow' on London and Paris; and Morris argues that fear of the Luftwaffe's potential 'was probably the single most important determinent of appeasement' (*The Roots of Appeasement*, 1991, p.181 and see P. M. H. Bell in *Secondary Sources*, p.92).

4   Economic decline had eroded Britain's capacity to rearm. As Chancellor of the Exchequer 1931–37, Chamberlain had nursed the economy back to health after the Great Depression. He shared the Treasury's insistence on the need to balance budgets in order to finance rearmament without setting off an inflationary spiral by excessive borrowing. He deprecated the unorthodox, open-ended financial measures necessary to fund all-out defence spending and expansion on a continental scale; and his defence measures, pegged at around £1650 million or 5 per cent of national income across a five-year period (Crozier, pp.136–7), were intended for deterrence and defence, not for all-out war. As late as early 1939, the Treasury warned that continued high defence spending 'may well result in a situation in which the completion of our material preparations against attack is frustrated by a weakening of our economic stability, which renders us incapable of standing the strain of war' (Kennedy in Martel, (ed.), p.152).

5   There was a clash between the Chiefs of Staff and the Treasury. The Chiefs of Staff believed that Britain's best hope of defeating Germany and Italy lay in a long war, in which the superior population and material resources of the Empire could be gradually deployed. The Treasury argued that given America's stated refusal to grant war loans on the pattern of World War I, Britain could only stand a year of war before its gold and dollar reserves ran out.

Chamberlain's apologists see him as a 'tough practitioner of *Realpolitik*' (Aster, p.240). They argue that on the evidence then available, to go to war in 1938 would have courted bankruptcy and defeat in a bad cause and a lost cause. A. J.

P. Taylor claims that 'the settlement at Munich was a triumph for British policy', a triumph for those who had courageously denounced the harshness and short-sightedness of Versailles' (Taylor, pp.234–5). What Chamberlain sought was not to prepare for war, but to avoid war altogether. Even a victorious war would mean an exhausted Britain, the decline of its international power and the break-up of its empire, while Russia, having sat by while the capitalist powers fought it out, would emerge the real winner, with the consequent spread of communism. Underlying 'appeasement' was a profound concern that war would destroy or revolutionize Britain's social and economic structure, the 'recasting of bourgeois Europe' achieved in the 1920s and the recovery attained after the Great Depression. The dominant liberal/conservative consensus of most Governments in power in Britain since 1922 looked back with aversion to the state control of society and the economy in World War I, and anticipated that their reimposition in a future war would lead, if Britain won, to a socialist Britain. At the time of the Rhineland crisis, Harold Nicolson had predicted that British intervention 'would only mean communism in Germany and France; and that is why the Russians are so keen on it' (*Diaries and Letters*, 1966, p.250). Chamberlain hoped that agreement with Germany over the Sudetenland would not only reduce international tensions but would bring about an Anglo-German *entente*, in which a pacified, stable Germany would continue to act as a bastion against communist Russia; and thus help to preserve the British way of life. On leaving to meet Hitler at Berchtesgaden, Chamberlain informed King George VI of his intention to attract Hitler by 'the prospect of Germany and England as the two pillars of European peace and buttresses against Communism' (quoted in Haslam, p.182).

Let us consider the counter-argument: that Chamberlain's appeasement policy was a contributory cause of World War II.

The case against appeasement was made by Alfred Duff Cooper, who resigned from the Government immediately after Munich, and by Churchill (who was in the political 'wilderness'). It was passionately revived in 1940 in *Guilty Men,* a polemical and personal attack on Chamberlain and his government by Michael Foot. Writing under the pseudonym 'Cato', Foot and two co-authors denounced Chamberlain for blindly contributing to the expansion of German power without regard to the likely consequences for Europe (including Britain). (For recent discussion see Sidney Aster, '"Guilty men": the case of Neville Chamberlain' in R. Boyce and E. M. Robertson (eds) *Paths to War,* 1989, pp.233–68; P. M. H. Bell, 'Appeasement', *Secondary Sources,* pp.84–102; R. A. C. Parker, *Chamberlain and Appeasement,* 1995 and *Churchill and Appeasement,* 2000; and Eric Goldstein, 'Neville Chamberlain, the British official mind and the Munich crisis' in I. Lukes and E. Goldstein (eds), *The Munich Crisis, 1938,* 1999, pp.276–92).

The immediate cost of Munich was:

1   The irreparable damage, military and economic to the rump Czechoslovakia, which lost its strategic frontier and strong fortifications in the Sudetenland (together with half its mining, chemical and timber industry, and some 86 per cent of its glass, ceramics and porcelain industry).

2   Disintegration of the rump Czechoslovakia (guaranteed by the four great powers at Munich), as Poland and Hungary followed Germany's example,

and Germany encouraged Slovakia to declare its independence as a German client-state. On 15 March 1939 German troops marched into Prague. Bohemia and Moravia – the Czech lands – became a German 'protectorate'. The only liberal and democratic state in Central Europe was finished off by brute force.

3   The further enormous disruption of the balance of power in Germany's favour, the accretion of Nazi prestige and a corresponding collapse of French and British standing with the abandonment of the rump Czechoslovakia. This involved the loss of the equivalent of 35 Czech divisions. Germany took enough military equipment from Bohemia and Moravia to supply 20 German divisions. The Skoda armament works in Prague and Pilsen expanded German arms production.

4   The lack of finality at Munich, despite Chamberlain's high hopes. Far from satisfying Hitler and bringing *détente* and international stability, Munich was immediately followed by a rapid and dangerous increase in European tensions. We now know that Hitler, baulked of the *Blitzkrieg* against Czechoslovakia (mentioned in the Hossbach Memorandum and detailed in a directive from Hitler in May 1938), regarded Munich as a failure. At the last moment he had pulled back from the brink. He persuaded himself that Chamberlain had tricked him not merely out of military victory over Czechoslovakia but even out of a successful military showdown with Britain and France (Weinberg, 1995, pp.111–19). At the same time, Munich increased Hitler's and Mussolini's contempt for the democracies ('little worms' was Hitler's description of Chamberlain and Daladier) and whetted their appetites for further aggression. 'In the wake of Munich, Hitler ordered a colossal increase in armaments – a five-fold increase in air strength, a trebling of munitions output' (R. Overy in Lukes and Goldstein, p.207). On 21 October 1938, three weeks after Munich, he gave orders for the 'liquidation of the remainder of the Czech state' J. Noakes and G. Pridham (eds) *Nazism 1919–1945*, 1988, p.724). On 15 March he sent his tanks into Prague. In April 1939 Mussolini seized Albania. In May, Italy and Germany signed a 'Pact of Steel'.

Appeasement was based on the premise that Hitler had specific, limited objectives; that these were open to discussion, delineation and satisfaction; and that they related to the revision of Versailles along lines of national self-determination. If this were so, then 'appeasement' should have satisfied every reasonable demand of German revisionism. Chamberlain also offered the return of former German colonies, or their equivalent. But Hitler was not interested in colonies. Nor was he interested any longer in discussion with Britain of the kind which had led to the Anglo-German naval agreement of 1935 (which he repudiated in April 1939). If the Hossbach memorandum is to be relied on, by November 1937 he had written off Britain and France as 'hate-inspired antagonists ... opposed to any strengthening of Germany's position' (*Primary Sources 2: Interwar and World War II*, Document I.24). What Hitler wanted from Britain was to be allowed to expand unimpeded into eastern Europe. After the Rhineland *coup*, and particularly after the Anschluss, Hitler's self-confidence and German propaganda became increasingly strident. Professions of peaceful intent were accompanied by open threats of military action. After Munich, Hitler cast off all restraint. At a meeting with 400 journalists and publishers on 10 November 1938, he frankly admitted that his peaceful protestations of the past had been a ruse for domestic and foreign consumption and a cover for rearmament: 'It was only out of necessity that for years I talked of peace' (*Germany and the Second World War*, Volume I, p.115).

What price appeasement, then, if the cause of the Sudeten Germans was merely a pretext, Munich a stepping-stone to aggression against non-Germans, as *Mein Kampf* and the Hossbach Memorandum suggest, as the French, the Russians and the British Foreign Office warned, and (though Taylor denies it) as Hitler's subsequent take-over of Bohemia-Moravia seems to demonstrate?

Chamberlain seems to have ignored or discounted these considerations; and, while he should not be criticized with benefit of hindsight, it is fair to blame him, as contemporary critics did, for failing to consider alternative policies if his perceptions turned out to be faulty. As the Russian ambassador in London, Maisky, commented, Chamberlain 'was playing with one card, on which he had put all his money' (quoted in C. Cross, *Life with Lloyd George*, 1975, p.197). For all his good intentions (as Aster, Parker and Goldstein demonstrate), his perceptions of Hitler were consistently wrong while his confidence in his own judgement remained boundlessly optimistic. He does not seem to have shown any awareness of the risks he ran by appeasement and which in fact materialized.

The immediate origins of World War II

Exercise   Please read Roberts, pp.434–9. Is there anything in the argument that Britain was responsible for the immediate outbreak of World War II? ■

Specimen answer   The immediate origin of World War II arose from a quarrel between Germany and Poland over Danzig and the Polish Corridor, one of Germany's last remaining grievances from the treaty of Versailles. It erupted into a European war through the intervention of Britain and France on Poland's side. Britain extended a guarantee of Poland's independence in March 1939, and complemented this with a military alliance in August. Britain and France declared war on Germany, not the other way round. □

What Hitler apparently wanted in September 1939 was a localized *Blitzkrieg* with Poland, not the general war for *Lebensraum* projected in the Hossbach Memorandum, for which Germany was not yet prepared. As with the Sudetenland, the German case for revision was not implausible: the return of Danzig to Germany and a German road-and-rail link to East Prussia across the Corridor. Again, Chamberlain's role is crucial to the question how and why war came. As D. C. Watt suggests, 'After Hitler, Neville Chamberlain is perhaps the single most important individual in the events of 1939' (p.76).

Why did Britain extend a guarantee to Poland on 31 March 1939? Remember that this constituted a complete reversal of British policy since 1919, reasserted only the year before over Czechoslovakia. Britain had expressly avoided commitments in eastern Europe; Austen Chamberlain had said that the Polish Corridor, was not worth 'the bones of a British grenadier'; the main point of

Neville Chamberlain's appeasement policy in 1938 had been to avoid making the 1919 eastern settlement a *casus foederis* (see Document I.27 in *Primary Sources 2: Interwar and World War II*). Why his *volte-face* in 1939?

1   Public opinion in Britain, which had shown overwhelming approval (McDonough queries this, pp.114–32), or at least relief at the Munich agreement, was outraged by Germany's march into Prague. Before Prague Hitler's demands had some appearance of legitimacy in terms of national self-determination for Germans. Hitler himself had publicly declared that he had no more demands in Europe and wanted no Czechs in the Reich (Speech, 26 September, 1938). Prague gave the lie to this, and appeasement began to lose its lustre.

2   The realization of the threat to Britain and France from the latest violent shift in the balance of power. Unless swift diplomatic action was taken, other states would draw their own conclusions from Anglo-French passivity and make their terms with Germany. There were fears that France itself might do so unless Britain took action to stiffen its morale. As it was, a German attack on Holland was (wrongly) thought to be imminent. In April, guarantees were extended to Romania and Greece.

3   Munich had given both Britain and France time to bring rearmament up to a level where both countries believed their armed forces at least capable of staving off defeat. In February 1939, the British government decided to throw financial caution to the wind by creating a full-scale continental army of 32 divisions. In March, it announced the doubling of the Territorial Army. In April it introduced military conscription and established a Ministry of Supply. Staff talks began with France.

Why no Anglo-Russian alliance in 1939? Why the Molotov-Ribbentrop Pact?

Against the advice of the Chiefs of Staff, Chamberlain did nothing to conclude an alliance with Russia before offering his unilateral guarantee to Poland. Such an alliance might have convinced Hitler that Chamberlain was serious. As it was, Hitler did not believe that Britain and France would fight, and provided they were without Russian support, he was prepared to risk a general war. Preparations to attack Poland in late summer 1939 went ahead. The Molotov-Ribbentrop non-aggression pact of August 23 1939 (see Roberts, p.437) made war inevitable. It gave Hitler the green light to attack Poland a week later in the conviction that Britain and France would not intervene, or that even if they did, he need not fear a war on two fronts. Ever since then, historians have debated whether Russia was serious about alliance with Britain and France in the spring and summer, or had intended a pact with Germany all along.

After Prague and Hitler's seizure of Memel in March 1939 Stalin was anxious to come to agreement with France and Britain. Germany openly threatened to strike eastward and might ally with Japan – a Russo-Japanese conflict raged on the Mongolian-Manchurian border from May to August. The French, equally anxious for alliance with Russia, were willing to overrule their allies in eastern Europe, since the reluctance of Poland and Romania to grant access to Russian troops was a stumbling-block to that alliance. Britain refused to treat these states as pawns in negotiations with Russia. It was Russia, not Poland, that Chamberlain attempted to treat as a pawn, his tactic being 'to keep Russia in the background without antagonizing her' (29 April, quoted in Haslam, p.214), or, as the Russians complained, to treat Russia 'like suspicious characters with whom one has business and does not greet in the street' (ibid., p.215).

Even when Molotov became Commissar of Foreign Affairs on 3 May, this did not necessarily signify, as is often supposed, that Russia had abandoned a policy of alliance with Britain and France for a pact with Germany. It was a sign that Stalin himself had come to take a more prominent part in directing Russia's foreign policy. It was a reminder to Britain and France to treat Russian offers seriously, Molotov warning: 'the Western Powers must unambiguously state whether they agree to the clear and simple Russian proposals or not' (quoted in Haslam, p.215).

Geoffrey Roberts (*The Soviet Union and the Origins of the Second World War*, 1995) contends that the protracted negotiations failed because Britain and Russia had in mind two incompatible purposes. After Munich, Russia believed that Hitler could no longer be deterred by a show of force: war was coming, the Soviet Union was overtly threatened, and what mattered was to form a military coalition. According to Roberts, Russia was serious about a military alliance with Britain and France and pressed negotiations until, in July and August, the possibility of a deal with Germany was perceived to be a better option, indeed the only realistic alternative once negotiations for a triple alliance collapsed.

What, then, did Britain hope to gain from negotiating with Russia? Without an alliance with Russia, Chamberlain's commitments to eastern Europe, as Lloyd George complained in the House of Commons, were 'the most reckless pledges that any country has ever entered into' (quoted in Lentin, 2001, p.111). Here we return to the question of Chamberlain's policy after March 1939.

How are we to account for Chamberlain's failure to conclude an alliance with Russia?

Once Chamberlain had given the guarantee to Poland, the only realistic hope of deterring Hitler lay in alliance with Russia. An opinion poll in June 1939 indicated that 84 per cent of the British public favoured an alliance (McDonough, p.84). Failure to clinch this lies with Chamberlain (See Taylor, 1964, pp.282–3). His dilatoriness throughout the spring and summer of 1939 suggests that he authorized negotiations reluctantly and only under parliamentary pressure, and that he had no serious intention of coming to terms with Russia. As has been noted, Chamberlain nurtured an inveterate and understandable suspicion of revolutionary communism. He expressed 'the most profound distrust of Russia', of her 'ability to mount an effective offensive even if she wanted to', and of 'her motives, which seem to me to have little connection with our ideas of liberty' (letter to his sister, 26 March 1939, quoted in Watt, p.180). According to one source he said he would 'resign rather than sign an alliance' with Russia, (quoted by Telford Taylor in Adams, p.133) Not only was he wholly 'sceptical of the value of Russian help' (letter to his sister, June 1939, quoted in Parker, 1993, p.236), especially after Stalin's purge of the Red Army in 1937, but he considered that appearing to negotiate with Russia at all was playing with fire, inflaming German fears of 'encirclement' and driving alleged German 'moderates' into Hitler's camp (6 May, 1939, Public Record Office, Kew, FO 371/23066). At the same time, according to A. J. P. Taylor, he seems to have felt that a show of negotiation with Russia might have a sobering effect on Hitler. He professed to believe that a statesman should never bluff (Aster, p.243). But brandishing the Russian card was surely a bluff: its aim – to deter Hitler by the spectre (though not the reality) of encirclement in order to force him to seek accommodation with Britain. As Taylor graphically puts it, Chamberlain was 'chalking a Red bogey on the wall in the hope that Hitler would then run away' (1965, p.447). His policy was fundamentally unsound. His carrot-and-stick approach to Hitler undermined the credibility of his policy both in Germany and Russia. Continual offers to Germany of peaceful revision of the German-Polish frontier, of colonies, of economic advantages, cut no ice with Hitler, while increasing Stalin's suspicions.

In the first place, Russia suspected Chamberlain (rightly) not merely of playing a double game but (wrongly) of aiming to embroil Hitler in war with Russia. In fact, the British government feared a repeat of Germany's victory over Russia in World War I, which would place European Russia under German control and enable Germany to turn on Britain and France. Second, and fatally, despite explicit warnings from the Chiefs of Staff of 'the very grave military dangers inherent in the possibility of any agreement between Germany and Russia', as late as the end of July Chamberlain refused to see that his policy would force Russia to come to terms with Germany. He 'could not bring himself to believe', he told the cabinet on 27 July, 'that a real alliance between Russia and Germany was possible' (quoted in Haslam, p.213). A low-level British military mission, without plenipotentiary powers and with instructions to stall, was sent to Russia – by sea – at the beginning of August, and was unable to give assurances on the crucial question: would Poland, if attacked by Germany, allow Soviet forces on its territory, or if not, would Britain overrule a Polish refusal?

Maisky, Russian Ambassador in London, told Harold Nicolson that 'he believes that Chamberlain hopes to get a compromise on the Danzig question, and that if he does that, he will allow the Russian negotiations to lapse. He says that he has a definite impression that the Government do not really want the negotiations to go through' (Nicolson, 20 July, 1939, p.406).

The evidence indeed suggests that Chamberlain had not renounced appeasement: he still hoped to settle the problem of Poland's frontiers on the Munich model. The guarantee to Poland was of Poland's 'independence', not its 'territorial integrity'. Danzig and the corridor remained negotiable.

In *Chamberlain and Appeasement* (1993), R. A. C. Parker agrees that Chamberlain should have seen that by summer 1939 Appeasement was a lost cause, and concludes that Chamberlain deliberately 'rejected effective deterrence. Chamberlain's powerful, obstinate personality and his skill in debate probably stifled serious chances of preventing the Second World War' (p.347).

A.W. Purdue and P. M. H. Bell (1997, pp.295–6) claim that there is 'little to be said for the view that an earlier and more enthusiastic approach by Britain and France could have succeeded' (Purdue, p.41). Even if Britain had acted with greater speed and conviction, both Purdue and Bell contend that Russia would still have closed with Hitler's offer of agreement. Hitler had far more to offer: territorial advance to the Curzon line in Poland; a sphere of influence in eastern Europe from Finland to Bessarabia and a non-aggression pact with Germany, that is, peace and expanding influence in return for mere neutrality. Britain and

France could offer nothing except a possible military alliance, which might or might not deter Germany; if it did not, Russia would be drawn into war, in order, as Stalin put it, to pull the chestnuts out of the fire for Britain and France. Geoffrey Roberts, on the other hand, argues that Russia was serious about a triple alliance. He emphasizes that Russia did not seriously consider the German option before late July, persevered with negotiations with Britain and France until the last moment, and responded to German offers in August only after abandoning all hope that Britain was in earnest. Even after the Molotov-Ribbentrop pact, he contends, Russia had no immediate plans to annex the states within its sphere of influence in eastern Europe. Concern for the security of Leningrad rather than brazen expansionism probably explains the hurried agreements forced on the Baltic states for the stationing of Soviet military bases (September-October 1939); and the same concern explains the demand on Finland for the lease of a naval base at Hango.

T. Uldricks argues that Stalin in 1939 was primarily motivated by *raison d'état* rather than by communist ideology. He was not inspired by an anti-fascist crusade or by the spread of revolution abroad. Not was territorial expansion his first priority. 'Stalin's principal objective was to preserve the country's national security' (in G. Gorodetsky (ed.) *Soviet Foreign Policy 1917–1991*, 1994, p.71) and a non-aggression pact with Germany seemed the best way of achieving this.

Despite the immediate territorial gains which Russia seized once war began, Stalin was chiefly aware of the pact as a breathing-space, in fact as a form of Soviet 'appeasement'. (Geoffrey Roberts, p.103–4). P. M. H. Bell (*Secondary Sources*, pp.84–102) suggests that the Nazi-Soviet pact might be described as 'the biggest single act of appeasement', legitimizing German occupation of far more territory than was conceded at Munich.

5   OPERATION 'BARBAROSSA': RUSSIA AND THE ORIGINS OF WORLD WAR II

For the course of World War II from September 1939 to 22 June 1941 see Roberts, pp.438–42. First came the so-called 'phoney war' in the west. Germany crushed Poland in a six–week '*Blitzkrieg*'. On 6 October, Hitler offered peace to Britain and France, who rejected it, but remained on the defensive. Hitler's next move came in April 1940, when the Germans struck north at Denmark and Norway, followed in May by '*Blitzkrieg*' in the west against Holland, Belgium, Luxemburg and France, culminating in Britain's retreat at Dunkirk and the capitulation of France in June 1940. Germany was now master of continental Europe from the North Cape and from the river Bug to the Atlantic (and by the spring of 1941 with the conquest of Yugoslavia and Greece – to the Mediterranean).

On 22 June 1941 began the third and greatest offensive of World War II, or any other war – Operation 'Barbarossa'. Three million Germans (assisted by 600,000 Finns, Rumanians and Hungarians) invaded the Soviet Union (see *Maps Booklet*, Map 9). In its scale, geographical and military, in its ideological dimension and in its ferocity and scale of casualties (of an estimated total of 50–60 million victims of World War II it is thought that casualties in the Soviet Union may have amounted to some 27 million),[8] the war between Germany and Russia was total war. The main theatre of World War II was unquestionably the eastern front where the Red Army took on some 70 per cent of the *Wehrmacht*.

Why did Hitler attack Russia? The question which historians have increasingly asked relates to how far war with Russia was (to use the phraseology adopted in the introduction to this unit) a *novus actus interveniens*, arising in the course of, but not essentially out of Germany's conquests in eastern and western Europe; or alternatively how far was Operation 'Barbarossa' what Germany had been leading up to all the time? How far was the intention to invade and destroy Russia connected with, a cause, or even *the* cause, the *causa causans,* of World War II? Finally, how far can a link be traced with Germany's conquest of Russia in World War I, and would such a link serve to validate the theory of a Thirty Years' War 1914–1945?

Russo-German relations 1939–41

The Molotov-Ribbentrop pact of August 1939 (supplemented by amendments on 28 September, when Lithuania was transferred to Russia's sphere), divided eastern Europe from the Baltic to the Black Sea into spheres of influence between Germany and Russia. Within a fortnight of Germany's attack on Poland, the Soviet army invaded Poland from the east, and annexed all territory up to the Curzon line. Between November 1939 and June 1940, Russia fought a war with Finland, annexed some Finnish territory, the three Baltic States (Estonia, Latvia, Lithuania) and the Rumanian province of Bessarabia. By 1941, Russia had recovered most of the territories lost to it in World War I. (See Roberts, Map 8, p.xxi). Meanwhile Russia assisted Germany's war economy with regular supplies of goods requested in German shopping-lists of February 1940 and January 1941, supplying most of Germany's needs in raw material and foodstuffs and rendering useless Allied attempts at an economic blockade. Russo-German relations 1939–41, were mutually advantageous and apparently friendly. Why, then, war in 1941?

1   It is possible to fashion an interpretation of events 1940–41 in the tradition of diplomatic historians such as A. J. P. Taylor, in order to trace a gradual deterioration in Russo-German relations, culminating in war, but war arriving from pressure of circumstances rather than from deliberate premeditation. (See H.W. Koch in *Secondary Sources*, pp.102–31.)

2   Another explanation is that Stalin was planning to attack Germany and that Hitler forestalled him with a pre-emptive strike. Hitler himself, addressing his generals in March 1941, took this line. He complained of Russian attitudes towards Finland and the Balkans, claimed a build-up of Russian troops 'along the demarcation line' separating the Russian and German

---

[8] This estimate represents direct loss due to German action, servicemen killed in action or fatally wounded, death from hunger and disease, casualties among partisans and other resistance fighters, civilians killed by enemy action, prisoners of war and Communist party members murdered in concentration camps (John Erickson in J. Erikson and D. Dilkes *Barbarossa*, 1994, pp.259–60). Soviet Military losses amounted to 8,700,000. Germany lost 5,600,000 men on the eastern front. See Mark Harrison in the *Course Reader*, p.223.

spheres of influence, and stated that 'we must count on an attack by Russia as a certainty' (see *Primary Sources 2: Interwar and World War II*, Document 1.1); and this interpretation has been revived more recently.

3   A related explanation is that Hitler came to see Britain's refusal to negotiate with Germany (Hitler held out offers of peace to Britain after the fall of Poland in October 1939 and of France in June 1940) in terms of British hopes of America and Russia. America, he believed, would not be ready to wage war before 1942. Russia must therefore be eliminated in 1941. This was how Hitler explained his intentions to his generals in July and December 1940 and again in January and March 1941. 'Russia is the last resort that England has on the Continent and we therefore have to anticipate Russia's attack against us' (*Primary Sources 2: Interwar and World War II*, Document II.1).

(For a summary of Russo-German relations 1940–41 see Roberts, p.441. For a detailed interpretation, see H.W. Koch in *Secondary Sources*, pp.102–31.)

To consider first the 'diplomatic' explanation. This sees differences between Russia and Germany emerging from Russia's exploitation of the Molotov-Ribbentrop pact. Russia was quick to consolidate its position after the fall of France in June 1940. With Germany now master of most of continental Europe, Russia was more vulnerable to attack than in 1939. Russia therefore rapidly advanced its frontiers westward in order to put as much territory as possible between its own hinterland and Germany's forces and at the same time to place its own forces on these frontiers. In so doing, however, Russia aggravated relations with Germany.

Russia's annexation of Bessarabia in June 1940 was within the spirit though not the letter of the pact, and Bessarabia had belonged to Russia until 1918; but Germany had aims of its own in Rumania, in particular the securing of the oil fields at Ploesti, vital to its war effort. German suspicions were also aroused by Russian claims on the Bukovina, which had never belonged to Russia; and though Stalin limited himself to the annexation of northern Bukovina, Germany was affronted. Russia in turn was offended by a German guarantee to Rumania and a rapid occupation of the rest of the country.

Russia attempted to force its 'protection' on Bulgaria in November 1940, Molotov staking Russian claims for a base there and pressing for control of the Turkish Straits, much to Hitler's irritation. In February 1941, German troops occupied Bulgaria. Stalin and Molotov were 'incensed' (G. Waddington in Erickson and Dilks, p.26). Another Russian grievance was Germany's attack in April 1941 on Yugoslavia, with which Russia had just concluded a treaty of friendship.

There was continuing friction over Finland. Finland was within Russia's sphere of influence under the Molotov-Ribbentrop pact; but Germany required supplies of nickel from the Finnish mines at Petsamo. German troops, with Finnish consent, crossed Finland *en route* for Norway, Finno-German staff conversations were held and a treaty of friendship was signed in December 1940.

Stated broadly, both Russian and German expansion under the pact had reached their limits and were heading towards a clash, as each state consolidated its gains or pushed for more. This is clear from discussions in Berlin in November 1940 between Molotov, Hitler and Ribbentrop. Ribbentrop sought to divert Russian ambitions away from eastern Europe by proposing a joint partition of the British empire between Russia, Germany, Italy and Japan. Molotov by contrast demanded clarification of existing rights under the 1939 pact, and pressed for Russian bases in Bulgaria and a German withdrawal from Finland. Hitler's declaration of war on Russia was to complain justifiably of Russia's intention to 'bolshevise and annex' the states in its sphere of influence and (more questionably) 'to attack Germany from the rear' (quoted in D. Volkoganov, in Erickson and Dilks, p.85). Did Hitler really feel threatened? Or was he rationalizing what he had already decided on, his irritation provoked by Russian demands in areas like Finland and Bulgaria which he had demarcated as take-off points for attack?

Did Stalin intend to attack Germany?

The question has been raised as to 'who was planning to attack whom in June 1941, Hitler or Stalin' (to quote the title of an article by Victor Suvorov). That Stalin planned to attack Hitler seems unlikely on the face of it in view of the poor performance of the Russian army against Finland in late 1939. Supplies to Germany under the Molotov-Ribbentrop pact and supplementary economic agreements in February 1940 and January 1941 were enormous. Never had there been such intensive trade between Russia and Germany. Russian deliveries were punctilious, and were even stepped up in the 18 months before the German attack (M. Zeidler, in B. Wegner (ed.), *From Peace to War*, 1997, pp.110–11). This suggests continuation of 'appeasement', of 'Danegeld' even, on Stalin's part. Stalin was unctuously servile, sending Hitler 'warmest congratulations' on the fall of France in June 1940, breaking off diplomatic relations with states defeated by Germany, including Yugoslavia in May 1941, and insisting in periodic communiqués on the cordiality of Russo-German relations, last of all on 14 June 1941, a week before the German attack.

All this might, of course, have been cover for a Russian surprise-attack. Stalin may well have thought eventual war with Germany to be inevitable and decided to strike first. If so, he failed to reckon that Hitler might beat him to it. Stalin apparently anticipated war in 1942. What is certain is an enormous military build-up of Russian forces between 1939 and 1941, from under 2 million men to over 5 million and from under 100 to over 300 divisions (see Geoffrey Roberts, p.319). In quantitative terms of *matériel*, Russia was more powerful than Germany. Alternatively this build-up may indicate Stalin's desire to deter an attack, not to start one himself. Certainly a partial Russian mobilisation and the transfer of troops to Russia's western borders in March 1941 were regarded by the German high command as defensive measures to counter Hitler's own huge concentration of forces for Barbarossa, and they welcomed it as facilitating their plans for encircling the Russian forces (Förster, in Wegner, pp.128–9). According to Jürgen Förster (ibid.), in May 1941 Stalin rejected a pre-emptive strike; and he thought that if a German attack did come, it would be preceded by German demands on Russia: a surprise-attack without a preliminary diplomatic offensive and an eventual ultimatum apparently never occurred to him.

The evidence suggests that Stalin wanted nothing more than to continue Russia's profitable benevolent neutrality and to propitiate Germany at all costs in order to avert war as long as possible; and that 'Barbarossa' took him completely by surprise. He did not believe that an attack was imminent, despite mounting evidence in the weeks before 22 June. He ignored British intelligence warnings of preparations for 'Barbarossa' as disinformation and denounced them as a provocation. He also suspected an Anglo-German pact directed against Russia, and his fears were fuelled by the arrival in Britain of Hitler's deputy, Rudolf Hess, in May 1941. On the eve of invasion, Stalin was 'torn between anxiety and fear of triggering off an unwanted war' (according to Marshal Zhukov, Gorodetsky in Wegner, p.357).

Hitler, *Mein Kampf*, and Operation 'Barbarossa'

In 1941 as in 1938, 1939 and 1940, it was Hitler who took the decision for war or peace. Weizsäcker, Secretary of State for Foreign Affairs, saw no threat to Germany from Russia, pointing out to Ribbentrop that hostilities between Germany and Russia would only prolong the war and give England new heart. Ribbentrop, agent of the non-aggression pact with Russia, and still nominally in charge of German foreign policy, sought to consolidate and extend Russo-German collaboration. Like the military, however, Ribbentrop was probably mesmerised by Hitler's apparent infallibility, demonstrated by an unbroken run of incredible and spectacular successes (Waddington, in Erickson and Dilks, pp.8–33). Hitler himself anticipated Russia's defeat in a matter of weeks. (So, for that matter, did the British Foreign Office, see H. Hinsley, in Erickson and Dilks, p.72).

Was 'Barbarossa' the outcome of ideas and plans which Hitler had entertained since the mid-1920s for the conquest of *Lebensraum* in the east?

Recapitulation

We have suggested in previous discussion of *Mein Kampf* that Hitler meant what he said about *Lebensraum*. Rich argues that in 1941 he put this into action, and that 'the primary purpose of Hitler's foreign policy and his fundamental aim in the Second World War was the realization of his long-range plan for the acquisition of *Lebensraum*' (Norman Rich, Course Reader, pp.128–9).

Exercise   Please re-read extract (b) from *Mein Kampf* in *Primary Sources 2: Interwar and World War II*, Document I.22. What does this suggest about Hitler's territorial ambitions with respect to Russia? ■

Discussion   Hitler rejects as inadequate the restoration of Germany's 1914 frontiers. In a future war of Germany's choosing, he anticipates 'the struggle for a future that will be worthy of our country', in order to 'lessen the discrepancy between our country' and the British empire and America. National Socialist foreign policy meant 'that the German people must be assured the territorial area which it is necessary for it to exist on this earth'. Hitler rejects overseas colonies. Germany's *Lebensraum* must be found in 'winning such territory for the settlement of our people as will extend the area of the Motherland'. Nationalist Socialists 'turn our eyes towards the lands of the East', i.e. 'Russia and the border States subject to her'. □

We have also seen that Hitler repeated these views at crucial moments (p.212). The Hossbach memorandum of 5 November 1937 (*Primary Sources 2: Interwar and World War II*, Document I.23) suggests that he had not changed his mind: 'The aim of German foreign policy was to make secure and to preserve the racial community and to enlarge it. It was therefore a question of space ... It was his unalterable resolve to solve Germany's problem of space at the latest by 1943–45'. At a meeting with twelve senior army commanders on 23 May 1939, Hitler stated that 'It is not Danzig that is at stake. For us it is a matter of expanding our living space in the East' (Noakes and Pridham, p.739).

In August 1939, Hitler stated that his ultimate object was not war with the west, but war with Russia (in conversation with Carl Buckhardt, 11 August 1939, Noakes and Pridham, p.739). For Hitler the Molotov-Ribbentrop pact was, like most of his international agreements, never more than a temporary expedient. On 17 October 1939, after the conquest of Poland, Hitler informed the supreme military commander, Field Marshal Keitel, of Poland's importance 'from a military point of view as an advanced jumping-off point' (Noakes and Pridham, p.928).

On 31 July 1940, Hitler informed his senior military advisers of his 'final decision' to 'finish off' Russia in 1941 (Förster in Wegner, p. 120). Military planning began in August 1940 and on December 18 Hitler signed Directive No.21 ordering the armed forces to be ready by May 1941 'to crush Soviet Russia in a quick campaign', advancing to a line running from Archangel to Astrakhan – Operation 'Barbarossa' (Noakes and Pridham, p.809). In January 1941 he told his military commanders 'Russia must be beaten' (Noakes and Pridham, p.813).

Jürgen Förster (in Wegner p. 121) argues that Russo-German disputes arising out of the Molotov-Ribbentrop pact or the question of how to force Britain to come to terms are side issues, which 'should not obfuscate the symbiosis in Hitler's war policy of calculation and dogma, strategy and ideology, foreign policy and racial policy.'

A new kind of 'total war'?

In *Primary Sources 2: Interwar and World War II*, Document II.1, General Halder gives an account of Hitler's address to the High Command in March 1941.

In the occupation of western Europe, German troops were, relatively speaking, on their best behaviour in their relations with civilians. The defeated western states, such as Denmark and Vichy France, retained a nominal independence as client-states of Germany.

Not so in the east (see *Maps Booklet*, Map 8). All pre-Versailles German territory was taken from Poland and re-incorporated into Germany. The remainder of German-conquered Poland, renamed the *Generalgouvernement*, was originally earmarked by its 'Governor-General', Hans Frank, after discussion with Hitler in March 1940, as 'a kind of reservation under German rule' for Poles and Jews, under the control of Himmler and the SS (quoted by T. Szarota in Wegner, p.49). Four months later, after further discussion with Hitler, Frank declared that the *Generalgouvernement* would remain 'an integral part of the German Reich'. It would be cleared of 'Poles as well as Jews', and resettled by Germans (ibid., pp.49, 50). By June 1941, 400,000 Poles reincorporated in the *Altreich* within Germany's 1918 boundaries were expelled outright; the remainder suffered humiliating degrees of discrimination as 'servants and slaves' (ibid., p.51, and Noakes and Pridham, pp.937–57). In the

Generalgouvernement, German policy towards the Polish intelligentsia was that it was to 'be rendered harmless and be put in concentration camps' (Noakes and Pridham, p.930). As for the Jews of Poland, mass murder began immediately, though it did not become a systematic Holocaust until after the invasion of Russia, when the main extermination camps were established in the *Generalgouvernement.*

'The attack on Poland was in some ways a rehearsal for the invasion of Russia' (G. L. Weinberg, *A World at Arms*, 1994, p.190). *Primary Sources 2: Interwar and World War II*, Document II.3 suggests that in the case of Russia, Hitler had in mind a similar ruthlessness, but on a far greater scale, and certainly a kind of war very different from his campaigns in the west: 'The war against Russia will be such that it cannot be conducted in a knightly fashion. This *struggle is a struggle of ideologies and racial differences and will have to be conducted with unprecedented, unmerciful, and unrelenting harshness*'(my italics – A. L.).

Exercise   Please read Field Marshal Keitel's orders for Barbarossa, 13 May 1941, *Primary Sources 2: Interwar and World War II*, Documents II.2 and II.3. What was significant about the intentions of the military with regard to the treatment of Russia? ■

Specimen answer   This order from the German commander-in-chief calls for 'ruthless action against any threat from the civilian population' shootings, 'collective despotic measures'. If the principle object of Barbarossa was *Lebensraum,* this was the literal implementation of Hitler's stated aims in *Mein Kampf* and in the Nazi party programme. It was to be brought about according to military plans approved by the German high command, through terror, subjugation and massacre. Plans for the invasion and occupation of Russia made specific provision for the subjection of the Slav peoples, mass murder and the destruction of communism. □

CONCLUSION: THE 'THIRTY YEARS' WAR' THESIS AGAIN

See Roberts Map 5 (p.xviii) and 8 (p.xxi) and read the chapter by Norman Rich in the *Course Reader*, pp. 125–41.

We have earlier noted parallels between Germany's 'almost megalomaniac' expansionism at the expense of Russia in World War 1 and Hitler's plans for *Lebensraum* in World War II. Fritz Fischer showed how the 'September programme' of 1914 for *Ostraum* – territorial expansion in the east – was not the monopoly of the military and political élite, but was shared by a wide section of German opinion, including academics and intellectuals as well as generals and industrialists. The Pan-Germans advocated pushing Russia back 'to the frontiers of pre-petrine Muscovy' by annexing Russian Poland, the Ukraine and the Baltic states. This programme was realized at Brest-Litovsk. Industrialists such as Thyssen called for annexation of the Don basin, Odessa, the Crimea and Caucasus. Ludendorff aspired to settle German colonists in Poland and the Ukraine and to deport the local populations. As Fischer points out, these 'grandiose' plans for *Ostraum* remained part and parcel of German war-aims until shortly before Germany's collapse in 1918 (Fischer, p.607).[9] The idea of gaining economic autarky from a colonial hinterland carved out of Russia seemed the perfect answer to the kind of economic blockade that had starved Germany of food and raw materials in World War I. We have also noted Hitler's frequently repeated intentions of turning western Russia into a *Lebensraum* that would make Germany economically self-sufficient and militarily unassailable. These were welcomed by the military and political élite and, as Arno Mayer points out, by important sections of the non-Nazi élites 'leading figures in business, the civil service, the churches and the intelligentsia' (*Why Did the Heavens Not Darken?*, 1988, p.203).

The argument for continuity, then, is that Germany's policy-makers and opinion-informers in 1914 quickly developed an appetite for territorial expansion as grandiose as Hitler's, or conversely, (as Taylor argues), that Hitler stands in a clear line of continuity and that German policy in the Second World War was a resumption of its policy in the First.

And yet the differences may be as revealing as the similarities. First, however much German appetites for expansion after 1914 grew with military success, as demonstrated at Brest-Litovsk in 1918, how convincingly does Fischer show that such desire for expansion was the root cause of World War I, that Germany went to war in order to realise these goals? (This issue is discussed in Units 5 and 6).

Secondly, for all the annexations at Brest-Litovsk, none of Ludendorff's plans for resettlement were carried out (perhaps there was not time). Poles had lived under German rule for 150 years. In World War I they served against Russia as German citizens in the German army. In the postwar plebiscites in 1921, the Polish-speaking inhabitants of Allenstein and Marienwerder voted to remain with Germany. The Germans in World War I played the nationalist card in encouraging Polish, Ukrainian and Balt separatism from the Russian empire. The contrasts with World War II were apparent from the first. While in 1915 the Germans approved the opening of the University of Warsaw in order to win Polish support, in 1939 the SS deported the academic staff of the University of Cracow to Sachsenhausen concentration camp as part of a policy to exterminate the Polish intelligentsia (Mayer, p.185). In World War I, captured Jewish officers in the Russian army were billeted in German-Jewish homes; in World War II, of the many hundreds of thousands of Soviet prisoners-of-war in German hands – 2 million by early 1942 – four out of five perished from starvation, disease, abuse or execution (Klaus-Jürgen Müller in Erickson and Dilkes, p.230). In World War II, while the Germans were at first greeted in the Ukraine as liberators from Communism, they soon made it plain that they were interested only in what Hitler called a 'war of extermination' (*Vernichtungskrieg*, 31 March 1941, quoted in Mayer. p.209); in the dismemberment of Russia, the extension of German rule to the Urals, the overthrow of the Soviet regime and of the '"Judaeo-bolshevik" world conspiracy' (Mayer, p.208); the subjugation, enslavement and 'ethnic cleansing' of Slavs and genocide of the Jews. In Document II.3 Hitler spoke of

[9] As Marc Ferro says, 'The programme came up a few years later, and can be found point for point in Hitler's *Table-Talk*' (M. Ferro, *The Great War 1914–1918*, 1991, p.141). *Hitler's Table-Talk 1941–1944* (1953), Oxford University Press, 1988. See, for example, pp. 4–5, 16, 24–5, 34–5, 37–8, 42–3, 53, 54, 68–70.

his officers' need 'to rid themselves of obsolete ideologies' and complained that the need for ruthlessness in the overriding of 'international law' and traditional military codes was 'beyond the comprehension of you Generals'. He underestimated the willingness of the *Wehrmacht*, the regular army, to co-operate in waging a total war of conquest and extermination, 'drenched in criminality' (K.-J. Müller, in Erickson and Dilkes, p.227).

Again, then, one is faced with the fundamental question: how far do the origins of World War II derive from Hitler and Nazism, how far from the 'German problem'? The Taylor school consider the two questions to be one and the same. They see Hitler as a natural outcome of German history, a more aggressive version of Bethmann Hollweg and Stresemann. Gordon Craig speaks for the discontinuity theory. For him, 'Hitler was *sui generis*, a force without a real historical past ... Both the grandiose barbarism of his political vision and the moral emptiness of his character makes it impossible to compare him ... with any other German leader' (*Germany 1866–1945*, 1978, p.543).

This, however, throws the question of the 'German problem' back on the German people, without whose support, as Taylor says (1964, p.26), 'he would have counted for nothing'. Certainly, German power plus Nazi ideology and Hitler's evil genius, made a fatal combination.

Chronology

1919	Treaty of Versailles
1920	US Senate votes against joining League of Nations
1921	Reparation Commission sets German debt (132,000,000,000 gold marks; £6,600,000,000)
1921	Hitler becomes leader of the NSGWP
1922	Russo-German treaty of Rapallo
1923	Franco-Belgian forces occupy the Ruhr
1924	Dawes Plan for reparations payments
1925	French evacuate the Ruhr
1925	Treaty of Locarno
1926	German-Soviet non-aggression pact (treaty of Berlin)
1926	Germany joins League of Nations
1927	Allied Military Control Commission withdrawn from Germany
October 1929	Wall Street Crash
1930	Allied evacuation of the Rhineland complete
1930	Reichstag elections with major gains by Nazis
1931	Hoover Moratorium on reparations
1933	Hitler appointed Chancellor
October 1933	Germany leaves League of Nations
January 1934	Germany and Poland conclude non-aggression pact
1934	Attempted coup in Austria and assassination of Dollfuss
1934	Death of German President Hindenburg. Hitler declared Führer (leader)

1935	Saar plebiscite – vote overwhelmingly for reincorporation into Germany
1935	Germany announces establishment of military airforce and reintroduction of universal military conscription
1935	Italy, France and Britain condemn German rearmament affirm interest in independence of Austria and Locarno agreements
1935	Mutual assistance pact between France and Russia
1935	Anglo-German naval agreement limiting German naval strength
1935	Italy invades Abyssinia: condemned by League of Nations
March 1936	Germany remilitarizes Rhineland and denounces Locarno
July 1936	Outbreak of Spanish Civil War
August 1936	Hitler's memorandum on the four-year plan
May 1937	Chamberlain succeeds Baldwin as Prime Minister
November 1937	Hossbach Memorandum
March 1938	Anchluss between Germany and Austria
September 1938	Munich settlement allows German annexation of Sudetenland
9 November 1938	Kristallnacht: Anti-Semitic pogrom in Germany
March 1939	Bohemia-Moravia occupied by German troops
March 1939	Lithuanian port of Memel seized by Germany
March 1939	Britain and France give guarantee to Poland
April 1939	Britain gives guarantees to Romania
April 1939	Hitler denounces Polish–German non-aggression pact of 1934 and Anglo-German naval agreement of 1935
April 1939	Italy invades Albania: Britain offers guarantee of assistance to Greece
May 1939	Italy and Germany sign Pact of Steel
23 August 1939	Russo-German (Ribbentrop-Molotov) non-aggression pact
25 August 1939	Britain and Poland sign Treaty of Alliance
1 September 1939	Germany invades Poland
3 September 1939	Britain and France declare war on Germany
17 September 1939	Russia invades Poland and annexes territory east of Curzon Line
October 1939	Poland surrenders to Germany
November 1939	Russia invades Finland
March 1940	Finland surrenders to Russia
April 1940	Germany invades Denmark and Norway
May 1940	Germany invades Holland, Belgium, Luxemburg, France
June 1940	Russia annexes Estonia, Latvia and Lithuania France signs armistice with Germany Russia annexes Bessarabia and northern Bukovina
November 1940	Inconclusive Russo-German talks
February 1941	Germany occupies Bulgaria
April 1941	Germany invades Yugoslavia
22 June 1941	Germany invades Soviet Union

References

Adams, R. J. Q. (ed.) (1995) *British Appeasement and the Origins of World War II*, Heath.

Adamthwaite, A. (1995) *Grandeur and Misery: France's Bid for Power in Europe 1914–40*, Edward Arnold.

Bainville, J. (1919, 1995 edition) *Les conséquences politiques de la paix*, éditions de l'Arsenal, Paris.

Bell, P. M. H. (1986) (2nd edn 1997) *The Origins of the Second World War in Europe*, Longman.

Berber, F. J. (ed.) (1936) *Locarno*, Hodge.

Boemeke, M., Feldman, G., Glaser, E. (eds) (1998) *The Treaty of Versailles. A Reassessment after 75 Years*, Cambridge University Press.

Boyce, R. and Robertson, E. M. (eds) (1989) *Paths to War: New Essays on the Origins of the Second World War*, Macmillan.

Bracher, K. D. (1973) *The German Dictatorship. The Origins, Structure and Effects of National Socialism* (trans. J. Steinberg), Penguin.

Bull, H. (ed.) (1986) *The Challenge of the Third Reich*, Clarendon Press.

Cato (Michael Foot, Peter Howard, Frank Owen), *Guilty Men*, Victor Gollanz 1940, reprinted with an introduction by John Stevenson, Penguin, 1998.

Charmley, J. (1989) *Chamberlain and the Lost Peace*, Hodder and Stoughton.

Churchill, W. S. (1948, 1967 edition) *The Second World War, Volume I: The Gathering Storm*, Cassell.

Craig, G. A. (1978, 1986 edition), *Germany 1866–1945*, Oxford University Press.

Cross, C. (1975) *Life with Lloyd George. The Diary of A. J. Sylvester 1931–45*, Macmillan.

Crozier, A. J. (1997) *The Causes of the Second World War*, Blackwell.

Donner, P. (1984) *Crusade: a Life against the Calamitous Twentieth Century*, Sherwood Press.

Emmerson, J. T. (1977) *The Rhineland Crisis 7 March 1936. A Study in Multilateral Diplomacy*, Maurice Temple Smith.

Erickson, J. and Dilkes, D, (1994) *Barbarossa. The Axis and the Allies*, Edinburgh University Press.

Eyck, E. (1967) *A History of the Weimar Republic*, Vol. II, 2nd edn, Harvard.

Ferro, M. (1988) *Hitler's Table Talk 1941–1944*, Oxford University Press.

Ferro, M. (1991) *The Great War 1914–1918*, Routledge.

Fest, J. C. (1977) *Hitler*, Penguin.

Fischer, F. (1986) *From Kaiserreich to Third Reich. Elements of Continuity in German History 1871–1945*, Allen and Unwin.

Germany and the Second World War. Volume I. The Build-up of German Aggression (1990), Clarendon Press, Oxford.

Germany and the Second World War. Volume IV. The Attack on the Soviet Union, (1998) Clarendon Press, Oxford.

Gorodetsky, G. (ed.) (1994) *Soviet Foreign Policy 1917–1991. A Retrospect*, Frank Cass

Haraszti, E. H. (1983) *The Invaders. Hitler Occupies the Rhineland*, Akadémiai Kiadó, Budapest.

Haslam, J. (1984) *The Soviet Union and the Struggle for Collective Security in Europe 1933–39*, Macmillan.

Hiden, J. (1996) *Republican and Fascist Germany*, Longman.

Hiden, J. and Farquharson, J. (1989) *Explaining Hitler's Germany. Historians and the Third Reich*, 2nd edn, Batsford.

Kennedy, P. (1985*) The Realities behind Diplomacy. Background Influences on British External Policy 1865–1980*, Fontana.

Kershaw, I. (1998) *Hitler 1889–1936: Hubris*, Allen Lane.

Laffan, M. (ed.) (1988) *The Burden of German History 1919–45*, Methuen.

Lee, M. M. and Michalka, W. (1987) *German Foreign Policy 1917–1933. Continuity or Break?*, Berg.

Lentin, A. (1985) *Guilt at Versailles. Lloyd George and the Pre-History of Appeasement*, Methuen.

Lentin, A. (1991, reprinted 1993) *The Versailles Peace Settlement. Peacemaking with Germany*, The Historical Association.

Lukes, I. and Goldstein, E. (eds) (1999) *The Munich Crisis, 1938. Prelude to World War II*, Frank Cass.

Margueritte, V. (1932) *Briand*, Flammarion.

Marks, S. (1976) *The Illusion of Peace. International Relations in Europe 1918–1933*, Macmillan.

Martel, G. (ed.) (1986) *The Origins of the Second World War Reconsidered. The A. J. P. Taylor Debate after Twenty-five Years*, Allen and Unwin.

Mayer, A. J. (1988, 1990 edition) *Why Did the Heavens not Darken? The 'final solution' in history*, Verso.

McDonough, F. (1998) *Neville Chamberlain, Appeasement and the British Road to War*, Manchester University Press.

Middlemas, K. (1972) *Diplomacy of Illusion. The British Government and Germany 1937–39*, Weidenfeld and Nicolson.

Mommsen, W. and Kettenacker, L. (eds) (1983*) The Fascist Challenge and the Policy of Appeasement*, Allen and Unwin.

Mommsen, W. (1996) *The Rise and Fall of Weimar Germany*, trans. E. Forster and L. E. Jones, University of North Carolina Press.

Morris, B. (1991) *The Roots of Appeasement. The British Weekly Press and Nazi Germany during the 1930s*, Frank Cass

Nicolson, H. (1966) *Diaries and Letters 1930–1939*, Collins.

Noakes, J. and Pridham, G., (eds) (1988) *Nazism 1919–1945*, Vol.3, *Foreign Policy, War and Racial Extermination*, University of Exeter.

Parker, R. A. C. (1993) *Chamberlain and Appeasement: British Policy and the Coming of the Second World War,* Macmillan.

Parker, R.A.C. (2000) *Churchill and Appeasement,* Macmillan.

Purdue, A. W. (1999) *The Second World War,* Macmillan.

Robbins, K. (1988, 2nd edn 1997) *Appeasement,* The Historical Association, Basil Blackwell.

Roberts, G. (1995) *The Soviet Union and the Origins of the Second World War,* Macmillan.

Robertson, E. M. (ed.) (1971) *The Origins of the Second World War. Historical Interpretations,* Macmillan.

Schwabe, K. (1985) *Woodrow Wilson, Revolutionary Germany and Peacemaking 1918–1919,* trans. R. and R. Kimber, University of North Carolina Press.

Sharp, A. (1991) *The Versailles Settlement: Peacemaking in Paris, 1919,* Macmillan.

Stone, G. and Sharp, A. (eds) (1999) *Anglo-French Relations in the Twentieth Century,* Routledge.

Suvorov, V. (1990) *Icebreaker. Who Started the Second World War?*

Taylor, A. J. P. (1964; first edn 1961) *The Origins of the Second World War,* Penguin.

Taylor, A. J. P. (1965) *English History 1914–1945,* Clarendon Press.

Watt, D. C. (1989, 1990 edition) *How War Came. The immediate origins of the Second World War,* Mandarin

Wegner, B. (ed.) (1997) *From Peace to War. Germany, Soviet Russia and the World 1939–1941,* Berghahn Books.

Weinberg, G. L. (1970) *The Foreign Policy of Hitler's Germany. Diplomatic Revolution in Europe 1933–1936,* Chicago University Press.

Weinberg, G. L. (1980) *The Foreign Policy of Hitler's Germany. Starting World War II 1937–1939,* Chicago University Press.

Weinberg, G. L. (1994) *A World at Arms. A Global History of World War II,* Cambridge University Press.

Weinberg, G. L. (1995) *Germany, Hitler and World War II. Essays in Modern German and World History,* Cambridge University Press.

Williamson, D. G. (1991) *The British in Germany. The Reluctant Occupiers,* Berg

Further reading

Dutton, David (2001) *Neville Chamberlain*, Arnold.

Grayson (1997) *Austen Chamberlain and the Commitment to Europe: British Foreign Policy, 1924–29*, Frank Cass.

Heater, D. (1994) *National Self-Determination. Woodrow Wilson and his Legacy*, St Martin's Press.

Hiden, J. (1977, 2nd edn 1993) *Germany and Europe 1919–1939*, Longman.

Keylor, W. R. (ed.) (1998) *The Legacy of the Great War. Peacemaking 1919*, Houghton Mifflin, New York.

Liulevrcius, V. G. (2000) *War Land on the Eastern Front. Culture, National Identity and German Occupation in World War I*, Cambridge University Press.

Neville, P. (1999) *Appeasing Hitler: Sir Neville Henderson*, Macmillan.

O'Riordan, Elspeth Y. (2001) *Britain and the Ruhr Crisis*, Palgrave.

Overy, R. J. (1987, 1994) *The Origins of the Second World War*, Longman.

Strohl, G. (2000) *The Germanic Isle. Nazi Perceptions of Britain*, Cambridge University Press.

Young, R. J. (1996) *France and the Origins of the Second World War*, Macmillan.

Index